FOUNDATIONS
OF ACCOUNTING

Edited by
RICHARD P. BRIEF
New York University

A GARLAND SERIES

Accounting Literature in the United States Before Mitchell and Jones (1796)

••••••••••••••••••••••••••••••

*Contributions by Four English Authors,
through American Editions, and
Two Pioneer Local Authors*

Edited with an introduction by
TERRY K. SHELDAHL

GARLAND PUBLISHING, INC.

NEW YORK & LONDON 1989

For a list of Garland's publications in accounting,
see the final pages of this volume.

Introduction copyright © 1989
by Terry K. Sheldahl

Library of Congress Cataloging-in-Publication Data

■ ■

Accounting literature in the United States before Mitchell and Jones (1796) :
contributions by four English writers, through American editions, and two
pioneer local authors / edited, with introductionby Terry K. Sheldahl.
p. cm.
Bibliography: p.
ISBN 0-8240-6131-4 (alk. paper)
1. Accounting—Early works to 1800. 2. Accounting—Early works to 1800—
Bibliography. I. Sheldahl, Terry K.
Hf5631.A26   1989
657—dc19   88-38984

Design by Renata Gomes

The volumes in this series are printed on
acid-free, 250-year-life paper.

Printed in the United States of America

To my parents,
Faye and Everett Sheldahl

ACKNOWLEDGMENTS
■■■■■■■■■■■■■■■■■■■■■■■■■■■■■■■■■■■■■■■

The summary given, on pages 3 and 4, of my personal introduction to each of the reprint selections points up the origin of this anthology, as with my other contribution to the series (Sheldahl 1988), in research travel of 1983 and '84. I am especially indebted in that connection to Phil Lapsansky of the Library Company of Philadelphia, Geraldine (Watkins) Yeager of Langsdale Library at the University of Baltimore, and Charles Latham, Jr., of the Episcopal Academy of Philadelphia. After Latham had advised me in 1983 of the work of Thomas Sarjeant, Lapsansky referred me to the microprint source (Shipton 1955–83) that would supply a number of references cited in chapter 1. In preparing the introductory chapter, I have benefited measurably from the generosity of the University of Mississippi in lending me numerous titles from the first Early American Imprints series (Shipton 1955–83) through interlibrary loan.

The scope of my debt to Peter McMickle of Memphis State University is apparent from the introduction and accompanying reference list. At a personal level, I especially appreciate his encouragement regarding this endeavor, and his ready consent to my use of unpublished material related to his new coauthored bibliography (McMickle and Jensen 1988).

As with my other current book, librarians Evelyn

Richardson and Linda Holmes of Savannah State College have been most helpful. Susan Morris of the Reference Department of the central library at the University of Georgia has once again assisted me superbly on a host of bibliographical matters.

Series editor Richard Brief has been wonderfully supportive throughout, even as I have failed by seven months to meet expectations of a year ago, when the table of contents and a capsule summary were submitted, regarding completion date. At Garland Publishing, whose financial assistance extended to this project, I wish to repeat my thanks to Ralph Carlson and his successor as vice president Leo Balk, and to their associate editor Brian Cook. I am again indebted to Dean Leo Parrish, Jr., for providing me with an appointment at Savannah State that is ideal for pursuing such work.

It is a geniune pleasure to thank the following libraries and individuals for supplying with reprint consent the contents of chapters 2–9:

1. Fisher—Historical Society of Pennsylvania; Carolyn Park, Collections Manager
2. Hutton—Library of Congress: Leonard Beck, Head (ret.), Rare Book and Special Collections Div.; James Gilreath, American History Specialist; and Elizabeth Harrison, Project Clerk, Photoduplication Div.
3. Sarjeant 1788, and
4. Sarjeant 1789—University of South Carolina: Thomas Cooper Library, Roger Mortimer, Head, Special Collections; and South Caroliniana Library, Charles Gay (microfilming)
5. Freeman—Portland Public Library, Portland, Maine; Edith H. McCauley, Special Collections Librarian
6. Sarjeant 1793—West Virginia University, Charles C. Wise, Jr., Library; Stokely B. "Jim" Gribble, Director,

providing microfilm

7. Dilworth—Lownes Collection, John Hay Library, Brown University; Jennifer B. Lee, Curator of Printed Books

8. Turner—John A. Albree Collection, Norwich University Library; Ann Turner, Director, and Paul Heller, Assistant Director.

Regarding Dilworth's book, finally, I also appreciate the kindness of Jane Hukill, director, and Zona Lindsay, assistant director, of the Delaware Campus Library at Widener University. For reprint use, if needed, in lieu of the Philadelphia edition, they loaned me the library's copy (from the Brandywine Valley History Collection) of the 1798 Wilmington printing. That gesture has permitted handwritten completion of the truncated photocopy pages.

Terry K. Sheldahl
School of Business, Savannah

CONTENTS

Acknowledgments   vii

1.   Introduction: Bibliographical Context, Selected Biographical Matter, and Prospective Nonbook Literature Searches   1

    Development of the Collection—Bibliographical Background   1
        Bentley and Leonard, 1934–35   1
        McMickle and Jensen, 1988   3

    Supplemental Biographical Coverage   7
        George Fisher   7
        Charles Hutton   11
        Thomas Dilworth   14
        Richard Turner   19

    Two Major Areas for Further Bibliographical Study of Early American Accounting   20
        Distribution of Accounting Literature
                                            20
        Nonbook Sources of Accounting Literature
                                            22
    Reference List   28

2. George Fisher's Bookkeeping Chapter, Unattributed, from Bradford's Manual, 1737   35

3. Charles Hutton's Single Entry *Course*, 1788
                                                        51

4. Thomas Sarjeant on Mercantile Arithmetic, 1788
                                                       137

5. Sarjeant's *Counting house*, The First Text Originating in the U. S., 1789   159

6. Samuel Freeman's Municipal Accounting Chapter, 1791   213

7. Sarjeant on Federal Currency, and Currency Exchange, 1793   241

8. Thomas Dilworth's *Book-keeper's assistant*, [1794]
                                                       293

9. The Rev. Richard Turner's *New introduction*, 1794
                                                       461

1

INTRODUCTION: BIBLIOGRAPHICAL CONTEXT, SELECTED BIOGRAPHICAL MATTER, AND PROSPECTIVE NONBOOK LITERATURE SEARCHES

CHAPTER 1

INTRODUCTION: BIBLIOGRAPHICAL CONTEXT,

SELECTED BIOGRAPHICAL MATTER, AND PROS-

PECTIVE NONBOOK LITERATURE SEARCHES

This volume of eighteenth-century accounting literature of the United

States, inclusive of the colonial period, relates closely to both Bentley

and Leonard's authoritative bibliography (1934-35), and the more comprehen-

sive pre-1821 study prepared for this series by McMickle and Jensen (1988).

My principal objectives, by way of introduction, are to spell out these

connections, and (subject to an unavoidable limitation) to supplement rele-

vant biographical coverage found in the new bibliography. Two broad new

directions of accounting bibliographical study are recommended in closing.

Development of the Collection--
Bibliographical Background

Bentley and Leonard, 1934-35

Published in Philadelphia and New York, respectively, in 1796 were

William Mitchell's "pioneer American text" A new and complete system of

book-keeping . . . (Bentley and Leonard 1934-35, 1:[9]), and an American

edition of (Edward Thomas) Jones's English system of book-keeping, by single

or double entry . . . (Evans 1903-55, s.v. "1796 AD: Jones, Edward Thomas").

It is not a recent discovery that accounting books were printed in the

United States at an earlier date. In introducing his celebrated collabor-

ation with Leonard, Bentley wrote (1934-35, 1:vi) that they had intention-

ally excluded "American editions" of works originating elsewhere. In that

connection he listed six foreign writers alphabetically, without dates.
They included Jones, whose new book was issued in two editions in London
in 1796 (Thomson 1963, 222), and three of the authors included in this
anthology--Thomas Dilworth, Charles Hutton, and Richard Turner.

Bentley and Leonard could have identified pre-1796 U.S. publications of
the texts by Dilworth and Turner by consulting volume 9, issued in 1925, of
Evans's American bibliography (1903-55, s.v. "1794 AD: Dilworth, Thomas.
The Young Book-keeper's Assistant:" and "Turner, Richard"). Although at
least the reprint source copies bear no such documentation, if these editions were copyrighted Leonard would presumably have identified the two
1794 titles in her review (Bentley and Leonard 1934-35, 1:[iii]) of national
copyright records. The 1788 work by Hutton that preceded the original copyright act (Bentley and Leonard 1934-35, 1:xiii) by two years is not listed
by Evans (1903-55, s.v. "1788 AD") or his successor Bristol (1970, s.v.
"1788"). Evans (1903-55, s.v. "1790 AD: Hutton, Charles") did find an
advertisement of a 1790 edition of Hutton's text reportedly published in
Burlington[, New Jersey], but Shipton and Mooney (1969, s.v. "[Hutton,
Charles . . .]") found no further evidence of such an imprint.

In terms of Bentley and Leonard's understanding (1934-35, 1:iv) of
"works on accounting" as books that deal "exclusively or primarily" with
accounting subject-matter, more recent research has generated only one
additional title prior to 1796, An introduction to the counting house (1789)
by Thomas Sarjeant. Chapter-length contributions by mysterious British
writer George Fisher, appearing in many editions (McMickle 1984, [48]), and
New England author Samuel Freeman have also been noted. In addition, at
least two publications with lesser accounting coverage have been identified
in the preparation of a new bibliography of early literature (McMickle and
Jensen 1988) to which this anthology is closely related.

McMickle and Jensen, 1988

Although planned and developed independently, my volume is in a real
sense a companion to McMickle and Jensen's valuable contribution (1988) to
the Foundations of Accounting series, The birth of American accountancy.
It reprints the principal pre-1796 titles identified in that work, plus
related selections from one of the six authors.

I am specifically indebted to McMickle and his colleagues for identification of the 1737 chapter traced to The instructor by George Fisher
(McMickle 1984); the 1788 printing of Charles Hutton's A course on book-
keeping (McMickle 1984, 36); and the municipal accounting chapter from
Samuel Freeman's manual The town officer, originating in 1791 (McMickle,
Jensen, and Wenzel 1986[1]). In the first connection, before seeing McMickle's
superb documentation (1984, 45) of the "double plagiarism" underlying the
bookkeeping section found in the fifth edition of the Bradfords' manual
The secretary's guide, I had arbitrarily inspected, in microprint, the preceding edition (Shipton 1955-83, no. 3139) instead. At the time I was
using only Shipton and Mooney's short-title bibliography (1969) of pre-1801
American imprints. Had I been able to supplement it with the Evans series
itself (1903-55, s.v. "1737 AD: Bradford, William [sic]"), I would have
found the 1737 title-page reference to bookkeeping.

I first became aware of the 1794 editions of the books by Thomas Dilworth and Richard Turner during visits of 1983 and '84 to the Library Company of Philadelphia and Langsdale Library, home of the Herwood Library of
Accountancy, at the University of Baltimore. The trip to Philadelphia led

3

---

[1]McMickle (1986) was introduced to Freeman's book The town officer
when in the 1970s he received a copy as a gift from the late William Holmes,
a Peat Marwick manager in Boston who is well remembered for his contributions to the study of accounting history.

indirectly also to my acquaintance through microprint edtitions (Shipton 1955–83, nos. 21445, 22127, 22870) with the three works by Thomas Sarjeant that are represented in this volume. In a subsequent article on that writer (Sheldahl 1985), I subsequently characterized his 1789 book as the first full-scale accounting text originating in the United States, broadly understood. This judgment has not been challenged by McMickle and Jensen (1987b, 21, 27).

Following up on a suggestion made at the close of the Sarjeant article (Sheldahl 1985, 29), and with the encouragement of editor Richard Brief, I developed a preliminary table of contents for this anthology late in 1986.[2] My revised prospectus of March 1987 listed the eight books or selections that follow. Six weeks after submitting it, I saw an abstract of a paper just presented by McMickle and Jensen (1987a) that identified two additional pre-1796 "American accounting works." When by happenstance I saw McMickle at another 1987 regional meeting a few days later, on May 1, I assured him at once that the anthology would not further infringe on his discoveries. After the meeting, I may have assisted the resumption of contact between Professors McMickle and Brief that would lead to publication of the new bibliography (McMickle and Jensen 1988).

In preparing to introduce this collection, I later inspected the two additions mentioned, The deputy commissary's guide by Maryland administrative official (McMickle and Jensen 1987b, 18) Elie Vallette (1774), and The

---

[2] Based on the Sarjeant article (Sheldahl 1985, 26), the original prospectus cited The American youth's instructor, a posthumous 1795 adaptation of The British youth's instructor by Daniel Fenning. I had uncritically associated it with the 1806 thirteenth edition of the British series, containing "a compendious method of book-keeping" Shipton and Mooney 1969, s.v. "Fenning, Daniel," first entry, "Fenning, Daniel, d. 1767"; and Thomson 1963, 217, quoted). Evans's entry (1903–55, s.v. "1795 AD: Fenning, Daniel. The American Youth's Instructor") reveals, however, that the 1795 book did not include the accounting section.

<u>rural oeconomy</u> by famed English agricultural authority (Hans 1951, 13)
Arthur Young (1776). The warrant for their inclusion within McMickle and
Jensen's comprehensive study (1987b, 16-19) is in no way questioned. None-
theless, due to the incidental nature of the accounting coverage found I
would not have included material from either book in my anthology even had
there been no personal commitment of the kind just reported.

In August of last year McMickle gave me a preliminary draft of the new
bibliography through 1808, twelve years short of the endpoint of the project
(McMickle and Jensen 1987b). At sixty-four pages, this manuscript is only
one-fourth the length of the eventual book ([Brief] 1988, 5, no. 10). I
understand, further, that in the process that led to the finished product
the draft material itself was heavily revised (McMickle 1988). By dint of
circumstance, however, I have access at this writing only to their 1987
coverage for purposes of introducing the reprinted literature without dup-
licating McMickle and Jensen's very able bibliographical and biographical
work. In what follows, then, I try to complement that coverage in the full
expectation that significant if indeterminate parts of the exposition will
be made redundant by the published bibliography (McMickle and Jensen 1988).

My only comment regarding <u>method</u> probably reflects no more than an
inadvertence in the preparation of preliminary front matter. As with the
prior abstract (McMickle and Jensen 1987a, 315), a limitation noted in
timely correspondence with editor Brief, the introduction to the draft manuscript (McMickle and Jensen 1987b, [v]) refers to only one general pre-
1801 source, Evans's massive <u>American bibliography</u> (1903-55). Two follow-up
works are essential additions to that remarkable study, however.

To the 39,162 Evans titles (1903-55), Bristol's <u>Supplement</u> (1970) adds
11,262 further imprints, of which Shipton and Mooney (1969, title, quoted,
1:v) include 10,035 in their "Short-Title Evans." The latter work should

5

be consulted as a concise alphabetical index to virtually the full Evans-
Bristol bibliography; as a key, relatedly, to the 1639-1800 Early American
Imprints microform series (Shipton 1955-83) based thereon, adding a substantial listing (Shipton and Mooney 1969, 1:xix-xxv, 2:xv-xxi (same list))
of source libraries; and as an authoritative guide to the many "ghost[s]" or
"serious bibliographical error[s]" (Shipton and Mooney 1969, 1:vi) found in
the Evans series. The value of such a source to an efficient search for
non-serial (Shipton and Mooney 1969, 1:v) publications from the period is
apparent.

　　　Granting that the short titles used do not provide the detail on contents that is found in the Evans entries (1903-55, excluding final volume),
my own review of Bristol (1970) and of Shipton and Mooney (1969) has dis-
closed no additional accounting titles. There is strong indirect evidence,
in any event, that McMickle and Jensen _did_ consult one or both of the two
sequels. They state (McMickle and Jensen 1987b, [v]) that there are "more
than 100,000 [total] entries" in the bibliographies by Evans and his successors for the period 1801-19, Shaw and Shoemaker (1958-83). Since the
early nineteenth-century study lists 51,960 titles (Shaw and Shoemaker
1958-83, vols. 1-20), it is evident that the stated total can be reached
only by including Bristol's Supplement (1970), at least as substantially
incorporated by Shipton and Mooney (1969).

　　　In their preliminary draft McMickle and Jensen (1987b) do not explain
the extension of coverage through 1820, a year beyond Shaw and Shoemaker's
endpoint. A possible rationale is the fact that, as indicated by the title
that _he_ used in bringing his study through 1798 and into '99, Evans himself
(1903-55, vols. 1-12) intended to cover American printing through 1820, the
year of commencement of the bibliography through 1861 developed earlier by

Roorbach (1852-61). In any event, Shoemaker's volume (1964) on that year would have been available for the extension of coverage to 1820.

Although it does not compromise their methods or results, finally, McMickle and Jensen (1987b, [v]) make a patent factual error in stating, indeed with emphasis (underscoring), that Evans's bibliography is not classified by subject-matter. To the contrary, the rear matter in every Evans volume (1903-55, for example, 1:433-42) includes a detailed subject classification. Only by historical accident do these thirteen indexes lack subject designations that would have served the specific purposes at hand.

Even in their preliminary version, McMickle and Jensen (1987b) supply extensive bibliographical and, often, biographical information pertinent to this collection. I have nothing to add to their prior coverage (McMickle, Jensen, and Wenzel 1986; inserted within McMickle and Jensen 1987b, 31-37) of Freeman, and have elsewhere (Sheldahl 1985) provided considerable background material on Sarjeant and his work. I shall accordingly at this point supplement the preliminary writeups (McMickle 1984, reproduced without tables and figures in following source, 1-15; and McMickle and Jensen 1987b, 20, 30, 38-43) on Fisher, Hutton, Dilworth, and Turner.

Supplemental Biographical Coverage
George Fisher

McMickle (1984, 46, 49) has ably discussed the absence of non-bibliographical information on George Fisher, and the long perpetuated myth that "he" was Ann Fisher Slack, whose book of fables and morality tales The pleasing instructor was apparently confused with Fisher's manual The instructor (Sheldahl 1985, 8). He has also listed nineteen U.S. or prior colonial printings of The [American] instructor between 1748 and 1833, providing full bibliographical data and specifying a source library for each edition or printing (McMickle 1984, [48]). Understandably omitted are four Evans listings from 1766-92 of ostensible printings by Hugh Gaine of New York that could not be located or confirmed by Shipton (1955-83) in developing the 1639-1800 Early American Imprints series (Shipton and Mooney 1969, s.v. "[Fisher, George . . .. The American Instructor . . ..]").

It is useful to supplement McMickle's 1984 references (44-47, 49) to the original American publisher of Fisher's bookkeeping chapter, and the contents and backgrounds of his principal works. In the former regard, Andrew Bradford, whose father William had become the first printer in both Pennsylvania and New York, was Philadelphia's leading printer prior to Franklin (Wroth 1938, 29-31, [59]). On December 22, 1719, he and a partner soon to withdraw introduced the American Weekly Mercury as the first colonial newspaper outside Boston. The Boston Gazette had appeared as the second one a day earlier. Andrew Bradford published the weekly continuously until his death in 1742, joined periodically on the masthead by his father although (Wroth 1938, 31) the elder Bradford resided in New York City throughout this time, starting its first paper in 1725. In some ways Philadelphia's Mercury, carried on (Wroth 1938, 31) until 1746 by the founder's widow, and New York's Gazette represented "the first form of chain journalism in this country" (Kobre 1944, 28, 37-39, quoting 38).

Coverage of accounts, if any, within Andrew Bradford's newspaper, available (Park 1988) in Philadelphia at the Historical Society of Pennsylvania, has not been determined. In the first two issues of 1735, however, the Mercury presented a seriously distorted unsigned version of an important essay on mercantile education by contemporary English bookkeeping writer William Webster (Sheldahl 1988, 147-48, 151-66, Webster's essay).

The instructor, the original source of the bookkeeping appendix published by Bradford in 1737, was one of the century's foremost general-

purpose manuals for _self_ instruction. The issuance of many colonial or
U.S. editions following the 1748 ninth edition, titled like most of the
later ones "The _American_ Instructor" (McMickle 1984, [48]), supports
Cremin's assertion (1970, 394) that it was "by far the most popular" one-
volume encyclopedic digest of "useful knowledge" of a day of limited formal
schooling opportunity.

As revealed by the title page reprinted by McMickle (1984, 47), the
scope of The American instructor (Fisher 1748) is remarkable. It covered
(Wroth 1938, 244)

> spelling, the three R's, letter writing, business accounts and forms,
> American geography and statistics, carpentry, mechanical rules, prices,
> rates, wages, the use of the sliding rule, guaging, dialling, dyeing,
> and color making. It included also [John] Tennant's Poor Planter's
> Physician, and gave instructions to the housewife in the care of linen,
> in the making of pickles, preserves, plasters, and wine . . ..

The medical self-instructor Every man his own doctor, or the poor planter's
physician had originated in Williamsburg and Philadelphia in 1734 (Wroth
1938, 242).

McMickle incorrectly conjectures (1984, 45-46) that within the printing firm Franklin and Hall, which would issue another edition of the book
in 1753, David Hall was primarily responsible for bringing out the initial
American version of Fisher's Instructor. In 1745, three years before publication, Benjamin Franklin had ordered two dozen copies of the British
work in preparation for developing a revised edition (Fisher 1748, title,
italicized except for 'American') "better adapted to these American colonies, than any other Book of like Kind." Franklin accordingly "omitted
portions of little use to colonial readers, corrected errors in the arithmetical section, and added significant features" that included the medical
writeup, capsule histories of the colonies, and his essay '"Advice to a
Young Tradesman, written by an Old One"' (Miller 1974, 237).

The 1748 preface (Fisher, [v]), published thirty-seven years (American Antiquarian Society (AAS) staff 1987, 81) before Philadelphia's first city directory, is signed, as it were, "Vale & Frurre." Those names are nowhere to be found in Shipton and Mooney's index (1969), for example. Presumably, however, they represent the Latin phrase '"[V]ale et freure"', meaning '"Goodby and enjoy"' (Morris 1988, emphasis in original).

George Fisher is known, beyond The instructor, for two series of arithmetic books. First, by 1722 he was listed as the editor (in effect) of new editions of Cocker's Arithmetic (McMickle 1984, 49). The reference, shown in the form used in the source, is to a celebrated text believed to have originated as a posthumous publication of English mathematician Edward Cocker's (1631-75). The book was brought out in 1678 by John Hawkins, probably a schoolmaster successor of Cocker's, and included an address by his fellow accounting writer John Collins, an early member of London's elite scientific body the Royal Society (The dictionary of national biography (D.n.b.) 1917, s.v. "Cocker, Edward"; and Thomson 1963, 205, 207). The D.n.b. entry just cited states that inclusive of Scots and Irish imprints, found also (Thomson 1963, 213) for Fisher's Instructor, at least 112 editions of Cocker's Arithmetic appeared; and lavishes praise upon a text noted for its rules, definitions, and examples.

Independently, George Fisher published Arithmetic in the pla[i]nest and most concise method . . ., originating in 1719 (McMickle 1984, 49). Peter Brynberg of Wilmington, Delaware, who three years earlier (Shipton and Mooney 1969, s.v. "Fisher, George," next-to-last entry) had reprinted The instructor, finally brought out an American edition of Fisher's Arithmetic in 1800. The author explained in his preface (Fisher 1800, vi) that he hoped to improve upon noted earlier writers including "Cooker" (shown

in the possessive form) as much as they had improved upon their own prede-
cessors. Fisher's coverage (1800, vi, quoted, [xi]-xii (Contents)) of the
four basic arithmetical operations, "with so much plainness and perspicuity,
and in such familiar and pertinent terms, that the meanest capacity may
understand and apply them properly," extended to a wide range of commercial
applications. Comparison is readily invited with Sarjeant's concise chapter
on mercantile arithmetic reprinted as chapter 4.

If Fisher is the most mysterious contributor to early American accounting literature, Charles Hutton, whose text stands next in line chronologic-
ally despite a half-century interval, is perhaps the most thoroughly known
of the authors.

Charles Hutton

Charles Hutton, 1737-1823, was one of England's outstanding mathemati-
cians and, using a contemporary (Hans 1951, 185) professional title, Teachers of Mathematics of his day. The son of a mining laborer and stepson of
a mining foreman, he began his teaching career at age eighteen in a village
near his native Newcastle-on-Tyne after himself working in the mines. Following diligent independent study and attendance at night classes held
there while teaching full time, Hutton opened his own mathematical school
in Newcastle in 1760, and also taught math at the leading local school
(D.n.b. 1917, s.v. "Hutton, Charles").

In Newcastle Charles Hutton taught mostly local artisans and merchants,
but many gentry as well attended adult classes that he offered within a
flourishing program that covered all areas of applied mathematics. Besides
conducting a school whose expansion required a new building, Hutton tutored
in affluent homes, and in that connection an influential squire placed a
considerable personal library at his disposal (Hans 1951, 109-10).

Hutton's Newcastle pupils included Elisabeth Surkes, whom he helped
become one of the most knowledgeable women of the age in mathematical and
scientific terms; and her future husband John Scott (Hans 1951, 110, 206), a
highly reactionary statesman in a long career as Britain's soliciter general,
attorney general, and lord chancellor. "[A]n unrelenting opponent of Cath-
olic emanicipation and of liberal reform" who became the first earl of
Eldon, Scott was virtual prime minister during the years 1807-12 (The
Columbia encyclopedia 3d, s.v. "Eldon, John Scott").

Charles Hutton published his first book in 1764 (D.n.b. 1917, s.v.
"Hutton, Charles"). Although the original primary title was soon dropped,
The schoolmaster's guide, or a complete system of practical arithmetic and
book-keeping . . . would go through at least twenty British printings or
editions through 1871. Both single and double-entry bookkeeping were covered in a section of the book published independently in 1838 (Thomson
1963, 219), fifty years after the former part as reprinted in this volume
had appeared in Philadelphia. Even earlier A course of book-keeping, according to the method of single entry had been published as a free-standing book
in London (McMickle and Jensen 1987b, 20). Although no record of such a
sequel has been found, a note to the "Advertisement" that opened the American edition (Hutton 1788, [iii]n) raised the possibility that if the text
were well received "a System of Double Entry m[ight] follow," presumably
also descended from the text first published by Hutton in 1764.

In 1773 Charles Hutton seized two professional opportunities that would
largely define the balance of his career. He began forty-five years as
editor of The Lady's Diary, an influential magazine of popular science and
mathematics directed especially toward a female audience that was noted for
brainteasing puzzles that attracted lively competition from among young and

older scholars alike. In 1775 the new editor published two volumes of selected problems and solutions from some seventy years of Diary issues (D.n.b. 1917, s.v. "Hutton, Charles"; and Hans 1951, 155-57).

After a very rigorous and competitive selection process, Charles Hutton was in 1773 also elected Professor of Mathematics at the Royal Military Academy at Woolwich, a London borough, where he would remain until retirement in 1807. Late in Hutton's teaching career Henry Clarke, a mathematician and teacher only a few years younger with a remarkably similar career and reputation, took the same post at the nearby Royal Military Academy at Great Marlow, with which he would move to Sandhurst in southern England in 1812. Evidently as a result of World War II bombing ravages, the two academies were merged at Sandhurst in 1946 (The Columbia-Viking desk encyclopedia 2d, s.v. "Woolwich"; D.n.b. 1917, s.v. "Clarke, Henry," "Hutton, Charles"; and Sheldahl 1988, 316-24). In a day in which as religious "Dissenters" they were barred from English degrees, both largely self-taught men received honorary doctorates from the University of Edinburgh, but although Clarke likewise had excellent credentials and prominent support only Hutton was admitted to the Royal Society (D.n.b. 1917, s.v. "Clarke, Henry," "Hutton, Charles"; and Hans 1951, 17 and 24, quoted, [247]).

A surveyor in Newcastle and an authority on navigation and related fields, Charles Hutton wrote a number of "clear and accurate" books in applied mathematics (D.n.b. 1917, s.v. "Hutton, Charles," quoting 353). His foremost contribution was a two-volume Mathematical and philosophical dictionary originating in 1795, and representing England's first dictionary of mathematics, physical science, and leading exponents of those fields (Hans 1951, 155; and Hutton 1815, 1:title).

There is one significant uncertainty regarding Hutton's 1788 American

13

text ([iii]): Who was the "W. W." who signed the opening advertisement?
Most likely it was someone readily identifiable, from the initials, with
printing or publishing in Philadelphia.

Based on inspection of the 'W' entries in Shipton and Mooney (1969, 2:
955-1017) and the three most contemporary city directories (Biddle 1791,
135-46 (40 "W. W." names); [Macpherson] 1785, 140-51 (42); and White 1785,
76-83 (24)), the editor was probably William Waring. He compiled New-Jersey
almanacs for the years 1788-92, and Philadelphia almanacs (Poor Will's), perhaps including pocket editions, for at least one additional year (Shipton
and Mooney 1969, s.v. "Waring, William. d. 1793," including bracketing of
name). Waring is listed by Biddle (1791, s.v. "Waring William," no comma)
as a schoolmaster, a vocation that might well have contributed to his
interest in a bookkeeping text.

While Charles Hutton was in the prime of his career when his work first
appeared in the United States, both Thomas Dilworth and Richard Thomas were
deceased when in 1794 their bookkeeping texts were published in American
editions. The date is imputed in the first case.

Thomas Dilworth

For a writer whose texts on arithmetic and the English language went
through innumerable editions, and whose accounting book (Thomson 1963, 220)
was also reprinted many times, Thomas Dilworth is surprisingly obscure. He
died in 1780, forty years after the initial appearance of his text A new
guide to the English tongue (Downey 1978, vi). Dilworth (1754, 1762, 1768,
1773, titles), shown as "Wappin" in first case) taught school on Wapping,
a famous street next to Tower Hill and the famous Tower of London. Wapping's history is steeped in intrigue and violence, particularly by way of
the hanging of "rebellious and otherwise violent sailors" such as, in 1701,

Captain Kidd. Near the infamous Execution Dock is the Prospect of Whitby, "once a smugglers' pub and now a tourists', with a fascinating riverside view" (Howell 1970, 109).

Despite its notoriety, Wapping enjoyed some distinction educationally in the 1700s. A mathematical school was opened there around 1720 by Thomas Haseldon, a past member of England's mercantile marine who had been a Teacher of Mathematics to the Royal Navy at Portsmouth. A fellow of the Royal Society beginning in 1739 who may still have been teaching in the '60s, Haseldon taught mathematics, navigation, and merchant's accounts and wrote textbooks in the first two fields (Hans 1951, 110-11).

From Dilworth's own generation was James Ferguson, an "eminent experimental philosopher, mechanist and astronomer" who moved to London from his native Scotland in 1740 at age thirty. Self-educated, he began his career as an instrument maker, and soon established himself nationwide as a writer and lecturer on mathematics and experimental science. Ferguson had a school at Wapping in 1766, four years before conducting a notable lecture series in Newcastle with assistance from Charles Hutton (Hans 1951, 145, quoted, 146).

Thomas Dilworth introduced The young book-keeper's assistant, reprinted from its first United States edition below, at some point between 1747 and '60. In the earlier year it was not noted alongside his arithmetic text on the title page of the first American edition of his English speller (Cohen 1974, 1:539; and Downey 1978, vi). In the later year the bookkeeping text was listed for sale by New York printer and bookseller (Keep 1909, 101-2) Hugh Gaine (Sheldahl 1985, 31, note 23). With the publication of the fourth edition in 1765 (The national union catalog, pre-1956 imprints (N.u.c.) 1968-81, s.v. "Dilworth, Thomas, d. 1780[.] The young book-keeper's assistant," entry 1) and the seventh twelve years later (Thomson 1963, 218), the bookkeeping text seems to have originated around midcentury.

In their preliminary draft, McMickle and Jensen (1987b, 30) cautiously stated that the first U.S. edition of The young book-keeper's assistant, undated, "is likely to have" appeared "between 1790 and 1794." More recent contact (McMickle 1988) reveals that they have since accepted the traditional dating (Evans 1903-55, s.v. "1794 AD: Dilworth, Thomas. The Young Book-keeper's Assistant"; and Shipton and Mooney 1969, s.v. "Dilworth, Thomas," next-to-last entry) at 1794. In Dilworth's day (1768, title) the book had been addressed in part to schools in English "Plantations and Colonies Abroad." Mentioned above, the slightly earlier writer William Webster cited by Dilworth (1768, [iv], [1794, iv]) as anticipating his own approach to accounting exposition is the subject of a chapter within another volume in this series (Sheldahl 1988, 144-50, 151-66, reprinted essay).

Dilworth's arithmetic text The schoolmaster's assistant (1773, title) covers in five sections whole numbers; "vulgar" or non-decimal fractions; decimals; questions and answers (sample problems and solutions); and duo-decimals, "commonly called Cross Multiplication." Parts 1 (Dilworth 1773, 1-110) and 3 (123-68), in particular, provide a wide variety of mercantile applications of the kinds reprinted, from Thomas Sarjeant's Elementary principles of arithmetic, in chapter 4. The coverage of decimal fractions includes, for example, annuities, leases, and real estate as well as more general treatment of interest calculations.

In 1797 William Milns ([iv]), a Londoner who had moved to New York three years earlier to continue his teaching and writing career in the New World (Sheldahl 1988, 335-43, biographical), wrote that the Assistant had gone through "upwards of one hundred editions," and was still widely used both in Europe and America. This rounded estimate is supported by documentation that in the United States (to oversimplify slightly) alone there were

23 or 24 printings of the book between 1773 and 1800 (Shipton and Mooney 1969, s.v. "Dilworth, Thomas . . .. The Schoomaster's Assistant," including one bracketed entry).

In the preface to his own book of commercial arithmetic, Milns further stated (1797, [iv-v]) that the section of questions and answers was nearly the only recommendation for Dilworth's text, while acknowledging that he had himself borrowed freely from the book, among a number of other arithmetics. In noting that even the book's strong point was marred for an American audience by the lack of reference to local currency, Milns could not have foreseen in 1797 that over the next thirty-five years four authors would bring out a dozen revisions adapting Dilworth's text specifically to the new nation (N.u.c. 1968-81, s.v. "Dilworth, Thomas . . .": "Dilworth's assistant" (or 'Assistant'), "Dilworth's Book-keepers assistant," "Federal calculator," "The federal calculator").

Thomas Dilworth's most famous book was probably A new guide to the English tongue. Explicitly addressed in 1762 (Dilworth, title), in part, to "the several English Colonies and Plantations abroad," it appeared in from 44 to 78 U.S. or prior colonial editions or printings between 1747 and 1800. The lower figure represents the number of volumes located for the first Early American Imprints microform series (Shipton 1955-83), while the higher one adds all additional printings listed (1903-55) by Evans (Shipton and Mooney 1969, s.v. "Dilworth, Thomas . . .. A New Guide to the English Tongue . . .," bracketed for the 34 non-verified listings.)

Dilworth's New guide was first and foremost a spelling text (Downey 1978, vi). It included, however, "A short, but comprehensive Grammar" (emphasis in original) of English, and a reader (Cohen 1974, 1:539; and Dilworth 1754, 1762, [1793], titles). Among at least a dozen English grammars to be imported or reprinted in America through the Revolutionary War period,

Dilworth's text was apparently the most widely used. Furthermore, its influence was felt during the early years of the newly formed republic and beyond. It is well documented, for example, that Abraham Lincoln used the book as a boy, according to one authority as the first text he studied (Downey 1978, xiv). It seems fitting that this "grammar of religious and moral living as well as . . . the English language" became in 1978 the first entry in a new series of historical texts on the evolution of American grammar (Dilworth [1793]; and Downey 1978, xiii, quoted, xv).

Another work by Thomas Dilworth was <u>Miscellaneous arithmetic: or a full account of the new calendar; with the several uses of the logarithms, and of multiplication and division by mon[e]y, &c.</u> Three parts (or chapters) of this seven-part book advertised within Dilworth's 1768 bookkeeping text ([ii]) dealt with ecclesiastical computation, as with the dating of Easter, under (<u>Columbia encyclopedia</u> 3d, s.v. "Calendar") the Gregorian calendar finally adopted in Britain and her colonies in 1752. Another one was probably the same elementary essay on the education of children shown as front matter within the 1773 edition (Dilworth, [ix]-xiv) of the arithmetic text, and separately published in Massachusetts in '82. Dilworth also published an astronomy book; a lengthy reply as "An advocate for the ladies" to a "scandalous" tract asserting "[t]he folly, sin, and danger of marrying widows and old women"; and an Anglican catechetical guide (<u>N.u.c.</u> 1968-81, s.v. "Dilworth, Thomas . . ." (or 'Thomas.'): "An advocate for the ladies," quoted, "The catechism of the Church of England explained," "An essay on the education of youth," "A new and complete description of the terrestial and celestial globes").

The second English author of an accounting text that was posthumously issued in the United States in 1794 came from the clerical rather than teaching ranks, and was still more broadly based as a writer than Dilworth.

Richard Turner

Richard Turner, c. 1724-1791, was a graduate of Magdalen "Hall," a
residential unit established alongside the Oxford "College" of the same
name in the fifteenth century that, in the manner of earlier student houses
opened at the university, had taken on a teaching role. In conjunction with
an older hall longer associated with Exeter College, Magdalen Hall gave rise
in the nineteenth century to Hertford College, named for the original donor
of land, circa 1301, that it occupies. Hertford's most famous graduate is
perhaps the twentieth-century satirist Evelyn Waugh (D.n.b. 1917, s.v.
"Turner, Richard (1724?-1791)," reference to Turner; and Hall and Frankl
1983, [6], 44-45, 50, otherwise).

Although he was a cleric within the Church of England, Turner in 1785
received an honorary Doctor of Laws degree from the University of Glasgow
in Scotland, where the Presbyterian Church (New Webster's universal encyclopedia 1987, s.v. "Church of Scotland") had secured established status
in 1690. He published at least three works in applied mathematics, dealing
respectively with guaging, trigonometry, and geometry. He also wrote on
geography, astronomy, and (in a tract not examined that appeared the year
of his death) education (D.n.b. 1917, s.v. "Turner, Richard (1724?-1791)").

A 1779 work on classical geography and a 1787 study of "Universal
History" attributed to the Rev. Mr. Turner by McMickle and Jensen, in
their preliminary manuscript (1987b, 38), belonged instead to his namesake
son. The younger Turner wrote several popular textbooks prior to his death
at age thirty-five, and is separately cited in the D.n.b. (1917, s.v.
"Turner, Richard (1753-88)"). Likewise listed (D.n.b. 1917, s.v. "Turner,
Thomas") is his brother Thomas, a famous potter described as "an excellent
chemist, . . . a thorough master of . . . porcelain manufacture, . . . a
skillful draughtsman, designer, and engraver, and . . . a clever musician."

Richard Turner, Sr.'s bookkeeping text (1794, title), oddly enough omitted from the D.n.b. writeup, was published in the United States by the Boston printing and bookselling firm Thomas and Andrews. Isaiah Thomas, later to develop a classic history of American printing (Thomas 1970) and to found the American Antiquarian Society (Staff 1987, 17-18), "was the leading American printer and publisher of his day" (McCorison 1970, x). Ebenezer Andrews had been a printing apprentice of his, and the two men extended their bookselling and, in the second case, printing business to Baltimore and Albany in 1794 and '96 (Thomas 1970, 181-82).

The careful work of McMickle and Jensen (1988) should largely conclude the identification of accounting books, chapters, and chapter sections published in the United States through 1820. Although isolated further book coverage may be found, it is time to turn bibliographical attention concerning the colonial and early national periods in new directions. Two inviting areas are the distribution of accounting literature, wherever published, in early America; and, granting that fruitful results can by no means be assured, nonbook accounting publication of the day.

Two Major Areas for Further Bibliographical Study of Early American Accounting

Distribution of Accounting Literature

Readers obtain published literature primarily through purchase (or gift) or borrowing. In colonial America and the early United States, books were sold through bookstores, auctions, subscription, and (not covered in the search noted below) peddling (Lehmann-Haupt 1952, 46-59). For lending purposes, many public libraries of one kind or another were formed (Sheldahl 1987, 21). To study a literature distribution is to review bookseller and library holdings, including (as recorded) those of personal collections.

Using Shipton and Mooney's index (1969) as my principal guide, I have through research travel in recent years examined roughly three hundred relevant titles, mostly bookstore and library catalogs, from the original Early American Imprints microform series (Shipton 1955-83). On the off chance that book information might be found, I have also inspected dozens of irrelevant broadsides. Although McMickle and Jensen's final listing (1988), pre-1801, may require reexamination of some items, every effort has been made to secure exhaustive coverage of the source. One implication of the review is that the literature reprinted in this volume was in general widely available, granting that particular editions or printings are not identified.

21

Philadelphia, New York, and Boston understandably predominate within book listings that provide reasonably broad coverage overall. The most serious limitation is negligible inclusion of Virginia, where printing was permanently introduced in 1730 following a brief effort of the 1680s (Wroth 1938, 38-39, 42). For the first thirty-six years there existed in Virginia only one press, allegedly "thought to be too much under the control of the governor" (Cappon and Duff 1950, 1:vi; and Thomas 1970, 552, quoted). Evans's assertion (1903-55, 3:447) that a Williamsburg bookseller maintained a press in 1763 stands unsupported by his own entries (s.v. "1763 AD").

A more than ample supply of book notices for Virginia, 1736-80, is available from a microfilm collection (Virginia Gazette 1950) of three Williamsburg newspapers of the period known as the "Virginia Gazette" (Cappon and Duff 1950, 1:vi; Kobre 1944, 81, 178-79, artificially distinguishing the paper brought out by William Hunter and his successors, 1751-80, from the one established by William Parks in 1736; and Thomas 1970, 552-58). The comprehensive subject index (Cappon and Duff 1950, s.v. "Books," especially "Books for sale, in Williamsburg, Va.") cites more than two hundred sales announcements, for example, together with hundreds of other book-related references. In assembling the first directory, evidently, of accounting literature locations through 1800, I plan to add a survey of Virginia Gazette book notices (1736-80) to the data obtained from the microprint collection (Shipton 1955-83).

The reference to newspapers calls attention to possible vast expansion of directory work, as the colonial Virginia newspapers were assuredly not distinctive in their day (and beyond) in carrying bookstore ads and other relevant items. Advertising, with books counted among the staples of coverage, "had become a permanent part of the [newspaper] institution" during its early development in seventeenth-century England (Kobre 1944, 8), and commonly accounted for nearly half of early American copy (Wroth 1938, 234). The reference likewise points up the principal source for advertising notices relative to accounting education and practice (Sheldahl 1987, especially 4, 10-11, 16-18), and a possible nonbook source of accounting literature itself. Along with newspapers, early American magazines are an unexplored potential source of accounting material.

Nonbook Sources of Accounting Literature

The first United States accounting journal was The Book-Keeper, which

with a title change along the way began a four-year run in 1880 ([Brief] 1988, 9, no. 25). Earlier business-related periodicals had included Hunt's Merchants' Magazine and Commercial Review, "a journal of commerce and finance" founded (Previts and Merino 1979, 49) in New York in 1839; and The Commercial Review of the South and West, or De Bow's Review, originating in New Orleans seven years later (Paskoff and Wilson 1982, 1, 2, quoted). Any expectation of a major serial literature in accounting prior to 1880, just

after the commencement of coverage in the first Accountants' index ([Brief]
1988, 9, no. 24), is tempered, however, by the mere five references found
under the terms "Accountants," "Accounts," and "Bookkeeping" in a major
index based on 239 English-language periodicals, including those published
by Hunt and De Bow, from 1802-81 (Poole [1891], titles, 1:xiv-xix, and s.v.
headings cited). Three references were to Hunt's . . ., including one of
unusual scope (254 pages, s.v. "Accounts"), and another one concerned a
two-part article from a New York banking journal.

Newspapers from the colonies and early states certainly promise a
wealth of primary information concerning not only the distribution of
accounting books, but also, principally through advertising by interested
parties, teaching and practice in the field. Valuable information on such
topics may have been found also in early magazines or other periodicals. A
highly problematic search for nonbook accounting literature, including in
the broadest sense the publication of actual accounting records, should thus
be combined or coordinated with work on related topics.

The potential scale of such study would invite participation over an
extended time by a substantial team of investigators, perhaps working under
the auspices of the Academy of Accounting Historians. Fellowship opportunities should be sought from the American Antiquarian Society (Staff 1987,
29, quoted, 167-68; and Anderson 1987, s.v. "American Antiquarian Society")
for study at that institution in Worcester, Mass., with its unmatched
holdings (as illustrated below) on "the territories that became the United
States of America," from their settlement by Europeans through 1876.

Kobre's highly readable survey (1944) of the colonial newspaper includes
interesting comparisons of the contents of leading papers. The first one,
disregarding a single issue produced in the same town fourteen years earlier,
originated in Boston in 1704 as a single small sheet printed on both sides

(Kobre 1944, 13, 17-18). Most colonial papers were four-page weeklies with extensive local advertising (Wroth 1938, 234). After 1750, however, one- or two-page "Postscripts," "Supplements," or "Extraordinaries" ('"Extras"') were added with some regularity, and by the time of the Revolutionary War there was movement toward semi-weekly publication. A Philadelphia newspaper that had introduced four political essays by Thomas Paine in 1776 became the first regularly issued American daily eight years later after having in the interim become an early tri-weekly paper. The number of English-language papers published in the colonies doubled between 1750 and '64, from 12 to 24, and doubled again by 1775, reflecting in the latter case the rise of politically motivated (patriot or loyalist) journalism (Kobre 1944, 96, 147-48, 154, 158, [174], quoted).

The foremost general bibliographical source on early newspapers remains Clarence Brigham's 1947 History and bibliography of American newspapers, 1690-1820, listing 2,120 titles (AAS staff 1987, 141). On another accounting, 1,934 papers had appeared by 1820 within the thirty states, inclusive of their prior history, that by then belonged to the union. More than 30 percent of them had lasted no more than a year, and fewer than 20 percent had survived for ten years or more (Wroth 1938, 232-33).

The American Antiquarian Society holds the world's finest collection of pre-1821 American newspapers, with 1,494 of the titles listed by Brigham. The society also maintains a full set of the largest microform collection, the Readex Early American Newspaper Series, 1690-1820, recorded both on opaque microprint cards and (so far as the reformatting has progressed) microfilm. Representing an ongoing project, the Readex series will ultimately include the full AAS collection, focused regionally on the northeast, as well as expanded further coverage (AAS staff 1987, 146; and Tracy 1988).

Another outstanding original collection is held by the world's largest library (Gurney and Apple 1981, title), the Library of Congress. Greenwood Press has (re)printed a 401-page index of eighteenth-century American newspapers listed by that institution (Hamilton 1988, 6, col. 2, entry 6). The Washington library has further supported newspaper research by assembling comprehensive indexes, so far as possible, of microform collections available in United States libraries ([United States] Library of Congress, 1973, 1978).

It is said (AAS staff 1987, 146) that while geneaological guides are often available for early newspapers, broader subject indexes generally are not. In any event, Milner's three-volume "Location and Subject Guide" (1977-82) to newspaper indexes should be very useful. An excellent subject index exists for Williamsburg's <u>Virginia Gazettes</u> (Cappon and Duff 1950). Indexed beyond the geneaological level through 1748 is the <u>Pennsylvania Gazette</u> (Milner 1977-82, 1:66), which after its founding by Franklin in 1729 as the successor to a paper introduced at the close of the preceding year became "the standard of comparison" and "the most interesting newspaper" in colonial America (Kobre 1944, 53-55, 61, quoted). With the apparent exception of the years 1846-49, the newspapers of Savannah, Georgia are indexed from their beginnings in 1763. Coverage through 1825 was provided through two New Deal WPA projects (General index . . . 1937, 1938, inspected in reviewing overall local indexing at the Georgia Historical Society in Savannah), although only the eighteenth-century volumes go beyond a proper-name format to supply meaningful subject classification.

The first (nonnewspaper) periodical, or <u>magazine</u>, to be issued in the colonies was a London title reprinted in Philadelphia in 1724. Seventeen years later Andrew Bradford and Franklin separately brought out short-lived magazines, Bradford after obtaining surreptitious notice of Franklin's plans. Two magazines started in Boston in 1743 were published for two or three years each. Through 1770, 20 periodicals were started; another one was launched during the Revolutionary War; and 79 serials made their first appearance during the balance of the century. It was reported fifty years ago that "[m]ore or less complete files remain[ed] of" 88 of the sum total of 100 titles (Wroth 1938, 236-37, 238, quoted).

The American Antiquarian Society reports today (Staff 1987, 147) that "[n]early all the eighteenth-century American . . . periodicals are represented" in its holdings, along with "a very large percentage" of magazines originating between 1801 and 1819. An Early American periodical index, 1743-1850 developed as a WPA project, and now available on Readex microprint cards, separately covers "authors, subjects, titles, poetry, and book reviews" for 370 publications (AAS staff 1987, 150). Already mentioned is Poole's Index ([1891]) for 1802-81 that includes English-language periodicals from other countries.

The AAS also owns the leading microfilm collection of early serial publications. The American Periodical Series for 1741-1835 was reissued by University Microfilms in Ann Arbor in 1979 (AAS staff 1987, 150; and Shipton and Mooney 1969, s.v. "The Mirror," entry 1).

The five-volume 1965 Union list of serials in libraries of the United States and Canada (Titus, description based primarily on 1:[iii-vi] ("Preface," "Introduction") reports the locations of 156,449 titles from throughout the world, listed alphabetically, that commenced publication before 1950. An annotated 1964 international bibliography (Freitag, based on iii, quoted, v, 127) of 1,218 union lists or similar documents compiled since 1859 ('76 in the U.S.), 60 percent or more of them since the Second World

War, includes

> newspapers, periodicals, annuals, services, government publications,
> proceedings of conferences and congresses, [and] the publications
> of learned societies.[3]

Only one of the 364 United States lists (221 of which are classified by

individual state) is cited under the heading "Commerce" within a subject

index that includes neither "Accounting" nor "Bookkeeping" (Freitag 1964,

1-37, 127, 142, from index).

The world's most comprehensive bibliographical source, finally, is

the Online Union Catalog supplied by the Online Computer Library Center,

the "OCLC" network. It reflects the merger of some 18 million records from

more than eight thousand libraries in 26 countries (Computer notes 1988,

A12). The valuable Worcester Area Cooperating Libraries Union List, which

includes the holdings of the AAS (Staff 1987, 148), is available both

through OCLC and in printed format.

I hope that this bare scratching of the bibliographical surface will

help stir interest in potential areas of historical work in American

accounting that obviously are wide open.

---

[3]The only recognized serial form excluded is the almanac, the subject
of a "monumental" 1962 reference work by Milton Drake (Freitag 1964, iii).
Fundamentally a "calendar with notations of astronomical and other data,"
the almanac took its place in the 17th and 18th centuries as (Columbia
encyclopedia 2d, s.v. "almanac")

> a full-blown form of folk literature, with notations of anniversaries
> and interesting facts, home medical advice, statistics of all sorts,
> jokes, and even fiction and poetry.

It would not be surprising in this light if one or more early almanac
compilers added accounting material of some kind. I found no such coverage
when in 1984, without having consulted Evans's bibliography (1903-55), I
looked over a few of the very numerous almanacs found in the first Early
American Imprints series (Shipton 1955-83). No doubt McMickle and Jensen
followed up on any hint of accounting subject-matter to be found in relevant Evans entries. Their partial 1987 draft (McMickle and Jensen, b),
at any rate, identifies no almanacs as sources of accounting literature.

REFERENCE LIST

American Antiquarian Society (AAS), Staff. 1987. The collections and
    programs of the American Antiquarian Society: A 175th-anniversary
    guide. Worcester, [Mass.]: AAS.

Anderson, Shirley, comp. 1988. Grants and fellowships. In Proceedings and
    Addresses of the American Philosophical Association 61 (June):893-934.

Bentley, Harry C., and Ruth S. Leonard. 1934-35. Bibliography of works on
    accounting by American authors. 2 vols. Boston: Harry C. Bentley.

Biddle, Clement. 1791. The directory or alphabetical list of house-keepers
    and persons in business. (Title shown in table of contents; identified on
    first page as "The Philadelphia Directory.") In The Philadelphia direc-
    tory, by Biddle, 1-147. Philadelphia: James & Johnson; microprint,
    Shipton 1955-83, no. 23205.

[Brief, Richard P., ed]. 1988 (from back page). Foundations of Accounting:
    A 36-volume series of books essential to an understanding of accounting,
    including 23 titles published for the first time. Catalog for series
    edited by Brief. New York: Garland Publishing.

Bristol, Roger P. 1970. Supplement to Charles Evans'[s] "American Bibli-
    ography." Charlottesville: University Press of Virginia, for Biblio-
    graphical Society of America and Bibliographical Society of University
    of Virginia.

Cappon, Lester J., and Stella F. Duff. 1950. Virginia Gazette index,
    1736-1780. 2 vols. Williamsburg: Institute of Early American History
    and Culture.

Cohen, Sol, ed. 1974. Education in the United States: A documentary
    history. 5 vols. New York: Random House.

The Columbia encyclopedia. 3d ed. 1963.

The Columbia-Viking desk encyclopedia. 2d ed. 2 vols. 1960. Used to
    supplement an incomplete copy of preceding source.

Computer notes. 1988. In The Chronicle of Higher Education 35 (September
    1):A12-A13.

Cremin, Lawrence A. 1970. American education: The colonial experience,
    1607-1783. New York: Harper & Row Publishers, Harper Torchbooks ed.

The dictionary of national biography (D.n.b.). 1917. 22 vols., as
    reprinted in slightly revised format, 1921-22, 1937-38, 1949-50.

Dilworth, Thomas. 1754. A new guide to the English tongue: In five parts. 15th ed. New York: J. Parker & W. Weyman; microprint, Shipton 1955-83, no. 7183.

_____. 1762. A new guide to the English tongue: In five parts. 23d ed. Reprint, from London edition, Philadelphia: W. Dunlap; microprint, Shipton 1955-83, no. 41259a.

_____. 1768. The young book-keeper's assistant: Shewing him, in the most plain and easy manner, the Italian way of stating debtor and creditor . . . . 5th ed. London: H. Kent.

_____. 1773. The schoolmasters assistant: Being a compendium of arithmetic, both practical and theoretical, in five parts. Philadelphia: [Joseph] Crukshank; microprint, Shipton 1955-83, no. 12752.

_____. [1793]. A new guide to the English tongue (as shown in reprint). Philadelphia: T. & W. Bradford; reprint, Delmar, N.Y.: Scholars' Facsimiles & Reprints (vol. 322), 1978. American Linguistics 1700-1900, Charlotte Downey, gen. ed.

_____. [1794]. The young book-keeper's assistant . . . . 12th ed. Philadelphia: Benjamin Johnson.

Downey, Charlotte, R.S.M. 1978. Introduction. In Dilworth [1793], reprint, v-xv.

Evans, Charles. 1903-55. The American bibliography of Charles Evans: A chronological dictionary of all books, pamphlets, and periodical publications printed in the United States from . . . 1639 . . . [through] 1800. 13 vols. [Chicago: Privately printed], vols. 1-12, and [Worcester, Mass.]: AAS, vol. 13; reprint, New York: Peter Smith, 1941-42, vols. 1-12, and [Gloucester, Mass.]: Peter Smith, 1962, vol. 13. The final volume was compiled by Clifford K. Shipton, who expanded the basic title from "American Bibliography," and substituted "1800" for "1820" in recognition that Evans's planned scale of coverage required a second massive project, to be undertaken by Shaw and Shoemaker (1958-83).

Fisher, George. 1748. The American instructor; or, young man's best companion. 9th ed. Philadelphia: B. Franklin & D. Hall; microprint, Shipton 1955-83, no. 6238.

_____. 1800. Arithmetic, in the plainest and most concise methods hitherto extant: With new improvements. The whole perused and approved of by the most eminent accountants . . . . Reprint, from London edition, Wilmington, [Del.]: Peter Brynberg; microprint, Shipton 1955-83, no. 37424.

Freitag, Ruth S., comp. 1964. Union lists of serials: A bibliography. Washington: [United States] Library of Congress, Reference Department, General Reference and Bibliography Division. Library Reference Series: Basic Reference Sources; reprint, Boston: Gregg Press, 1972.

General index to contents of Savannah, Georgia, newspapers, 1763–1799 (9 vols.), 1800–1805 (4), 1806–1810 (6). 1937. WPA [Works Progress Administration] official project no. 165-34-6999. Supervised by committee of Savannah Historical Research Association. Georgia Historical Society collection, Savannah, Ga.

General index to contents of Savannah, Georgia, newspapers, 1811–1815 (2 vols.), 1816–1820 (4). 1938. WPA official project no. 465-34-3-148. Supervised by committee of Savannah Historical Research Association. Georgia Historical Society collection.

Gurney, Gene, and Nick Apple. 1981. The Library of Congress: A picture story of the world's largest library. Rev. ed. New York: Crown Publishers.

Hall, Michael (text), and Ernest Frankl (photographs). 1983 (renewal of 1982 copyright). Oxford. 3d ed. Englewood-Cliffs, N.J.: Prentice-Hall.

Hamilton, Edward R., Bookseller. 1988. Bargain Books (monthly catalog). September 2. Falls Village, Conn.

Hans, Nicholas. 1951. New trends in education in the eighteenth century. London: Routledge & Kegan Paul. International Library of Sociology and Social Reconstruction, ed. W. J. H. Sprott (founded by Karl Mannheim).

Howell, Francis. 1970. London: Gazeteer. In The Shell guide to England, ed. John Hadfield, 96–147. New York: American Heritage Press, a subsidiary of McGraw-Hill, 1970.

Hutton, Charles. 1788. A course of book-keeping, according to the method of single entry . . . . Philadelphia: Joseph James.

_____. 1815. Philosophical and mathematical dictionary: . . . Mathematics, astronomy, and philosophy, both natural and experimental . . . . New ed. 2 vols. London: For the author and numerous booksellers.

Keep, Austin Baxter. 1909. The library in colonial New York; reprint, New York: Burt Franklin (Lenox Hill), 1970. Research & Source Works Series, no. 638.

Kobre, Sidney. 1944. The development of the colonial newspaper. [New York?: For the author (inferred from copyright page)]; reprint, Gloucester, Mass.: Peter Smith, 1960.

Lehmann-Haupt, Hellmut. In collaboration with Lawrence C. Wroth and Rollo G. Silver. 1952. The book in America: A history of the making and selling of books in the United States. 1952. 2d ed. New York: R. R. Bowker Co.

[Macpherson, James]. 1985. Macpherson's directory, for the city and suburbs of Philadelphia . . . . Philadelphia: Francis Bailey; microprint, Shipton 1955-83, no. 19067.

McCorison, Marcus A. 1970. Preface to this edition. In Thomas 1970, ix-xiii.

McMickle, Peter L. 1984. Young man's companion of 1737: America's first book on accounting? (emphasis added). Abacus 20 (June):34-51.

_____. 1986. Presentation by McMickle, Wenzel, and Jensen (1986). Annual meeting of American Accounting Association, Southeast Region, Greenville, S.C. April 18.

_____. 1988. Conversations with Terry K. Sheldahl, March 22 (by telephone), August 15 (Orlando, Florida).

McMickle, Peter L., and Paul H. Jensen. 1987a. An investigation and compilation of all purported eighteenth century works on accounting published in America. (An abstract.) In Collected papers of the thirty-nith annual meeting: Southeast Region, American Accounting Association, ed. Elliott L. Slocum, 315-17. Atlanta: Georgia State University. (Dated based on conference dates as given, April 23-25, 1987.)

_____. 1988. The birth of American accountancy: A compilation and review of works on accounting published in America prior to 1821. New York [and London]: Garland Publishing. Foundations of Accounting, ed. Richard P. Brief. (Cited as in [Brief] 1988, 5, entry 10.)

McMickle, Peter [L.], and Paul [H.] Jensen, producers, eds., and contributing authors. 1987b. The birth of American accountancy. Partial preliminary draft of McMickle and Jensen 1988, distributed in connection with presentation of August 18 at American Accounting Association 1987 national meeting, Cincinnati, Ohio.

McMickle, Peter [L.], Loren [A.] Wenzel, and Paul [H.] Jensen. 1986. The town officer: The earliest American work on municipal accounting? (emphasis added). School of Accountancy, Fogelman College of Business and Economics, Memphis State University. Working Paper Series, no. 86-12, April.

Miller, C. William. 1974. Benjamin Franklin's Philadelphia printing, 1728-1766; A descriptive bibliography. Philadelphia: American Philosophical Society.

Milner, Anita Cheek. 1977-82. Newspaper indexes: A location and subject guide for researchers. 3 vols. Metuchen, N.J. and London: Scarecrow Press.

Milns, William. 1797. The American accountant, or, a complete system of practical arithmetic. Containing . . .. New-York: J. S. Mott for Milns; microprint, Shipton 1955-83, no. 32479.

Morris, Susan D. 1988. Letter to Terry K. Sheldahl, September 6. Reference Department, Main Library, University of Georgia.

The national union catalog, pre-1956 imprints (N.u.c.). 1968-81. 754 vols.

New Webster's universal encyclopedia. 1987. New York: Bonanza Books.

Park, Carolyn. 1988. Letters to Terry K. Sheldahl, April 28, May 13. Collections Manager, Historical Society of Pennsylvania.

Paskoff, Paul F., and Daniel J. Wilson, eds. 1982. The cause of the South: Selections from "De Bow's Review," 1846-1867. Baton Rouge and London: Louisiana State University Press.

Poole, William Frederick. With William I. Fletcher, associate ed. [1891]. Poole's index to periodical literature. Rev. ed. 2 vols. [Boston: Houghton, Mifflin & Co.]; reprint, New York: Peter Smith, 1939, as two-part first volume of 6-vol. series covering 1802-1906, maintaining title through a succession of compilers.

Previts, Gary John, and Barbara Dubis Merino. 1979. A history of accounting in America: An historical interpretation of the cultural significance of accounting. New York: John Wiley & Sons, Ronald Press div.

Roorbach, O[rville] A., comp. and arr. 1852-61. Bibliotheca Americana. Catalogue of American publications, including reprints and original works, 1820 to 1852, inclusive, and three supplements with related titles, extending coverage through 1860. 4 vols.; reprint, New York: Peter Smith, 1939.

Sarjeant, Thomas. 1789. An introduction to the counting house; or, a short specimen of mercantile precedents, adapted to . . . the United States of America. Philadelphia: Dobson and Lang, for Sarjeant; microprint, Shipton 1955-83, no. 22127.

Shaw, Ralph R., and Richard H. Shoemaker, comps. 1958-83. American bibliography: A preliminary checklist, 1801 to 1819. 23 vols. New York (nos. [1-19]), or Metuchen, N.J. and London ([20-23]): Scarecrow Press. Vols. 1-19 supply yearly listings, while nos. 20-23 include addenda and three indexes. The final volume was prepared by Frances P. Newton.

Sheldahl, Terry K. 1985. America's first recorded text in accounting: Sarjeant's 1789 book. In The Accounting Historians Journal 12 (Fall): 1-42.

_____. 1987. Accounting education in eighteenth-century America. Rev., March. Working paper, Savannah, Ga. Draft of December 1985 appears in Proceedings: Dedication Seminar of the Accounting History Research Center at Georgia State University, comp. and ed. Norman X. Dressel (dec.), Elliot L. Slocum, and Alfred R. Roberts, 83-130. [Atlanta]: Academy of Accounting Historians, 1988.

Sheldahl, Terry K., ed., with general and individual introductions. 1988. Education for the mercantile countinghouse: Critical and constructive essays by nine British writers, 1716-1794. New York and London: Garland Publishing. Foundations of Accounting, ed. Richard P. Brief.

Shipton, Clifford K., ed. 1955-83. Early American Imprints. Series 1, 1639-1800. Microprint collection, titles 1-49,197 (omitting newspapers, periodicals in general, "ghosts," and items not available or reproducible). New York: Readex Microprint Corp., and Worcester, Mass.: AAS. Includes reissue of titles. Production after 1974 appears to have concerned correction and refinement.

Shipton, Clifford K., and James E. Mooney. 1969. <u>National index of American imprints through 1800: The short-title Evans.</u> 2 vols. [Worcester]: AAS, and [New York?]: Barre Publishers.

Shoemaker, Richard H., comp. 1964. <u>A checklist of American imprints for 1820. Items 1-4390.</u> New York and London: Scarecrow Press.

Thomas, Isaiah. 1970. <u>The history of printing in America, with a biography of printers & an account of newspapers.</u> Ed. Marcus A. McCorison. New York: Weathervane Books. Based on 2d ed. [Albany, N.Y.: Joel Munsell, for AAS, 1874, 2 vols].

Thomson, Hugh W. 1963. Bibliography: Books on accounting in English. In <u>Accounting in England and Scotland: 1543-1800. Double entry in exposition and practice,</u> by B[asil] S. Yamey, H[arold] C. Edey, and Thomson, 202-26. London: Sweet & Maxwell, 1963; reprint, New York and London: Garland Publishing, 1982. Accountancy in Transition, ed. Richard P. Brief.

Titus, Edna Brown. 1965. <u>Union list of serials in libraries of the United States and Canada.</u> 3d ed. 5 vols. New York: H. W. Wilson Co. Sponsored by Joint Committee on Union List of Serials, with cooperation of U.S. Library of Congress.

Tracy, Joyce Ann. 1938. Telephone conversation with Terry K. Sheldahl, September 7. Curator of Newspapers and Serials, AAS.

Turner, the Rev. R[ichard]. 1794. <u>A new introduction to book keeping, after the Italian method, by debtor and creditor . . . .</u> 1st American ed., from 3d English ed. Boston: I. Thomas and E. T. Andrews.

[United States] Library of Congress. Processing Department, Catalog Publication Division. 1973. <u>Newspapers in microform, United States, 1948-1972.</u> Washington: Library of Congress.

_____. 1978. <u>Newspapers in microform, United States, 1973-1977.</u> Washington: Library of Congress.

Vallette, Elie. 1774. <u>The deputy commissary's guide within the province of Maryland . . . .</u> Annapolis: Catharine Green and Son; microprint, Shipton 1955-83, no. 13742.

The Virginia Gazette, 1736-1780 (three newspaper series). 1950. Microfilm collection, 6 reels. Williamsburg: Institute of Early American History and Culture.

White, Francis. 1785. <u>The Philadelphia directory . . . .</u> Philadelphia: Young, Stewart, and M'Culloch; microprint, Shipton 1955-83, no. 19385.

Wroth, Lawrence C. 1938. <u>The colonial printer.</u> 2d ed. N.p.: Southworth-Anthoensen Press; reprint, Charlottesville: Dominion Books, div. of University Press of Virginia, 1964.

[Young, Arthur]. 1776. <u>Rural oeconomy: or essays on the practical parts of husbandry . . . .</u> 2d ed. Reprint, from London edition, Philadelphia: James Humphreys, Jr.; microprint, Shipton 1955-83, no. 15226.

2

GEORGE FISHER'S BOOKKEEPING CHAPTER, UNATTRIBUTED, FROM BRADFORD'S MANUAL, 1737

THE
Secretary's GUIDE,
OR
Young Man's Companion.
In FOUR Parts:
CONTAINING,

PART I. Directions for Spelling, Reading and Writing true ENGLISH, with the Pronunciation, &c.

PART II. How to write Letters of Compliment, Friendship, or Business; with proper directions for external and internal Superscriptions, and other Things necessary to be understood in that Affair.

PART III. Arithmetick made Easy, and the Rules thereof explained and made familiar to the Capacities of those that desire to Learn. With a short and easy Method of SHOP and BOOK-KEEPING, MERCHANT's Accompts, &c. And TABLES, how to lay out and measure Land, Gauging Vessels, Measuring Boards, Glass, round or square Timber, Buying or Selling any thing by the Hundred: Also a Table of Interest at 6 or 8 per Cent.

PART IV. Forms of the most useful Writings, such as, Bills, Bonds, Letters of Attorney, Indentures, Bonds of Arbitration, Awards, Umpirages, Deeds of Sale, Deeds of Gift, Assignments, Leases and Releases, Counter Securities, Declarations of Trust, with many other useful Writings, Bills of Exchange, &c. With Monthly Observations in Gardening, Planting, Grafting, and Inoculating Fruit Trees, and the best time to prune them.

To which is added,

The FAMILY COMPANION:

Containing Rules and Directions, how to make *Cyder, Mead, Wines* of our own Growth, &c. With a Collection of choice and safe Remedies, very useful in Families.

The Fifth Edition, greatly Enlarged and carefully Corrected.

Philadelphia: Printed and Sold by ANDREW BRADFORD, at the Sign of the *BIBLE.* MDCCXXXVII.

36

Rules and Directions for BOOK-KEEPING, or *Merchant's-Accompts.*

IT is not without good Reason that moſt People of Buſineſs and Ingenuity, are deſirous to be Maſters of this Art, if we conſider the Satisfaction that naturally ariſes from an Account well kept; the Pleaſure that accrues to a Perſon by ſeeing what he gains by each Species of Goods he deals in, and his whole Profit by a Year's Trade; and thereby alſo, to know the true State of his Affairs and Circumſtances; ſo that he may, according to his Diſcretion, retrench or enlarge his Expences, &c. as he ſhall think fit.

Of the Books in Uſe.

THE Books of principal Uſe, are the *Waſte-Book,* the *Journal,* and the *Leidger.*

Waſte-Book.

IN this Book muſt be daily written whatever occurs in the way of Trade; as Buying, Selling, Receiving, Delivering, Bargaining, Shipping, &c. without Omiſſion of any one Thing, either Bought or Sold, &c. as Money Lent or Received at Intereſt: But not Money Received or Paid for Goods Sold or Bought at any Time; for that will come of Courſe, and muſt be entered into the *Caſh-Book,* from whence it is poſted into the *Leidger.*

The *Waſte-Book* is rul'd with one Marginal Line, and three Lines for Pounds, Shillings, and Pence; and the Day of the Month, and Year of our Lord, is inſerted in the be middle of the Page. In this Book any one may write, and, on occasion, any thing may be altered or blotted out, if not well entered, or any Error be made.

Journal.

INto this Book every Thing is posted out of the *Waste-Book*, but in other Terms, in a better Stile, and in a fairer Hand, without any alteration of Cyphers or Figures; and every Parcel, one after another (promiscuously set) without Intermission; to make the Book, or several Entries of it, of more Credit and Validity, in Case of any Law Dispute, or other Controversy that may happen between Merchant and Merchant. In this Book you are to distinguish the Debtor and Creditor, (or in quainter Terms, the *Debet* and *Credit:*) And to this Book you must have recourse for the Particulars of an Account, which in the *Leidger* are entered in Grofs, that is, in one Line. In this Book also, the Day of the Month must be placed in the middle of the Page; and is Ruled with double Marginal Lines, for References to the *Leidger*; and with three Lines for Pounds, Shillings, and Pence; as the *Waste-Book*.

Of the Leidger.

FRom the *Day-Book* or *Journal* (as derived from the *French*) all Matters or Things are posted into the *Leidger*, which by the *Spaniards* is called *El libr Grande*, as being the biggest Book, or chief of Accompts. The Left hand side of this Book is the *Debtor*, and the Right the *Creditor*, and the *Numbers* and *Folios* of each must be alike, as, 45 *Debtor*, and also 45 *Creditor*. The Day of the Month (in this Book) by most is set in a narrow Column on the Left hand, and the Month on the Left of that: But the Number in the narrow Column to the Right of that; and at the Head of each Folio the Name

of

of the Place of Refidence, and the Year of our Lord
as thus :

London, Anno————————————1736.

But the Examples of thefe feveral Books hereafter
following, will make the foregoing Hints of them much
more intelligible.————And as I am upon the Subject
of *Book-keeping*, I will take this as a univerfal Text,
(for fo it is) *viz.*

*All Things Received, or the Receiver, are Debtors to
the Things Delivered, or the Deliverer.*

38

Wafte-Book Entry.

		l.	s.	d.
	London, January 1. 1736. Bought of *William Wilkins* of *Nortonfalgate*, 120 Yards of white Sarcenet, at 2 s. 3 d. per Yard, to pay in 2 Months. ————	13	10	00
1 —— 2	*The Journal Entry of the fame.* Wrought Silks Debtor to *William Wilkins* l. 13--10 for 120 yards of white Sarcenet, at 2 s. 3 d. per yard, to pay in 2 Months. ————	13	10	00
	In this Example, the Account of Wrought Silks is the Receiver, and therefore Debtor to William Wilkins *the Deliverer.*			
	Again, *Wafte-Book Entry.* January 4. Sold *Henry Hartington* 246 lb. nett of Indigo Lahore, at 6 s. 6 d. per lb. to pay at 3 Months. ————	79	19	00

Journal

		l.	*s.*	*d.*
3	*Journal Entry.*			
—	Henry Hartington Dr. to Indigo,			
4	for 246 *lb.* nett, at 6 *s.* 6 d. *per*			
	lb. to Pay in 3 Months ———	79	19	oo

Once more.		

			l.	*s.*	*d.*
	Waste-Book Entry.				
	Bought of *George Goodinch* sen. *viz.*				
	Cheshire Cheese 430 C. }				
	½ at 23 *s.* 4 d. *per* C. }	*l.* 502--5			
	Butter 50 Firkins qt. nett }				
	2800 *lb.* at 3 *d. per* lb. }	35--0			
	to pay at 6 Months ———		537	c5	oo

			l.	*s.*	*d.*
—	*Journal Entry.*				
5	Sundry Accounts Dr. to Geo. Good-				
	inch, *l.* 537--05 ——— *viz.*				
4	Cheese of Cheshire for }				
	430 C. ½ at 23 *s.* 4 d. }	*l.* 502--5			
	per C. }				
5	Butter for 50 Firkins, }				
	qt. nett 2800 *lb.* at 3 d. }	35--0			
	per lb. } ———		537	05	oo

			l.	*s.*	*d.*
	Waste-Book.				
	Sold *James Jenkings* ——— *viz.*				
	White Sarcenet 50 Yards }	*l.* 7--10--0			
	at 3 *s. per* yard ——— }				
	Indigo Lahore 50 *lb.* }	17--10--0			
	at 7 *s. per* pound ——— }		25	oo	oo

			l.	*s.*	*d.*
	Journal Entry of the last.				
6	*James Jenkings* Dr. to sundry Ac-				
—	counts, *viz.*				
7	To white Sarcenet for }				
	50 yards, at 3 *s. per* }	*l.* 7--10--0			
	yard. }				
8	To Indigo Lahore for }				
	50 *lb.* at 7 *s. per* lb. }	17--10--0			
	———		25	oo	oo

S

39

From these few Examples of Entry, it may be observed, That an experienced Person in Accompts, and a good Writer, may keep a *Journal* without a *Waste-Book*, or a *Waste-Book* without a *Journal*, since they both import one and the same Thing, though they differ a little in Words or Expression: For the Leaves of both are numbered by Pages, or Parcels.

But however, I shall give Methods of keeping each, as far as room will give Leave.

(1)
The Waste-Book.

London, *January* 1st, —————————— *1736.*

An Inventory of all my Effects of Money, Goods, and Debts, belonging to me A. B. of London, *Merchant,*— viz.

	l.	*s.*	*d.*
In Cash for Trading Occasions ——————— 3500-00-0			
In Tobacco 4726 *lb.* at 9 *d* per lb. } 177-04-6			
In Broadcloth 6 pieces, at 50 *s.* per piece — } 15-00-0			
Dowlass 1000 Ells, at 2 *s.* 4 *d.* per Ell—— } 116-13-4			
Canary Wines 9 Pipes, at 30 *l.* per Pipe — } 270-00-0			
Due to me from *Henry* *Bland,* per Bond — } 60-00-0	4158	17	10

40

Journal

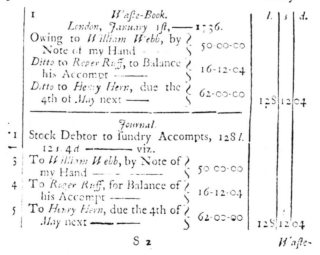

(1)

Journal.

Inventory, &c as before.

		l.	s.	d.
—	Sundry Accompts Dr. to *Stock*, 4138 *l.* 17 *s.* 10 *d.* —— *viz.*			
1	Cash for Trading Occasions *l.* 3500-00-0			
	Tobaccoes 4726 *lb.* at 9 *d.* per lb. } 177-04 6			
1	Broadcloths 6 pieces at 50 *s.* per piece —— } 15-00 0			
1	Dowlas 1000 Ells, at 2 *s.* 4 *d.* per Ell. —— } 116-13-4			
1	Canary Wines 9 Pipes, at 30 *l.* per Pipe —— } 270-00-0			
3	*Henry Bland* due on Bond — 60-00-0			
		4138	17	10

I shall make one Page serve both for *Waste-Book* and *Journal Entries*, as well to save room, as to have both Methods of Entry under Eye, to make them more intelligible and useful to the Reader, he hereby being not obliged to turn over Leaf to see their Difference of Entry.

1	*Waste-Book.*	l.	s.	d.
	London, January 1*st*, —— 1736.			
	Owing to *William Webb*, by Note of my Hand - } 50-00-00			
	Ditto to *Roger Ruff*, to Balance his Accompt —— } 16-12-04			
	Ditto to *Henry Hern*, due the 4th of *May* next —— } 62-00-00	128	12	04

Journal.

•1	Stock Debtor to sundry Accompts, 128 *l.* 12 *s.* 4 *d.* —— *viz.*			
3	To *William Webb*, by Note of my Hand —— } 50-00-00			
4	To *Roger Ruff*, for Balance of his Accompt —— } 16-12-04			
5	To *Henry Hern*, due the 4th of *May* next —— } 62-00-00	128	12	04

S 2

Waste-

Wafte-Book.   2

	London, *Febr.* 2d. ——— —— 1736.				
	Sold *Thomas Townfend :* *viz.*		*l.*	*s.*	*d.*
	246 *lb.* of *Virginia*-Cut Tobacco ⎰ at 14 *d. per* lb. ——— ⎱	14-07-00			
	460 Ells of Dowlafs, at 3 *s.* ⎰ *per* Ell ——— ——— ⎱	69-00-00			
			83	07	00
	Feb. 2. *Journal.*				
6	*Thomas Townfend* Debtor to Sundries, *viz.*				
1	To Tobacco for 246 *lb.* at 14 *d.* ⎰ *per* lb. ——— ⎱	14-07-00			
1	To Dowlafs for 460 Ells, at ⎰ 3 *s. per* Ell.——— —— ⎱	69-00-00			
			83	07	00
	Wafte-Book. Ditto 24th.				
	Bought of *Leonard Legg* 4 Pipes of Canary, at 28 *l. per* Pipe ——— —— To pay in 6 Months.		112	00	00
	Ditto 24th. *Journal.*				
1	Canary Wines Debtor to *Leonard Legg* for 4 Pipes, at 28 Pounds *per* Pipe ———		112	00	00
2	To pay in 6 Months.				

The fhort Lines ruled againft the Journal Entries are, or may be termed Pofting Lines, and the Figure on the Top of the Line denotes the Folio of the Leidger where the Debtor is entered ; and the Figure under the Line fhews the Folio of the Leidger, where the Credit is entered ; and the other fmaller Figures againft the fundry Debtors,

Debtors, or sundry Creditors (whether Goods or Persons) shew also in what Folios of the Leidger they are posted. And the Figures in the narrow Column towards the Left-hand of the Pounds, Shillings and Pence Lines, direct to the Folio in the Leidger where the *Debet* or *Credit* is posted; that is, to the Accompt of the Goods or of the Person, immediately following the Words *To* or *By*; the first being proper to the Left or *Debet* Side in the Leidger; and the other used always on the Right or *Credit* Side of the Folios in the Leidger.

There are several other Books used by Merchants besides those Three before-mentioned; as the *Cash-Book*, which is ruled as the Leidger, and folio'd likewise; wherein all Receipts of Money are entered on the Left-hand Folio, and Payments on the Right; specifying in every Entry, the Day of the Month, (the Year being set on the Top) for what, and for whose Account the Money was received, or paid; and the Total *Debet* and *Credit* of each Side, is to be posted into the Leidger, to the Accompt of Cash therein, in one Line of either Side, *viz.* To, or By sundry Accompts, as *per* Cash-Book, Folio, &c. which is to be done once a Month, or at Discretion; and the Particulars of each Side, Article by Article, are to be posted into the Leidger to the proper Accompts unto which they belong; with References in the Cash-Book to the several Folio's in the Leidger; and carry the Balance over Leaf in the Cash-Book; by which you may know at any time what Cash you have, or ought to have by you.

Another Book, is a Book of Charges of Merchandize, wherein are to be entered the Custom and petty Charges of any Shipp'd Goods; as Porteridge, Wharfage, Warehouse-room, &c. and once a Month are transferred into the Cash-Book on the Credit Side, making Reference to the Book of Charges of Merchandize; and likewise the same in the Dr. Side of the same Accompt in the Leidger for the Particulars thereof.

The

43

The next Book I shall name, is the Invoice Book, or Book of Factories: In this Book are to be copied all Invoices, or Cargozones of Goods shipp'd, either for Accompts proper or partable; and also of Goods received from abroad, which must always be entered on the Left-side, leaving the Right-side Blank; and on the Advice of the Disposal of Goods sent abroad, and also on the Sale of Goods received from abroad, enter them on the Blank or Right-side; so that at first View may be seen how the Accompt stands, &c.

The next is a Bill-Book, wherein are entered Bills of Exchange accepted, and when they become due; and when paid, made so in the Margin.

The next is a Book of Houshold Expences, for the monthly Charge spent in House-keeping; likewise Apparel, House-rent, Servants Wages, and Pocket Expences; and this may be monthly summ'd up, and carried to the Credit of Cash.

Besides the above-mentioned, there must be a Book to copy all Letters sent abroad, or beyond the Seas; wherein the Name of the Person or Persons to whom the Letter is sent, must be written pretty full, for the readier finding the same.

The next is (and what is very necessary) a Receipt Book, wherein are given Receipts for Money paid, and expressed for whose Account or Use, and for what it is received; to which the Receiving Person must set his Name for himself, or some other, with the Year and Day of the Month on the Top.

Lastly, a Note or Memorandum Book, to minute down Affairs that occur, for the better Help of Memory; which is of great Use, where there is Multiplicity of Businets.

Having given an Account of the several Books and their Use, the next Thing necessary will be to give some few Rules of Aid, to enable the Book-keeper to make proper Entries, and to distinguish the several Debtors and Creditors, *viz.*

First, For Money received, make Cash Dr. to the
Party

Party that paid it, [if for his own Account] and the Party Cr.

Secondly, Money paid, make the Receiver Dr. [if for his own Account] and Cash Cr.

Thirdly, Goods bought for ready Money, make the Goods Dr. to Cash, and Cash Cr. by the Goods.

Fourthly, Goods sold for ready Money, just the contrary, *i. e.* Cash Dr. and the Goods Cr.

Fifthly, Goods bought at Time; Goods bought are Dr. to the Seller of them, and the Seller Cr. by the Goods.

Sixthly, Goods sold at Time, just the contrary, *i. e.* the Party that bought them is Dr. to the Goods, and the Goods Cr. by the Party.

Seventhly, Goods bought, part for ready Money, and the rest at Time : First make the Goods Dr. to the Party for the Whole. Secondly, make the Party Dr. to Cash for the Money paid him in part of those Goods.

Eighthly, Goods sold, part for ready Money, and the rest at Time : First make the Party Dr. to the Goods for the Whole. Secondly, Cash Dr. to the Party received him in part of those Goods.————Or either of these two last Rules may be made Dr. to Sundries ; as Goods bought, Dr. to the selling Man for so much as is left unpaid, and to Cash for so much paid in ready Money : And so the contrary for Goods sold.

Ninthly, When you pay Money before it is due, and are to have Discount allowed you ; make the Person Dr. to Cash for so much as you pay him, and to Profit and Loss for the Discount ; or make the receiving Man Dr. to Sundries, as before.

Profit and Loss is Dr.

To Cash for what Money you pay and have nothing for it ; as Discount of Money paid you before due, and to Abatement by Composition, Houshold Expences, *&c.*

Per Contra Cr.

By Cash for all you receive, and deliver nothing for it ; as Discount for prompt Payment, any Legacy left

you,

you, Money received with an Apprentice, and by the Profit of every particular Commodity you deal in, by Ships in Company, by Voyages, &c.

To balance or clear an Accompt when full written.

1. IF the Dr. Side be more than the Credit, make the Old Accompt Cr. by the New ; and if the contrary, make the New Accompt Dr. to the Old : But if the Dr. Side be lefs than the Credit, then make the Old Accompt Dr. to the New, and the New Accompt Cr. by the Old, for fuch a Reft or Sum as you fhall find in the Accompt.

2. An Accompt of Company, wherein you have placed more received of another than his Stock ; then add as much on the *Debet* Side as you find on the *Credit* Side ; to the End that, in the New Accompt you may have fo much *Debet* as you put in, and fo much *Credit* as you have received.

3. In Accompts of Merchandize, you muft enter the Gain, or Lofs, before you make the Old Accompt Cr. by the New, and the New Dr. to the Old, for the Remainder of Goods unfold.

4. In the Foreign Accompts, which you are to keep with a double Margin, or Column, for Dollars, Crowns, or any Foreign Coins whatfoever, which have been received or paid by Bills of Exchange, for Goods fold by Factors or Correfpondents, or bought by them for the Accompt before ; here you muft firft balance the faid inward Margin of Dollars, Crowns, &c.

To remove an Accompt full written to another Folio.

Sum or add up the Dr. and Cr. Sides, and fee the Difference ; which place to its oppofite : As admit the Cr. fide exceeds the Dr. then you are to write the Line in the Old Accompt to balance on the Dr. fide, to anfwer the Line on the Cr. fide of the New Accompt.

How

*How to Balance at the Year's End, and thereby to know
the State of your Affairs and Circumstances.*

YOU muſt make an Accompt of Balance on the next
void Leaf or Folio of your Leidger to your other
Accompts ; but after you have ſo done, do not venture to
draw out the Accompt of Balance in the ſaid Folio, till
you have made it exact on a Sheet of Paper, Ruled and
Tituled for that Purpoſe ; becauſe of Miſtakes or Errors
that may occur or happen in the Courſe of balancing your
Leidger ; which are to be rectified, and will cauſe E-
raſements or Alterations in that Accompt, which ought
to be very fair and exact ; and after you have made it
to bear in the ſaid Sheet, Copy fair in the ſaid Accompt
of Balance in the Leidger.

The Rules for Balancing are theſe, *viz.*

1ſt, Even your Accompt of Caſh, and bear the Nett
Reſt to balance Dr.

2dly, Caſt up all your Goods Bought, and thoſe Sold,
of what Kind ſoever, in each Accompt of Goods ; and
ſee whether all Goods Bought, be Sold, or not ; and if
any remain Unſold, value them as they coſt you, or according to the preſent Market Price, ready Money ; and
bear the Nett Reſt to balance Dr.

3dly, See what your Goods or Wares ſeverally coſt,
and alſo how much they were ſold for, and bear the Nett
Gain or Loſs, to the Accompt of Profit and Loſs.

4thly, Even all your Drs. and all your Crs. in order
as they lie, and bear the Nett Reſt of every ſeveral Dr.
and Cr. to balance.

5thly, Even your Voyages, your Factors Accompts,
and Charges of Merchandize, or any other Accompts,
wherein is either Gain or Loſs, and bear the Nett Gain
or Loſs to the Accompt of Profit and Loſs ; and the
Goods unſold to balance.

T

6thly,

6thly, Even the Accompt of Profit and Lois, and bear the Nett Reft to Stock or Capital, as an Advance to your Stock or Capital.

7thly, Even your Stock, and bear the Nett Reft to balance Cr.

Then caft up the Dr. and Cr. fides of your Balance; and if they come out both alike, then are your Accompts well kept; otherwife you muft find out your Error by pricking over your Books again, to fee whether you have entered every Dr. and Cr. in the Leidger as you ought.

Note, *By pricking over the Books is meant an Examining every Article of the Journal, againft the Leidger, and marking it thus, -- or thus †; and upon a fecond Examination thus ‡; and upon a third Examination thus ‡-- or any other Marks.*

Note alfo, *In all Accompts of Goods, you muft keep a Column in the Middle of the Leaf, of each fide, for Number, Weight, or Meafure.*

And alfo Note, *That the Money, Wares, or Goods remaining in your Hands, and the Debts owing to you, muft ever balance with the Nett Stock and Debts owing by you.*

Though what hath been faid in relation to Book-keeping, and the feveral Rules thereunto belonging, may feem a little abftrufe to the altogether unlearned therein; yet there is no fuch mighty Difficulty to obftruct them as they may imagine: For thefe following Hints may render what hath been already faid, intelligible to any ordinary Capacity.

1ft, Stick clofe to the Text, or General Rule beforementioned, *viz.* That all Things Received, or the Receiver, are Debtor to all Things Delivered, or the Deliverer; for this Rule holds good in all Cafes.

2dly, When the Dr. (whether Perfon or Goods) is known, the Cr. is eafily underftood, without mentioning it: For if *A* be Dr. to *B,* then *B* is Cr. by *A,* for what Sum foever it be: Alfo, if Goods be Dr. to *C,* then *C* is Cr. by thofe Goods, for the Sum they amount to. ——

This

This I mention, becaufe that moft Authors (if not all) that I have met with on the Subject of Book-keeping, fpend a great many Words which I think might be faved, in declaring the Creditor, as well as fhewing the Debtor, when it may be underftood, as aforefaid.

3*dly*, This Art of *Italian* Book-keeping, is called *Book-keeping by double Entry*, becaufe there muft be two Entries; the firft being a Charging of a Perfon, Money, or Goods; and the fecond, a Difcharging of a Perfon, Money, or Goods.

4*thly*, *Strictly Note*, That if the Firft Entry be on the Dr. or Left-hand fide of your Leidger; the next, or Second Entry, muft always be made on the Right or Credit fide of your Leidger: For whenever one Perfon or Thing is Charged, then always another Perfon or Thing is Difcharged for the fame Sum, let it be what it will.

And fo it is in Balancing or Evening an Account, and carrying it to another Folio: For if the Old Account be evened by Balance on the Credit Side, then the New Accompt muft be Debited or Charged on the *Debet* Side, for the Sum that Balanced the Old Account.

Much more might be faid to this *Art of Book-keeping* if I had room; but I have plainly fpoke to the Principal Fundamentals thereof, which I hope may be fufficient for the Inftruction and Improvement of any intelligent Reader.

49

Of

3

CHARLES HUTTON'S
SINGLE-ENTRY
COURSE, 1788

A

COURSE OF

Book - Keeping,

According to the Method of

SINGLE ENTRY;

———————

*With a description of the Books, and directions for using them:
very useful either for young Book-keepers entering into
Business, or for Teachers in their Schools, &c. &c.*

Extracted from the Works of
CHARLES HUTTON, L. L. D. F. R. S.
*And Professor of the Mathematics in the Royal military Academy,
Woolwich.*

With sundry Alterations and Additions, by the Editor.

PHILADELPHIA,
PRINTED BY JOSEPH JAMES IN CHESNUT-STREET.
M.DCC.LXXXVIII.

ADVERTISEMENT.

The great *Utility* and *Want* of a fuitable Specimen of *Single Entry*, in our Schools, are obvious; and Doct. Hutton's, being adopted by fome judicious Teachers, in Preference to any other they knew of, it was conceived that a Republication of it, feparate from the other excellent Works of that learned Author, with fuch Alterations and Additions as would ftill better adapt it to the Occafion, would be acceptable to many.   It is hoped the Liberty taken therein can give no Offence to him or others, as it is done, not with a View to private Emolument, but for general Convenience and public Good.   The Difference between this and the Original may be beft known by comparing them, without enlarging here.

PHILADELPHIA, 12 Mo. 10th, 1788.   W. W.

If this fhould meet with Approbation, perhaps a Syftem of Double Entry may follow.

54

T H E
A U T H O R'S
P R E F A C E.

IT is very neceſſary that almoſt every perſon who is intended for buſineſs, ſhould learn a courſe of Book-Keeeping of this kind, becauſe it is uſed in almoſt every ſhop. The Italian method alone is not ſufficient; for it is a frequent complaint among the Merchants, &c. who uſe this method, that their boys, having learnt only the Italian form, when they firſt come to buſineſs, are almoſt as ignorant in the management of their Books, as if they had never learnt any method. There are ſome who have not time to learn, or perhaps a capacity to underſtand a complete courſe of the Italian method: There are alſo many intended for ſuch kinds of buſineſs, that the Italian method would be thrown away upon them; to all ſuch then this method will be extremely uſeful. And even ſuppoſing a boy were intended for a buſineſs which requires the Italian method alone, I would notwithſtanding, have him taught this firſt, if it were only to facilitate his acquiſition of the other.

This method is ſo eaſy, that it may alſo be taught, in a few weeks time to young Ladies, as well as to young Gentlemen.

BOOK-KEEPING

Is the art of keeping Books of Accounts.

DESCRIPTION OF THE BOOKS.

The principal Books of Accounts are the DAY-BOOK, and the LEDGER; to which may be added a Memorandum book, Expence book, &c. the forms and ruling of which, may be sufficiently known by inspecting the following specimen.

THE DAY-BOOK

Contains entries of the several articles in the successive order of their dates; making each person Dr. *to* what he becomes accountable for, or Cr. *by* what is received of him on account. The dates are in the middle of the page, and in the margin are written the numbers of the Ledger folios, to which the respective articles are posted.

THE LEDGER

Is the grand Book of accounts, wherein all the several articles of each particular person or account, which lie scattered, in different parts of the Day-Book, are collected into spaces allotted for them; the Dr. and Cr. fronting one another on opposite sides of the same folio, and shewing the whole state of the account at once. The Alphabet to the Ledger readily points out the folio in which any account is opened.

B

Being prepared with Books ruled in the proper form, copy one month's accounts into the Day-Book; omitting the figures in the left hand margin, and leaving the money column's blank; minding not to begin an entry at the bottom of a page when there is not fufficient room for it. See Day-Book page 9 and 10.

Then on a flate or wafte paper calculate the amounts of the feveral articles, at their refpective prices, and carry them out correctly into the columns, placing units under units, tens under tens, &c.

POSTING.

The next Step is to poft, or transfer the entries from the DAY Book to the LEDGER, thus;

Open an account in the LEDGER for the firft perfon who ftands Dr. or Cr. in the DAY BOOK, i. e. write his name and the contraction Dr. on the left hand page of the folio, and CONTRA Cr. on the right: then, if the perfon be Dr. poft the article to the Dr. fide, entering the YEAR in the margin, oppofite to the name, and the MONTH and DAY in the fame line with the article; but if he be Cr. enter it in like manner on the Cr. fide; obferving that an article on the Dr. fide begins with the Word To, and on the Cr fide with BY: then turn imediately to the DAY-BOOK Margin, and there fet the number of the LEDGER folio againft the entry, to fhow that it is poſted, and where to: laſtly, inſert the name under the proper letter in the ALPHABET. See James Elford's, account &c. Ledger A.

Leaving room for articles of a future date in the account already open'd, open an account for the next entry in the DAY-BOOK, and poſt it in like manner; thus proceed with all the DAY-BOOK entries, taking them ſucceſſively as they ſtand, (except thoſe marked 'paid" in the margin, which are to be comitted) obſerving that when a name occurs, for whom an account is already open'd in the LEDGER, it muſt be poſted to that account without opening another, unleſs the ſpace aſſign'd it be ſill'd, then it is to be transferr'd to another folio. See Lucy Berry's account LEDGER A. folio 2 and 9. This done, take the entries of another month, (more or leſs) into the DAY-BOOK, and poſt them to the LEDGER as before.

BALANCING

When the Dr. ſide of a perſon's account is heavier than the Cr. ſide, he is in debt, by ſo much as is the difference; but when the Cr. ſide is the greater the balance is due to him: hence, by that ingeniouſly contrived and excellent book, the LEDGER with its ALPHABET, we can not only turn to any perſon's account, and ſee immediately how it ſtands, but alſo aſcertain the GENERAL STATE of the STOCK, thus,

Open an account of STOCK, either on a feparate paper or in the LEDGER (as in LEDGER A folio 11)and in the Cr. fide enter the amount of the CASH in hand, and other property in poffeffion, eftimated as nearly as may be; then by adding up the two fides of of each account in the LEDGER, on a loofe paper, and taking their difference, the feveral debts receivable are brought to the Dr. of STOCK, and thofe payable to the Cr. fide : the difference of the two fides of the STOCK account will then fhew the NEAT ESTATE.

When LEDGER A is filled transfer the unbalanced accounts to a fecond LEDGER, diftinguifhed by B, as in this fpecimen, where they ftand open for future entries, and fo from LEDGER B to C &c. as occafion may require.

THE MEMORANDUM BOOK

Contains minutes of fuch occurrences as are not to be pofted to the Ledger ; being a better mode of recording them, than writing fuch memorandums in the Day-Book.

THE EXPENCE BOOK

Exhibits the expenditures of cafh for apparel, furniture, the various exigencies, of houfe-keeping &c. &c.

DAY-BOOK.

1789.

Philadelphia Firſt Mo. 1ſt. 1789.   £. S. D.

I	**James Elford,** of Bath, **Dr.**			
	To 15 yards of fine broad cloth, at 13 ſ 6d	10	2	6
	24 ditto of ſuperfine - - 18 9	22	10	0
		32	12	6

I	**George Robſon,** of York, **Dr.**			
	To 12 gallons of palm ſack at - - 6 ſ 8d	5	2	0
	17 ditto. - port-red - - 5 8	4	16	4
	9 ditto - - claret - - 8 9	3	18	9
		13	17	I

I	**Mary Maſterman,** **Dr.**			
	To 1½ lb green tea, - - at 16 ſ 0d	1	4	0
	2¼ congou, - - at 9 6	1	1	4½
	¼ ſtone of ſugar - - 5		1	3
	A lump of ſugar, weight 20½ lb, at 0 8		13	8
		3	0	3½

61

62

	First Mo. 9th, 1789.		£.	S.	D.
2	*Lucy Berry,* **Dr.**				
	To 9¼ *yards of silk,* - at 12 ∫ 9d		6	1	1¼
	13 *ditto* - *flowered ditto* - 15 6		10	1	6
			16	2	7¼
	——— 20 ———				
2	*Jonas Moore,* . **Dr.**				
	To a ream of thick post paper - -		1	0	0
	——— 27 ———				
2	*James Wilson,* Schoolmaster, **Dr.**				
	To 6 *Schoolmasters guides* - at 2 ∫ 3d		0	13	6
	3 *Doz. copy books* - - 2 6			7	9
	2 *Quires foolscap* - - 0 10			1	8
	1 *ditto thin post* - - 1 0				8
			1	3	8

Second Mo. 5th, 1789.

		£.	S.	D.
3	**Abel Ableman,** *Dr.*			
	To a Ledger ruled - . -	0	15	0
	5C Quills - - at £0 2 6	0	12	6
	3 Reams, thick post - 1 0 0	2	0	0
	6 Quires pot . . . 8	0	4	0
	40 Reams, blue demy - . 5 6	11	0	0
	2 Pen knives and an Inkstand - .	0	6	0
	- 12 .	15	17	6
3	**William Winton,** *Dr.*			
	To 20 oz. of Nutmegs at of 3	0	5	0
	5¼ lb Coffee - . 4 0	1	2	0
	3¼ Cocoa - - . 2 4	0	7	7
	4 Almonds - . 1 0		4	0
	8¼ Raisins - - . 0 7		4	11½
		2	3	6½

B

63

——- Second Mo. 20th, 1789. ——-

			£	S.	D.
3	**William Watson,** *Dr.*				
	To 2 Gallons of Rum at - - 10 ʃ 0		1	0	0
	4 Brandy, - 10 6		2	2	0
	3 Eng. Gin, - 5 0		0	15	0
	-- 27 --		3	17	0

		£	S.	D.
2	**Jonas Moore** *Cr.*			
	By Cash received of him in full.	1	0	0

——- Third Mo. 10th, 1789. ——-

		£	S.	D.
4	**Jesse Sling,** *Dr.*			
	To a Silver Punch Bowl weighing - - 23oz 4dwt 0gr at 5ʃ10	6	15	4
	a Tankard - 10 3 6 6 2	3	2	8
	a Tea Pot and Lamp 30 5 12 7 3	11	19	5¼
	6 Plates - - 73 11 5 6 1	22	7	5¼
	18 Spoons - 41 0 10 6 3	12	16	4½
		56	1	4

64

——— *Third Mo.* 22d, 1789. ———

			£.	S.	D.
1 **George Robſon,** *of York,* **Dr.**					
To 27¼ *Gallons Sherry* at - 6ſ 2			8	11	1¼
22¼ *Rheniſh* - 6 4			7	2	6
34 *Liſbon* - - 4 10			8	4	4
			23	17	11¼

——— *Fourth Mo.* 7th, 1789. ———

4 *Thomas Lawſon,* **Dr.**					
To 7½ *Yds. of ſcarlet Cloth* at 21ſ 0			7	17	6
4 *ſuperfine Blue* - 20 0			4	0	0
¼ *Velvet* - - - 18 0				4	6
30 *Gold Lace* - - 10 6			15	15	0
			27	17	0

——— 12 ———

2 *Lucy Berry,* **Dr.**					
To 11¼ *Yds. Luſtring* - at 6ſ 10			4	0	3¼
14 *Brocade* - 11 3			7	17	6
			11	17	9¼

65

---- Fourth Mo. 24th, 1789. ----

	£.	S.	D.
Mary Masterman, **Cr.**			
By Cash received of her in full - -	3	0	3¼

---- 25 ----

4 David Johnson, **Dr.**			
To 5 Gallons Lamp-Oil - at 4ſ 2	1	0	10
3¦ Train-Oil - - 3 0		10	6
¼ Sweet-Oil - - 12 6		9	4½
	2	0	8½

---- Fifth Mo. 3d, 1789. ----

1 James Elford, **Dr.**			
To 27 Yds. of yard-wide Cloth at 8ſ 4	11	5	0
16 Drugget - - 6 3	5	0	0
12 Serge - - - 2 10	1	14	0
32 Shalloon - - 1 8	2	13	4
	20	12	4

66

Fifth Mo. 7th, 1789.

Paid		£.	S	D.
	Phebe Bradey, Dr.			
	To 1 Hhd. of Malaga, qt. 93 Gallons at 6ſ 8	31	o	o

10

4	**Thomas Lawſon,** Dr.			
	To 7 Yds of ſuperfine Cloth at 19ſ 6	6	16	6
	12 Shalloon - - 2 4	1	8	0
	1 Doz. and 9 Coat-Buttons - 2 6		4	4½
	2 do. 8 Waiſtcoat do. - 1 3		3	4
		1	12	2½

5	**Nicholas Norton,** of Durham, Dr.			
	To 9 Pair of Worſted Stockings at 4ſ 6	2	o	6
	6 Silk do. - 15 9	4	14	6
	17 Thread do. - 5 4	4	10	8
	23 Cotton do. - 4 10	5	11	2
	14 Yarn do. - 2 4	1	12	8
	18 Womens Gloves - 4 2	3	15	0
	19 Yds. Flannel - - 1 7½	1	10	0½
		23	15	4½

C

Fifth Mo. 20th, 1789.

			£.	S.	D.
4	**Thomas Lawson,** *Cr.*				
	By a Bill on Capt. James Dixon		10	0	0
5	**Capt. James Dixon,** *Dr.*				
	To Thomas Lawson's Bill on him for		10	0	0

-------- 20 --------

			£.	S.	D.
4	**David Johnson,** *Dr.*				
	To 13 Cheshire Cheeses weighing				
	- - 5C 3Qr 12lb at £1 12 6		9	10	4¼
	25 Gloucester 3 0 18 1 8 0		4	8	6
	47 Stilton - 1 2 5 3 4 8		3	8	11¼
			17	7	10

-------- 26 --------

			£.	S.	D.
5	**Mary Shields,** *Dr.*				
	To 8lb Rice - - at of 4¼			3	0
	3¼ Currants - - 0 5			1	5¼
	2 Quarts Vinegar - - 0 6			1	0
			0	5	5¼

68

Sixth Mo. 3d, 1789.

		£.	S.	D.
5	*James Dixon,* **Dr.**			
	To 7qr. 3 Bufh. Wheat, at £1 8 0	10	6	6
	9 7 Rye - - 1 1 6	10	12	8¼
	17 4 Oats - - 0 10 8	9	6	8
	6	30	5	5½
Paid	*Job Farmer,* **Cr.**			
	By 25 Bufh. of Oats - at 2f 6	3	2	6
	12			
4	*Jeffe Sling,* **Cr.**			
	By a Bank-note receiv'd by the Servant	20	0	0

69

----- *Sixth Mo.* 17th, 1789. -----

				£	S.	D.
1	**Mary Mafterman,**		*Dr.*			
	To 14*lb* hard Soap — — at o*f* 6				7	0
	7 foft do. — — — 0 5				2	11
	3½ Starch — — 0 5¼				1	7¼
	3¼ Blue — — 1 4				4	8
	40 Raifins — — 0 4½				15	0
	3 Doz. Candles — — 5 9				17	3
	----- 21 -----			2	8	5¼
1	**Mary Mafterman,**		*Cr.*			
	By 40 Yds. of Ruffia Sheeting at 2*f* 2			4	6	8
	----- 24 -----					
5	**James Dixon,**		*Cr.*			
	By 30 Yds. Federal Rib — at 6*f* 8			10	0	0

70

——————— *Sixth Mo. 28th, 1789.* ———————

					£		D.
4	**David Johnson,**			**Dr.**			
	To 17lb Cream Cheese	- at	£0 0 7½		0	10	7½
	53 Stone 3lb Bacon	-	0 4 8		12	8	4
	15¼ Firkins Butter	-	1 8 0		21	14	0
					34	12	4

——— *Seventh Mo. 3d.* ———

					£		D.
6	**Fanny Dawson,** of *Liverpool,*			**Dr.**			
	To 14 Yds. blue Ribbon	- at	0f 7½		0	8	9
	21 white do.	- -	0 6		0	10	6
	12¼ Lace	-	3 6		2	3	9
	9 Pair Kid Gloves	-	2 4		1	1	0
					4	4	0

——— *7* ———

					£		D.
2	**James Wilson,** Schoolmaster,			**Cr.**			
	By Cash receiv'd in full	-	-		1	3	8
5	**Nicholas Norton,**			**Cr.**			
	By Cash receiv'd of him on Account	-			22	10	0

71

--- Seventh Mo. 10th, 1789. ---

		£.	S.	D.
6 *Robert Retail,*	*Dr.*			
To 24¼ lb Royal Green Tea at 18ſ 6		22	13	3
21¼ Imperial - 24 10		25	10	0
35¼ beſt Bohea - 13 10		24	14	6¼
17¾ Coffee - - 5 4		4	14	2¼
25 double-refin'd Sugar - 1 1¼		1	8	1¼
9 Sugar Loaves wt. 137 lb. 0 7¼		4	5	7¼
		83	5	9

--- 17 ---

6 *Charles Anderſon,*	*Dr.*			
To 6 Mahogany Chairs - at 18ſ6		5	11	0
2 Elbow do. - 25 0		2	10	0
2 Pier Glaſſes • 36 0		3	12	0
		12	4	0

72

			£.	S.	D.
6 **Charles Anderson,**		**Dr.**			
To 25 Yds. Curtain-Stuff	at	2ſ 2	2	14	2
12 Ticking	-	1 3	0	15	0
3 Stones Feathers	-	25 0	3	15	0
2 Pier Tables	-	50 0	5	0	0
28			12	4	2
5 **James Dixon,**		**Dr.**			
To 12 Buſh. Peas	- at	2ſ 9	1	13	0
9 Beans	-	3 5	1	10	9
17 Malt	-	4 8	3	9	4
25 lb. Hops	- -	1 4	1	3	4
			8	16	5

73

			£.	S.	D.
	———— *Eighth Mo.* 1*st*, 1789. ————				
3	*William Winton,* Dr.				
	To 10 *Grofs of Bottles* - at 22*f* 0		11	0	0
	9 *fmall do.* - 15 0		6	15	0
	2 *doz. Wine-Glaffes* - 4 6			9	0
	3 *D:canters* - 1 2			3	6
	——— 7 ———		18	7	6
3	*Abel Ableman,* Cr.				
	By an Order on Doctor James for -		10	0	0
	Cafh in full - - -		5	17	6
			15	17	0
7	*Doctor James,* Dr.				
	To Abel Ableman's Order on him for		10	0	0

74

--- *Eighth Mo.* 12,*th* 1789. ---

4 *David Johnson,*		*Cr.*	£	*s.*	*D.*
By Cash in Part	-	-	50	0	0

16

6 *Charles Anderson,*		*Cr.*			
By 5 *Packs of Hops*	-	*at* 48*s*	12	0	0

18

6 *Charles Anderson,*		*Dr.*			
To a Mahogany Bed-stead	-		2	10	0
2 *Stools*	-	*at* 5*s* 3	0	10	6
a Poker, Tongs and Fender	-		1	0	0
2 *other Setts of Irons*		15 0	1	10	0
			5	10	6

E

--- *Eighth Mo. 21ſt, 1789.* ---

7	*Conrade Compound* of Exeter *Dr.*		£.	S.	D.
	To 21*lb.* Cochineal — at 29ſ 6		30	19	6
	6¼ Opium — — 6 4		1	19	7
	53 Scammony — 8 10		23	8	2
	1 Mercury — — 12 2			12	2
			56	19	5

--- 26 ---

7	*John Baker* *Dr.*				
	To 5 Groſs of Braſs-Buttons — 18ſ 0		4	10	0
	2 White Do. — 15 0		1	10	0
	7 Doz. Pair of Buckles — 2 2		9	2	0
	12 Trunk-Locks — 0 10			10	0
	6 Chamber Do. — 2 6			15	0
			16	7	0

76

——————— Ninth Mo. 3d, 1789. ———————		£	S.	D.
8	Sarah March **Dr.**			
	To 8 Sarcenet Hoods - at 4 ſ 3	1	14	0
	——————— 4 ———————			
2	James Wilson, Schoolmaster, **Dr.**			
	To 6 Hutton's Arithmeticks - at 2 ſ 3		13	6
	1 Thous. Pinions - -		2	6
	3 Doz. Copy-Books - 2 6		7	6
	3 Quires thin Post - 1 0		3	0
	Lowth's Eng. Grammar - -		2	4
		1	8	10
Paid	Jonas Moore, **Dr.**			
	To Huttons Book-keeping - -		6	0

77

---------- Ninth Mo. 6th, 1789. ---

		£.	S.	D.
2	*Lucy Berry,* *Dr.*			
	To 12½ Yds of Sattin - at 10ʃ 8	6	10	8
	9			
5	*Nicholas Norton,* *Cr.*			
	By a Bank Note for - -	20	0	0
	12			
2	*Lucy Berry,* *Dr.*			
	To 11¼ Yds. Velvet - at 18ʃ	10	4	9
2	*James Wilson,* Schoolmaster, *Dr.*			
	To the Universal Penman - -	1	5	0
	16			
8	*Sarah March,* of Chester, *Dr.*			
	To 17 Indian Fans - at 3ʃ 10	3	5	2

78

-------- Ninth Mo. 18th, 1789. --------

		£	S.	D.
1	*Mary Masterman,* *Dr.*			
	To Cash in full - -	1	18	2¼

-------- 22 --------

		£	S.	D.
2	*Lucy Berry,* *Cr.*			
	By Cash receiv'd of the Steward -	20	0	0

-------- 24 --------

		£	S.	D.
6	*Charles Anderson,* *Cr.*			
	By Cash in full - -	17	7	8

-------- 27 --------

				£	S.	D.
8	*Sarah March,* *Dr.*					
	To 21 Yds. Silver Ribbon -	*at*	2ʃ 2	2	5	6
	11¼ *fine Lace* -		10 6	6	0	9
				8	6	3

F

79

--- Tenth Mo. 2d, 1789. ---

		£	S.	D.
8	Samuel Edwards, Dr.			
	To 14 *lb.* Flax, - at 1∫	0	4	0
	4			
8	Robert Barber, *of Briftol, Stationer,* Cr.			
	By 30 Reams of Fools Cap Paper at 12∫ 6	18	15	0
	5			
2	Lucy Berry, Cr.			
	By Cafh in Part - -	19	0	5
	6			
9	Lucy Berry, Dr.			
	To 27¼ Yds. Holland - at 5∫ 6	7	11	3
4	David Johnfon, Cr.			
	By Cafh in full - -	4	1	6

80

---- Tenth Mo. 10th, 1789. ----

		£.	s.	D.
9	**Matthew Milton,** *Dr.*			
	To 40 Ells of Dowlas — at 1ſ 6	3	0	0
	34 Diaper — 1 4½	2	6	9
	31 Holland — 5 8	8	15	8
	13	14	2	5
9	**Lucy Berry,** *Dr.*			
	To 40 Yds. of Irish Cloth at 3ſ 4	6	13	4
	15			
9	**Henry Foster,** *Dr.*			
	To 2½ Cwt. Iron — at 18ſ 9	2	6	10½
	18			
9	**Mary Gray,** *Dr.*			
	To Cash lent her — •	7	10	0

81

--- Tenth Mo. 21th, 1789. ---

		£.	S.	D.
9	**Mary Gray,** *Cr.*			
	By 3 ps. Irish Cloth, quant. 87 Yds. at 2ſ 2	9	8	0
	23			
7	**John Baker** *Cr.*			
	By Cash in part	10	0	0
8	**Sarah March** *Dr.*			
	To 9 pair Kid-Gloves at 2ſ 2	0	19	6
	5 Doz. Pair Lamb ditto 1 2	3	10	0
	12 Ps. of Bobbin 6	0	6	0
		4	15	6
	27			
1	**George Robſon,** *Cr.*			
	By Cash in full	37	15	0

82

—— *Tenth Mo.* 30*th*, 1789. ——

					£	S.	D.
8	**Samuel Edwards,**			**Dr.**			
	To 12 *lb* of Flax	-	*at*	10*d*		10	0
	14 *ditto*	-	-	9		10	6
					1	0	6

—— *Eleventh Mo.* 4*th.* ——

					£	S.	D.
9	**Matthew Milton,**			**Cr.**			
	By 30 Gallons of Brandy	-	*at*	8ʃ 6	12	15	0
	Cash in full	-	-		1	7	5
					14	2	5

————— 7 —————

					£	S.	D.
10	**Samuel Simpson,**			**Dr.**			
	To 3 Sugar Loaves, wt. 32¼ *lb*		at 8¼*d*		1	3	0¼

————— 13 —————

				£	S.	D.
1	**James Elford,**		**Cr.**			
	By an Assignment on Dr. James for	-		50	0	0

83

G

Eleventh Mo. 13th, 1789.

		£.	S.	D.
7	**Doctr. James,** Dr.	50	0	0
	To James Elford's Affignment on him for			
	15			
5	**James Dixon,** Cr.	42	3	9
	By 3 Ps. of Holland qt. 112½ Ells at 7ſ 6			
5	**James Dixon,** Dr.	3	3	10¼
	To Cafh in full - -			
	20			
10	**Samuel Simpfon,** Dr.	0	5	2
	To 15½ lb of Currants - at 4d			

84

Eleventh Mo. 22d, 1789.

		£	S	D.
10	Thomas Grey, Dr.			
	To 2 Doz. Knives and Forks - at 15ʃ 0	1	10	0
	a Set of China - -	2	10	0
	18 China Plates - 2 3	2	0	6
	3 Diʃhes - - 4 6		13	6
	a Mahogany Tea-Board -		10	6
	26	7	4	6
10	Thomas Grey, Cr.			
	By 42 Ells of Holland - at 5ʃ 6	11	11	0
	28			
4	Jeʃʃe Sling, Cr.			
	By Caʃh in Full - -	36	1	4

85

Eleventh Mo. 29th, 1789.

			£	S.	D.
10 **Samuel Simpson,** *Dr.*					
To 17¼ lb of Malaga Raisins	at 0f 5¼			7	10¼
19¼ Raisins of the Sun —	0 6			9	10¼
17 Rice — —	0 3¼			4	11¼
8¼ Pepper —	1 6			12	4¼
13 Oz. Cloves —	0 9			9	9
			2	4	10¼

Twelfth Mo. 1st.

			£	S.	D.
2 **James Wilson,** Schoolmaster, *Cr.*					
By Cash in full — —			2	13	10

2

			£	S.	D.
9 **Matthew Milton,** *Cr.*					
By 20 Yds. Broad-Cloth	at 22f 6		22	10	0

86

——————— *Twelfth Mo. 3d*, 1789. ·——————

		£·	S.	D.
3	*Able Ableman,* **Dr.**			
	To a Pipe of Wine - -	25	0	0
	—————— 6 ——————			
3	*William Winton,* **Cr.**			
	By 30 Gallons Brandy - at 7∫ 6	11	5	0
	By Cash in full - -	9	6	0$\frac{1}{2}$
		20	11	0$\frac{1}{2}$
	————— 8 —————			
10	*Thomas Hunter,* **Dr.**			
	To 3 Chaldrons of Coals at £· 1 15	5	5	0
	————— 10 —————			
3	*William Watson,* **Cr.**			
	By Cash in full - -	3	17	0

H

87

——— *Twelfth Mo. 10th, 1789.* ———

			£.	S.	D.
7	Doctr. James,	Cr.			
	By Cash in Composition £. 20 19				
	By Profit and Loss, lost by him 39 10		60	0	0
	——— 13 ———				
9	Henry Foster,	Cr.			
	By Cash in full - -		2	6	0¼
	——— 15 ———				
4	Thomas Lawson,	Cr.			
	By 3C. 2qrs 14lb Tobacco at £. 4 a Cwt.		14	10	0
	——— 18 ———				
5	Mary Shields,	Dr.			
	To a Lump of Sugar wt. 22¼lb at 8½d			16	1¼

88

——— *Twelfth Mo. 19th, 1789.* ———

			£·	S	D.
9	*Lucy Berry,*	*Cr.*			
	By Cash in full	- -	20	0	0
	20				
10	*Samuel Simpson,*	*Cr.*			
	By Cash in full	- -	3	13	0.
	22				
6	*Fanny Dawson,*	*Cr.*			
	By Cash in full	- -	4	4	0
	23				
11	*Edward Young,*	*Dr.*			
	To 3C. 1qr Cheese - at 30s		4	17	6
	24				
6	*Robert Retail,*	*Cr.*			
	By a Bill on Thomas Lawson for		50	0	0

--- *Twelfth Mo. 24th, 1789.* ---

		£.	S.	D.
4	*Thomas Lawson,* **Dr.**			
	To *Robert Retail's* Bill on him for -	50	0	0
5	*Mary Shields,* **Cr.**			
	By Cash in full - -	1	1	6¼
	29			
8	*Sarah March,* **Cr.**			
	By Cash in full - -	18	0	11
9	*Mary Gray,* **Cr.**			
	By 15 Yds Velvet - at 10/	7	10	0
	30			
10	*Thomas Grey,* **Cr.**			
	By Cash borrowed of him -	37	10	0
	31			
3	*William Watson,* **Dr.**			
	To 1 Year's Rent, due this Day -	40	0	0

90

LEDGER
A.

The ALPHABET *to*

A	fo	B	fo	C	fo
Ableman Abel	3	*Baker John*	7	*Compound Conrade*	7
Anderson Charles	6	*Barber Robert*	8		
		Berry Lucy (9)	2		

D		E		F	
Dixon James	5	*Elford James*	1	*Foster Henry*	9
Dawson Fanny	6	*Edward Samuel*	8		

G		H		IJ	
Gray Mary	9	*Hunter Thomas*	10	*Johnson David*	4
Grey Thomas	10			*James Doctor*	7

K		L		M	
		Lawson Thomas	4	*Masterman Mary*	1
				Moore Jonas	2
				March Sarah	8
				Milton Matthew	9

the LEDGER.

N	fo	O	fo	P	fo
Norton Nicholas	5				

Q		R		S	
		Robſon George	1	Sling Jeſſe	4
		Retail Robert	6	Shields Mary	5
				Simpſon Samuel	10

T		UV		W	
				Wilſon James	2
				Vinton William	3
				Watſon William	3

X		Y		Z	
		Young Edward	11		

1789			James Elford,	Dr.	£.	S.	D.
1 Mo	1		To Sundries - -		32	12	6
5 Mo	3		To Sundries - -		20	12	4
					53	4	10

1789			George Robson,	Dr.			
1 Mo	1		To Sundries - -		13	17	1
3 Mo	22		To ditto - - -		23	17	11½
					37	15	0½

1789			Mary Masterman,	Dr.			
1 Mo	4		To Sundries - -		3	0	3½
6 Mo	17		To ditto - - -		2	8	5½
9 Mo	18		To Cash in full - -		1	18	2¼
					7	6	11¼

94

1789	Contra	Cr.	£.	S	D.
11 Mo 12	By a Bill on Dr. James for		50	0	0
	By Account, Ledger B, fol. 1.		?	4	10
			55	4	10

1789	Contra	Cr.			
10 Mo 27	By Cash in full		37	15	$0\frac{1}{2}$

1789	Contra	Cr.			
4 Mo 24	By Cash in part - -		3	0	$3\frac{1}{4}$
9 Mo 21	By 40 Yds. of Russia Sheeting at 2/2		4	6	8
			7	6	$11\frac{1}{4}$

K

1789			Lucy Berry,		Dr.	£.	S.	D.
1 Mo	9		To Sundries	-	-	16	2	7½
4 Mo	12		To Sundries	-	-	11	17	9½
9 Mo	6		To 12¼ Yds. of Sattin	at 10ſ8		6	10	8
	12		To 11¼ Yds. of Velvet	18 0		10	4	9
						44	15	10

1789			Jonas Moore,		Dr.			
1 Mo	20		To a Ream of Paper	-		1	0	0

1789			James Wilſon,		Dr.			
1 Mo	27		To Sundries	-	-	1	3	8
8 Mo	24		To ditto	-	-	1	8	10
9 Mo	12		To the Univerſal Penman	-		1	5	0
						2	13	10

96

(**2**)

1789	Contra	Cr.	£.	S.	D.
9 Mo 22	By Cash received of the Steward		20	0	0
10 Mo 5	By Cash in part —		19	0	5
	By Account at fol. 9 —		5	15	5
			44	15	10
1789	Contra	Cr.			
2 Mo 27	By Cash in full — —		1	0	0
1789	Contra	Cr.			
7 Mo 7	By Cash in full — —		1	3	8
12 Mo 1	By Cash in full — —		2	13	10

97

98

1789			Abel Ableman,	Dr.	£.	S.	D.
2 Mo	5		To Sundries	- -	15	17	6
12 Mo	3		To a Pipe of Wine	-	25	0	0

1789			William Winton,	Dr.			
2 Mo	12		To Sundries	- -	2	3	6½
8 Mo	1		To Sundries	- -	18	7	6
					20	11	0½

1789			William Watson,	Dr.			
2 Mo	20		To Sundries	- -	2	7	0
12 Mo	31		To 1 Year's Rent	·	40	0	0

1789			*Contra*	*Cr.*	£.	S.	D.
8 Mo	7		By Sundries - •		15	17	6
			By Account, Ledger B. fol. 1.		25	0	0
1789			*Contra*	*Cr.*			
12 Mo	6		By Sundries - -		20	11	0½
1789			*Contra*	*Cr.*			
12 Mo	10		By Cash in full		3	17	0
21 Mo	31		By Account, Ledger B. Fol. 1		40	0	0

L

1789	Jeſſe Sling,	Dr.	£.	S.	D.
3 Mo 10	To Sundries — —		56	1	4
1789	Thomas Lawſon,	Dr.			
4 Mo 7	To Sundries — —		27	17	0
5 Mo 10	To ditto — —		8	12	2¼
12 Mo 24	To Robert Retail's Bill on him for		50	0	0
			86	9	2¼
1789	David Johnſon,	Dr.			
4 Mo 25	To Sundries — —		2	0	8¼
5 Mo 20	To Sundries — —		17	7	10
6 Mo 28	To Ditto. — —		34	12	11¼
			54	1	6

100

1789			Contra	Cr.	£.	S.	D.
6 M.	12		By a Bank Note	-	20	0	0
11 M.	28		By Cash in full	- -	36	1	4
					56	1	4

1789			Contra	Cr.			
5 M.	20		By a Bill on Captain James Dixon		10	0	0
12 Mo	15		By 3C.2qrs.14lb, Tobacco at £.4 a Cwt.		14	10	0
			By Account, Ledger B. Fol. 1.		61	19	2½
					86	9	2½

1789			Contra	Cr.			
8 Mo	12		By Cash in part	-	50	0	0
10 M.	6		By Cash in full	- -	4	1	6
					54	1	6

1789		Nicholas Norton,	Dr.	£.	S.	D.
5 Mo	14	To Sundries		23	15	4¼
		To Account, Ledger B. Fol. 2.		18	14	7¾
				42	10	0

1789		James Dixon,	Dr.			
5 Mo	20	To Thomas Lawson's Bill on him for		10	0	0
6 Mo	3	To Sundries		30	5	10¼
7 Mo	28	To Ditto		8	16	5
11 Mo	15	To Cash in full		3	1	10¼
				52	3	9

1789		Mary Shields,	Dr.			
5 Mo	26	To Sundries		0	5	5¼
12 Mo	18	To a Lump of Sugar wt. 22¼lb. at 8¼d.		0	16	1¼
				1	1	6¼

102

1789		Contra	Cr.	£.	S.	D.
7 Mo	7	By Cash in part —		22	10	0
9 Mo	9	By a Bank Note — —		20	0	0
				42	10	0

1789		Contra	Cr.			
6 Mo	24	By 30 Yds. Federal Rib, at 6ſ 8d		10	0	0
11 Mo	15	By 3 Ps. of Holland qt. 112½ Ells a 7ſ6		42	3	9
				52	3	9

1789		Contra ſ	Cr.			
12 Mo	24	By Cash in full — —		1	1	9½

104

1789			Fanny Dawson,	Dr.	£.	S	D.
7 Mo	3		To Sundries		4	4	0
1789			Robert Retail,	Dr.			
7 Mo	10		To Sundries		84	3	5¼
1789			Charles Anderson,	Dr.			
7 Mo	17		To Sundries		11	13	0
7 Mo	24		To Ditto.		12	4	2
8 Mo	13		To ditto		5	10	6
					29	7	8

1789	Contra	Cr.	£.	S.	D.
12 Mo 22	By Cash in full - -		4	4	0

1789	Contra	Cr.	£.	S.	D.
12 Mo 24	By a Bill on Thomas Lawson, for		50	0	0
	By Account, Ledger B. Fol. 2.		34	3	5½
			84	3	5½

1789	Contra	Cr.	£.	S.	D.
8 Mo 16	By 5 Packets of Hops, at 48ſ		12	0	0
9 Mo 24	By Cash in full		17	7	8
			29	7	8

105

1789			Doctor. James,	Dr.	£	S.	D.
8 M	7		To Abel Ableman's Order.		10	0	0
11 M	13		To James Elford's Assignment on him		50	0	0
					60	0	0

1789			Conrade Compound,	Dr.			
8 Mo	21		To Sundries	-	-	56	19	5

1789			John Baker,	Dr.			
8 Mo	26		To Sundries	-	-	16	7	0

106

1789	Contra	Cr.	£.	S.	D.
12 Mo 10	By Sundries		60	0	0

1789	Contra	Cr.			
	By Account, Ledger B. Fol. 2.		56	19	5

1789	Contra	Cr.			
10 Mo 23	By Cash in part		10	0	0
	By Account, Ledger B. Fol. 3.		6	7	0
			16	7	0

1789			Sarah March, . Dr.	£.	S.	D.
9 Mo	3		To 8 Sarcenet Hoods, at 4f3	1	14	0
9 Mo	16		To 17 Indian Fans, at 3f10	3	5	2
9 Mo	27		To Sundries - -	8	6	3
10 Mo	23		To Ditto - -	4	15	6
1789			Samuel Edwards, Dr.			
10 Mo	2		To 14lb Flax, at 1f -	0	14	0
10 Mo	30		To Sundries - -	1	0	6
1789			Robert Barber, Dr.			
			To Account, Ledger B. fol. 2.	18	15	0

108

1789	Contra	Cr.	£.	S.	D.
12 Mo 29	By Cash in full -		18	0	11

1789	Contra	Cr.			
	By Account Ledger B. Fol. 2.		1	14	6

1789	Contra	Cr.			
10 Mo 4	By 30 Reams of Paper at 12/6		18	15	0

109

1789			Lucy Berry,	Dr.	£.	S.	D.
			To Account at Fol. 2.		5	15	5
10 Mo	6		To 27¼ Yds. Holland, at 5/6		7	11	3
	13		To 40 Yds. Irish Cloth, at 3/4		6	13	4
					20	0	0
1789			Matthew Milton,	Dr.			
10 Mo	10		To Sundries — —		14	2	5
			To Account Ledger B. Fol. 3.		22	10	0
1789			Henry Foster,	Dr.			
10 Mo	15		To 2 Cwt. of Iron, at 18/9		2	6	10¼
1789			Mary Gray,	Dr.			
10 Mo	18		To Cash lent her		7	10	0
			To Account Ledger B. Fol. 3.		9	8	6
					16	18	6

110

1789	Contra		Cr.	£.	S.	D.
12 Mo 19	By Cash in full - -			20	0	0

1789	Contra		Cr.	£.	S.	D.
12 Mo 4	By Sundries - -			14	2	5
12 Mo 2	By 20 Yds. Broad Cloth, at 22/6			22	10	0

1789	Contra		Cr.			
12 Mo 13	By Sundries - -			2	6	10

1789	Contra		Cr.			
10 Mo 21	By 3 Ps. Irish Cloth, 87 Yds. at 2/2			9	8	6
12 Mo 29	By 15 Yds. Velvet, at 10s.			7	10	0
				16	18	6

O

112

1789			Samuel Simpson,	Dr.	£.	S.	D.
11 M.	7		To 3 Sugar Loaves, wt. 32½ lb. at 8½d		1	3	0½
11 M.	20		To 15½ lb. Currants, at 4d.			5	2
11 M.	29		To Sundries, - -		2	4	10½
					3	13	0½
1789	10		Thomas Grey,	Dr.			
11 M.	22		To Sundries - -		7	4	6
			To Account, Ledger B. Fol. 3.		41	16	6
					49	1	0
1789			Thomas Hunter,	Dr.			
12 Mo	8		To 3 Chaldrons of Coals, at £. 1 15		5	5	0

1789	*Contra*		*Cr.*	£.	S.	D.
12 Mo 20	By Cash in full	-		3	13	0¼

1789	*Contra*		*Cr.*	£.	S.	D.
11 Mo 20	By 42 Ells Holland, at 5/6			11	11	0
12 Mo 30	By Cash borrowed	-		37	10	0
				49	1	0

1789	*Contra*		*Cr.*	£.	S.	D.
	By Account Ledger B. Fol. 3.			5	5	0

113

1789	Edward Young,	Dr.	£.	S.	D.
12 Mo 23	To 3C. 1qr. Cheese, at 30ſ.		4	17	6

114

1789	Stock	Dr.	£.	S.	D.
12 Mo 31	To N. Norton, due to him,		18	14	7½
	To Robert Barber, -		18	15	0
	To Matthew Milton, -		22	10	0
	To Mary Gray, - -		9	8	6
	To Thomas Grey, - -		41	16	6
	To Balance, my neat Worth, -		916	18	7
			1028	3	2½

1789	Contra	Cr.	£.	S	D.
	By Account Ledger B. Fol. 3.		4	17	6

1789	Contra	Cr.	£.	S	D.
12 Mo 31	By Amount Inventory of my Cash and other Effects }		789	10	0
	By James Elford, due to me -		3	4	10
	By Abel Ableman, - -		25	0	0
	By William Watson, - -		40	0	0
	By Thomas Lawson, -		61	19	2½
	By Robert Retail, - -		33	5	9
	By Conrade Compound, -		56	19	5
	By John Baker, - -		6	7	0
	By Samuel Edwards, -		1	14	6
	By Thomas Hunter, - -		5	5	0
	By Edward Young, -		4	17	6
			1028	3	2½

P

LEDGER
B.

118

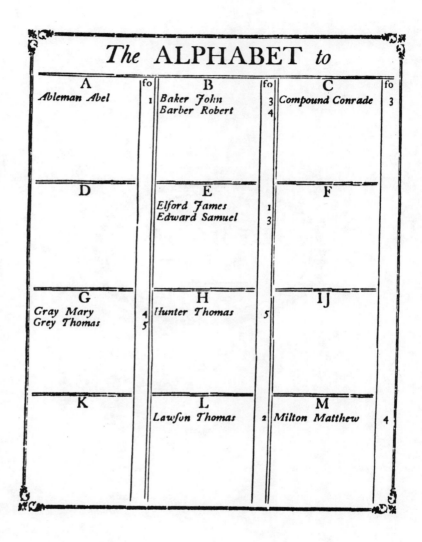

A		fo	B		fo	C		fo
Ableman Abel		1	*Baker John*		3	*Compound Conrade*		3
			Barber Robert		4			
D			E			F		
			Elford James		1			
			Edward Samuel		3			
G			H			IJ		
Gray Mary		4	*Hunter Thomas*		5			
Grey Thomas		5						
K			L			M		
			Lawson Thomas		2	*Milton Matthew*		4

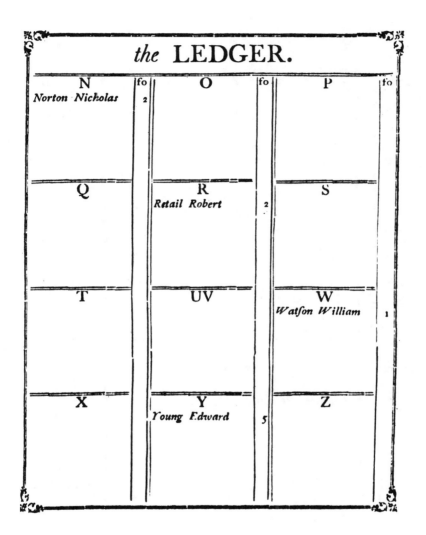

the LEDGER.

N	fo	O	fo	P	fo
Norton Nicholas	2				
Q		R		S	
		Retail Robert	2		
T		UV		W	1
				Watson William	
X		Y		Z	
		Young Edward	5		

119

120

1789	*James Elford,*	*Dr.*	£.	S.	D.
	To Account at Ledger A. fol. 1		3	4	10
1789	*Abel Ableman,*	*Dr.*			
	To Account Lndger A. fol. 3		25	0	0
1789	*William Watson,*	*Dr.*			
	To Account Ledger A. fol. 3		40	0	0

1789	Contra	Cr.	£.	S.	D.
1789	Contra	Cr.			
1789	Contra	Cr.			

Q

1789	Thomas Lawson,	Dr.	£.	S.	D.
	To Account Ledger A, Fol. 4		61	19	2¼
1789	Nicholas Norton,	Dr.			
1789	Robert Retail,	Dr.			
	To Account Ledger A, Fol. 6		33	5	9

122

1789	Contra	Cr.	£.	S.	D.
1789	Contra	Cr.			
	By Account Ledger A, Fol. 5		18	14	7½
1789	Contra	Cr.			

123

1789	Conrade Compound,	Dr.	£.	S	D.
	To Account Ledger A, Fol. 7		56	19	5

124

1789	John Baker,	Dr.			
	To Account Ledger A, Fol. 7		6	7	0

1789	Samuel Edwards,	Dr.			
	To Account Ledger A, Fol. 8		1	4	6

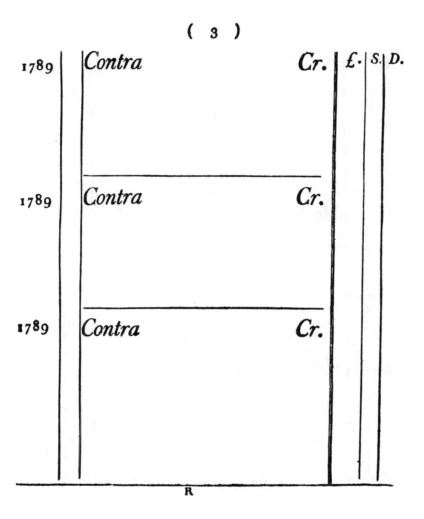

1789	Robert Barber,	Dr.	£.	S.	D.
1789	Matthew Milton,	Dr.			
1789	Mary Gray,	Dr.			

126

1789	*Contra*	*Cr.*	£.	S.	D.
	By Account Ledger A, Fol. 8.		18	15	0
1789	*Contra*	*Cr.*			
	By Account Ledger A, Fol. 9		22	10	0
1789	*Contra*	*Cr.*			
	By Account Ledger A, Fol. 9		9	8	6

127

128

1789	Thomas Grey,	Dr.	£.	S.	D.
1789	Thomas Hunter, Dr. To Account Ledger A, Fol. 10		5	5	0
1789	Edward Young, Dr. To Account Ledger A, Fol. 11		4	17	6

1789	Contra	Cr.	£.	S.	D.
	By Account Ledger A, Fol. 10		41	16	6
1789	Contra	Cr.			
1789	Contra	Cr.			

R

129

130

MEMORANDUMS.

1789		
1 Mo	5	*Hired Martha Maid, at 4/6 per Week.*
	12	*Paid an agreeable Visit to A. B.*
	20	*Appointed to attend at the State-House, on the 27th Inst. at 4 P. M.*
2 Mo	3	*Let my House in Fifth-Street to Jonas Johns, at £. 40 per Ann. payable quarterly.*
	28	*Miles Cleaver agrees to furnish me with Wood for the ensuing 12 Months, Hickory at 22/6 per Cord, Oak at 15/.*
3 Mo	17	*Bought a Horse and Chaise of M. N. to pay in 3 Months.*
4 Mo	20	*Entered Patty and Phebe, at J. I's School.*
	28	*X. Y. sailed for Liverpool.*
5 Mo	10	*A remarkable Aurora Boreales.*
	25	*A heavy Shower of Hail, uncommon at this Season.*
6 Mo	15	*Commenced Boarding with J. P.*

THE
EXPENCE
BOOK.

1789		EXPENCES, Viz.	£.	S.	D.
1 Mo	2	Laid out in Market		13	4
	4	Paid for a new Carpet	0	5	
	7	——— for a Load of Hay	1	16	
		The Shoemaker's Bill	12	17	4
	8	The Baker's Bill	1	2	6
	9	Marketing	3	12	9
	14	½ Doz. Chairs	7	10	
	16	Phebe's School Bill	2	12	6
	21	Repairing the Clock	1	2	6
	23	6 Cords Wood at 30f with hauling and sawing	10	16	
	30	70 lb. Beef, at 3½	1		5
		Expended this Month	49	8	4
2 Mo	1	J. Seller's Bill for Cloth and Trimmings	8	12	7
	6	Marketing	1	8	5
	9	Sweeping the parlour & Kitchen Chims.		8	
	12	Taylor's Bill	5	10	9
		Paid Polly Money for Needle-Work.	1	2	6
	20	Sundries		7	2
	23	Taxes	2	15	6
	26	1 Piece Linen, Handkerchiefs, &c.	5	5	6
	28	Paid Jane Cook in Part of her Wages	3		
			27	18	5
3 Mo	1	Paving the Yard	5	10	6
	5	A Barrel of Flour	1	15	
		Carried forward	7	5	6

1789	EXPENCES, *Viz.*	*L.*	*S.*	*D.*
3 Mo	Brought forward - -	7	5	6
6	A Gammon, 7∫6, Bruſhes 6∫3		14	
12	5 Buſhels Apples, 10∫6 Turnips 1∫3		13	9
18	Stable Rent - -	5	10	
19	Marketing - -		16	6
25	A Stove - -	6	10	
29	A Quarter's Wages to John -	3		
		24	9	9
4 Mo 4	A Coffee Mill, 8∫ 1 Doz Candles 10∫		18	
10	Mending the Tongs and And-Irons		4	10
16	Sand and Black-Ball -		1	6
21	1 lb. Tea, 10∫ 6 lb. Sugar 4∫3		14	3
23	Oyſters - -		5	
30	Mending the Chaiſe -	2	10	
		4	12	7
5 Mo 6	Daniel Dun's Bill for Grocery	16	9	10
12	1 Caſk Wine - -	30		
20	Marketing - -	7	2	6
31	A Bed and Bedding -	22	10	
		77	2	4
6 Mo 7	Doctor's Bill - -	20		
10	Nurſe's Wages .. -	5	10	
24	Sundries - -		5	6
	Carried forward	25	25	6

134

		EXPENCES, Viz.	£.	S.	D.
1789		Brought forward - -	25	15	6
6 Mo	30	Marketing - -	4	2	2
			29	17	8
		Thus proceeding through the Year.			
		Brought from 1 Month -	49	8	4
		2 Month -	27	18	5
		3 Month -	24	9	9
		4 Month -	4	13	7
		5 Month -	77	2	4
		6 Month -	29	17	8
		Expended these 6 Months	213	10	8

135

ERRATA. For the Day-Book.

PAGE 1	LINE 7	for 6/8	read 8/6
2	10	7/9	7/6
do	12	8/0	1/0
4	14	£. 11 19 5¼	£. 10 19 9¼
7	9	1 12 2½	8 12 2½
9	4	10 12 8¼	10 12 3¾
11	6	34 12 4	34 12 11¼
12	4	24 10	24
do	14	12 4	11 13
18	3	Yds. 12¼	12¼ Yds.
24	7	3 3 10¼	3 1 10¼

ERRATA. For the Ledger.

FOL. 1	LINE 8	for Part	read Full.
do	do	9 Mo.	6 Mo.
3	do	21 Mo.	12 Mo.
5	7	£. 30 5 10¼	£. 30 5 5¼
do	10	1 1 9¼	1 1 6¼
9	7	2 6 10	2 6 10¼

4

THOMAS SARJEANT ON MERCANTILE ARITHMETIC, 1788

PREFATORY NOTE

At the close of the accounting book reprinted
as chapter 5, Sarjeant (1789, 52) corrects
eleven errors, principally numerical, found in the
1788 arithmetic book from which the following
selection is drawn. Five of them, from text pages
62, 63, 69, and 70, relate to this chapter.

ELEMENTARY PRINCIPLES

OF

ARITHMETIC;

WITH THEIR APPLICATION TO THE

TRADE AND COMMERCE

OF THE

UNITED STATES OF AMERICA.

IN EIGHT SECTIONS.

By *THOMAS SARJEANT,*

LATE MASTER OF THE MATHEMATICAL SCHOOL IN THE
ACADEMY OF THE PROTESTANT EPISCOPAL CHURCH,
IN THE CITY OF PHILADELPHIA.

FOR THE USE OF SCHOOLS AND PRIVATE EDUCATION.

PARVUM PARVA DECENT.　　HOR. EP.

PHILADELPHIA:

PRINTED BY *DOBSON* AND *LANG* FOR THE EDITOR;
AND SOLD BY T. DOBSON, IN SECOND STREET, AND
BY W. PRITCHARD, IN MARKET STREET.

M.DCC.LXXXVIII.

Suppoſe a Loaf of $8\frac{1}{4}$ lb. coſt 1s. 5d. when Wheat is at 7s. a bu. what muſt be paid for 8 oz. of Bread when Wheat is at 5s. 3d. a buſh. ?　　　　　　　　　　　　　　　A. $\frac{3}{4}$d.

Suppoſe £.13 10 be received for the intereſt of a certain ſum for 9 mon. at £.5 per cent. per an. what was the ſum of money lent ?　　　　　　　　　　　　　　A. £.360.

If 1 lb. 4 oz. of Bread be bought for 2d. when Wheat is at 6s. a buſh. what weight may be bought for 1s. when Wheat is at 5s. 6d. a buſh. ?　　　　　A. 8 lb. 2 oz. 14 dr.

If 25 men working 12 hours a day, can do a piece of work in 28 days, how many men can do the ſame in 13 days, working 15 hours a day ?　　　　　　　　　A. 43 men.

If 4 Ells Eng. make 8 Braces at Leghorn ; and 30 Braces at Leghorn 27 Braces at Venice ; how many Ells Eng. are equal to 81 Braces at Venice ?　　　　　A. 45 Ells Eng.

140

If 5 lb. at London make $4\frac{1}{2}$ at Amſterdam ; and 45 lb. at Amſterdam 56 lb. at Thoulouſe ; how many lb. at Thoulouſe are equal to 112 lb. at London ?　　　　　A. $125\frac{11}{17}$.

If 24 Men in 18 days eat 50s. worth of Bread when Wheat is at 5s. a buſh. how much will ſerve 32 men 30 days, when Wheat is at 6s. a buſh. ?　　　　　A. £.6 13 4.

If when Wheat is at 6s. a buſh. £.6 13 4 worth will ſerve 32 men 30 days ; how much will 24 men eat in 18 days, when Wheat is 5s. a buſh. ?　　　　　[A. 50s. worth.

SECTION THE FIFTH.

MERCANTILE ARITHMETIC.

EXCHANGE.

DEFINITION XXIV.

EXCHANGE is the Converſion of any Sum of Money of one Country, State, &c. to its equivalent in another.

DEF. XXV. CONTINENTAL Exchange is the Converſion of Spaniſh Dollars into the American Currencies, and of the
American

American Currencies into *Spanish Dollars* ; together with the Conversion of the different *American Currencies* into *each other*.

TAB. XXII. *The Value of* DOLLARS *in the several* STATES.

No. of Doll.	N. Hampsh. Massachusett R. Island, Connecticut, Virginia.			New-York, and N. Carolina.			N. Jersey, Pennsylvan. Delaware, and Maryland.			S. Carolina, and Georgia.		
1	£. 0	6	0	£. 0	8	0	£. 0	7	6	£. 0	4	8
5	1	10	0	2	0	0	1	17	6	1	3	4
10	3	0	0	4	0	0	3	15	0	2	2	6
15	4	10	0	6	0	0	5	12	6	3	10	0
20	6	0	0	8	0	0	7	10	0	4	13	4
30	9	0	0	12	0	0	11	5	0	7	0	0
40	12	0	0	16	0	0	15	0	0	9	6	8
50	15	0	0	20	0	0	18	15	0	11	13	4
60	18	0	0	24	0	0	22	10	0	14	0	0
70	21	0	0	28	0	0	26	5	0	16	6	8
80	24	0	0	32	0	0	30	0	0	18	13	4
90	27	0	0	36	0	0	33	15	0	21	0	0
100	30	0	0	40	0	0	37	10	0	23	6	8
200	60	0	0	80	0	0	75	0	0	46	13	4
300	90	0	0	120	0	0	112	10	0	70	0	0
400	120	0	0	160	0	0	150	0	0	93	6	8
500	150	0	0	200	0	0	187	10	0	116	13	4
1000	300	0	0	400	0	0	375	0	0	233	6	8

PART I. *Any Number of Spanish Dollars being given, to find their Value in the several American Currencies.*

DIR. XX. Take the value of a Dollar *(Tab. XXII.)* in the given State, in Aliquot parts from the number of Dollars.

	Doll.		£.	s.	d.
Reduce	35	to N. England &c. Currency.	10	10	0
Reduce	56	to N. York &c. Cur.	22	8	0
Reduce	131	to N. Jersey &c. Cur.	49	2	6
Reduce	748	to S. Carolina &c. Cur.	174	10	8
Reduce	1000	to N. England &c. Cur.	300	0	0
Reduce	1000	to N. York &c. Cur.	400	0	0

Reduce

	Doll.		£.	s.	d.
Reduce	1000	to N. Jersey &c. Cur.	375	0	0
Reduce	1000	to S. Carolina &c. Cur.	233	6	8
Reduce	6780	to N. England &c. Cur.	2034	0	0
Reduce	6780	to N. York &c. Cur.	2712	0	0
Reduce	6780	to N. Jersey &c. Cur.	2542	10	0
Reduce	6780	to S. Carolina &c. Cur.	1582	0	0
Reduce	10560	to N. England &c. Cur.	3168	0	0
Reduce	10560	to N. York &c. Cur.	4224	0	0
Reduce	10560	to N. Jersey &c. Cur.	3960	0	0
Reduce	10560	to S. Carolina &c. Cur.	2464	0	0

PART II. *A Sum of Money being given in either of the American Currencies, to change the same to Spanish Dollars.*

DIR. XXI. Reduce the value of a Dollar in the given State to the lowest denomination, and the given sum to the same denomination, and divide the latter by the former.

£.	s.	d.		Doll.
Reduce 10	10	0	N. England &c. Cur. to Dollars	35
Reduce 22	8	0	N. York &c.	56
Reduce 49	2	6	N. Jersey &c.	131
Reduce 174	10	8	S. Carolina &c.	748
Reduce 300	0	0	N. England &c.	1000
Reduce 400	0	0	N. York &c.	1000
Reduce 375	0	0	N. Jersey &c.	1000
Reduce 233	6	8	S. Carolina &c.	1000
Reduce 2034	0	0	N. England &c.	6780
Reduce 2712	0	0	N. York &c.	6780
Reduce 2542	10	0	N. Jersey &c.	6780
Reduce 1582	0	0	S. Carolina &c.	6780
Reduce 3168	0	0	N. England &c.	10560
Reduce 4224	0	0	N. York &c.	10560
Reduce 3960	0	0	N. Jersey &c.	10560
Reduce 2464	0	0	S. Carolina &c.	10560

OBS. XXIII. *Dir. XX.* and *XXI.* are equally applicable to the Purchasing or Disposing of *State Securities*, &c.

What is the Value of £.275 in Loan Office Certificates, at 4s. 6d. in the Pound ?　　　A. £.61 17. 6

What Quantity of Loan Office Certificates may be bought for £.61 17 6, at 4s. 6d. in the Pound ?　　A. £.275.

Land Office Certificates at 3s. 9d.—what must be given for £.500 worth?　　　A. £.93 15.

What

What sum in Land Office Certificates at 3*s*. 9*d*. in the Pound
will £.93 15 purchase ?   *A.* £.500.
What sum must be given for £.1000 Continental Certificates
at 4*s*. 2*d*. in the Pound ?   *A.* £.208 6 8.
I lay out £.208 6 8 in Continental Certificates at 4*s*. 2*d*. in
the Pound—to what amount will it purchase ? *A.* £.1000.

PART III. *A Sum of Money being given in the Currency
of one State, to find its value in that of another.*

Dir. XXII. As the value of a Dollar in the given State :
is to the given sum : : so is its value in the required State :
to the sum required.

What is the value of £.205 10 N. Hampshire Currency in
N. Carolina ?   *A.* £.274.
What is the value of £.195 10 Massachusetts-Bay Currency
in Pennsylvania currency ?   *A.* £.244 7 6.
Bring £.130 2 6 Virginia currency to S. Carolina currency.
                                          £.101 4 2.
Find the value of £.274 N. York currency in Rhode-Island
currency.   £. 205 10.
Reduce the Sum of £.336 16 in N. Carolina currency to
N. Jersey currency.   £.315 15.
Reduce £.166 0 3 N. York to S. Carolina currency.
                                          £.96 16 9¾
Required the amount of £.244 7 6 Maryland money, in
Connecticut.   £.195 10.
Required the amount of £.315 15 Delaware currency in N.
York currency.   £ 336 16.
What is the worth of £.260 8 9 Pennsylvania currency in
Georgia ?   *A.* £.162 1.
Turn £.101 4 2 S. Carolina to Massachusetts-Bay cur-
rency.   £.130 2 6.
What is the value of £.96 16 9¾ at Charleston, S. Carolina,
in N. York currency ?   *A.* £.166 0 3.
Turn £.162 1 Georgia currency into Pennsylvania currency.
                                          £.260 8 9.

Cont. XII. To reduce the New England and
Virginia Currencies——

——*To New York and North Carolina,* ADD one third
part of the New Hampshire &c. sum to itself.

Reduce *N. Eng.* &c. Currency, to *N. York*, &c. Currency.

£.205	10	0	=	£.274	0	0
1700	8	6¼	=	2267	4	9
10000	0	0	=	13333	6	8 (Con. 15.)

CONT. XIII. ——*To New Jersey, Pennsylvanie, Delaware, and Maryland;* ADD one fourth part of the Sum to itself.

Reduce *N. Eng.* &c. Currency, to *N. Jersey*, &c. Currency.

£.195	10	0	=	£.244	7	6
9000	10	4	=	11250	12	11
50000	0	0	=	62500	0	0 (Con. 18.)

CONT. XIV. ——*To South Carolina and Georgia;* MULTIPLY the given Sum by 7, and DIVIDE the Product by 9.

Reduce *N. Eng.* &c. Currency to *S. Carolina*, &c. Currency.

£.130	2	6	=	£.101	4	2
9004	14	6	=	7003	13	6
45001	1	0	=	35000	16	4 (Con. 21.)

CONT. XV. To reduce the Currencies of New York and North Carolina——

——*To the Currencies of New England and Virginia;* SUBTRACT one fourth part of the N. York &c. Sum from itself.

Reduce *N. York*, &c. Currency to *N. Eng.* &c. Currency.

£.274	0	0	=	£.205	10	0
2267	4	9	=	1700	8	6¼
13333	6	8	=	10000	0	0 (Con. 12.)

CONT. XVI. ——*To New Jersey, Pennsylvania, Delaware, and Maryland;* SUBTRACT one sixteenth part.

Reduce *N. York*, &c. Currency, to *N. Jersey*, &c. Currency.

£.336	16	0	=	£.315	15	0
2000	0	0	=	1875	0	0
35791	14	4	=	34492	4	8¼ (Co. 19.)

CONT. XVII. ——*To South Carolina and Georgia Currencies;* MULTIPLY the Sum by 7, and DIVIDE the Product by 12.

Reduce

Reduce *N. York*, &c. Currency to *S. Carolina*, &c. Currency.

£.166	0	3	=	£.96	16	9¾
1575	19	6	=	919	6	4½
12000	13	0	=	7000	7	7 *(Con.22.)*

CONT. XVIII. To reduce the Currencies of New Jersey, Pennsylvania, Delaware, and Maryland——

——*To the New England and Virginia Currencies;* SUBTRACT one fifth part.

Reduce *N. Jersey*, &c. Currency, to *N. Eng.* &c. Currency.

£.244	7	6	=	£.195	10	0
11250	12	11	=	9000	10	4
62500	0	0	=	50000	0	0 *(Con.13.)*

CONT. XIX. ——*To New York and North Carolina Currencies;* ADD one fifteenth part.

Reduce *N. Jersey*, &c. Currency, to *N. York*, &c. Currency.

£.315	15	0	=	£.336	16	0
1875	0	0	=	2000	0	0
34492	4	8¼	=	36791	14	4 *(Con.16.)*

CONT. XX. ——*To South Carolina and Georgia,* MULTIPLY by 28, and DIVIDE the Product by 45.

Reduce *N. Jersey*, &c. Currency, to *S. Carolina*, &c. Curren.

£.260	8	9	=	£.162	1	0
686	15	3	=	427	7	0
2777	3	1½	=	1728	0	2 *(Con.23.)*

CONT. XXI. To reduce the Currencies of South Carolina and Georgia——

——*To the New England and Virginia Currencies,* MULTIPLY the given Sum by 9, and DIVIDE by 7.

Reduce *S. Carolina*, &c. Currency, to *N. Eng.* &c. Currency.

£.101	4	2	=	£.130	2	6
7003	13	6	=	9004	14	6
35000	16	÷	=	45001	1	0 *(Con.14.)*

CONT. XXII. ——*To New York and North Carolina Currencies;* MULTIPLY by 12, and DIVIDE the Product by 7.

Reduce·

145

Reduce *S. Carolina*, &c. Currency, to *N. York*, &c. Curren.

£.96	16	9¾	=	£.166	0	3
919	6	4½	=	1575	19	6
7000	7	7	=	12000	13	0 (Con. 17.)

CONT. XXIII. *To New Jersey, Pennsylvania, Delaware, and Maryland Currencies;* MULTIPLY by 45, and DIVIDE by 28.

Reduce *S. Carolina*, &c. Currency, to *N. Jersey*, &c. Curren.

£.162	1	0	=	£.260	8	9
427	7	0	=	686	16	3
1728	0	2	=	2777	3	1½ (Co. 21.)

SIMPLE INTEREST,

146

INSURANCE, COMMISSION, BROKERAGE, FACTORAGE, together with the purchasing of STOCKS, PAPER MONEY, &c. may with propriety be reduced to the same Directions.

DEF. XXVI. *Simple Interest* is the Money allowed for the Use of any Sum of Money, at a certain *Rate per cent. per ann.* that is, at a certain Rate for the Use of £.100 for a year.

DEF. XXVII. The *Principal* is the Sum lent.

DEF. XXVIII. The *Amount* is the Principal and Interest added together.

DEF. XXIX. *Insurance* is an Allowance *per cent.* and sometimes *per ann.* for Protection from loss by Fire, Sea, &c.

DEF. XXX. *Commission, Brokerage,* and *Factorage,* are Allowances, at a certain Rate *per cent.* for Buying or Selling Goods for another.

DEF. XXXI. *Stocks* are Public Funds, in which £.100 is sometimes worth *less* and sometimes *more* than £.100, and is accordingly said to be *under* or *above* PAR.

DIR. XXIII. *Multiply* the Principal or given Sum by the Rate *per cent.* and that Product, *divided* by 100, (*Cont. VIII.*) is the Interest, &c. for one Year.

What is the Interest of £.396 for one year, at £.3 *per cent. per ann.?*　　　　　　　　　　*A.* £.11 17 7.

What is the Interest of £.184 16 for a year, at £.4 *per cent. per ann.?*　　　　　　　　　　*A.* £.7 7 10.

What is the Interest of £.125 10 for a year, at £.6 *per cent. per ann.?*　　　　　　　　　　*A.* £.7 10 7.

What

What is the Amount of £.365 for a year, at £.6 *per cent.*
per ann. ?   A. £.386 18.

What is the Commiffion for difpofing of Goods valued at
£.1250, at £.7 *per cent.*?   A. £.87 10.

What is the Infurance of £.500, at £.10 *per cent.*? A. £.50.

What is the value of £.125 Stock, at £.85 *per cent.* ?
                                          A. £.106 5.

DIR. XXIV. If the Rate *per cent.* is lefs than a Pound,
or confifts of Pounds, with parts of Pounds or Shillings,
Pence, &c. work by *Aliquot* parts.

What is the Brokerage of £.238, at 5s. *per cent.*?
                                          A. 11s. 10¾d.

Find the Brokerage of £.429, at 6s. *per cent.*   £.1 5 8¾.

Find the Infurance of £.663, at 7s. *per cent.*   £.2 6 4¾.

At 7s. 6d. *per cent.* what is the Commiffion for buying Goods
to the Amount of £.281 10 6 ?   A. £.1 1 1½.

Find the Infurance of £.827, at 11s. *per cent.*   £.4 10 11½.

What is the Factorage for difpofing of Goods to the amount
of £.796 2 7, at 18s. 4d. *per cent.*?   £.7 5 11¼.

Find the Commiffion for purchafing Goods to the amount of
£.849, at £.1 8 *per cent.*   £.11 17 8½.

Find the Infurance of £.93, at £.1 9 *per cent.* £.1 6 11½.

At £.2 4 6 *per cent.* what muft a Factor receive for felling
Goods to the Sum of £.111 19 6 ?   A. £.2 9 9¾.

What is the Intereft of £.215 18 6 for one year, at £.3½,
or £.3 10 *per cent. per ann.* ?   A. £.7 11 1¾.

Find the Intereft of £.198 13 4 for a year, at £.4¼ or
£.4 5 *per cent. per ann.* ?   A. £.8 8 10½.

Find the Intereft of £.75 15 for one year, at £.3¾ *per cent.*
per ann. ?   A. £.2 16 9¾.

What is the Amount of £.238 10 6 for a year, at £.4½
per cent. per ann. ?   A. £.249 17 1.

Find the Amount of £.145 7 4 for a year, at £.5¼, or
£.5 15 *per cent. per ann.*   £.153 14 6.

What is the Intereft of £.750, at £.6¼ *per cent. per ann.* ?
                                          A. £.46 17 6.

What is the Purchafe of £.312 10 Bank Stock, at £.94½
per cent. ?   A. £.295 6 3.

Find the Value of £.250 Stock, at £.96¼ *per cent.*
                                          £.240 12 6.

CONT. XXIV. When Stock is *above* PAR, find its value
at the Excefs only, and *add* it to the given Sum.

                                          Find

Find the Purchase of £.480 14 India Stock, at £.103¼ per cent. £.496 6 5¼.

At £.109½ per cent. what is the value of £.178 10 India Annuities ? A. £.195 9 1¾.

If South Sea Stock be at £.125¾ per cent. what sum will £.1340 5 6 of it sell for ? A. £.1685 7 10¾.

OBS. XXIV. The Method of Purchasing of Stocks may be applied to PAPER MONEY.

What is the Value of £.25 of Paper Money, at £.95 10 per cent. ? A. £.23 17 6.

Find the Value of £.470 of Paper Money, when depreciated to £.82¼ per cent.? £.386 11 6.

What is the worth of £.987 12 6, at £.75 per cent. ? A. £.740 14 4½.

148

DIR. XXV. If the Interest, or Insurance, is required for several Years; *multiply* the Interest, &c. for one Year by the number of them.

Find the Interest of £.150 18 for 2 years, at £.6 per cent. per ann. ? £.18 2 1½.

Find the Interest of £.95 14 8 for 3 years, at £.3¼ per cent. per ann. ? £.9 6 7½.

What is the Insurance of £.100 10 6 for 4 years, at £.3½ per cent. per ann.? A. £.14 1 5.

What is the Amount of £.270 19 for 5 years, at £.3¾ per cent. per ann. ? A. £.311 15 0½.

DIR. XXVI. If ¼, ½ or ¾ of a Year, or any Number of Months are required, take *Aliquot* parts of the Interest for a Year.

Find the Interest of £.100 for ½ a Year, at £.6 per cent. per ann. £.3.

What is the Insurance of £.243 10 9 for 1¾ Years, at £.2 12 6 per cent. per ann. ? A. £.11 3 1¾.

Find the Interest of £.349 15 for 2½ Years at £.4 per cent. per ann. ? £.34 19 5¾.

Find the Amount of £.281 11 6 for 3¼ Years, at £.5 per cent per ann. ? £.327 6 6¾.

What is the Interest of £.105 12 for 3¾ Years, at £.4½ per cent. per ann. ? A. £.17 16 3¾.

What is the Amount of £.1210 for 4¼ Years, at £.4¾ per cent. per ann. ? A. £.1454 5 4½.

Find

Find the Intereſt of £.150 10 for 3 Months, at £.4 *per cent. per ann.?* A. £.1 10 1.

Find the Amount of £.128 15 for a Year and 7 Months, at £.5 *per cent. per ann.?* £.138 18 $10\frac{1}{4}$.

What is the Intereſt of £.245 10 6 for 2 Years and 10 Months, at £.$3\frac{1}{4}$ *per cent. per ann.?* A. £.22 12 $1\frac{3}{4}$.

Dir. XXVII. For Weeks ſay, As 52 Weeks : are to the Intereſt for a Year : : ſo are the Weeks given : to the Intereſt required.

What is the Intereſt of £.500 for 14 Weeks, at £.$3\frac{1}{2}$ *per cent. per ann.?* A. £.4 14 $2\frac{3}{4}$.

Find the Intereſt of £.218 10 for 19 Weeks, at £.$4\frac{1}{4}$ *per cent. per ann.?* £.3 7 $10\frac{1}{2}$.

What is the Inſurance of £.3851 15 6 for 1 Year and 9 Weeks, at £.$4\frac{1}{2}$ *per cent. per ann.?* A. £.372 15 $4\frac{1}{2}$.

Find the Amount of £.389 14 6 for 1 Year and 25 Weeks, at £.$4\frac{3}{4}$ *per cent. per ann.?* £.417 2 $8\frac{1}{4}$.

Dir. XXVIII. For Days ſay, As 365 Days : are to the Intereſt for one Year : : ſo are the Days given : to the Intereſt required.

What is the Intereſt of £.80 5 for 120 Days, at £.3 *per cent. per ann.?* A. 15*s*. $9\frac{3}{4}$*d*.

Find the Intereſt of £.189 16 6 for 341 Days, at £.$3\frac{1}{4}$ *per cent. per ann.?* £.5 15 3.

What is the Intereſt of £.2000 from May 10 to July 28, at £.$4\frac{1}{2}$ *per cent. per ann.?* A. £.19 9 7.

Find the Amount of £.5240 from Jan. 1 to April 20, in a Leap Year, at £.$4\frac{3}{4}$ *per cent. per ann.* £.5315 0 $2\frac{1}{2}$.

What is the Inſurance of £.3948 10 for 1 Year 240 Days, at £.$10\frac{3}{4}$ *per cent. per ann.?* A. £.703 11 3.

At £.$4\frac{3}{4}$ *per cent. per ann.* what is the Amount of £.189 10 3 for 2 Years and 359 Days? A. £.216 7 4.

EQUATION OF PAYMENTS.

Def. XXXII. *EQUATION of PAYMENTS* finds a mean time for Paying the whole of ſeveral Sums, due at various times.

Dir. XXIX. *Multiply* each Sum by its Time, and *divide* the Total of the Products by the *Whole Debt*.

What

What is the equated time of £.10 due at 2 Months, £.18 due at 3 Months, and £.22 due at 8 Months ?   *A.* 5 *Mon.*

What is the mean time for paying £.100 at 1 Week, £.200 at 3 Weeks, and £.100 at 5 Weeks ?   *A.* 3 *Weeks.*

What will be the equated time of £.9 due at 15 Days, £.23 at 8 Days, and £.58 at 31 Days ?   *A.* 23 *Days.*

Find the equated time of £.20 at 1 Month, £.50 at 3½ Months, and £.76 at 5 Months.   3 *Months,* 28 *Days.*

C owes D £.25 due 29 Days hence, £.120 due 1 Year 3 Days hence ; but agreeing with D to pay it at one payment—find the time.   309 *Days.*

E owing F £.10 9 due in 4 Days, £.12 10 due in 9 Days, and £.45 15 due in 3 Weeks, is desirous of paying F at one equated time ; when is it ?   *A.* 16 *Days.*

G buys of H on Oct. 10, Goods to the value of £.120 19 6, to pay £.50 Nov. 7, and the rest Dec. 15, but desires to pay at a mean time ; what day will it be ?

150

A. 50 *Days,* or *Nov.* 29.

REBATE, or DISCOUNT.

Def. XXXIII. *REBATE,* or *DISCOUNT,* is an *Allowance* for the Payment of Money, Bills, &c. before they become due.

Dir. XXX. *When the Discount is at a certain Rate in the Pound,* take it by Aliquot parts from the given Sum.

What is the Discount of £.47 10, at 1s. 8d. in the Pound ?
A. £.3 19 2.

What is the Present Worth of a Bill of £.125, Discount allowed at 1s. in the Pound ?   *A.* £.119. 15.

What is the Discount of £.350, at 6d. in the Pound ?
A. £.8 15.

Dir. XXXI. *When the Discount is at a certain Rate* per cent. per ann.—find the Amount of £.100 at the Rate and Time given ; then say, As that Sum : is to £.100 : : so is the given Sum : to the Present Worth, which, *subtracted* from the given Sum, gives the *Discount* required.

What is the Present worth of £.365 for a Year, at £.5 *per cent.* ?   *A.* £.347 12 4½.

What is the Discount of £.100 for 6 Months, at £.5 *per cent. per ann.* ?   *A.* £.2 8 9½.

What is the Rebate of £.500 for 9 Months, at £.5 *per cent. per ann.* ?   *A.* £.18 1 5¼.

Find

Find the Preſent Worth of £.140 10 due 11 Months hence, at £.$4\frac{1}{2}$ *per cent. per ann.* £.134 18 8.

Find what preſent money will pay a debt of £.50 due 8 Months hence, at £.4 *per cent. per ann.* £.48 14 $0\frac{1}{4}$.

At £$4\frac{3}{4}$ *per cent. per ann.* what is the Diſcount of £.110 15 due 11 Weeks hence? *A.* £.1 2 $0\frac{1}{2}$.

At £.5 *per cent. per ann.* what is the Rebate of £.85 13 4 for 27 days? *A.* 6*s.* $3\frac{3}{4}$*d.*

What preſent money will diſcharge a Bill of £.75 15, which has 3 Weeks to run, at £.$4\frac{1}{4}$ *per cent.*? *A.* £.75 11 $3\frac{1}{2}$.

What is the Preſent Worth of a £.20 Note due 53 Days hence, at £.5 *per cent.* Diſcount? *A.* £.19 17 $1\frac{1}{4}$.

Find the Diſcount of £.100, to be paid ½ at 3 Months, and ½ at 6 Months, at £.$4\frac{1}{2}$ *per cent.* £.1 13 $1\frac{3}{4}$.

Find the Rebate of £.96 16 payable ¼ at 2 Months, and the reſt at 5 Months, at £.5 *per cent.* £.1 13 $7\frac{3}{4}$.

A Perſon has £.500 owing him, due 1 Year 9 Days hence; 151
but wanting money, gets it diſcounted at £.$4\frac{3}{4}$ *per cent. per an.* what does he receive? *A.* £.476 15 11.

COMPOUND INTEREST.

DEF. XXXIV. *COMPOUND INTEREST* is Intereſt upon Intereſt, for the time it remains unpaid after it is due, at the ſame Rate as on the Principal.

DIR. XXXII. Find the firſt year's Intereſt, and *add* it to the Principal; then find the Intereſt of this Amount; and ſo continue to *add* every year's Intereſt for the time given. *Subtract* the firſt Principal from the laſt Amount, and it gives the Compound Intereſt required.

What is the Compound Intereſt of £.150, forborne 2 Years, at £.$3\frac{1}{2}$ *per cent. per ann.*? *A.* £.10 13 8.

Find the Compound Intereſt of £.345, forborne $2\frac{1}{2}$ Years, at £.4 *per cent. per ann.* £.35 12 $3\frac{1}{4}$.

At £.$3\frac{3}{4}$ *per cent. per ann.* what is the Amount of £.925 for 3 Years, at Compound Intereſt? *A.* £.1033 0 3.

What will be the Compound Intereſt of £.115 5, forborne $2\frac{1}{4}$ Years, at £.$4\frac{1}{4}$ *per cent. per ann.*? *A.* £.11 6 $8\frac{1}{4}$.

Find the Amount of £.450 10, forborne $3\frac{1}{2}$ Years, at £.$4\frac{1}{2}$ *per cent. per ann.* Compound Intereſt. £.525 13 $2\frac{1}{2}$.

At £.5 *per cent. per ann.* what is the Amount of £.2459 for 3 Years, 7 Mon. Compound Intereſt? *A.* £.2929 12 $5\frac{3}{4}$.

What is the Compound Intereſt of £.4093, forborne 4 Years, 10 Months, 15 Days, at £.5 *per cent. per ann.*?

A. £.1099 14 $5\frac{1}{2}$.

ALLOWANCES in MERCHANDISE.

DEF. XXXV. *GROSS* is the Whole Weight of any Commodity, before the following Deductions are made : —

DEF. XXXVI. *Tare* is an Allowance for what contains the Goods ; as, a *Hogshead, Chest,* &c.

DEF. XXXVII. *Tret* is an Allowance for Waste, Dust, &c. and is always 4 *lb.* in 104, or $\frac{1}{26}$.

DEF. XXXVIII. *Cloff* is an Allowance on some Goods for the turn of the scale, and is generally 2 *lb.* for every 3 *cwt.*

DEF. XXXIX. *Suttle* is the Remainder, when some Allowances are made.

DEF. XL. *Neat Weight* is what remains when all Deductions are made.

152

DIR. XXXIII. From the *Gross* SUBTRACT what is allowed, and the Remainder is *Neat.*

Gross 8141 *lb.* Tare 242 *lb.* how many *lbs.* neat ? *A.* 7899.
Gross 17 *cwt.* 2 *qr.* Tare 1 *cwt.* 3 *qr.* 4 *lb.* how much Neat ?
A. 15 *cwt.* 2 *qr.* 24 *lb.*
Gross 2 *cwt.* 27 *lb.* Tare 2 *qr.* 9 *lb.* how much Neat ?
A. 1 *cwt.* 2 *qr.* 18 *lb.*
Gross 9 *cwt.* 1 *qr.* 14 *lb.* Tare 156 *lb.* how much Neat ?
A. 7 *cwt.* 3 *qr.* 26 *lb.*
Gross 98 *cwt.* 21 *lb.* Tare 1210 *lb.* how many *lbs.* Neat ?
A. 9787 *lb.*

DIR. XXXIV. *When the Tare is at a certain Allowance by the Barrel, Hogshead, &c.* MULTIPLY *it by the Number of Barrels,* &c.

What is the neat weight of 6 *hhd.* weighing Gross 29 *cwt.* 3 *qr.* 10 *lb.* allowing Tare at 3 *qr.* 7 *lb.* a *hhd.* ?
A. 24 *cwt.* 3 *qr.* 24 *lb.*
What is the neat weight of 9 *barr.* of Oil, weighing Gross 18 *cwt.* 1 *qr.* Tare 1 *qr.* 8 *lb.* a *bar.?* *A.* 15 *cwt.* 1 *qr.* 12 *lb.*
In 7 Butts, each 5 *cwt.* 2 *qr.* 14 *lb.* Gross, and Tare, a *bt.* 3 *qr.* 18 *lb.* how much Neat Weight ? *A.* 33 *cwt.*
In 16 Bales of Silk, each 3 *cwt.* 3 *qr.* Gross, and Tare, 19 *lb.* a Bale, how many *lbs.* Neat weight ? *A.* 6416 *lb.*

DIR. XXXV. *If the Tare is at a certain Allowance a cwt.* take Aliquot parts of an *cwt.* by which DIVIDE the Gross.

Find

Find the Neat weight of 11 Casks, weighing Gross 21 *cwt.* 2 *qr.* 4 *lb.* allowing Tare 16 *lb.* a *cwt.* 18 *cw.* 1 *qr.* 24 *lb.*

Find the Neat weight of 8 Bags, each 8 *cwt.* 1 *qr.* 7 *lb.* Gross, deducting Tare 14 *lb.* a *cwt.* 58 *cwt.* 0 *qr.* 21 *lb.*

What is the Neat weight of 20 Bales of Cloth, each 2 *cwt.* 3 *qr.* allowing Tare 7 *lb.* a *cwt.* *A.* 51 *cwt.* 2 *qr.* 7 *lb.*

What is the Neat weight of 26 Barrels of Anchovies, each 24 *lb.* Tare 8 *lb.* a *cwt.* ? *A.* 5 *cwt.* 0 *qr.* 20 *lb.*

In 7 *hhd.* each 6 *cwt.* 0 *qr.* 14 *lb.* Gross, deducting Tare 10 *lb.* a *cwt.* how many *lb.* Neat ? *A.* 4374 *lb.*

DIR. XXXVI. *To find the Tret*, DIVIDE what remains, after the Tare is deducted, by 26, because 4 *lb.* is $\frac{1}{26}$ of 104 *lb.*

Find the Neat weight of 8 *cwt.* 3 *qr.* 20 *lb.* Gross, 1 *cwt.* 2 *qr.* Tare, and Tret 4 *lb.* in 104. 7 *cwt.* 0 *qr.* 16 *lb.*

Find the Neat weight of 23 *cwt.* 1 *qr.* Gross, Tare 18 *lb.* a *cwt.* Tret 4 *lb.* in 104. 18 *cwt.* 3 *qr.* 2 *lb.*

What is the Neat weight of 4 *hhd.* each 3 *cwt.* 3 *qr.* Gross, Tare 3 *qr.* 7 *lb.* a *hhd.* Tret as before ? *A.* 11 *cwt.* 1 *qr.* 6 *lb.*

What is the Neat weight of 84 *cwt.* 0 *qr.* 20 *lb.* Gross, allowing Tare 21 *lb.* a *cwt.* and Tret as usual ?

A. 65 *cwt.* 3 *qr.* 3 *lb.*

In 7 Jars of Oil, each 2 *qr.* 10 *lb.* Gross, Tare 13 *lb.* a Jar, Tret as usual ; how many Neat Gallons of 7½ *lb.* each ?

A. 47 *gal.* 4½ *lb.*

DIR. XXXVII. *To find the Pounds Cloff,* MULTIPLY the *cwt.* in the Remainder after finding the Tret, by 2, and DIVIDE the Product by 3.

Gross 24 *cwt.* 1 *qr.* 10 *lb.* Tare 4 *cwt.* 2 *qr.* 18 *lb.* Tret as usual, and Cloff 2 *lb.* in 3 *cwt.* how much Neat ?

A. 18 *cwt.* 3 *qr.* 8 *lb.*

Gross 9 *cwt.* 3 *qr.* 24 *lb.* Tare 1 *cwt.* 2 *qr.* Tret as usual, Cloff 2 *lb.* in 3 *cwt.* how much neat ? *A.* 8 *cwt.* 0 *qr.* 11 *lb.*

What is the Neat weight of 9 *cwt.* 2 *qr.* Gross, Tare 16 *lb.* a *cwt.* Tret and Cloff as usual ? *A.* 7 *cwt.* 3 *qr.* 4 *lb.*

What is the Neat weight of 15 *cwt.* 1 *qr.* 7 *lb.* Gross, Tare 15 *lb.* a *cwt.* Tret and Cloff as usual ? *A.* 12 *cwt.* 2 *qr.* 21 *lb.*

In 4 Barrels of Oil weighing Gross, as follows, viz. N°. 1. 3 *cwt.* 2 *qr.*—N°. 2, 4 *cwt.* 1 *qr.* 17 *lb.*—N°. 3, 2 *cwt.* 3 *qr.* N°. 4, 3 *cwt.* 3 *qr.* 20 *lb.* Tare, 1 *qr.* 8 *lb.* a Barrel; Tret and Cloff as usual ; how many Neat Gallons ?

A. 189 *gal.* 3 *qts.*

BARTER

BARTER.

DEF. XLI. *BARTER* adjufts the Exchanging one Commodity for another, fo as that neither party fhall fuftain Lofs.

DIR. XXXVIII. The Price of two Commodities being given, *to find the Difference of their Total Values*, find the Value of each, and SUBTRACT the one from the other.

What is the difference in Value between 4 *yds.* of Cloth at 17*s.* 6*d.* a *yd.* and a *cwt.* of Sugar at 7*d.* a *lb.* ?   *A.* 4*s.* 8*d.*

A barters with B 48½ *yds.* at 3*s.* 4*d.* a *yd.* for 38 *ells* at 4*s.* 2*d.* what is the difference of Value ?   *A.* 3*s.* 4*d.*

C and D barter ; C gives 30 *gall.* of Brandy, at 12*s.* 6*d.* a *gall.* and D gives 60 *ells* of Holland at 5*s.* 2½*d.* an *ell* ; which muft pay the balance, and how much ?

            A. D £.3 2 6.

154

DIR. XXXIX. *To know how much of one Commodity muft be given for another,* find how much the given Commodity is worth, and then find what quantity of the other this Sum will purchafe.

How much Tea at 9*s.* a *lb.* fhould be given in Barter for 2 *cwt.* 3 *qr.* of Sugar, at £.3 a *cwt.* ?   *A.* 18 *lb.* 5¼ *oz.*

What quantity of Coffee at 5*s.* 3*d.* a *lb.* muft be given for 72 *lb.* of Chocolate, at 4*s.* 6*d.* a *lb.* ?   *A.* 61 *lb.* 11¼ *oz.*

How much Tobacco at £.5 12 6 a *cwt.* is equal in value to 3½ *cwt.* of Snuff, at £.6 10 a *cwt.*?   *A.* 4*cwt.* 0 *qr.* 4¾ *lb.*

If 8 *cwt.* 1 *qr.* of Hops were given for 336 *gal.* of Oil at 2*s.* 6*d.* a *gal.* what were they a *cwt.* ?   *A.* £.5 1 9¾.

What was that Cloth a Yard, 99 *yds.* of which were given for a *hbd.* of Wine, at 6*s.* 1¼*d.* a *gall.* ?   *A.* 3*s.* 10¾*d.*

E agrees to take of F 7 *cwt.* 2 *qr.* of Tobacco at £.4 14 6 a *cwt.* and to pay him £.20 down, and the reft in Hops at £.5 a *cwt.* what quantity muft he have ?

            A. 3 *cwt.* 0 *qr.* 9 *lb.*

DIR. XL. *To find a Proportional Barter Price,* fay, As the Ready Money Price of the one : is to its Barter Price : : fo is the Ready Money Price of the other : to its Barter Price.

Suppofe Wheat at 19*s.* a Load ready money, and Cloth at 5*s.* 9*d.* a Yard ready money, and in Barter the Wheat is raifed to £.1 ; what muft the Cloth be raifed to a *yd.* in bartering for the Wheat ?   *A.* 9*s.* 10¾*d.*

                     G has

G has Sugar at £.3 a *cwt.* ready money; but in bartering
with H for Tea, worth 6*s.* a *lb.* ready money, will have
£.3 5 a *cwt.*—what muſt the Tea be raiſed to, and how
much of it given for 7 *cwt.* of Sugar ?   *A.* 6*s.* 6*d.*—70 *lb.*

I has Coffee at 5*s.* a *lb.* and 30½ *gal.* of Brandy at 11*s.* 9*d.* a
gal. which he barters with K for £.20 caſh, and a Suit of
Clothes worth £.5 5, and agrees to have Board and Lodg-
ing for the reſt, at £.30 a Year; how many Days Board
muſt he have ?   *A.* 181.

L O S S AND G A I N.

DEF. XLII. *LOSS and GAIN* diſcovers the Profit or
Loſs on Goods, and teaches to regulate their Prices to any
propoſed Gain or Loſs.

DIR. XLI. *To find the Gain or Loſs by any Commodity,*
find the Difference between its Coſt and Produce.

Bought 137 *lb.* of Chocolate, at 4*s.* 1½*d.* a *lb.* and ſold it at
4*s.* 9*d.* a *lb.* what was the Gain ?   *A.* £.4 5 7½.

If 12 *cwt.* 3 *qr.* of Tobacco was ſold for £.75 4, and bought
at £.5 15 a *cwt.* was it at Gain or Loſs ?

A. £.1 17 9 *gain.*

Ale bought at £.3 a *bar.* and retailed at 8*d.* a *qt.* what was
the Profit on 50 *bar.*?   *A.* £.63 6 8.

Sold 3 *cwt.* 2 *qr.* of Sugar for £.12 5, which coſt £.3 5 6 a
cwt. what is the Gain a *cwt.*?   *A.* 4*s.* 6*d.*

DIR. XLII. *To find the Gain or Loſs per cent.*—ſay, As
the Coſt : is to the Produce :: ſo is £.100 : to a fourth
Number—the difference between which and £.100 is the
Gain or Loſs required.

Cloth bought at 17*s.* 9*d.* a *yd.* and ſold at 18*s.* 4*d.* what is
the Gain *per cent.* ?   *A.* £.3 5 8½.

Sugar bought at £.3 5 6 a *cwt.* and ſold at £.3, what was the
Loſs *per cent.*?   *A.* £.8 7 11½.

If Tea was ſold at 9*s.* 6*d.* a *lb.* which coſt £.53 15 8 a *cwt.*
what was the Gain or Loſs *per cent.*?   *A:* £.1 1 8¼ *loſs.*

DIR. XLIII. *To find the Coſt,* ſay, As £.100 increaſed
or diminiſhed by the Gain or Loſs : is to £.100 :: ſo is
the Produce : to the Coſt.

If Cheeſe was ſold for £.2 3 a *cwt.* at £.10 *per cent.* profit,
what did it coſt a *cwt.* ?

A. £.1 19 1.
Sold

Sold Goods for £.86, by which I gained £.9 10 4 *per cent.* what was the Sum I paid for them ? *A.* £.78 10 6.

Bought a Cheft of damaged Hyfon Tea, which I retailed at 12*s.* 6*d.* a *lb.* at £.16 13 4 *per cent.* Lofs, what was the Prime Coft ? *A.* £.84.

DIR. XLIV. *To find the Selling Price*, fay, A's £.100 : is to £.100 increafed or diminifhed by the required Gain or Lofs *per cent.* : : fo is the Prime Coft : to the Selling Price.

What muft Sugar be fold for a *lb.* to gain £.12 *per cent.* if an *cwt.* cofts £.3 6 8 ? *A.* 8*d.*

Suppofe 99 *ells* of Cambric coft £.44 11, what fhould a *yd.* be fold for, to gain £.14 *per cent.* ? *A.* 8*s.* 2½*d.*

At £.37 10 *per cent.* Lofs, what muft I fell Red Port at a *gal.* if the Pipe coft £.63 ? *A.* 6*s.* 3*d.*

DIR. XLV. *The Gain or Lofs at a certain Selling Price being given, to find the Gain or Lofs at a fuppofed Selling Price*, fay, As the given Selling Price : is to £.100 increaf-ed or diminifhed according to the given Rate : : fo is the fuppofed Selling Price : to a fourth Number—the difference between which and £.100 is the fuppofed Gain or Lofs.

Bought a quantity of Flaxfeed, which I fold at 4*s.* a *bufh.* at £.4 *per cent.* Lofs, what would have been the Lofs *per cent.* at 3*s.* 6*d.* ? *A.* £.16.

If by felling Cloth at 8*s.* a *yd.* I gain £.9 *per cent.* what will be the gain *per cent.* at 8*s.* 7*d.* ? *A.* £.16 18 11½.

Sold a Plantation for £.3500, by which I loft £.12 10 *per cent.*—what would have been the Gain or Lofs *per cent.* if I had fold it for £.4750 ? *A.* £.18 15 *gain.*

FELLOWSHIP.

DEF. XLIII. *FELLOWSHIP* is a Rule which propor-tions any Sum or Number according to two or more Sums or Numbers given, fo as to fhew the Share, Gain, or Lofs, &c. on each.

DIR. XLVI. When *no time* is mentioned, ADD together the feveral Sums or Numbers; and fay, As their Total : is to the whole Gain or Lofs, &c. : : fo is each Sum or Num-ber : to its Gain or Lofs.

Divide the number 480 into parts which fhall bear a true pro-portion to 2, 4, and 6. 80 + 160 + 240 = 480.

A puts

A puts in £.70, and B £.80, and trading together gain £.25;
   what is each man's fhare?   *A.* £.11 13 4. B £.13 6 8.
C puts in £.74, and D £.98 ftock, by which they gain £.30 10;
   what are their fhares?   *A.* C £.13 2 5¼. D £.17 7 6½.
E, F and G by their partnerfhip gain £.720; E put in £.20
   and F £.30, as often as G put in £.40.—what is each perfon's fhare?   *A.* E £.160. F £.240, G £.320.
H and I export 155 pieces of Cloth, which were loft at fea;
   H's part was to I's as 2 to 3; what is each man's lofs, at
   £.5 8 a Piece?   *A.* H £.334 16. I £.502 4.
Two Gentlemen, K and L, jointly buy an Eftate, and clear by
   it the firft Year £.409 16. I demand each Gentleman's
   fhare, K having paid 7 Guineas as often as L paid 9 Guineas?   *A.* K £.179 5 9. L £.230 10 3.
M and N trading together, had the misfortune to lofe
   £.48 16 9. M's ftock was £.129, and N's £.240 15;
   what fhare muft each perfon fuftain of the lofs?

157

      A. M £.17 0 9¼. N £.31 15 11½.
Three Tradefmen, O, P and Q, make a joint ftock; O put
   in £.28, P £.30, and Q £.50 5, by which they gained
   £.19 4. I demand each man's proper fhare of the gain?
      A. O £.4 19 3¾. P £.5 6 5. Q £.8 18 3.
R, S, T and U joined in trade, making a Stock of £.600, and
   in a fhort time gained as follows, viz. R £.25, S £.20,
   T £.15, and U £.7 10; what was each man's Stock?
      A. R £.222 4 5¼. S £.177 15 6½.
         T   133 6 8.   U   66 13 4.
A Perfon breaking owes V £.50, W £.75 9, X £.128, and
   Meffrs. Y and Z £.207 6 6, and his effects being found
   worth £.240, it is required to find each Creditor's Divi-
   dend?   V £.26 0 10¼. W £. 39 5 11¾.
         X   66 13 4¾.   Y, Z. 107 19 9.

DIR. XLVII. When the Sums or Numbers are connected
with time, MULTIPLY each of them into its time, and ADD
the Products; then fay, As the Sum of thefe Products : is
to the whole Gain or Lofs, &c. : : fo is each Sum or Number : to its Gain or Lofs.

Two Perfons, A and B, having joined in trade, gained £.39 8.
   A had £.56 in 5 Months, and B £.64 in 4 Months; what
   were their fhares?   *A.* A £.20 11 7½. B £.18 16 4¼.
C, D and E by partnerfhip loft £.60. C had £.40 in 21
   Days, D £.50 in 32 Days, and E had £.62 in 48 Days;
   what did each lofe?
      A. C £.9 6 1¼. D £.17 14 6. E £.32 19 4½.
                                             F began

F began trade *March* 1, with £.500 ftock, and on *May* 1 takes
in G as a partner, with £.300 ftock ; they caft up their
Accounts *Sep.* 29, and find their gain £.99 8 ; what are
their fhares ?   *A.* F £.69 11 11¾. G £.29 16.

A Perfon dying, left £.750, after his wife's death, to his two
Sons, to be divided in proportion to their ages, and the time
each fhould conduct himfelf with fobriety.   H, aged 30,
refrained from drink 5 Weeks, and I, aged 25, but 5 Days ;
find their portions.   H £.670 4 3.   I £.79 15 8¾.

A Grazier rents a Field of Grafs, for which he is to pay £.30 ;
and by putting in 19 Horfes 12 Days ; 25 Oxen 18 Days ;
and 56 Sheep 13 Days, it is eaten up ; what did each parcel coft him keeping ?

A. Horfes £.4 17 3½. *Oxen* £.9 12 0¼. *Sheep* £.15 10 3.

K and L made a joint Stock for a Year, and gained £.75 10 6.
K put in at firft £.130, and 2 Months after £.25. L put in
at firft £.70, at 3 Months' end £.40 more, at 4 Months after this £.54, but 1 Month before the expiration of the Year
he took out £.20.   I demand their dividends.

K £.41 18 7¾.   L £.33 11 10.

158

5

THOMAS SARJEANT'S
COUNTING HOUSE,
THE FIRST TEXT
ORIGINATING
IN THE U. S.,
1789

PREFATORY NOTE

As this chapter title implies, the text (Sarjeant 1788)
to which the following book was a "necessary supplement"
(Sarjeant 1789, [3] (following title page), emphasis deleted)
is not fundamentally an acccounting work. Chapters 4 and 7,
together with part 1 of the 1789 book (Sarjeant, {15}–18), present
accounting-related material by Sarjeant that extends the coverage
of this collection beyond bookkeeping.

AN INTRODUCTION

TO THE

COUNTING HOUSE;

OR,

A SHORT SPECIMEN OF

MERCANTILE PRECEDENTS,

ADAPTED

TO THE PRESENT SITUATION OF THE

TRADE AND *COMMERCE*

OF THE

UNITED STATES OF AMERICA.

FOR THE USE OF SCHOOLS AND PRIVATE EDUCATION.

By *THOMAS SARJEANT.*

INTENDED AS A SUPPLEMENT TO THE ELEMENTARY PRINCIPLES OF ARITHMETIC.

PHILADELPHIA;
PRINTED BY DOBSON AND LANG FOR THE *EDITOR;*
AND SOLD BY T. DOBSON AND W. POYNTELL IN SECOND STREET; AND W. PRITCHARD, T. SEDDON, AND RICE & Cº. IN MARKET STREET.
MDCC LXXXIX.

AFTER the Publication of the Elementary Principles of Arithmetic, it was suggested to the Editor by some Gentlemen, for whose opinion he entertains the greatest deference, that an Abstract of the Course of Mercantile Instructions attempted in the Academy of the Protestant Episcopal Church in this City, would be a necessary Supplement to that Work, as well as a proper Addition to bind with it.

If any Apology is requisite for the Imperfections of the Attempt, it may in some measure be deduced from the Want of Uniformity in different Counting Houses, and from the utter impossibility of Exhibiting many of the Mercantile Forms by Letter Press.

162

To obviate Objections which may arise from its Brevity, it may be replied, that Specimens of Invoices, Foreign Bills of Exchange, the Cash, Housekeeper's and other Subsidiary Books would have been added, but they were inadmissible in a first Course of Instructions, and would have swelled the Work to a size and price, totally improper for the Use of those for whom it is intended.

The Editor lays no claim to Originality.—Considerable parts of the Treatise were selected, at distant periods, without the least view to Publication, from those Authors which were best adapted to the particular views of the Young Gentlemen immediately under his care, and though they have been altered on a variety of accounts, they probably bear some resemblance to those parts of the Treatises from which they were Extracted. His principal Object is, to furnish a Compendium for American Youth, in which the Fundamental Principles of a Mercantile Education are communicated in a more Concise and Intelligible Manner, than in any other Introductory Treatise in the English Language.

PHILAD. March 18, 1789,

FOR THE USE OF SCHOOLS AND PRIVATE EDUCATION.

Juſt Publiſhed, by the ſame Author,

I. SELECT Arithmetical Tables. On an half ſheet, to bind with Cyphering Books. Price 6*d.*

II. Elementary Principles of Arithmetic, with their Application to the Trade and Commerce of the United States of America. Small octavo. Price, 2/6. Fine paper, 3/9.———☞ *This is an attempt at a Cheap, Concise and Portable School Book, adapted to the Uſe of* THESE STATES, *and reduced to a Scientific Form. It contains, excluſive of the Uſual Branches of the Science, the moſt ample Inſtructions for finding the Diſcount on Paper Money, and the Value of all kinds of Public Securities; and for converting the various American Currencies into each other. It is diveſted of uſeleſs rules, unneceſſary remarks, and every thing uneſſential to ſuch a Practical Knowledge of the Subject, as is ſufficient for the Generality of Youth.*

163

III. A Synopſis of Logarithmical Arithmetic, in which the Nature of Logarithms, and their Application, are made eaſy to thoſe who have not ſtudied higher branches of Mathematics. Price 3/9.

IV. A Paradigm of Inflections of Words in the Engliſh Language. Price 3 *d.*

V. Mr. Harriſon's Rudiments of Engliſh Grammar. A New Edition, reviſed, corrected and much improved. Price 1/6.

IN THE PRESS,

VI. BRACHYGRAPHY. A Compendious Syſtem of SHORT HAND, adapted to the various Arts, Sciences and Profeſſions. After the manner of the late Mr. *Thomas Gurney,* Short Hand Writer for near forty years in the different Engliſh Courts of Judicature.

———————

☞ *The Elementary Principles of Arithmetic, and the Introduction to the Counting Houſe, may be had, bound together, at Half a Dollar; or on fine paper at 5ſ. They contain a complete Introductory Courſe of Mercantile Inſtructions. An Uniformity will be found in both Treatiſes, which will beſt diſcover and recommend itſelf in thoſe Schools in which they may be introduced.*

SECTION THE FIRST.

BILLS OF PARCELS.

DEFINITION.

A BILL of PARCELS is an Account given by the Seller to the Purchaser, of the Goods purchased, their Quality, Quantity, Value, &c.

165

	PHILADELPHIA, Jan. 12, 1789.	
Mr. William Moor,		
	Bought of Patrick Kingston.	
Irish linen, 25 *yards*,	at 3*s*. 9*d*. a *yd*.	£.4 13 9

	NEW-YORK, Dec. 19, 1788.	
Mr. John Williams,		
	Bought of Samuel Smith.	
6 *galls*. Madeira Wine,	at 14*s*. 6*d*. a *gall*.	£.
10 *galls*. Spirits	at 4*s*. 9*d*.	
		£.6 14 6

	LANCASTER, July 1, 1788.	
Miss Quincy,		
	Bought of Simon Thompson & Cᵒ.	
4½ *yds*. Persian,	at 6*s*. 6*d*. a *yd*.	£.
9 *yds*. Shalloon,	at 2*s*. 2*d*.	
19 *yds*. Garnet Silk,	at 5*s*. 8*d*.	
		£.7 16 5

B

PHILADELPHIA, Nov. 18, 1788.

Mrs. Mackenzie,

Bought of Samuel Nathan.

A pair of Paſte Ear-rings,			£.2 12 6
A Garnet Hoop Ring,			1 1 0
1 *doz.* of Table Spoons, *wt.* 21 *oz.*	at 6*s.* 9*d.* an *oz.*		
3 *doz.* of Tea d°. *wt.* 9 *oz.* 7½ *dwt.*	at 7*s.* an *oz.*		
			£.14 0 10¼

READING, Sept. 4, 1788.

Mrs. Richardſon,

Bought of Samuel Ward.

3 *lb.* Green Tea,	at 9*s.* a *lb.*	£.	
3¼ *lb.* Bohea d°.	at 8*s.*		
166 ¼ *lb.* Fine Hyſon,	at 18*s.*		
10 *lb.* Sugar,	at 1*s.* 3*d.*		
1½ *oz.* Nutmegs,	at 1*s.* 6*d.* an *oz.*		
		£.3 12 3	

CHARLESTON, July 3, 1788.

Mr. James Smithſon,

Bought of Edward Heſſon.

Poland Starch,	¾ *cwt.*	at	£.2 12 6 a *cwt.*	£.
Fine Muſtard,	¼	at	7 7 0	
Anchovies,	3 *jars*,	at	2 3 a *jar.*	
Beſt Capers,	7 *lb.*	at	1 2 a *lb.*	
Chamber Oil,	3 *gall.*	at	3 4 a *gall.*	
Sallad Oil,	1 *qt.*	at	8 6	
				£.5 5 3½

LONDON, July 1, 1788.

Mr. Wm. Smith,

Bought of Martin Jones & C°.

10½ *yds.* Yorkſhire Camblets,	at £.0 1 10 a *yd.*	£.	
13¼ --- Mancheſter Velvet,	at 1 3 0		
17¾ --- Thickſet,	at 0 9 0		
19½ --- Indian Dimity;	at 0 3 0		
13¼ --- Shalloon,	at 0 2 8		
17¾ --- Perſian,	at 0 6 0		
		£.34 4 1	

NEW-YORK, NOV. 9, 1788.

Mrs. Jane Somerset,

Bought of Edmund Brisk & C°.

			s.	d.		
12¾ yds.	Rich broaded Sattin,	at	18	6	a yd.	£.
6	Mohair,	at	4	2		
25¼	Paduasoy,	at	11	8		
15½	Flowered Damask,	at	8	8		
34¼	Poplin,	at	3	0		
12½	Italian Mantua,	at	7	6		
30	Double Taffaty,	at	2	9		

£.48 8 9½

PHILADELPHIA, June 30, 1789.

Mr. Jonathan Marriot,

Bought of George Grocer & C°.

Sugar,	cwt.	17 2 17	at	£.1	13	10	a cwt. £.
Raisins,		12 1 19	at	1	14	5	
Tobacco,		4 0 12	at	4	19	4	
Rice,		1 0 15	at	2	16	4	
Pepper,		1 3 19	at	3	12	4	
Brimstone,		2 1 19	at	1	19	1	
Bees Wax,		2 2 12	at	1	18	4	

£.91 9 9½

B O O K   D E B T S.

DEFINITION. *Bills of Book Debts* are taken from the Ledger, or other Book of the Seller; giving an account of the several Articles, with their Value, and the Date when each Parcel was sold and delivered.

Mr. John Abrahams,

Dr. to James Cordwainer.

1788.		£.	s.	d.
Jan. 9.	A pair of Women's Callimanco Shoes,		9	6
Feb. 17.	A pair of Women's Leather Shoes,		7	0
Mar. 18.	A pair of Men's Shoes,		11	3
April 7.	Two pair of d°.	1	5	0
June 1.	A pair of Boots,	2	5	0

Mrs. Denbigh,
                                     Dr. to John Butcher.

1788.				£.	s.	d.
Jan. 18.	Neck of Lamb,				1	2
21.	Marrow bones				1	3
Feb. 12.	Breaft of Veal,	*wt.* 8 *lb.* at 4¼ a *lb.*				
16.	Loin of Pork,	8 *lb,* at 4¼				
Mar. 19.	Rump of Beef,	18 *lb.* at 4¼				
April 21.	Quarter of Lamb,				4	6

Mr. William Barber,
                                     Dr. to Samuel Cowes.

168

1788.				£.	s.	d.
July 7.	Turpentine Oil,	2 *cwt.*	at	7	0	0
Aug. 19.	Saltpetre,	1 *cwt.*		6	0	0
Sept. 1.	Gunpowder,	7 *lb.*			17	6
Oct. 9.	Roach Allum,	1 *cwt.*		1	4	0
Nov. 18.	Brimftone,	2 *cwt.*		2	8	0
Dec. 19.	Pearl Afhes,	3 *cwt.*		3	12	0

Mr. Chriftopher Lenox,
                                     Dr. to James Lukens.

1788.			£.	s,	d.
May 1.	Red Port,	2 *doz.*	1	9	0
	Lifbon,	1 *doz.*	1	8	0
	Mountain,	½ *doz.*		18	0
	Very old Mountain,	½ *doz.*	1	0	0
July 7.	Madeira,	1 *gall.*		17	6
	Champagne,	1 *doz.*	2	0	0
Oct. 12.	Red Port,	2 *doz.*	2	18	0
	White d°.	1 *doz.*	1	5	0

The Hon. Wm. Wycherley, Efq.
                                     Dr. to Samuel Silverfmith.

1787.		oz.	dwt.	gr.		s.	d.	
May 22.	A fet of Silver Caftors, *wt.*	25	10	10	at 7	9		£.
June 4.	Half *doz.* Soup Plates,	85	14	15	at 6	6		
26.	Teapot and Lamp,	29	16	15	at 6	4		
Aug. 12.	Punch bowl,	67	0	16	at 6	10		
Oct. 18.	A *doz.* Silver Spoons,	33	11	10	at 6	2		

£.80 8 11

Memorandum.

Bought at Mrs. Fanciful's Sale, *Nov.* 18, 1788

		£.	s.	d.
LOT 1.	4 Sauce pans,	0	18	0
2.	4 Small d°. and a Tea kettle,	0	10	6
3.	A brass fish kettle and skillet,	0	9	0
48.	3 pair Jars and 2 Beakers,	4	10	0
49.	1 pair of fine Swanskin Blankets,	1	15	6
81.	A Lady's travelling Dressing Box,	4	12	0

£.

A Week's Disbursements.

1789.

	£.	s.	d.
June 17. Paid for Horse Hire,	0	17	0
————Shoes and Boots,	2	19	0
————Ream of Paper,		14	6
————Dozen of Candles,		7	6
————3 *yds*. of Cloth,	2	14	0
Taylor's Bill,	7	14	3
Quarter's Rent,	5	0	0
Journeymen's Wages,	7	13	0
Sundries for Housekeeping,	1	17	6

RECEIPTS.

DEFINITION. A *Receipt* is a written acquittance, or discharge from a debt, given by the Receiver to the Payer; and is either in *full*, or in *part*, on a Person's *own* account, or on that of *another*.

1. *To Bills of Parcels, or Book Debts.*

[IN FULL.] Received payment (or, the Contents in full).
James Trusty.

[IN PART.] Received the Sum of Five Pounds on Account.
James Trusty.

£.5 0 0

[FOR ANOTHER.]   Received payment for Mr. James Trusty.
William Cashkeeper.

☞ *If the Bill is not paid when delivered in, the Date must be added at the time of payment.*

II. *SEPARATE RECEIPTS of various kinds, on a Person's* OWN *Account, or* IN PARTNERSHIP.

Received *July* 19, 1787, of Mr. John Dennis Sixteen Pounds Ten Shillings, in full of all demands.

£.16 10   John Joseph.

Received *May* 14, 1788, of Thomas James Esq. One Hundred Pounds, in full of all demands.

£.100   Martha David.

170

Received *Jan.* 15, 1786, of Mr. James Farmer Eighteen Pounds Ten Shillings, in full for a Quarter's Rent due at Christmas last.

£.18 10   Jonas Landlord.

Received *Oct.* 15, 1787, of Benjamin Bond Esq. Fifteen Pounds Fifteen Shillings, in full for half a Year's Salary due *Sept.* 30 last.

£.15 15   Edward Dormer.

Received *Feb.* 19, 1782, of Mrs. Mary Brookes Three Pounds, in full for an half Year's Interest on Fifty Pounds, due the 10th instant.

£.3   Samuel Bird.

Received *July* 9, 1788, of Mr. Ambrose Foster a Note of his Hand for Ten Pounds, which, when paid, will be in full of all demands.

Elisabeth Newman.

Received *June* 1, 1785, of Mr. William Johnson Twenty Pounds on Account.

£.20   James Cummings.

Received *June* 4, 1787, of Mrs. Sarah Smith, Ten Pounds, in part of a Note of Hand for Twenty-five Pounds.

£.10   Daniel Emerson.

Received *April* 10, 1788, of Mr. Edward Connor, by the hands of Mr. James Wilson, One Hundred Dollars, on Account, for Mason's Work done by me

100 *Dollars.* Moses Marble.

Received *July* 1, 1787, of Mr. William Jones One Hundred and Thirty-five Pounds, on Account, for Self and Partner. William Newcomb.

£.135

Received *Feb*, 2, 1789, of Mr. William Chaloner, Sixty-four Pounds Fifteen Shillings, in full of all demands.

£.64 15 Watkins, Jones & Cº.

III. *SEPARATE RECEIPTS*, *given on* ANOTHER *Person's Account.*

171

Received *March* 18, 1789, of Mr. William Dimsdale, Five Pounds, for the Use of Mr. John Holland.

£.5 Thomas Markham.

Received *August* 9, 1781, of Mrs. Eliz. Johnson Eighteen Dollars and an half, on Account, for Mr. James West.

18½ *Dollars.* Benjamin Banker.

Received *Nov.* 13, 1785, of Mess. Bond & Cº. Forty-six Pounds Ten Shillings and Ninepence, on Account, for my master Mr. James Dunn.

£.46 10 9 Christopher Collector.

Received *Feb.* 18, 1789, of Mrs. Mary Orchard Fifteen Pounds, for a Quarter's Rent, due *Jan.* 1. last, to my mother Eliz. Langley. James Langley.

£.15

Received *Dec.* 24, 1788, of James Plenty Esq. Seventy-one Pounds Sixteen Shillings and Fourpence, for Plumbers' and Glaziers' Work, at Newtown Place, done by my father William Builder. Sophia Builder.

£.71 16 4

☞ *In Receipts, Promissory Notes, &c. the words* THE SUM OF *are sometimes inserted immediately before the Money is mentioned.*

PROMISSORY NOTES.

DEFINITION. A *Promissory Note* is a writing given as a Security for some valuable consideration, as Money, Goods, &c. promising to pay the Sum, &c. mentioned, at a time appointed.

PHILADELPHIA, *Jan.* 1, 1789.

I promise to pay to Mr. William Woolston, on demand, Ten Pounds, for value received.

£.10   Moses Michael.

CHARLESTON, *Sept.* 4, 1788.

I promise to pay to Mr. Robert Williams, or Bearer, on demand, Twenty Pounds Six Shillings, the value received.

172   £.20 6   Oliver Mark.

BOSTON, *Aug.* 5, 1785.

I promise to pay to Mrs. Eliz. Owen, or Order, on demand, Ninety-five Pounds, value received.

£.95   Richard Benjamin.

NEW-YORK, *Feb.* 18, 1788.

I promise to pay to Mr. Joseph Dearman, or Order, at Ten Days after Date, One Hundred Dollars, value received.

100 *Dollars.*   Ann Dennis.

BURLINGTON, *Oct.* 12, 1788.

I promise to pay to Mrs. Ann Masters, or Bearer, at One Month after Date, Seven Pounds Sixteen Shillings and Three-pence, for value received.

£.7 16 3   Mary Adams.

NEWCASTLE, *Sept.* 15, 1785.

I promise to pay to Thomas Burr Esq. or Order, at Twenty-eight Days after Date, One Hundred and Fifty Pounds, for Self and Partner, value received.

£.150   Luke Mortimer.

TRENTON, *March* 1, 1787.

I promise to pay to Sylvanus Urban Esq. or Order, One Thousand Pounds, value received, on, or before the first Day of June next.

£.1000   Noah Smithson.

Witnesses—Moses Green,
          Martha Dennis,

BRISTOL, *Dec.* 1, 1788.

I promiſe to pay to Mr. Jacob Nathaniel, or Bearer, on demand, Fifty Pounds, for Meſſ. Jackſon and C°.

James Martin.

£.50

PITTSBURGH, *Aug.* 12, 1787.

Borrowed and Received of Mrs. Jane Jones Thirty-five Pounds Twelve Shillings, which I promiſe to pay at Two Months after Date.   Samuel Johnſon.

£.35 12

LONDON, *Sept.* 4, 1782.

I promiſe to pay to Sir James Cricket, or Order, on demand, One Thouſand Pounds, value received, for Meſſ. Jones, Wilſon, Martin, and Benſon.

£.1000   Edward Manſel.

173

RICHMOND, *May* 1, 1784.

Twenty-one Days after Date I promiſe to pay to the Hon. Lewis Owens Eſq. or Order, Seventy-five Pounds, value received, for my Father Thomas Unwin.

£.75   Jonas Unwin.

PHILADELPHIA, *Nov.* 12, 1787, Received of Mr. James Turny a Bill of Exchange, at Three Months, on Meſſ. Atkinſon & C°. Merchants in Front ſtreet, for Two Hundred Pounds, for which I promiſe to be accountable, on demand.   Zachariah Young.

£.200

Received of Mrs. Barbara Allen Three Hundred and Five Ounces of Silver Plate, which I promiſe to be accountable for on demand. Witneſs my hand, at NEW YORK, this 17th *June*, 1774.   James Chandler.

Twelve Months after Date, I promiſe to pay to the Rev. Peter Pious, or his Order, One Hundred and Twenty-five Pounds, which I this day borrowed and received, with Intereſt on the ſame at Six *per cent. per ann.* Witneſs my hand, at PHILADELPHIA, this 22d *April*, 1788.

David Goodman.

£.125 0 0 *Principal.*
      Intereſt.
———— —
———— *Amount.*

C

LONDON, *July* 19, 1786.

We, jointly and feparately, promife to pay to James Mar-
fhall Efq. or Order, One Hundred and Eighty Pounds,
for value received; Forty Pounds, part thereof, at One
Month after date, Sixty Pounds at Two Months, and
Eighty Pounds at Three Months after date, with Intereſt
on each payment, at Six *per cent. per ann.* till it becomes
due.   James Sampſon.
                                                     Timothy Truſty.

£.40   *at One Month.*
  60   *at Two Months.*
  80   *at Three Months.*
─────
 180
─────

BILLS of EXCHANGE.

DEFINITION.   A *Bill of Exchange* is an Order for Money to
be received in *one* place, for the value paid in *another.*

────────

£.35   NEW-YORK, *July* 10, 1788.
    At fight, pay Mr. Jonathan Montgomery, or Order, Thirty-
       five Pounds, for value received, and place it to Account,
       as by advice from, Sir,
                                   Your humble Servant,
To Mr. John Smith, }   John Sherman.
Mercht. at Albany. }

£.150   LONDON, *July* 1, 1788.
    At Twenty-eight Days fight, pay Mr. William Cummings,
       or Order, One Hundred and Fifty Pounds, for value re-
       ceived, without further advice, and place it to Account.
                                   Yours, &c.
To James Sherman, Efq. }   Adam Bowman.
Merchant in Cornhill. }

£.457 12 6   BALTIMORE, *July* 18, 1788.
    One Month after date, pay Mr. Thomas Johnſon, or Order,
       Four Hundred and Fifty-ſeven Pounds, Twelve Shillings
       and Sixpence, Pennſylvania Currency, value received of
       Simon Jones, Efq. and place it to Account, as by advice
       from,
                                   Sir, your humble Servant,
To Meſſ. James and Newton, }   Samuel Maſon.
Merchants in Philadelphia. }

1000 *Doll.*

PHILADELPHIA, *Nov,* 10, 1787.

At Thirty Days fight, pay to Meſſ. Atkins and Foſter, or Order, One Thouſand Dollars, Specie, value received of Captain James Marſhall, and place it to Account, as by advice from, Sir,

To James Banner, Eſquire,
Mercht. in Charleſton, S. C.

Your humble Servants,
Dimſdale & Manton.

£.500

LANCASTER, *Oct.* 14, 1788.

On the firſt of December next, pay to Charles Drummond, Eſq. or Order, Five Hundred Pounds, for value received, and place it to account, without farther advice from,
Sir, yours, &c.

To Col. James Oliver,
Philadelphia.

William Town.

175

A P P L I C A T I O N.

Bills of Parcels.

Mrs. A goes to the Store of Mr. B. in Boſton, on *Feb.* 2, 1789, and buys 3 *yds.* of long Lawn, at 19*s.* 6*d.* a *yd.*—$\frac{3}{4}$ yd. of Book Muſlin, at 19*s.* 6*d.* a *yd.*—14 *yds.* of fine Iriſh Linen, at 7*s.* 9*d.* a *yd.*—and 12 *yds.* of Striped Linen, at 4*s.* 9*d.* a *yd.*——*Make out the Bill.*

Make a Bill and Receipt for the following Articles, bought *Mar.* 1, 1719, by **Mr. C.** of Meſſ. D, E & Cº. Grocers in Lancaſter. —7 cwt. 3 qr. 15 *lb.* of Loaf Sugar, at £.5 5 a *cwt.*—14 *cwt.* 1 qr. Lump dº. at £.4 10.—2 bags of Coffee, each *wt.* 3 *qr.* at 1*s.* 7*d.* a *lb.*—and a box of Soap, *wt.* 14 *cwt.* at 5$\frac{3}{4}$*d.* a *lb.*

Mr. F's ſervant purchaſes on his maſter's account, *Dec.* 14, 1788, of Mr. G, of New-York, 3 *lb.* of Green Tea, at 15*s.* a *lb.* —1$\frac{1}{2}$ *lb.* of Hyſon, at 20*s.*—7 *lb.* of Bohea, at 4*s.* 2*d.*—10 *lb.* of Sugar, at 7$\frac{1}{2}$*d.*—and 3$\frac{1}{2}$ *oz.* of Nutmegs, at 1*s.* 9*d.* *Make out the Bill.*

H buys of K of Charleſton, *April* 1, 2$\frac{1}{2}$ *cwt.* of Turpentine Oil, at £.3 10 a *cwt.*—1$\frac{1}{2}$ *cwt.* of ſtrained Turpentine, at £:1 4. —5 *cwt.* of Burgundy Pitch, at £.1 17.—1$\frac{1}{2}$ *tuns* of White Wine Vinegar,

Vinegar, at 4s. 2d. a gall.—4 cwt. of Starch, at £.2 7 a cwt.—
and 5 cwt. of Gunpowder, at 2s. 6d. a lb. Exhibit the form of
the Bill.

Book Debts.

L is indebted to M, as appears by the Account in the Ledger,
for the following Articles.—1788, *March* 29, to 18 *gall.* Palm
Sack, at 18s. 6d. a *gall.*—*April* 13, to 35 *gall.* of Red Port, at
9s. 4d.—*May* 26, to 17 *gall.* Sherry, at 16s. 6d.———— 31, to
19 *gall.* of Rhenish, at 12s. 8d. and *July* 13, to 32 *gall.* of Burgundy, at £.1 2 6. *Make out the Bill, and write a Receipt to it,
as Clerk to M, it being paid* July 20, *by* N. O, *Esq.*

Make out a Bill for the following Book Debt, of P. Q, *Esquire,
from the Ledger of* R, *and write a Receipt in full, as received of* S,
the house steward. 1789, *Jan.* 2, To a flank of Beef, 7 *lb.* at 4d.
————4, To a rib of Beef, 9½ *lb.* at 4½d.————7, A leg of Mutton,
8 *lb.* at 4¼d.————10, A Neat's Tongue at 2s. 6d.————12, A leg
of Lamb, 5s. 6d.————17. A round of Beef, 19 *lb.* at 4¼d. a *lb.*
————23. A loin of Veal, 5¾ *lb.* at 4¾ a *lb.*

Orders.

Make out Bills for the following Goods.

READING, *July* 10, 1788.
Gentlemen,
Please to send by the first opportunity 16 *ells* of Dowlas, at
1s. 4d. an ell; 22½ *ells* of Holland, at 3s. 4d. ; a piece of Cam-
brick at £.8 10, quality as before ; 85 *yds.* of Diaper at 1s. 10d.
and 19½ *yds.* of Damask, at 4s. 3d.—The Amount shall be remitted on the receival of the Goods.

Yours, &c.

Messrs. Masham and Co. }
Merchts. in Philadelphia. }   James Jackson.

ALBANY, *July* 15, 1788.
Mess. Howard and Deacon,
As the last Goods answered my expectation, you may draw
on me for the balance whenever you think proper ; and send
by the Stage, as soon as possible, 10½ *yds.* of Yorkshire Cloth,
at 13s. ; 7 *yds.* of fine Spanish Black, at 12s. 6d. ; 6¾ *yds.* of fine
grey

grey Cloth, at 31*s*. 6*d*.; 16¾ *yds*. of Frieze, at 7*s*.; 4 *yds*. of second Drab at 30*s*.; 5⅞ *yds*. of superfine Spanish Cloth, at 33*s*.; and 31 *yds*. of livery Scarlet Cloth, at 26*s*.

I am, Gentlemen, &c.

Messrs. Howard and Deacon, }   John Merriman.
Merchts. in New-York.

Receipts.

Write Receipts for the following circumstances, and supply Names,
Dates, &c. where they are wanting.

T receives of U, on *Feb*. 1, 1789, £.25 13 on Account.

V pays W, on *Jan*. 16, £.15 4, in full of all demands.

Y receives of Z, *Jan*. 16, £.18 for a Quarter's Wages, due *Jan*. 1.

A pays B, Esq. £,120 for a half Year's Rent due *Feb*. 4, 1788.

C receives of Mess, D, E & Cº. £.160 10 on account of F. G, Esquire.

I pay £.60 in part for Self and Partner.

One pays another £.37 10, in full for a Year's Interest on £.625, due the first of last month.

A son receives £.18 16 for his father, and gives a Receipt in full of all demands.

Miss H receives £.7 10 in part of a Bill, and gives a Receipt in her mother's name.

I received of the Hon. K. L, Esq. by the hands of his steward, £.1000, on Account.

July 18, 1788, I paid £.150 18 6, in full, for M, to N, Clerk to Mess. O, P, & Cº. and took his Receipt.

Promissory Notes.

Write a Note in the name of Q, for £.10, payable to R, or Order, on demand, and date it *July* 10, 1788.

I owe a person £.17 10, and give him a Note on demand, but not payable to order, *Aug.* 14. 1787.

A merchant owes Mrs. S. £.125, and gives her a Note for it, payable to herself or order, one Month after date.

I am to have a Note from a person who owes me £.25, payable to myself, or Bearer, seven Days after date.

My brother lends me One Hundred Dollars, and as a security, is to have my Note payable on demand, but not negotiable.

178

My servant gives a Note to a merchant for £.500, payable to Order, 14 days after date.

I advanced a person £.20 on *Jan.* 1, 1789, and he gives his Note to pay it to me, or Order, on or before *May* 1.

T, son of U, borrows of V. W, Esq. £.80 for the use of his father, and gives a Note for it, payable to V. W, Esq. or Bearer, at Three Months after date.

Bills of Exchange.

Mess. Newson and Smithson, Merchants in Philadelphia, are indebted to Mr. John Dolland of Trenton £.60; for which sum, *July* 6, 1788, Mr. D. draws on Mess. N. and S. in favour of Mr. Moses Sampson, or Order, at a Month after date, without further advice. *Make the Draught.*

Jan. 1, 1789, I drawed for £.1000 Pennsylvania Currency, on James Reynolds, Esq. of New-York, payable to Mess. Johnson & C°. or Order, at 10 Days sight, as by advice.

Make a Draught for £.150, dated *July* 10, 1788, payable at a Month, as by advice, to Mrs. Ann Palmer, or Order.—*Drawer,* James Hewson of Pittsburgh—*Drawees,* Martin, Thames and Newberry, Philadelphia.

☞ *The Pupil may be further exercised by being required to write Receipts, Promissory Notes, or Bills of Exchange, founded on the circumstances of either of the Bills of Parcels, Book Debts, &c. at the discretion of the Tutor.*

SECTION THE SECOND.

BOOK-KEEPING by SINGLE ENTRY.

DEFINITION.

BOOK-KEEPING is an Art, which teaches the Method of recording, and difpofing the Accounts of Tranfactions in a courfe of Trade.

Book-keeping by SINGLE ENTRY is principally made ufe of by Retail Traders, Store-keepers, &c. and requires only a *Wafte,* or *Day Book,* and a *Ledger.*—It contains an Account of all *Cafh* lent or borrowed, *Debts* difcharged or contracted, and *Goods* fold or bought on *Credit.*

☞ *A Courfe of Book-keeping of this kind is requifite, becaufe in many Trades it is entirely fufficient.—In others, the Italian Method is wholly unapplicable.—It is alfo neceffary as Introductory to that Method, and to facilitate its Acquifition.*

DAY BOOK.

The DAY BOOK is ruled with a Marginal Line at the left hand, for a reference to the folio of the Ledger, and three Columns at the right for £. *s. d.*

GENERAL DIRECTION. The Perfon to whom a fum of Money is lent, a Debt difcharged, or Goods fold, is DEBTOR.—The Perfon of whom a fum of Money is borrowed, a Debt contracted, or Goods bought, is CREDITOR.

LEDGER.

The page of the LEDGER is ruled with a Column at the left hand for the Month and Day, and two fets of Columns for *£. s. d.* in *Debtor* and *Crediter;* with a fpace between for a reference

ference to the Day Book. The *Debtor* Column contains the Debts the Person has contracted, and on what accounts ; the *Creditor* shews what Payments he has made, and of what kind ; and the *difference* shews the Balance between the parties.

      ☞ *Some Book-keepers allow two opposite pages, as in the Italian Method, instead of the double Columns here recommended.*

     GENERAL DIRECTION. A Folio, or part of a Folio, must be opened for each Person's Account, as in the Specimen : Then, once a week, or as often as convenient, transfer the Day Book Entries.—First, put the Day of the Month in the Column appropriated to that purpose ; afterwards the name of the Commodity, if one alone, or the word *Sundries*, if more than one ; then the Sum Total in its proper Column, as it Dr. or Cr. respectively. In the intermediate space, add the Folio of the Day Book from which the Entry is posted. Lastly, in the Marginal Column of the Day Book, place the Number of the Folio of the Ledger to which the Entry is transferred.

     To BALANCE THE LEDGER, open a new Account at the End, by the Title *BALANCE DR.* and *CR.* as in the Specimen. To the *Debtor* Column of this Account will be brought the *Debts due to you*, and to the Creditor what *Debts you owe*.

     Then add the Dr. and Cr. Columns of each Person's Account separately, and *if both columns are even*, neither party is indebted to the other, and the work is done.

     If the *Debtor* Column is the greater, and the Person is indebted to you, add the difference to the Creditor Column to make them even, prefixing the words, *Carried to the next Ledger*, and specifying the Folio—Then in the Balance Account make *Balance Dr.* to the Person for the same sum ; and on opening a new Ledger, make the Person Dr. for the sum, prefixing the words *Brought from the last Ledger*, and add the Folio.

     If the *Creditor* Column is the greater, and you are indebted to the Person, add the difference to the Debtor Column to make them even, prefixing the words *Carried to the next Ledger*, and specifying the Folio—Then in the Balance Account make *Balance Cr.* by the Person for the same sum ; and on opening a new Ledger, make the Person Cr. for the sum, prefixing the words *Brought from the last Ledger*, and add the Folio.

Specimen of the DAY BOOK.

		£.	s.	d.
	PHILADELPHIA, January 1, 1789.			
5	*Thomas Drake, Dr.*			
	A pipe of Gallipoly oil, at *s. d.* 3 6 a *gall.*	22	1	0
	— 2 —			
5	*Samuel Griffiths, Dr.*			
	Half a pipe of Red Port, at *£. s.* 51 10 a *pipe.*	25	15	0
	— 3 —			
5	*John Woolſton, Cr.*			
	6 pieces of Broad Cloth, 45½ yds. each, at *s. d.* 16 3	221	16	3
	— 5 —			
5	*Thomas Wilſon, Eſq. Dr.*			
	2 cwt. Hyſon Tea, at *s. d.* 11 9 a *lb.*			
	1½ Green, at 13 6			
	3 Bohea. at 4 9			
		324	16	0
	— 6 —			
6	*Mrs. Newton, Dr.*			
	10 ells Dowlaſs, at *s. d.* 1 7 an *ell.*			
	12 yds. Holland, at 3 6 a *yd.*			
	4½ Muſlin, at 11 0			
		5	7	4
	— 7 —			
5	*John Woolſton, Dr.*			
	Caſh and Bank Notes on account,	150	0	0
	— 8 —			
6	*William King, Cr.*			
	Caſh borrowed on demand,	60	0	0

D

			£.	s.	d.
	PHILADELPHIA, January 9, 1789.				
6	John Cornman, Cr.				
		s. d.			
	6 qrs. Wheat,	at 43 6 a qr.			
	10 Barley,	at 25 9			
	14 buſh. Malt,	at 4 2 a buſh.			
			28	16	10
	——— 10 ———				
5	Thomas Drake, Cr.				
		s. d.			
	2½ cwt. Brown Soap,	at 56 0 a cwt.			
	36 lb. Bohea Tea,	at 4 3 a lb.			
			14	13	0
	——— 12 ———				
6	William King, Dr.				
		s. d.			
	40 doz. Candles,	at 6 6 a doz.			
	30 Mould d°.	at 7 6			
	7 cwt. Tallow,	at 31 6 a cwt.			
			35	5	6
	——— 13 ———				
5	Thomas Wilſon, Eſq. Cr.				
	Caſh and Bank Notes, on Account,		100	0	0
	Draught on Williamſon & C°. on Account,		100	0	0
			200	0	0
	——— 14 ———				
5	Samuel Griffiths, Cr.				
		£. s.			
	2 pps. Red Port,	at 47 0 a pipe			
	1½ Liſbon,	at 45 0			
	6 doz. Madeira,	1 15 a doz.			
			172	0	0
	——— 15 ———				
6	Mrs. Newton, Dr.				
	Caſh lent on demand,		15	0	0
	——— 16 ———				
5	Thomas Drake, Dr.				
		s. d.			
	31½ cwt. Hops,	at 45 6 a cwt.	71	13	3

182

PHILADELPHIA, January 17, 1789.

		£.	s.	d.
6	*William King, Cr.*			
	Check on the Bank, 60 *dollars.*	22	10	0

— 19 —

		£.	s.	d.
6	*John Cornman, Dr.*			
		s. d.		
	$14\frac{1}{2}$ *cwt.* Virginia Tobacco, at 1 9 a *lb.*	142	2	0

— 20 —

		£.	s.	d.
6	*Mrs. Newton, Dr.*			
		s. d.		
	$45\frac{1}{2}$ *yds.* Broad Cloth, at 17 6 a *yd.*			
	$24\frac{1}{2}$ Irish Linen, at 3 9			
		44	8	$1\frac{1}{2}$

— 21 —

		£.	s.	d.
5	*Samuel Griffiths, Dr.*			
		s. d.		
	$10\frac{1}{2}$ *cwt.* Bar Iron, at 20 3 a *cwt.*	10	12	0

— 22 —

		£.	s.	d.
6	*William King, Cr.*			
		s. d.		
	144 *bush.* Virginia Coals, at 1 3 a *bush.*	9	0	0

— 23 —

		£.	s.	d.
5	*John Woolston, Dr.*			
		s. d.		
	25 *lb.* Hyson Tea, at 13 0 a *lb.*			
	7 Coffee, at 4 9			
		17	18	3

— 24 —

		£.	s.	d.
6	*Mrs. Newton, Dr.*			
		s. d,		
	7 *yds.* Fine Silk, at 12 6 a *yd.*			
	9 Flowered d°. at 14 9			
	10 Florentine at 11 6			
		16	15	3

— 25 —

		£.	s.	d.
5	*Thomas Wilson, Esq. Cr.*			
	Draft on Jackson & C°. on Account,	100	0	0

183

LEDGER.

	PHILADELPHIA, January 27, 1789.		£.	s.	d.
6	*John Cornman*, Cr.				
	3 pieces Irish Linen, 25½ yds.	*s. d.* at 3 9	14	6	10½
	————— 28 —————				
5	*Thomas Drake*, Cr.				
	Public Securities,	valued at	60	0	0
	————— 29 —————				
5	*John Woolston*, Dr.				
	Cash in full,		53	18	0
	————— 30 —————				
6	*Mrs. Newton*, Cr.				
	Check on the Bank,	150 dollars,	56	5	0
	Cash in full,		25	5	8½
			80	10	8½
	————— 31 —————				
6	*William King*, Dr.				
	Cash in full,		56	4	6

184

Specimen of the LEDGER.

ALPHABET.

Balance,	Page 6	*King*, Wm.	Page 6
Cornman, John	6	*Newton*, Mrs.	6
Drake, Tho.	5	*Wilson*, Tho. Esq.	5
Griffiths, Samuel	5	*Woolston*, John	5

1789.	*Thomas Drake,*	Debtor.		F.	Creditor.		
Jan. 1	Gallipoly oil,	22	1	0	1		
10	Sundries,				2	14 13	0
16	Hops,	71 13	3		2		
28	Public Securities,				4	60 0	0
31	Carried to the next Ledger,					19 1	3
	£	93 14	3			93 14	3

1789.	*Samuel Griffiths,*	Debtor.			Creditor.		
Jan. 2	Red Port,	25 15	0	1		
14	Sundries,			2	172 0	0
21	Bar Iron,	10 12	0	3		
31	Carried to the next Ledger,	135 13	0			
	£	172 0	0		172 0	0

185

1789.	*John Woolſton,*	Debtor.			Creditor.		
Jan. 3	Broad Cloth,			1	221 16	3
7	Sundries,	150 0	0	1		
23	Sundries,	17 18	3	3		
29	Caſh in full,	53 18	0	4		
	£	221 16	3		221 16	3

1789.	*Thomas Wilſon, Eſq.*	Debtor.			Creditor.		
Jan. 5	Sundries,	324 16	0	1		
13	Sundries,			2	200 0	0
25	Draft,			3	100 0	0
31	Carried to the next Ledger,				24 16	0
	£	324 16	0		324 16	0

186

1789.	Mrs. Newton,	Debtor.			F.	Creditor.		
Jan. 6	Sundries,	5	7	4	1			
15	Cash,	15	0	0	2			
20	Sundries,	44	8	1½	3			
24	Sundries,	16	15	3	3			
30	Sundries,				4	81	10	8⅕½
	£.	81	10	8½		81	10	8½

1789.	William King,	Debtor.				Creditor.		
Jan. 8	Cash,				1	60	6	0
12	Sundries,	35	5	6	2			
17	Bank Check,				3	22	10	0
22	Coals,				3	9	0	0
31	Cash-in full,	56	4	6	4			
	£.	91	10	0		91	10	0

1789.	John Cornman,	Debtor.				Creditor.		
Jan. 9	Sundries,				2	28	16	10
19	Tobacco,	142	2	0	3			
27	Irish Linen,				4	14	6	10½
31	Carried to the next Ledger,					98	18	3½
	£.	142	2	0		142	2	0

1789.	Balance,	Debtor.				Creditor.		
Jan. 31	Thomas Drake,	19	1	3	5			
	Samuel Griffiths,				5	135	13	0
	Thomas Wilson, Esq.	24	16	0	5			
	John Cornman,	98	18	3½	6			
	£.	142	15	6½		135	13	0

✠✠✠✠✠✠✠✠✠✠✠✠✠✠✠✠✠✠✠✠✠✠✠✠✠✠✠✠✠✠✠✠

SECTION THE THIRD.

BOOK-KEEPING by DOUBLE ENTRY.

BOOK-KEEPING by DOUBLE ENTRY is generally made ufe of by Wholefale Traders, Merchants, &c. and requires a variety of Books, the principal of which are, the Wafte Book, Journal, and Ledger. It is fo denominated becaufe every Article has a DOUBLE ENTRY of *Debtor* and *Creditor*.

This method of Book-keeping is the moft perfect ever invented.—It contains Accounts of the Merchant's Stock in Trade, of every Perfon he deals with, and every Commodity he deals in, his Profit or Lofs by any branch of Trade, his Income, Expenditure, &c.

☞ *It is alfo called the* ITALIAN *Method, from its being firft ufed by the* Genoefe *and* Venetians, *while they held the trade between* Europe *and the Eaft Indies, before the difcovery of a paffage thither by the Cape of Good Hope.*

WASTE BOOK.

The WASTE BOOK is ruled exactly fimilar to the Day Book in the Courfe by Single Entry. It contains a plain Narrative or Memorandum of every occurrence in Trade, as it happens in the ordinary courfe of bufinefs.

JOURNAL.

The JOURNAL is ruled as the Day Book.—In this, every circumftance of the Wafte Book is expreffed in a more methodical and Commercial Form, as preparatory to the Ledger.

L E D G E R.

In the LEDGER, two oppofite pages are allotted for each Perfon, Commodity, &c. *That* on the left hand for the Debtor Entries, and *that* on the right, for the Creditor. Each page is ruled as the Day Book; with an additional Column at the left hand of the £. *s. d.* for a Folio reference, and fometimes an additional Column at the left hand of the page, to feparate the Month and Day. As it contains the promifcuous and particular Articles of the other Books, collected under their refpective general heads, it requires an Alphabet to be prefixed.

The Accounts of which the Ledger is compofed, are the following, viz.

I. *Account of Stock.* This it the Merchant's Account of himfelf, and the term *Stock* is fubftituted for his own name.—It contains on the Debtor fide his Debts at opening the Books; on the Creditor, the Amount of all his property, as Cafh, Goods, Debts, &c.

II. *Account of Cafh.* The Debtor fide of this Account contains the Cafh on hand at opening the Books, and what is received in the courfe of Trade; the Creditor fide contains the difburfements.

III. *Accounts of Goods.* The Debtor fides fhew the Goods on hand, and what have been purchafed, with the price; the Creditor fides what have been fold, and what they have produced.

IV. *Accounts of Perfons.* The Debtor fides fhew what Debts they have contracted, and on what accounts; the Creditor, what payments they have made, and of what kind.

V. *Account of Profit and Lofs.* The Debtor fide fhews the Lofs by any Article of Merchandife, and alfo all incidental expences; the Creditor fide fhews the Gain, &c.

VI. *Account of Balance.* The Debtor fide fhews the feveral branches of the Merchant's property when the Books are clofed; and the Creditor fide fhews the Debts he owes.

Other Accounts are fometimes inferted, adapted to the particular Circumftances or Inclination of the Merchant, and the various branches of commerce in which he is engaged.

188

DIRECTIONS.

THE WASTE BOOK. The firſt thing neceſſary is an *Inventory* of the Merchant's whole eſtate, or a particular Account of all his *Property* or *Effects*, as *Caſh, Commodities, Debts*, &c.---which, together, are called STOCK. The manner of making this Inventory may be ſeen in the Specimen; and as in entering the various Tranſactions in Buſineſs, only a plain narrative is required, no particular directions need be given.

THE JOURNAL. A Tranſaction in the Journal conſiſts of, what has been termed, an Entry and a Narration.

The *Entry* aſcertains the proper Debtor and Creditor, and is expreſſed in one line---thus; *Cheeſe Dr. £.12 to Cyder.* The Creditor Entry is always underſtood to be the reverſe of the Debtor---thus; *Cyder Cr. £.12 by Cheeſe.*

189

The *Narration* is the expreſſion of the other material parts of the Tranſaction in as many lines as are neceſſary, and differs but little from the Waſte Book Entry.

The words *Sundry Accounts*, or *Sundries*, are made uſe of when either the Dr. or Cr. is complex, or is compoſed of various particulars.

Almoſt the whole myſtery of Book-keeping conſiſts in the Art of *Journalizing;* and writers on the ſubject have uſually burdened the Learner with a multitude of particular Rules for every circumſtance which occurs in buſineſs. They may, however, all be reduced to the two following, as will appear by the ſubſequent Application of them to the various Tranſactions in the annexed Specimen.

RULE I. *Whatever the Merchant poſſeſſes, or receives, or whoever is accountable to him, is* DEBTOR; *and if he aſks* on what account? *the anſwer ſhews the* CREDITOR.

RULE II. *Whatever be parts with, and every perſon to whom he is accountable, is* CREDITOR; *and if he aſks* on what Account? *the anſwer ſhews the* DEBTOR.

APPLICATION of the preceding RULES.

DATE.	TRANSACTIONS, &c.	DEBTOR.	CREDITOR.
Jan. 1	Property	Sundry Accounts	Stock
	Debts	Stock	Sundry Accounts
2	Purchaſe for ready money	Commodity	Caſh

E

Date, Transactions, &c.	Debtor.	Creditor.
Jan. 3 Sale for ready money	Caſh	Commodity
5 Houſekeeping ex-pences	Profit and Loſs	Caſh
6 Received a legacy	Caſh	Profit and Loſs
7 Purchaſe on credit	Commodity	Seller
8 Sale on credit	Purchaſer	Commodity
9 Purchaſe for ready money, and	Commodity	Caſh part
Part credit	Commodity	Seller the reſt
10 Sale for ready money	Caſh, part	Commodity
and Part credit	Purchaſer the reſt	Commodity
12 Paid Interest	Profit and Loſs	Caſh
13 Caſh won	Caſh	Profit and Loſs
14 Paid Poor's Tax	Profit and Loſs	Caſh
15 Gift	Profit and Loſs	Caſh
16 Borrowed money	Caſh	Lender
17 Paid Salary	Profit and Loſs	Caſh
19 Lent money	Borrower	Caſh
20 Barter	Commodity recd.	Commodity deliv.
21 Drawer of a Bill	Bills receivable	Drawee
22 Drawee to a Bill	Drawer	Bills payable
23 Received a Bill	Caſh	Bills receivable
24 Paid a Bill	Bills payable	Caſh
25 Shipped Goods to a Factor	Voyage	Commodity
Expences thereon	Voyage	Caſh
28 The Goods ſold	Factor	Voyage
Profit	Factor	Profit and Loſs
31 The Factor remits	Commodity	Factor
Expences attending	Commodity	Caſh

190

Example. The Journal is opened with the Inventory. The Property, conſiſting of Caſh, Goods, Debts owing to the Merchant, &c. is expreſſed (by Rule I.) *Sundry Accounts Drs.* £.374 10 *to Stock,* in the Entry ; and the Narration conſiſts of an enumeration of each particular, as in the Waſte Book. The Debts owing by the Merchant are expreſſed (by Rule II.) *Stock Dr.* £.18 *to Sundry Accounts,* and the particulars alſo Narrated as in the Waſte Book.

Thus, it is evident, that the whole Art of Journalizing conſiſts of nothing more than the application of the *two foregoing Rules* to every Tranſaction in the Courſe of Buſineſs.

OBSERVATION I. When an Entry of the Waste Book is Journalized, it is usual to write the letter *J.* in the marginal line, or the word *Posted*, or sometimes only *P.*

OBSERVATION II. When a Journal Entry is transferred to the Ledger, a reference is made both to the Dr. and Cr. Folio, by a Fractional expression in the marginal line; the *Numerator* referring to the *Debtor* folio, and the *Denominator* to the *Creditor.* But when the *Drs.* are more than one, the *Crs.* need only be mentioned once under the lower *Dr.*—and where there are more *Crs.* than one, the *Drs.* need only be expressed over the first *Cr.*

☞ *To accommodate the Pupil with the opportunity of comparing the Waste Book and Journal with each other, they are here placed on opposite pages, and not formed into distinct books, as in Real Business.*

THE LEDGER. TO OPEN THE LEDGER—At the top of the opposite pages allotted for the Stock Account, in some conspicuous or ornamental hand, on the *Dr.* side, write the Date of the Year, the words *Stock Dr.* F, for the folio reference, and £. *s. d.* each at the head of their respective columns, as in the Specimen; and on the *Cr.* side the words *Per contra Cr.* with the Date, Reference, and £. *s. d.* as before.

Then in the first Journal Entry, as. *Sundry Accounts* are *Drs.* £.374 *to Stock*, it is implied that *Stock* is *Cr.* £.374 *by Sundry Accounts*; on the *Cr.* side, therefore, write the words *By Sundry Accounts*, place the Sum, Month and Day of opening the Books, with the Reference, in the Columns allotted to each particular.

And as each Article has a Double Entry, in the same manner open pages, or parts of pages, as may be necessary for each of the particular Accounts Drs. to Stock, viz. Cash, Hops, Wine, Broad Cloth, and John Woolston; on the *Dr.* side of each of these Accounts write the words *To Stock*, specifying the particulars as in the Journal, placing the Sum, Month, Day and Reference as before directed.

In the second Entry *Stock* is *Dr.* £.18 *to Sundry Accounts.* On the *Dr.* side, therefore, of the Stock Account, write the words *To Sundry Accounts*, specifying the Sum, &c. as before: And as it is implied that *Sundry Accounts* are *Crs.* £.18 *by Stock*, open, as before, pages, or parts of pages, for each particular, viz. Thomas Drake, and Samuel Taylor; in the *Cr.* side of each of which Accounts, write the words *By Stock*, expressing the particulars as in the Journal, and supply the Sum, &c, as before.

The Ledger being thus opened, write these respective Heads of Accounts under their proper letters in the Alphabet, and add the number of the page of the Ledger in which they were inserted.

To Enter the Transactions, &c, of the Journal into the Ledger, see in the Alphabet if proper pages are allotted for the Accounts, both *Dr.* and *Cr.* of the Entry; if not, let such be opened, according to the preceding Directions.—Then, in the Entry of *Jan.* 2, for instance, *Cheese Dr.* £.10 2 6 to *Cash*, a new Account must be opened for *Cheese*, on the *Dr.* side of which write the words *To Cash*, expressing as much of the Narration as convenient, in one line; place the Month, Day, and Sum in their proper columns, and in the folio reference insert 1, that being the number of the folio of the Cash Account where the same Entry is made *Cr.*

As the Entry also implies *Cash Cr.* £.10 2 6 *by Cheese*, in the *Cr.* side of the Cash Account write the words *By Cheese*, expressing, as before, as much of the Narration as can be contained in one line. The Date, and Sum, must be put in their proper columns, and in the folio reference 3, because the Account of Cheese, where the same Entry is *Dr.* is the third folio. No other example is necessary of a Simple Entry, as they are exactly similar; nor of a Complex one, because in the Directions for Journalizing, in page 30, they are all reduced to Simple Entries.

To Balance the Ledger, open a new Account at the End, by the title of *Balance Dr.* and *Per contra Cr.*

Account of Cash.

Add up the *Dr.* and *Cr.* sides separately, the difference shews the Cash remaining on hand. Make *Cash Cr. by Balance* for the Sum, and in the Balance Account, *Balance Dr. to Cash* for the same sum.—The *Cr.* side of this Account can never exceed the *Dr.* because no man can pay more Cash than he receives.

Account of Goods.

(1.) When the Whole remains *unsold*, as in Sugar, make the *Commodity Cr. by Balance* for the Whole, at prime cost, and *Balance Dr. to the Commodity* for the same quantity, at the same sum.

(2.) When the Whole is *sold*, as in Cyder, find the difference between the Cost and Produce, for which sum make the *Commodity Dr. to Profit and Loss* if it is Gained; or *Cr. by Profit and Loss* if it is Lost.

(3.) When a *part* remains unsold, make the *Commodity Cr. by Balance* for what remains, at prime cost; and *Balance Dr. to the Commodity* for the same. Then find the difference between the *Dr.* and *Cr.* sides of the Account, and make the *Commodity* also *Dr. to Profit and Loss* for the Gain; or *Cr. by Profit and Loss* for
the

the Lofs.—The difference fhews the Gain on that particular branch of Trade if the *Cr.* fide exceeds, or Lofs if the *Dr.* exceeds.

Account of Perfons.

Add the *Dr.* and *Cr.* fides feparately, and then obferve,

(1.) When both fides are *even*, neither party is indebted to the other, and the work is done.

(2.) When the *Dr.* fide is the greater, which is when the Perfon is indebted to the Merchant, make the *Perfon Cr. by Balance* for the difference, and *Balance Dr. to the Perfon* for the fame fum.

(3.) When the *Cr.* fide is the greater, which happens when the Merchant is indebted to the Perfon, make the *Perfon Dr. to Balance* for the difference, and *Balance Cr. by the Perfon* for the fame fum.

Account of Profit and Lofs.

193

Add the *Dr.* and *Cr.* fides—Then,

(1.) If the *Dr.* fide is the greater, make the *Account Cr. by Stock* for the difference, as fo much Loft by Trade ; and make *Stock Dr. to Profit and Lofs* for the fame fum.

(2.) If the *Cr.* fide is the greater, make the *Account Dr. to Stock* for the difference, as fo much Gained by Trade ; and *Stock Cr. by Profit and Lofs* for the fame fum.

Account of Balance.

As the *Dr.* fide is fuppofed to be the greater, make them equal by putting *Balance Cr. by Stock* for the difference, as the Neat of the Merchant's Eftate ; and, in the Stock Account, make *Stock Dr. to Balance* for the fame fum.

Account of Stock.

Add each fide feparately, and if the fums are equal, the Book of Accounts has been correctly kept, if not, they muft be examined in order to difcover the Error.

OBSERVATION. As the Profit and Lofs Account fhews the alterations which have been made in the Merchant's circumftances by Trade ; the Stock, with the Profit and Lofs added or fubtracted, gives the Balance; and the Balance, with the Profit or Lofs added or fubtracted, gives the Stock—The Stock and Balance, therefore, prove each other.

Specimen of the WASTE BOOK.

	£.	s.	d.
— PHILADELPHIA, January 1, 1789. —			

P.

INVENTORY
Of the PROPERTY of T. S. taken this day.

	£.	s.	d.	£.	s.	d.
Cash,	100	0	0			
Hops, 10 *bags*, at £.3 0 a *bag*,	30	0	0			
Wine, 4 *pipes*, at 20 5 a *pipe*,	81	0	0			
Broad Cloth, 6 *pieces*, at 25 10 a *piece*,	153	0	0			
John Woolston owes on demand,	10	10	0			
				374	10	0

P.

DEBTS.

	£.	s.	d.	£.	s.	d.
To Thomas Drake on bond,	16	0	0			
To Samuel Taylor on account,	2	0	0			
				18	0	0

——— 2 ———

	£.	s.	d.
P. Bought of Samuel Newton half a *ton* of Cheshire Cheese, at £.20 5 a *ton*, for which I paid ready money,	10	2	6

——— 3 ———

	£.	s.	d.
P. Sold to John Williams 4 *bags* of Hops, at £.4 10 a *bag*, for which I received ready money,	18	0	0

——— 5 ———

	£.	s.	d.
P. Paid Housekeeping Expences last month,	4	15	0

——— 6 ———

	£.	s.	d.
P. Received a Legacy left me by my Uncle,	5	0	0

——— 7 ———

	£.	s.	d.
P. Bought of Samuel Taylor 2 *hhds.* of Tobacco, at £.10 6 a *hhd*, to pay in 3 months,	20	12	0

194

Specimen of the JOURNAL.

		£.	s.	d.
	——— PHILADELPHIA, January 1, 1789. ———			
	Sundry Accounts Drs. £.374 10 in Stock.			
		£.	s.	d.
1	Cash,	100	0	0
1	Hops, 10 *bags*, at £.3 0 a *bag*, 30	0	0	
2	Wine 4 *pipes*, at 20 5 a *pipe*, 81	0	0	
2	Broad Cloth, 6 *pieces*, at 25 10 a *piece*,153	0	0	
2/1	John Woolston, by note on demand, 10	10	0	
		374	10	0
1/2	*Stock Dr. £.18 to Sundry Accounts.*			
	To Thomas Drake on bond, 16	0	0	
3	To Samuel Taylor on account, 2	0	0	
		18	0	0
	——— 2 ———			
3/1	*Cheese Dr. £.10 2 6 to Cash.*			
	Paid for half a *ton* of Cheshire,	10	2	6
	——— 3 ———			
1/1	*Cash Dr. £.18 to Hops.*			
	Received for 4 *bags*,	18	0	0
	——— 5 ———			
3/1	*Profit and Loss Dr.£.4 15 to Cash.*			
	For Houshold Expences,	4	15	0
	——— 6 ———			
1/3	*Cash Dr. £.5 to Profit and Loss.*			
	Received my Uncle's Legacy,	5	0	0
	——— 7 ———			
4/3	*Tobacco Dr. £.20 10 to Samuel Taylor.*			
	For 2 *hhds.* at £.10 6, to pay in 3 months,	20	12	0

195

———— PHILADELPHIA, January 8, 1789. ————

	£.	s.	d.
P. Sold Samuel Griffiths one piece of Broad Cloth, at £.28 10, to be paid at a month,	28	10	0

———— 9 ————

P. Bought of Tho. Wilson, Efq. 4 *bbds.* of Cyder, at
£.2 5 a hogfhead.

			£.	s.	d.			
Paid Cafh,	£.5	0	0			
Due at a month,	4	0	0			
				9	0	0

———— 10 ————

P. Sold to Samuel Taylor 2 pipes of Wine, at £.25 a
pipe.

Cafh received,	£.30	0	0		
Due on demand,	20	0	0		
			50	0	0

———— 12 ————

	£.	s.	d.
P. Paid Thomas Drake a Quarter's Intereft, due the firft inftant,	0	4	0

———— 13 ————

	£.	s.	d.
P. Won this day at Quadrille,	2	2	0

———— 14 ————

	£.	s.	d.
P. Paid Poor's Tax due the firft inftant,	0	2	6

———— 15 ————

	£.	s.	d.
P. Dined with the Hon. G. W, Efq. and gave his fervants,	0	5	0

———— 16 ————

	£.	s.	d.
P. Borrowed of William King, to pay on demand, with Intereft at £.6 *per cent. per ann.*	10	0	0

———— 17 ————

	£.	s.	d.
P. Paid my Bookkeeper's Salary, due the firft inftant, and other Expences,	15	0	0

———— 19 ————

	£.	s.	d.
P. Lent Andrew Thompfon, to be paid on demand,	5	0	0

196

		£.	s.	d.
——— PHILADELPHIA, January 8, 1789. ———				
$\frac{1}{2}$	*Samuel Griffiths Dr. £.28 10 to Broad Cloth.* For a *piece*, to be paid at a month,	28	10	0
——— 9 ———				
$\frac{3}{1}$ 4	*Cyder Dr. £.9 to Sundry Accounts.* To Cash paid, £.5 0 0 To Tho. Wilson, Esq. at a month, 4 0 0	9	0	0
——— 10 ———				
1 3 2	*Sundry Accounts Drs. £.50 to Wine.* Cash in part for 2 *pipes*, £.30 0 0 Samuel Taylor on demand, 20 0 0	50	0	0
——— 12 ———				
$\frac{3}{1}$	*Profit and Loss Dr. 4s. to Cash.* For Thomas Drake's Interest,	0	4	0
——— 13 ———				
$\frac{1}{3}$	*Cash Dr. £.2 2 to Profit and Loss.* Won at Quadrille,	2	2	0
——— 14 ———				
$\frac{3}{1}$	*Profit and Loss Dr. 2s. 6d. to Cash.* Paid Poor's Tax,	0	2	6
——— 15 ———				
$\frac{3}{1}$	*Profit and Loss Dr. 5s. to Cash.* Gave the Hon. G. W's servants,	0	5	0
——— 16 ———				
1 4	*Cash Dr. £.10 to William King.* Borrowed at £.6 *per cent.* Interest,	10	0	0
——— 17 ———				
$\frac{3}{1}$	*Profit and Loss Dr. £.15 to Cash.* For Bookkeeper's Salary and other Expences,	15	0	0
——— 19 ———				
$\frac{5}{1}$	*Andrew Thompson Dr. £.5 to Cash.* Lent, to be paid on demand,	5	0	0

F

197

		£,	s.	d.
— PHILADELPHIA, January 20, 1789. —				
P. Bartered 4 *hhds.* of Cyder, at £.3 a *hhd.* for half a *ton* of Gloucester Cheese, at the same value,		12	0	0
— 21 —				
P. Drawn a Bill on John Woolston, payable at sight,		5	0	0
— 22 —				
P. Thomas Drake has drawn a Bill on me, to be paid at sight,		10	0	0
— 23 —				
P. John Woolston paid the Bill which I drew on him,		5	0	0
— 24 —				
P. Paid the Bill to Thomas Drake,		10	0	0

198

— 25 —				
P. Shipped 2 *cwt.* of Cheshire Cheese in the Golden Swan, John Streeton master, consigned to John Cornman at New York, marked as in the margin.				
Cheese valued at £.2 10 0				
X Paid Freight, &c. 0 12 0				
X		3	2	0
— 28 —				
P. Received advice that my Factor has received and sold the Cheese.				
Sold for £.6 10 0				
Charges deducted, 0 18 6				
		5	11	6
— 31 —				
P. Received from my Factor, John Cornman of New York, a Chest of Sugar.				
Neat Weight, *cwt.* 3 2, at £.4 8 0				
Paid Freight, &c. here, 1 0 0				
		5	8	0

——— PHILADELPHIA, January 20, 1789. ———

		£.	s.	d.

Cheese Dr. £.12 to Cyder.

$\frac{3}{3}$ Received half a *ton* of Gloucester Cheese for 4 *hhd.* at £.3 a *hhd.* 12 0 0

——— 21 ———

Bills Receivable Dr. £.5 to John Woolston.

$\frac{5}{2}$ To be paid at sight, ... 5 0 0

——— 22 ———

Thomas Drake Dr. £.10 to Bills Payable.

$\frac{2}{5}$ To pay at sight, ... 10 0 0

——— 23 ———

Cash Dr. £.5 to Bills Receivable.

$\frac{1}{5}$ Received John Woolston's Bill, ... 5 0 0

——— 24 ———

Bills Payable Dr. £.10 to Cash.

$\frac{5}{1}$ Paid Thomas Drake's Bill, ... 10 0 0

——— 25 ———

$\frac{5}{3}$ *Voyage to New York Dr. £.3 2 to Sundry Accounts.*

To Cheese, 2 *cwt.* of Cheshire, at £.2 10 0

1   To Cash paid Freight, &c.   0 12 0

     3 2 0

——— 28 ———

$\frac{6}{5}$ *John Cornman Dr. £.5 11 6 to Sundry Accounts.*

To Voyage to New York,   £.3 2 0

3   To Profit and Loss gained by } 2 9 6

   Selling the Cheese, }

     5 11 6

——— 31 ———

$\frac{6}{6}$ *Sugar Dr. £.5 8 to Sundry Accounts.*

To John Cornman for *cwt.* 3 2, at £.4 8 0

1 To Cash paid Freight, &c. here,   1 0 0

     5 8 0

Specimen of the LEDGER.

✛✛✛✛✛✛✛✛✛✛✛✛✛✛✛✛✛✛✛✛✛✛✛✛✛✛✛✛✛✛✛✛✛✛✛✛

1789.	STOCK	DR.	F.	£.	s.	d.
Jan. 1	To Sundries, as in the Journal, -		1	18	0	0
	To Balance, for the Neat of my Eftate,		6	367	14	6
				385	14	6

200

✛✛✛✛✛✛✛✛✛✛✛✛✛✛✛✛✛✛✛✛✛✛✛✛✛✛✛✛✛✛✛✛✛✛ ✛✛✛ ✛ ✛

1789.	CASH	DR.				
Jan. 1	To Stock, - - ready money,		1	100	0	0
3	To Hops, - - - - -		1	18	0	0
6	To Profit and Lofs, - a legacy, -		3	5	0	0
10	To Wine, - - - -		2	30	0	0
13	To Profit and Lofs, - won at Quadrille,		3	2	2	0
16	To William King, - borrowed, -		4	10	0	0
23	To Bills receivable, - John Woolfton,		5	5	0	0
				170	2	0

✛✛✛✛✛✛✛✛✛✛✛✛✛✛✛✛✛✛✛✛✛✛✛✛✛✛✛✛✛✛ ✛✛✛ ✛ ✛

1789.	HOPS	DR.				
Jan. 1	To Stock, - 10 *bags*, at £.3 a *bag*,		1	30	0	0
	To Profit and Lofs gained, - -		3	6	0	0
				36	0	0

Specimen of the LEDGER.

++

1789.	PER CONTRA	CR.	F.	£.	s.	d.
Jan. 1	By Sundries, as in the Journal, -		1	374	10	0
	By Profit and Loss gained by Trade, -		3	11	4	6
				385	14	6

++

201

1789.	PER CONTRA	CR.				
Jan. 2	By Cheese, - - - - -		3	10	2	6
5	By Profit and Loss, - houshold expences,		3	4	15	0
9	By Cyder, - - - - -		3	5	0	0
12	By Profit and Loss, - interest, -		3	0	4	0
14	By Profit and Loss, - poor's tax, -		3	0	2	6
15	By Profit and Loss, - G. W's servants,		3	0	5	0
17	By Profit and Loss, - salary, &c. -		3	15	0	0
19	By Andrew Thompson, lent, - -		5	5	0	0
24	By Bills Payable, - Tho. Drake, -		5	10	0	0
25	By Voyage to New York, - freight, &c.		5	0	12	0
31	By Sugar, - - - freight, &c.		6	1	0	0
	By Balance remains on hand, -		6	118	1	0
				170	2	0

++

1789.	PER CONTRA	CR.				
Jan. 3	By Cash recd. for 4 *bags*, at £.4 10 a *bag*,		1	18	0	0
	By Balance remains 6 *bags*, at £.3 -		6	18	0	0
				36	0	0

L E D G E R.

1789.	WINE	DR.	F.	£.	s.	d.
Jan. 1	To Stock, for 4 *pipes*, at £.20 5 a *pipe*, ·		1	81	0	0
	To Profit and Lofs gained, - ·		3	9	10	0
				90	10	0

✠✠✠✠✠✠✠✠✠✠✠✠✠✠✠✠✠✠✠✠✠✠✠✠✠✠✠

1789.	BROAD CLOTH	DR.				
Jan. 1	To Stock, for 6 *pieces*, at £.25 10 a *piece*,		1	153	0	0
	To Profit and Lofs gained, - ·		3	3	0	0
				156	0	0

202

✠✠✠✠✠✠✠✠✠✠✠✠✠✠✠✠✠✠✠✠✠✠✠✠✠✠✠

1789.	JOHN WOOLSTON	DR.				
Jan. 1	To Stock, by Note on demand, ·		1	10	10	0
				10	10	0

✠✠✠✠✠✠✠✠✠✠✠✠✠✠✠✠✠✠✠✠✠✠✠✠✠✠✠

1789.	THOMAS DRAKE	DR.				
Jan. 22	To Bills payable, - one drawn at fight,		5	10	0	0
	To Balance, · due to him, -		6	6	0	0
				16	0	0

1789.	PER CONTRA	CR.	F.	£.	s.	d.
Jan. 10	By Cafh in part for 2 *pipes*, at £.25 a pipe,		1	30	0	0
	By Samuel Taylor for the reft.	-	3	20	0	0
	By Balance remains, - - 2 *pipes*,		6	40	10	0
				90	10	0

✠✠✠✠✠✠✠✠✠✠✠✠✠✠✠✠✠✠✠✠✠✠✠✠✠ ✠ ✠✠✠ ✠ ✠

1789.	PER CONTRA	CR.				
Jan. 8	By Samuel Griffiths, - - a *piece*, at	4	28	10	0
	By Balance remains, - - 5 *pieces*,	6	127	10	0
			156	0	0

203

✠✠✠✠✠✠✠✠✠✠✠✠✠✠✠✠✠✠✠✠✠✠✠✠✠ ✠ ✠✠✠ ✠

1789.	PER CONTRA	CR.				
Jan. 22	By Bills receivable, - one drawn at fight,	5	5	0	0
	By Balance remains due on demand, -	5	5	10	0
			10	10	0

✠✠✠✠✠✠✠✠✠✠✠✠✠✠✠✠✠✠✠✠✠✠✠✠ ✠ ✠✠✠ ✠ ✠

1789.	PER CONTRA	CR.				
Jan. 1	By Stock on bond, - - -	1	16	0	0
			16	0	0

1789.	SAMUEL TAYLOR	DR.	F.	£.	s.	d.
Jan. 10	To Wine, - - due on demand,		2	20	0	0
	To Balance due to him, - - -		6	2	12	0
				22	12	0

1789.	CHEESE	DR.				
Jan. 2	To Cash paid for 10 *cwt.* of Cheshire, at £.1 0 3 a *cwt.* - - - -		1	10	2	6
20	To Cyder, barter'd for 10 *cwt.* of Gloucester, at £.1 4 0 a *cwt.* -		3	12	0	0
	To Profit and Loss gained. - -		3	0	9	6
				22	12	0

1789.	PROFIT AND LOSS	DR.				
Jan. 5	To Cash, - a month's houshold expences, -		1	4	15	0
12	To Cash, - Tho. Drake's Interest, -		1	0	4	0
14	To Cash, - paid poor's tax, - -		1	0	2	6
15	To Cash, - given G. W's servants, -		1	0	5	0
17	To Cash, - bookkeeper's salary and expences,		1	15	0	0
	To Stock gained by Trade, - -		1	11	4	6
				31	11	0

1789.	CYDER	DR.				
Jan. 9	To Cash in part for 4 *bbds.* at £.2 5 -		1	5	0	0
	To Tho. Wilson, Esq. for the rest, -		4	4	0	0
	To Profit and Loss gained, - -		3	3	0	0
				12	0	0

204

1789.	PER CONTRA	CR.	F.	£.	s.	d.
Jan. 1	By Stock on account, - - -		1	2	0	0
7	By Tobacco, - to pay in 3 months,		4	20	12	0
				22	12	0

✛✛✛✛✛✛✛✛✛✛✛✛✛✛✛✛✛✛✛✛✛✛✛✛

1789.	PER CONTRA	CR.				
Jan. 25	By Voyage to New York, - 2 cwt. of Cheshire, at £.1 5 - - -		5	2	10	0
	By Balance remains 8 cwt. of Cheshire, -		6	8	2	0
	By Balance remains 10 cwt. of Gloucester,		6	12	0	0
				22	12	0

205

✛✛✛✛✛✛✛✛✛✛✛✛✛✛✛✛✛✛✛✛✛✛✛✛

1789.	PER CONTRA	CR.				
Jan. 5	By Cash, - a legacy left by my uncle,		1	5	0	0
13	By Cash, - won at Quadrille, -		1	2	2	0
	By Hops gained, - - - -		1	6	0	0
	By Wine gained, - - - -		2	9	10	0
	By Broad Cloth gained, - - -		2	3	0	0
	By Cheese gained, - - - -		3	0	9	6
	By Cyder gained, - - - -		3	3	0	0
	By John Cornman, voyage to N.York gained,		6	2	9	6
				31	11	0

✛✛✛✛✛✛✛✛✛✛✛✛✛✛✛✛✛✛✛✛✛✛✛✛

1789.	PER CONTRA	CR.				
Jan. 20	By Gloucester Cheese in barter for 4 hhds. at £.3 - - - - -		3	12	0	0
				12	0	0

G

1789.	THO. WILSON, ESQ.	DR.	F.	£.	s.	d.
	To Balance due to him, - - -		6	4	0	0

✠✠✠✠✠✠✠✠✠✠✠✠✠✠✠✠✠✠✠✠✠✠✠✠✠✠✠✠✠✠✠

1789.	TOBACCO	DR.				
Jan. 7	To Samuel Taylor, 2 *hhds.* at £.10 6 -		3	20	12	0

206

✠✠✠✠✠✠✠✠✠✠✠✠✠✠✠✠✠✠✠✠✠✠✠✠✠✠✠✠✠✠✠

1789.	SAMUEL GRIFFITHS	DR.				
Jan. 8	To Broad Cloth, - to pay at a month,		2	28	10	0

✠✠✠✠✠✠✠✠✠✠✠✠✠✠✠✠✠✠✠✠✠✠✠✠✠✠✠✠✠✠✠

1789.	WILLIAM KING	DR.				
	To Balance due on demand to him, -		6	10	0	0

1789.	PER CONTRA	CR.	F.	£.	s.	d.
Jan. 9	By Cyder remains due at a month, —		3	4	0	0

1789.	PER CONTRA	CR.				
	By Balance remains, — — 2 *hhds*,		6	20	12	0

207

1789.	PER CONTRA	CR.				
	By Balance remains due to me, —		6	28	10	0

1789.	PER CONTRA	CR.				
Jan. 16	By Cash borrowed on demand, —		1	10	0	0

1789.	ANDREW THOMPSON	DR.	F.	£.	s.	d.
Jan. 19	To Cash, - - lent on demand,		1	5	0	0

✠✛✠

1789.	BILLS RECEIVABLE	DR.				
Jan. 21	To John Woolston, - - at sight,		2	5	0	0

✠✛✠

1789.	BILLS PAYABLE	DR.				
Jan. 24	To Cash, - - - paid the Bill,		1	10	0	0

✠✛✠

1789.	VOYAGE TO NEW YORK	DR.				
Jan. 25	To Cheshire Cheese, - - 2 cwt.	C		2	10	0
	To Cash paid Freight, &c. - -	C		0	12	0
				3	2	0

208

1789.	PER CONTRA	CR.	F.	£.	s.	d.
	By Balance remains due to me, -		6	5	0	0

1789.	PER CONTRA	CR.				
Jan. 23	By Cash, - - received the Bill,		1	5	0	0

209

1789.	PER CONTRA	CR.				
Jan. 22	By Thomas Drake, - - at sight		2	10	0	0

1789.	PER CONTRA	CR.				
Jan. 28	By John Cornman, who has received the Cheese, - - - - -		6	3	2	0
				3	2	0

1789.	JOHN CORNMAN	DR.	F.	£.	s.	d.
Jan. 28	To Voyage to New York, - -		5	3	2	0
	To Profit and Loss gained, - -		3	2	9	6
				5	11	6

✠✠✠✠✠✠✠✠✠✠✠✠✠✠✠✠✠✠✠✠✠✠✠✠✠ ✠✠✠ ✠ ✠

1789.	SUGAR	DR.				
Jan. 31	To John Cornman, a chest, wt. cwt. 3 2 qr.		6	4	8	0
	To Cash, - paid Freight, &c. here,		1	1	0	0
				5	8	0

210

✠✠✠✠✠✠✠✠✠✠✠✠✠✠✠✠✠✠✠✠✠✠✠✠✠ ✠✠✠ ✠ ✠

1789.	BALANCE	DR.				
Feb. 1	To Cash remains on hand, - -		1	118	1	0
	To Hops, remains 6 bags, at £.3 a bag, -		1	18	0	0
	To Wine, remains 2 pipes, at £.20 5 a pipe,		2	40	10	0
	To Broad Cloth, remains 5 pieces, at £.25 10		2	127	10	0
	To John Woolston, remains due on demand,		2	5	10	0
	To Cheshire Cheese, 8 cwt. at £.1 0 3 a cwt.		3	8	2	0
	To Gloucester do. 10 cwt. at £.1 4 0 a cwt.		3	12	0	0
	To Tobacco, - 2 bbls. at £.10 6 -		4	20	12	0
	To Samuel Griffiths, - due to me,		4	28	10	0
	To Andrew Thompson, - due to me,		5	5	0	0
	To John Cornman, - - due to me,		6	1	3	6
	To Sugar, - - a chest, 3 cwt. 2 qr.		6	5	8	0
				390	6	6

1789.	PER CONTRA	CR.	F.	£.	s.	d.
Jan. 31	By Sugar, - received a Cheſt, at		6	4	8	0
	By Balance remains due to me, -		6	1	3	6
				5	11	6

✠✠✠✠✠✠✠✠✠✠✠✠✠✠✠✠✠✠✠✠✠✠✠✠✠✠✠✠✠✠✠✠✠

1789.	PER CONTRA	CR.		£.	s.	d.
	By Balance, remains a Cheſt, with charges, valued at - - - - -		6	5	8	0
				5	8	0

211

✠✠✠✠✠✠✠✠✠✠✠✠✠✠✠✠✠✠✠✠✠✠✠✠✠✠✠✠✠✠✠✠✠

1789.	PER CONTRA	CR.		£.	s.	d.
Feb. 1	By Thomas Drake, - due to him,		2	6	0	0
	By Samuel Taylor, - - due to him,		3	2	12	0
	By Thomas Wilſon, Eſq. - due to him,		4	4	0	0
	By William King, - - due to him,		4	10	0	0
	By Stock, for the Neat of my Eſtate, -		5	367	14	6
				390	6	6

ALPHABET.

		Page			Page
B	*Balance*, - -	6	K	*King*, Will. - -	4
	Bills, receivable, -	5	P	*Profit and Loss*, -	3
	Bills, payable, -	5	S	*Stock*, - - -	1
	Broad Cloth, - -	2		*Sugar*, - -	6
C	*Cash*, - - -	1	T	*Taylor*, Sam. -	3
	Cheese, - - -	3		*Thompson*, Andrew, -	5
	Cornman, John, -	6		*Tobacco*, - -	4
	Cyder, - - -	3			
D	*Drake*, Tho. -	2	V	*Voyage to New York*, -	5
G	*Griffiths*, Sam. -	4	W	*Wilson*, Tho. Esq, -	4
				Wine, - - -	2
H	*Hops*, - - -	1		*Woolston*, John, -	2

212

THE END.

ERRATUM, IN THE BOOK-KEEPING.

In the Ledger by Double Entry, Fol. 2. Cr. side, line 19.
read *Fol.* 6. for *Fol.* 5.

The following ERRATA in the *Arithmetic*, have been discovered
since its Publication.

PAGE 52, line 6, for 517 read 587.—for 513 7 6 read
513 12 6.—line 31, for £96 6 9 read £96 16 9. P. 62, line 25,
for 311 read 321.—line 32, for $1\frac{3}{4}$ read $8\frac{3}{4}$. Page 63, line 16,
for $4\frac{1}{4}$ read $8\frac{1}{4}$. Page 69, line 6, for *I has Coffee* read *I has 89 lb.
of Coffee*. Page 70, line 3, for *chest* read *cwt.* Page 74, line 2,
for $\frac{18}{480}$ read $\frac{18}{3760}$. Page 85, line 7, for £.94 4 read £.19 4.
Page 93, line 43, for *Huntingtonford* read *Huntingfora*.

6

SAMUEL FREEMAN'S MUNICIPAL ACCOUNTING CHAPTER, 1791

THE

TOWN OFFICER;

OR THE

POWER AND DUTY OF

SELECTMEN,	* CONSTABLES,
TOWN CLERKS,	* COLLECTORS OF TAXES,
TOWN TREASURERS,	* SURVEYORS OF HIGH-WAYS,
OVERSEERS OF THE POOR,	* SURVEYORS OF LUMBER,
ASSESSORS,	* — FENCE VIEWERS,

AND OTHER TOWN OFFICERS.

As contained in the Laws of the Commonwealth of Massachusetts:

With a variety of FORMS for the use of such Officers.

TO WHICH ARE ADDED,

THE POWER AND DUTY OF *TOWNS, PARISHES* AND *PLANTATIONS*;

And a plain and regular *Method* to keep Accounts of the Expenditures of Monies voted by a Town; upon an inspection of which, the state of its Finances may at any time be known.

By SAMUEL FREEM.

[With the Priviledge of Copy Right.]

PORTLAND:

Printed by BENJAMIN TITCOMB, Jun. MDCCXCI.

A
Plain and Regular METHOD to keep
ACCOUNTS
OF THE EXPENDITURES OF MONIES
VOTED BY A TOWN;

Upon an Infpection of which, the State of its FINANCES may at any time be known.

AS one of the great Objects of Government is to guard and defend the Property of its Subjects ; as no public Meafures engage the attention of a People more than thofe which affect their Intereft, and require by way of Taxes a part of their Property for public Ufes ; and as nothing will enfure a cheerful acquiefcence in fuch meafures but an Affurance that the Monies thus taken from them are applied to the Ufes for which they were defigned ; it is of importance in all Communities, that proper Regulations fhould be eftablifhed, whereby it may clearly appear, that fuch Monies are faithfully expended, and regularly accounted for. Too much care cannot be taken in this Bufinefs, as it relates to the raifing and applying of Taxes required for the fupport of Government, and the Exigencies of a State ; and it muft be happy for the People of any State, to have fuch a Plan eftablifhed, as fhall provide effectual Checks upon the feveral
Officers

Officers through whose hands their Monies are to pass ; and as shall exhibit at any time, such a state of the Expenditures thereof, as will satisfy every reasonable Person who may inspect the same.

Whether such a Plan has been adopted, or is now wanted in this State or not, it is not for me to enquire. My design is to form a regular Plan for keeping the Accounts of a Town, by which its Inhabitants may at any time know whether the Monies which they may have voted at any Meeting, be raised, collected and expended, agreeably to their views in voting them. To these ends, it will be necessary for the Town to establish the following

217

R E G U L A T I O N S.

1. THAT after every annual, or other Meeting, at which any Money should be voted to be raised,* the Town Clerk should make out two Lists or Accounts, of the Sums voted, expressing therein the particular Purposes for which they are to be raised, and deliver one of them to the Selectmen, and the other to the Assessors of the Town. And

When Monies voted for any purpose shall be by the Town appropriated to any other, or transferred to the general Account of Monies unappropriated, a Certificate thereof should be made out by the Clerk, and delivered to the Selectmen.

R 2.

---

* *Previous to the voting of any Monies, it is proper that an Estimate of the Sums proposed to be raised, should be laid before the Town, that the Town may have opportunity to consider the same, and judge whether upon a general view thereof, it would be expedient to raise the whole Sum therein mentioned : and if not, what part thereof.*

2. That when the Monies voted fhall be affeffed, the Affeffors fhould certify to the Selectmen and alfo to the Treafurer, the amount of the feveral Tax Bills committed to the Collectors, (including the overlay‑ings) together with any Additions or Abatements they may have made therein.

3. That no Sums be paid by the Treafurer but by an Order of the Selectmen in writing, expreffing what Appropriations they are to be paid out of.

4. That the Selectmen draw no Orders upon the Treafurer for the application of any Monies, nor He pay any, but for fuch purpofes as may have been pre‑vioufly determined by the Town.

5. That no appropriation be altered, but by an ex‑prefs Vote of the Town.*

6. That at every annual *March* or *April* Meeting, the Selectmen fhould exhibit to the Town a State of their Accounts, having previoufly fettled with the Treafurer, and examined into the ftate of the Collec‑tors' Bills.

7. That the Town Clerk deliver to the Selectmen, a Lift of the Accounts allowed, or Sums voted to Per‑fons at any Meeting ; and alfo, a Copy of all other Votes refpecting Money matters.

Having

---

* *In this cafe a transfer fhould be made from the Account of Expenditure of Monies voted for the purpofe firft intended, to an Account ftated for the Expenditure of the fame Money, for the purpofe to which it fhall be fo al‑tered, or voted to be appropriated.*

Or, The Account firft mentioned may be balanced by the Account of Mo‑nies unappropriated ; and fo much of the Monies contained in this Account as may be wanted, appropriated for the purpofe, and an Account thereof fta‑ted as abovementioned : and this laft method I prefer, as hereby, you may take more or lefs of the Monies contained in the Account laft mentioned, as may be wanted, and not only fo, but all the appropriation of furplus Monies will appear in one view.

Having thefe REGULATIONS eftablifhed, the Selectmen,† whofe Duty it fhould be to keep the Accounts aforefaid, in a Book provided for the purpofe,
fhould obferve the following

R U L E S.

1. State a general ACCOUNT of MONIES voted by the Town, (*See
No.* I.) and on the debit fide thereof, enter the amount of the fame from
the Account of Monies voted by the Town as made out by the Town
Clerk, which fhould be recorded in the Book aforefaid.

This Account will be balanced by the Account of Monies affeffed.
(No. II.)

2. State an ACCOUNT of MONIES affeffed, (No. II.) and enter on the
debit fide thereof, the amount of the Monies voted, and the amount of
the overlayings in the Collectors' Bills.

This Account will be balanced by the Accounts of the feveral Collectors. (No. III. & IV.)

3. State Accounts with the feveral COLLECTORS (No. III. & IV.) and
charge therein the amount of the Bills committed to them, with the
Additions to the fame.

Thefe Accounts will be balanced by the feveral Accounts following,
viz. 1. The Treafurer's Account (No. XIII.) upon the Collector's
producing his Receipts, when they exhibit their Accounts of the Monies
they may have collected.* 2. The Account of Monies unappropriated
(No. V.) for the amount of the Abatements ; and 3. The Account of
Expenditure of Monies voted for the Treafurer's and Collectors' Commiffions. (No. XI.)§

4. State an ACCOUNT of MONIES belonging to the Town unappropriated, (No. V.) In this Account you are to give credit 1. For the
Sums overlaid in the Tax Bills, with the Additions to the fame. 2.
The furplus of Monies, or Monies voted for any particular purpofe and
not expended. 3. Monies acquired by the Town in other ways than
by Affeffments from the Polls and Eftates of the Inhabitants.

                                                           This

---

† *Perhaps inftead of committing this Bufinefs to Selectmen, it would be
expedient (if a Law were provided for the purpofe) that a* TOWN AC-
COUNTANT *fhould be chofen to perform it.*

* *In many, and perhaps moft Towns, it is cuftomary for the* Treafurer
*to fettle with the Collectors. Upon the prefent Plan, the Bills are to be fet-
tled (and perhaps in other cafes it would be beft they fhould be) by the* Selectmen.

§ *When the Selectmen fettle with the Collectors, they fhould make out a
Certificate to the Treafurer, of the Sums allowed to the refpective Collectors
for their Commiffions for collecting.*

This Account will be balanced, when the Monies are appropriated, by the Accounts of Expenditures thereof for the purposes to which they may be applied. In this Plan I have supposed them to be voted for 1. A Work House (No. XIV.) 2. A Bridge (No. XV.) and 3. To make up what was deficient in the Monies voted for Treasurer's and Collectors' Commissions, (No. XI.)

5. State an ACCOUNT of the EXPENDITURE of each Sum voted for any particular purpose, (No. VI. VII. VIII. IX. X. XI. XIV. XV.) and give credit therein for the amount of such Sums respectively. All these Accounts, except that of Monies voted for the Commissions of the Treasurer and Collectors (No. XI.) will be balanced by the Account of Orders drawn by the Selectmen upon the Treasurer, (No. XII.) if all of it should be made use of ; or, when the whole should not be wanted for the purpose intended, (as in No. VII.) by the Account of Monies unappropriated. (No. V.)

NOTE. The Account of Expenditure of Monies voted for the Treasurer's and Collectors Commissions, will be balanced 1. By their respective Accounts (No. III. IV. & XIII.) and 2. By the Account of Monies unappropriated (No. V.)

6. State an ACCOUNT of ORDERS drawn by the SELECTMEN upon the TREASURER† (No. XII.) and credit therein the several Orders drawn upon the Treasurer, (or rather the Amount of the several Orders taken from a particular Account thereof, which should be entered as they may from time to time be drawn, in a part of the Selectmen's Book allotted for the purpose, or in a Book by itself, if it should be judged more convenient.

This Account will be balanced by the Treasurer,s Account (No. XIII.)*

7. State an Account with the Town TREASURER (No. XIII.) and herein charge him with the Sums paid to him by the several Collectors‡
(No.

---

† *If it should be thought best to keep an Account of each year's Tax by itself, you may state different Accounts of Orders drawn, specifying in each, out of which Tax the Sums therein mentioned are to be paid. Thus "Account of Orders drawn upon the Treasurer for payment of Monies out "of Tax No.——or Tax of such a year."*

* *When occasion may require that Orders be frequently drawn for payment of Monies appropriated to a particular purpose, it would be best to charge them as they may be drawn, to the Persons in whose favour they be drawn. And when the whole shall be drawn for, to balance his or their Accounts by the Account of Orders &c. charg'd in one Sum.*

‡ *The practice in some Towns for the Treasurer to charge himself with the whole Bills, and on a Settlement to charge back what remains unpaid, and afterwards to recharge himself with the remainder, and so on, is improper, and liable to mistakes. By the present Plan, which proposes that the Collectors' Bills should be settled by the Selectmen, this inconvenience will be avoided*

(No. III. & IV.) and any other Sums which he may have received on account of the Town. (See Account No. V.)

This Account will be balanced 1. By the amount of the Selectmen's Orders (No. XII.) and 2. By the Treasurer's Commissions (No. XI.)

N. B. No credit should be given to the Treasurer for any Orders drawn upon him by the Selectmen, until such Orders be produced, and, by a receipt thereon, it appears that they be paid.

OBSERVATIONS.

1. By this Method of keeping the Town Accounts, you may upon inspection, know 1. The amount of all the Monies voted by the Town. 2 The amount of the Sums assessed and committed to the Collectors. 3. What Sums the Collectors have paid into the Treasury, and what remains in their own hands, or in their Bills uncollected. 4. The exact state of the Treasurer's Accounts. Or, generally, whether the Monies voted be assessed and expended ; If expended, whether they be expended for the purposes for which they were raised, or if not expended, whether they be in the Treasurer's or Collectors' hands ; or, whether they remain in the Collectors' Bills uncollected. Also, what Monies belong to the Town unappropriated.

☞ By a due attention to the Appropriations, there will always, (except in cases of absconding or insolvent Persons,) be a sufficiency of Money in the Treasurer's hands or in the Collectors Bills to answer the purposes for which the same was voted to be raised.

2. You will observe that the Accounts herein stated, are all balanced : This will be the case only when the Sums set in the Collectors' Bills are compleatly collected, and the same together with the Monies belonging to the Town wholly expended.

3. You will also observe, that when an Entry is made on one side of any Account, another is invariably made on the opposite side of the Account referred to.

4. That the amount of the two Accounts of Monies voted, and Monies unappropriated, deducting the Abatements charged in the Account last mentioned, are equal to the amount of the several Accounts of Monies expended.

NOTE.

To prevent confusion in mixing the former Transactions of a Town with future ones, it may be well for the Inhabitants of any Town, who should approve of the present Plan to settle with their Treasurer and Collectors, —enter a state of their Accounts in a distinct Book, and compare the amount of the Sums in their hands with their former Votes for raising Money. If on such Settlement, it should be found that there will not be sufficient Sums in their hands to answer the purposes designed, let what may so remain be applied thereto so far as it will go, and let the Town vote as much more Money as will be necessary to make up the deficiency, of the Expenditure of which, an Account may be stated as in other cases. If there should be a surplus, let it be paid when collected into the Treasury, charged to the Treasurer.

rer, and entered on the Credit fide of the Account of Monies unappropriated, to be appropriated whenever the Town fhould fee fit.

FORMS.

I.

Account of Monies voted by a Town.

AT a legal Meeting of the Inhabitants of the Town of P——holden at the——in faid Town, April 4, 1791.

The following Sums were voted to be raifed by an Affeffment upon the Polls and Eftates of the Inhabitants of faid Town according to law, for the purpofes hereafter expreffed, viz.

For the fupport of Schools.	£300
For the fupport of the Poor.	250
For building a School-houfe.	150
For the payment of Accounts allowed by the Town.	200
For Contingencies.	50
For the Treafurer's and Collectors' Commiffions.	50

In the whole   £1000

II.

Affeffors' Certificate of the amount of Monies affeffed &c.

To the Selectmen of the Town of P——+ or,
To the Treafurer of the Town of P——

THE following is a State of the Affeffments made by us upon the Polls and Eftates of the Inhabitants of faid Town, which we have committed to the Collectors thereof to collect, viz.

One Bill dated——committed to Mr. G. W. ⎫ amounting, with the overlayings to ⎭	£625
Another dated——(or of the fame date *as the cafe may be*) committed to Mr. D. N. amounting, with the overlayings, to ⎭	415

Carried over   £1040

The

+ *If the Selectmen fhould be Affeffors, this Certificate will to them be unneceffary. They ought however to enter the fubftance of it in their Book.*

222

		£1040
Brought over		£1040
The Sum voted by the Town		1000

Overlaid	40
Overlaid in the State Tax Bill dated——committed to Mr. G. W.	14
Overlaid in a County Tax Bill dated——committed to Do.	6
Overlaid in a State Tax Bill dated——committed to Mr. D. N.	6
Overlaid in a County Tax Bill dated——committed to Do.	4

P   A. D. 17   W. S.   P. W.   H. M. } Affessors.   £70

III.

223

Account of Orders drawn by the Selectmen on the Town Treasurer.

		*	£.	s. d.
1791.	To pay C. C. towards his falary as a School Master.	6	80	
	To pay J. L. towards his do.	6	70	
	To pay the Overfeers of the Poor.	7	100	
	To pay A. B. the Committee for building the School Houfe.	8	100	
	To pay for charges incurred in taking care of fundry perfons vifited with the Small Pox.	10	30	
	To pay fundry Accounts allowed by the Town.	9	200	
1792.	To pay S. F. School Mafter.	6	50	
	To pay C. C. do.	6	20	
	To pay J. L. do.	6	30	
	To pay S. F. do.	6	50	
	To pay the Overfeers of the Poor.	7	100	
	To pay the Committee for building a School Houfe.	8	50	
	To pay for repairing the Bridge over—— River, partly carried away by the Frefhet.	10	20	
Entered in Account No. XII.			£ 900	
				To

* *The figures in this Column, point to the Accounts ftated in this Book. In the Selectmen's Book fimilar References fhould be made, either in the Number of the Account, or in the Page wherein the fame may be ftated.*

To pay the Committee for building a Work } House.	14	200
To pay sundry Persons for Work on —— } Bridge.*	15	78
To pay sundry other Persons for materials } for said Bridge.*	15	25
To pay the Committee for building a Work } House.	14	100

Entered in Account No. XII.   £403

IV.
Exhibition of a Collector's Bill.

P   17

MR. G. W. one of the Collectors for the said Town of P——exhibited to the Selectmen, according to Law an Account of Monies by him collected, towards his Town Bill, dated —— for raising the Sum of £———and the Overlayings of a State State Tax Bill dated—the said Overlayings being £— and produced Receipts of the Treasurer for the following Sums paid into the Treasury of said Town, viz.

One Receipt dated——	for	£106
One ditto dated——	for	238
One ditto dated——	for	84

In the whole   £428

NOTE. *The Receipts should be left with the Selectmen and filed, and they should give the Collector a Certificate of the Amount, as follows; viz.*

P   17

MR. G. W. exhibited to us sundry Receipts of the Town Treasurer, for Monies paid into the Treasury, towards his Tax Bill dated——for £——viz. [*Here insert the date and sums as above*] amounting in the whole to £428. for so much of which Bill, this shall be a discharge.   S. F. W. S. J. T. Selectmen.

P.   17

MR. G. W. exhibited to the Selectmen a further account of Monies by him collected towards his

---

* *If the Orders be given to individual Persons, they are to be entered accordingly. I enter them here in gross for the sake of brevity.*

his bills dated———[as above mentioned] and produced Treasurers Receipts as follows, viz.

One dated——— for   143
One dated——— for   55
————
£198

It appears by a Certificate from the Affeffors that they have made Additions to faid Bills as follows, viz.

To the Town Tax Bill dated———to the amount of £. 10
To the State Tax Bill dated———to the amount of   5
————
15

They have alfo made Abatements as follows, viz.

From the faid Town Tax Bill dated———   5
From the faid State Tax Bill dated———   3
————
£8   17

M R. D. N. exhibited to the Selectmen an Account of the Monies by him collected, towards his Tax Bills committed to him to collect, viz.

Town Tax Bill dated——— and overlaid in a State Tax Bill dated———
and produced Receipts from the Treasurer, as follows, viz.

One dated———for   196
One dated———for   219
————
£415

It appears by a Certificate from the Affeffors, that they have made Additions to the faid Bills as follows, viz.   To the Town Bill dated——— 7
To the State Bill dated———3
————
£10

They have alfo made Abatements as follows, viz.

From the faid Town Bill dated——— 4
From the faid State Bill dated———2
————
£6

P 17 Further Additions made to D. N's. Bills viz.

To the Town Bill dated——— 3
To the State Tax Bill dated———2
————
£5   Further

S

225

Further Abatements made from said Bills, viz.

From the said Town Bill dated——— 2
From the said State Bill dated ——— 1
——
£3

V.

Selectmen's Certificate to the Treasurer of the Sums allowed to a Collector for his Commissions.

P   17

To E. I. Treasurer of said Town.

Sir,

THIS is to certify to you that the Commissions allowed to Mr. G. W. on a settlement of his Bill for
collecting the Sums therein contained, amount to the
Sum of £———

S. F. W. S. J. T.   Selectmen.

VI.

STATE *of the Town's* FINANCES, *as exhibited to the* TOWN *by the* SELECTMEN.

P   April 1792.

THE Selectmen exhibit to the Town, the following state of its Finances, and Estimate of Monies wanted for the ensuing year, viz.

State of the Collectors' Bills.

G. W's. Bill dated——— 625
Overlaid in a State Tax Bill dated——— 14
Ditto in a County Tax Bill dated——— 6
Additions to said Bills 15
——
£660

Paid by him into the Treasury 626
Abated from his Bills 8
His Commissions 26
Remains in his Bills uncollected 000
——
£660

D. N.

226

D. N's Bill dated——— 415
    Overlaid in a State and County Tax Bill 10
    Sundry Additions made to said Bills 15

          £440

    Paid by him into the Treasury 415
    Sundry Abatements 9
    His Commissions 16
    Remains in his Bill uncollected 00

          £440

State of the Treasury.

Paid to the Treasurer by G. W. Collector 626
Ditto   by D. N. 415
Received by him for Fines 10
    Ditto for a debt due from A. B. 30
    Ditto of the State Treasurer 50
    Ditto from C. D. as a Donation 200

          £1331

The amount of Orders drawn upon
    him by the Selectmen. £900
    His Commissions in part 8   908

Remains in the Treasury £ 423

Amount of Sums remaining in the Treasury, and in the Collectors' Bills, viz.

    In the Treasury 423
    In the Collectors' Bills, viz.
    In G. W's. Bill 000
    In D. N's. Bill 000

        Total £ 423

Estimate.

For the support of Schools £ 400
For the support of the Poor 130
To (make up with what was voted last
    year to) pay the Treasurers' and Col-
    lectors' Commissions. 20
For the Treasurer's and Collectors'
    Commissions the present year. 70   30

    (Carried over) £620

(Brought over)   620
For building a Work-House   300
For building a Bridge over——River,   103
For future appropriations   100

Amounting in the whole to   £1123
Whereupon, Voted, that the Sum of £423 be appropriated for the following purposes, viz.
To make up the deficiency for Commissions £20
For building a Work-House   300
For building a Bridge over——River   103

—— 423

and that the Sum of £700 be raised upon the Polls and Estates of the Inhabitants of said Town, for the other purposes mentioned in said Estimate.*

228

A C C O U N T S.

I.

ACCOUNT *of* MONIES *voted by the* TOWN.   Dr.

	See page		£
1791.	134	To sundry Accounts of the Expenditures of Monies voted Ap. 4. 1791. (S. No. VI, VII, VIII, IX, X, XI, XIV, XV,) the amount whereof is	1000

CONTRA   Cr.

1791.	134	By Account of Monies assessed (No. II.)	1000

II.

ACCOUNT *of* MONIES *Assessed.*   Dr.

1791.	134	To Account of Monies voted by the Town, (No. I.)	1000

(Carried over)

* *If the Estimate be not agreeable to the Inhabitants of the Town, they will before they vote the same, amend it as they see fit.*

			Brought over	1000
	135	To Account of Monies unappropriated (No. V) for the amount of the Sums overlaid in the Collectors' Bills.	70
				1070

CONTRA

Cr.

1791.	135	By G. W. Collector (No. III.)	645
	135	By D. N. Ditto (No. IV.)	425
			1070

III.

G—— W—— Collector,

Dr.

1791.	134	To Account of Monies assessed (No. II.) for the amount of a Tax Bill dated——	625
		To new Account for the Balance	35
			660
	135	To Account of Monies assessed (No. II.) for the Sums overlaid in a State and County Tax Bill, dated——	20
	137	To Account of Monies unappropriated (No. V.)for the Additions to the above Tax Bill	10
	137	To Ditto (No. V.) for Additions to the State Tax Bill, dated——	5
		*	£35

CONTRA.

Cr.

1791.	136	By E. I. Town Treasurer (No. XIII.)	£428
	136	By Ditto (No. XIII.)	198
	137	By Account of Monies unappropriated (No. V) for Abatements in the Town Tax Bill dated——	5
	137	By Ditto (No. V.) for Abatements in the State Tax Bill dated——	3
	138	By Account of Expenditure of Monies voted for Commissions (No. XI.) for his Commissions on the Bills charged on the other side.*	26
			£660
		By Balance of the last Account	£35

* *The Dr. and Cr. of these Accounts for the greater conveniency of printing are here entered on the same side of the Book, but in the Select men's Book they will be entered on opposite pages, according to the usual way of keeping Accounts.*

IV

IV.

D—— N—— *Collector,*   *Dr.*

	134	To Account of Monies affeffed (No. II.) for the amount of a Tax Bill dated ———	415
		To New Account for the Balance.	25
	137		
			£440
	137	To Account of Monies affeffed (No. II.) for the Sums overlaid in a State and County Tax Bill dated. ———	10
	137	To Account of Monies unappropriated (No. V.) for Additions to the Tax Bill dated———	7
	137	To Ditto (No. V.) for Additions made to the State Bill dated———	3
	137	To Ditto (No. V.) for further Additions made to the Town Tax Bill dated———	3
	137	To Ditto (No. V.) for further Additions made to the State Bill dated———	2
			£25

Contra.   *Cr.*

1791.	139	By E. I. Town Treafurer (No. XIII).	415
	137	By Account of Monies unappropriated (No. V.) for Abatements made from the Town Bill dated———	4
	137	By Ditto (No. V. for Abatements made from the State Bill dated———	2
	138	By Ditto (No. V.) for Ditto made from the Town Bill dated———	2
	138	By Ditto (N. V.) for ditto made from the State Bill dated———	2
	139	By Account of Expenditures of Monies voted for Commiffions, (N. XI).	16
			£440
		By Balance of the laft Account	£25

V.

ACCOUNT *of Monies belonging to the* TOWN *unappropriated.*

1791.	137	To G. W. (No. III) for Abatements made from his Bills dated——— and———	8
	137	To D. N. (No. IV) for Ditto made from his Bill dated——— and———	9
	138	To new Account for the Balance, being the Amount of the nett fum belonging to the Town unappropriated.	423
			£440

230

1792.	139	To Account of Expenditure of Monies voted for paying the Treasurer's and Collectors' Commiffions (N. XI).	20
	140	To Account of Expenditure of Monies voted towards building a Work Houfe (N. XIV).	300
	140	To Account of Expenditure of Monies voted by the Town to build a Bridge over—— River. (XV.)	103

£423
CONTRA.
Cr,

1791.	135	By Account of Monies affeffed (No. II) for the amount of the fums overlaid in the Tax Bills committed to G. W. and D. N.	70
	137	By G. W. Colle&or (No. III)for Additions to his Bills dated——and——	15
	137	By D. N. Colle&or (No.IV.)for Additions to his Town Bill dated——	10
	137	By Ditto (No. IV.) for Ditto to his State Bill dated——	5
		By Account of Expenditure of Monies voted for the Poor, (No. VII.) £— being fo much more than was wanted for that purpofe.	50
	139	By E. I. Treafurer, (No. XIII) for Fines by him received.	10
	139	By Ditto (No. XIII) which he received of A. B. for a Debt due to the Town.	30
	139	By Ditto (No. XIII) he received of the State Treafurer to reimburfe what the Town paid for Supplies to the State Poor.	50
	139	By Ditto (No. XIII) for what he received of C. D. as a Donation to the Town.	200

£440

| 1791. | | By Balance of the laft Account. | £423 |

VI.

Expenditure of MONIES *voted by the* TOWN *for the fupport of* SCHOOLS.
Dr.

| 1791 | 135 | To Account of Orders drawn by the Sele&men (No. XII)for fundry Orders drawn in favor of C. D. and other Schoolmafters. | £300 |

CONTRA   Cr.

| 1791. | 134 | By Account of Monies voted by the Town, (No. I) | £300 |

VII

VII.

Expenditure of MONIES *voted by the* TOWN *for the support of the Poor.*   **Dr.**

1791.	135	To Account of Orders drawn by the Select-men (No. XII) for two Orders drawn in favor of the Overseers of the Poor.	200
		To Account of Monies unappropriated (V.)	50
			250

CONTRA.   **Cr.**

| 1791. | 134 | By Account of Monies voted by the Town (I.) | 250 |

VIII.

Expenditure of MONIES *voted by the* TOWN *for building a School House.*   **Dr.**

| 1791. | 135 | To Account of Orders drawn by the Selectmen (XII) for two Orders in favor of the Committee for building a School House. | 150 |

CONTRA.   **Cr.**

| 1791. | 134 | By Account of Monies voted by the Town (No 1) | 150 |

IX.

Expenditure of MONIES *voted by the* TOWN *for payment of Accounts allowed by the* TOWN.*   **Dr.**

| 1791. | 135 | To Account of Orders drawn by the Select-men, (XII.) | 200 |

CONTRA.   **Cr.**

| 1791. | 134 | By Account of Monies voted by the Town, (No. I.) | 200 |

  X.

---

* *If any should desire to know the particular amount of each kind of the ex-pences contained in the Accounts here referred to, the same may be collected and kept in a distinct part of the Selectmen's Book unconnected with the Accounts here stated——Or, to be more particular, an Account of each kind of ex-pence (or rather an Account of the Expenditures of Monies voted to defrey the same) may be stated in like manner with the other Accounts of Expendi-tures, and this Account No. IX. balanced by them. An Account may then be stated with each Person to whom the sums contained in the several Accounts voted by the Town are to be paid, by which personal Accounts the said Account of Expenditures respectively may be balanced, and the said per-sonal Accounts in their turn balanced by the Account of Orders drawn by the Selectmen upon the Treasurer.*

X.

Expenditure of MONIES *voted by the* TOWN *for Contingencies.* Dr.

| 1791 | 135 | To Account of Orders drawn by the Selectmen (XII) for two Orders drawn, viz. one to pay charges incurred on account of the Small Pox, *l.*30 ; the other for repairing——— Bridge *l.*20. | £50 |

CONTRA. Cr.

| 1791 | 134 | By Account of Monies voted by the Town (I.) | £50 |

XI.

Expenditure of MONIES *voted by the* TOWN *to pay the the Commiffions of the Treafurer and Collector.**

1791	138	To G. W. Collector (III)	£26
	138	To D. N. Ditto (IV.)	16
	139	To E. I. Treafurer (XII.)	8
			£50
1792		To E. I. Treafurer (XIII.)	£20

CONTRA. Cr.

1791	134	By Account of Monies voted by the Town (I.)	£50
	139		
1792		By Ditto (I.)	£20

XII.

Account of ORDERS *drawn by the* SELECTMEN *upon the Town Treafurer.* Dr.

| 1791 | 135 | To E. I. Treafurer (XIII.) | £900 |
| 1792 | 136 | To Ditto (XIII) | £403 |

T CONTRA.

---

* If the Accounts of thofe Perfons who may have received Orders on the Treafurer, as charged in the Account of Expenditures, fhould not be fettled by the Selectmen, it is proper the Selectmen fhould certify the amount of fuch Orders to fuch Committee of the Town as may be appointed to examine and adjuft faid Accounts.

233

CONTRA.   Cr.

| 1791 | 135 | By fundry Accounts of Expenditures of Monies voted by the Town, (See No. VI. VII. VIII.IX. X. | £900 |
| 1792 | 140 | By Account of Monies voted by the Town for building a Work-Houfe, (XIV.) and a Bridge over——River, (XV.) | £403 |

XIII.

E. I. TREASURER *of the* TOWN *of* P.*   Dr.

234

1791	136	To G. W. Collector (III.)	£428
	137	To Ditto (III).	198
	138	To D. N. Collector (IV.)	415
	139	To Account of Monies unappropriated (V.) for Monies received by the Treasurer, viz.	
		For Fines, £10	
		For a Debt due from A. B. 30	
		From the State Treasurer, 50	
		From C. D. as a Donation 200	290
1792		To Balance of laft Account	£1331
			£423

CONTRA.   Cr.

1791	135	By Account of Orders drawn by the Selectmen, (XII)	£900
	139	By Account of Expenditure of Monies voted for the Treaſurer's and Collectors' Commiſſions, (XI.)	8
		By new Account for Balance.	423
			£1331
1792	140	By Account of Expenditure of Monies voted for the Treaſurer's and Collectors' Commiſſions, (XI.)	£20
	136	By Account of Orders drawn by the Selectmen, (XII.)	403
			£423

---

* *The Treaſurer's Account ſhould be fettled by the Selectmen, and ſettled annually, previous to the March or April Meeting.*

XIV.

Expenditure of MONIES *voted by the* TOWN *for building*
a WORK-HOUSE. Dr.

1792	136	To Account of Orders drawn by the Select-men (XIII) for two Orders in favor of the Committee for building said House.	£300
		CONTRA. Cr.	
1792	140	By Account of Monies voted by the Town, (I.)	£300

XV.

Expenditure of MONIES *voted by the* TOWN *for building*
a Bridge over——*River.* Dr.

1792	136	To Account of Orders drawn by the Select-men (XII) for sundry Orders drawn for pay-ment of work and materials for said Bridge.	£103
		CONTRA. Cr.	
1792	140	By Account of Monies voted by the Town, (I.)	£103

235

THE

TREASURER's ACCOUNTS

may be kept in the manner following, viz.

1. When he shall have received from the Affessors a Certificate of the Amount of the Sums committed to the several Collectors,§ to record the same (in a Book provided for the purpose) as in Page 134, 135.

2. To State in said Book—1. An Account of the Collectors Bills.— 2. * An Account with each Collector—3. An Account of Monies be-longing to the Town.—4. An Account with the Town.——Then

3. To enter—1. On the Credit side of the " Account of the Collec-tors Bills" the amount of the same, together with any Additions that may be made thereto when the same shall be certified to him by the Af-fessors,; and on the debit side thereof, whatever Abatements may be
made

---

§ *To the form of this Certificate, when given to the Treasurer, as inserted in Page* 134 *next to mentioning the amount of the Collectors Town Bills, re-spectively, it should have been inserted, "* which he is to collect *and pay in to you on or before the day of next."*

* *The use of these Accounts, is to know from time to time, what Monies are accounted for by the respective Collectors, toward the Bills committed to them to collect—for it being incumbent on the Treasurer to issue Warrants against them, when they are remiss in their Duty, it is proper he should know how far they perform the same.*

made and certified as aforesaid, and 2. To charge the several Collectors with the Sums contained in their respective Bills, with the Additions, and to give them credit for the Abatements.

4. To give the Collectors credit, and charge the " Account of Collectors Bills" with their Commissions, when certified to him by the Selectmen.

5. When the Collectors make any payments to him, to enter the same to their credit, and on the debit side of the "Account of Collectors' Bills.——Also to give the Town credit for whatever Sums he shall receive of the Collectors or any other person on Account of the Town, and place the same on the Debit side of the Account of Monies belonging to the Town.——and

6. To charge the Town with the Orders drawn upon him by the Selectmen, and give credit for the same in the " Account of Monies belonging to the Town."

The Accounts thus kept will stand as follows :——

I.

236

		ACCOUNT *of* COLLECTORS BILLS.	Dr.
1791.	137	To G. W. Collector (No. II) for the Amount of the Abatements made from his Bills.	5
	137	To Ditto for Ditto.	3
	136	To Ditto received of him.	428
	137	To Ditto Ditto.	198
	137	To D. N. Collector (No. III) for the Amount of the Abatements made from his Bill.	6
	138	To Ditto for Ditto.	3
	137	To Ditto received of him.	415
	138	To G. W. (No. II.) for his Commissions as per Certificate of the Selectmen dated ——	26
	139	To D. N. (No. III.) for Ditto, per Ditto dated——	16
			£1100

CONTRA.

			Cr.
1791	134	By G. W. Collector (N. II.) for the amount of his Bill dated——	625
	135	By Ditto overlaid in a State Tax Bill committed to him dated——	14
	135	By Ditto overlaid in a County Bill committed to him dated——	6
	134	By D. N. Collector (No. III) for the amount of his Bill dated——	415
	135	By Ditto overlaid in a State Tax Bill committed to him dated——	6
	135	By Ditto overlaid in a County Tax Bill committed to him dated——	4
		Carried over	£1070

Brought over   £1070

	137	By G. W. (No. II) for Additions to his Bill dated ———	10
	137	By Ditto for Ditto	5
	137	By D. N. (No. I) for Additions to his Bill dated—	10
	137	By Ditto for Ditto	5

£1100

11.

G—— W——, *Collector,*   *Dr.*

1791	134	To Account of Collector's Bills, (No. I) for the Amount of a Bill dated———	£625
	135	To Ditto overlaid in a State Bill dated———	14
	135	To Ditto overlaid in a County Tax Bill dated———	6
	137	To Ditto for Additions made to his Bill dated———	10
	137	To Ditto for Ditto to his Bill dated———	5

£660

CONTRA.   *Cr.*

1791	137	By Account of the several Collectors Bills(No. I.) for the amount of the Abatements made from his Bill dated———	£5
	137	By Ditto for Ditto dated———	3
	136	By Ditto received of him	428
	137	By Ditto received of him	198
	138	By Ditto for his Commissions	26

£660

111.

D—— N——, *Collector,*   *Dr.*

1791	134	To Account of Collectors Bills, (No. I) for the Amount of a Bill committed to him to collect dated———	415
	135	To Ditto overlaid in a State Bill dated———	16
	135	To Ditto overlaid in a County Bill, dated———	4
	137	To Ditto for Additions to his Bill dated———	7
	137	To Ditto for Additions to his State Bill dated———	3
	137	To Ditto for further Additions to his Bill dated———	3
	137	To Ditto for Additions made to the State Bill dated———	2

£440

CONTRA

237

CONTRA.   *Cr.*

1791	137	By Account of Collectors' Bills (No. I) for the amount of the Abatements made from his Bill dated———	A
	137	By Ditto for Abatements made from his State Bill dated———	2
	138	By Ditto for further Abatements made from his Town Bill dated———	2
	138	By Ditto for Ditto made to his State Bill dated———	1
	134	By Ditto received of him	415
	138	By Ditto for his Commissions as per Certificate of the Selectmen	16
			2440

IV.

Account of MONIES *belonging to the* TOWN.   *Dr.*

1791	136	To Account with the Town (No. V) for the Sums received of G. W. Collector	428
	137	To Ditto received of Ditto	193
	137	To Ditto received of D. N. Collector.	415
	139	To Ditto for Fines received of———	10
	139	To Ditto received of A. B. for a Debt due from him to the Town	30
	139	To Ditto received of the State Treasurer	50
	139	To Ditto received of C. D. as a Donation to the Town	200
			£1331

CONTRA.   *Cr.*

1791	135	By Account with the Town (No. V.) for the Amount of Orders drawn upon me by the Selectmen	900
	136	By Ditto Ditto	403
	139	By Ditto for my Commissions	28
			£1331

V.

The TOWN *of* P———   *Dr.*

1791	135	To Account of Monies belonging to the Town (No. IV) for the Amount of the Selectmen's Orders drawn upon me	900
	136	To Ditto for Ditto	403
	139	To Ditto for my Commissions	28
			£1331

CONTRA

Contra. Cr.

1791	136	By " Account of Monies belonging to the Town" (IV) for a Sum received of G. W. Collector.	428
	137	By Ditto received of Ditto	198
	137	By Ditto received of D. N. Collector	415
	139	By Ditto received for Fines, of———	10
	139	By Ditto received of A. B. for a Debt due from him to the Town.	30
	139	By Ditto received from the State Treasurer	50
	139	By Ditto received of C. D. as a Donation to the Town.	200
			£1331

239

7

SARJEANT ON FEDERAL CURRENCY, AND CURRENCY EXCHANGE, 1793

THE

Federal Arithmetician,

OR, THE

Science OF *Numbers,*

IMPROVED.

By Thomas Sarjeant.

PHILADELPHIA:

PRINTED AND PUBLISHED BY THOMAS DOBSON.

·1793·

[*Price* ONE DOLLAR]

THE
FEDERAL
ARITHMETICIAN.

PART THE *FOURTH.*

244

The *FEDERAL DENOMINATIONS, or Money of Account—Table—The FEDERAL COINS—Table—Federal Notation—The Fundamental Rules—Their Application—The Valuation of different Denominations of Federal Money—The Valuation of the Impoſt—The Application of the Doctrine of Aliquot Parts to the Federal Denominations.*

PRINCIPLES.

I.

(*ARTICLE* 130.) **B**Y an ordinance of CONGRESS, of July 6, 1785, and another of August 8, 1786, Accounts in the United States are to be kept in *Dollars, Dimes, Cents,* and *Mills.*

II.

(131.) Theſe denominations perfectly correſpond with decimal Fractions, increaſing and decreaſing in a *decuple* proportion.

G 2 III. *The*

III.

(132.)   *The* TABLE *for* ACCOUNTS.

Dollars.	Dimes.	Cents.	Mills.
D.	d.	c.	m.
1	10	100	1000
	1	10	100
		1	10

IV.

(133.) The names of the inferior denominations de-
note their values as compared with the money Unit,
the DOLLAR; thus *dime*, comes from the French word
dixme or *dime*, ten—*cent*, from the Latin word *centum*,
an hundred—and *mill* is part of the Latin word
mille, a thousand.

245

V.

(134.) It was also determined that there shall be
Two Gold; Four *Silver*; and Two Copper, Coins.

G O L D.

The EAGLE, so denominated from its impression of
the *American* Eagle, to contain 246·268 grains of
Fine Gold, of the value of 10 Dollars.

The HALF-EAGLE, to be stamped in the same manner, and to contain 123·134 grains, of the value of
5 dollars.

S I L V E R.

The DOLLAR, or *Money Unit* of the United States
to contain 375·64 grains of Fine Silver.

The HALF-DOLLAR to contain 187·82 grains.

The DOUBLE-DIME, in value, one-fifth of a Dollar,
and to contain 75·123 grains.

The DIME, value, a tenth part of a Dollar, and to
contain 37·564 grains.

C O P P E R.

A CENT, in value, ten Mills, or an hundredth part
of a Dollar, and to weigh 5·76 drams, Averdupoise.

An

An HALF-CENT, value, 5 mills, the two hundredth part of a Dollar in the same proportion.

VI.

(135.)   *The* TABLE *for* COINS.

Eagle.	h.-eag.	dol.	h.-dol.	d. dime.	dime.	cent.	h.-cent.
I	2	10	20	50	100	1000	2000
	I	5	10	25	50	500	1000
		I	2	5	10	100	200
			I	2.5	5	50	100
				I	2	20	40
					I	10	20
						I	2

246

VII.

(136.) It was moreover ordained, that the standard for Gold and Silver shall be eleven parts Fine, and
one Alloy; and that the Mint Price of a pound Troy
weight of uncoined Gold shall be 209 Dollars, 7 Dimes,
and 7 Cents; and of uncoined Silver, 9 Dollars, 9
Dimes, and 2 Cents.

NOTATION.

VIII.

(137.) Sums may be separated as in Compound
Numbers, by dots; or, as in books of accounts, by
lines, thus, Fifteen Dollars, Six Dimes, Four Cents,
and Two Mills, may be written, either

Dolls. d.   c.   m.   Dolls. d. c.   m.
     15 ·· 6 ·· 4 ·· 2; or, 15 | 6 | 4 | 2.

But as dimes, cents, and mills, can each be expressed by a Single Figure only, they are sufficiently
conspicuous without these distinctions, if the value of
the unit or lower figure be expressed or understood.
Thus, 15642, if mills are expressed or understood,
may be considered as standing for mills only; or,
which is the same thing, by separating them by dots

and prefixing the respective denominations, for the sum of 15 dollars, &c. as before.

IX.

(138.) But the method best adapted to practical purposes is the decimal form of expression by a single separation, in which the sum will appear either as a *mixed* or a *pure* decimal. Thus, the same sum may be written

$$15\cdot642 \, Dolls. \quad \text{or,} \quad 15D. \quad 642$$
$$156\cdot42 \, dimes. \quad\quad 156d. \quad 42$$
$$1564\cdot2 \, cents. \quad\quad 1564c. \quad 2$$

The value of the several denominations is here ascertained (as before) by having the value of the unit figure, or that immediately to the left of the decimal point (which indicates all the superior figures) particularly specified.

X.

(139.) The most convenient form of separation for general use, is that where the point is placed to the left of dimes, in which the whole sum assumes the general denomination of dollars.

The 15 to the left of the decimal point may be read 15 dollars, or 1 eagle 5 dollars; and the 624 as decimals of a dollar, the 6 dimes being Primes, the 4 cents, Seconds; and the 2 mills, Thirds.

XI.

(140.) CONGRESS, however, in the Impost, and other Acts, have only made use of the two denominations of *Dollars* and *Cents*; in which the figure in the Tens place of Cents is understood to be Dimes, and the Mills, if any, are expressed in fractions of Cents: Thus the article of *Unwrought Steel*, for instance, is rated at 56 cents, for 5 dimes and 6 cents; *molasses*, at 2½ cents instead of 2 cents and 5 mills; and that of *twine* or *packthread*, at 200 cents, which is only another expression for 2 Dollars.

☞ *The places beyond mills may be denominated as in Decimals, Fourths, Fifths, &c. There are some instances in which it may be necessary to retain them, but in general they may be disregarded.*

REDUCTION

REDUCTION.

PROPOSITION the TWENTY FIFTH.

To REDUCE *a sum of Money from one Denomination to its equivolant in another.*

DIRECTION.

(141.) Remove the decimal point *one* place to the *right hand*, for each denomination, if the Reduction is *descending*, or to the *left*, if *ascending*.

EXAMPLES.

Ex.	Dollars.		Dimes.		Cents.		Mills.
1.	1·000	=	10·00	=	100·0	=	1000
2.	4·908	=	49·08	=	490·8	=	4908
3.	13·600	=	136·00	=	1360·0	=	13600
4.	561·361	=	5613·61	=	56136·1	=	561361

248

PROPOSITION the TWENTY SIXTH.

To Add, Subtract, Multiply, or Divide the FEDE-RAL DENOMINATIONS.

DIRECTION.

(142.) Operations are performed exactly as in Decimals.

ADDITION.

Ex. 5. Mills.	Ex. 6. Cents.	Ex. 7. Dimes.	Ex. 8. Dollars.
341	467·1	961·31	4516·123
72	310·3	41·50	710·345
156	72·1	6·30	67·89
580	5·6	47·61	1234·5
310	831·5	3·59	678·9
700	73·0	900·78	1463·145
2459	1759·6	1961·09	8675·903

Ex. 9.

Ex. 9.	*Ex.* 10.	*Ex.* 11.	*Ex.* 12.
D. d. c. m.	D|d|c|m	Dollars.	Dollars.
3··4··1··3	41|1|5|7	45|301	1051·123
6··1··2··1	31|5|6|	7|62	·136·003
5··3··6··1	7|6|1|7	46|3	100·5
7··8··2··3	3|3|2|	74|121	7007·413
5··1··6··9	9|3|1|4	51|6	90·001
8··3··5··1	18|3|6|1	73|93	6000
36··2··3··8	111|3|2|9	298|872	14385·040

SUBTRACTION.

249

Ex. 13.	*Ex.* 14.	*Ex.* 15.	*Ex.* 16.
Dollars.	Dollars.	Dollars.	Dollars.
4·512	36·071	591·362	7315·1
1·351	24·793	513·706	21·378
3·161	11·278	77·656	7293·722

MULTIPLICATION.

Ex.	Multiplicand. Dollars.	Multiplier.		Product. Dollars.
17.	25·36	×	6	= 152·16
18.	417·2	×	10	= 4172
19.	6·134	×	12	= 73.608
20.	·007	×	36	= ·252
21.	35·008	×	100	= 3500·8
22.	146·3	×	1571	= 229837·3
23.	·798	×	2314	= 1846·572
24.	3·5	×	94631	= 331208·5
25.	4·7361	×	573108	= 27142967·988
26.	9181·53	×	1200000	= 11017836000

DIVISION.

DIVISION.

Ex.	Dividend. Dollars.		Divisor.		Quotient. Dollars.
27.	478	÷	2	=	239
28.	5761·123	÷	7	=	823.017
29.	1431·051	÷	3·4	=	420·89
30.	39165·c06	÷	123	=	318·414
31.	4736·827	÷	4·076	=	1162·1
32.	9604·687	÷	52·04	=	184·56
33.	100000	÷	6781	=	14·747
34.	141·156	÷	6·781	=	20·816
35.	5·361	÷	197·3	=	·02717
36.	1234567	÷	10000	=	123·4567

250

APPLICATION.

37. Add 4D. 3d. 7c. and 9m.—15D. od. and 8c.—7c. and 5m.—1D. and 1 m.—375D. and 57D. 4d. 8c. and 7m. together.   453D. od. 3c. 2m.

38. Add 45·031———37·1———5·21———3·003———·507 and ·004 dollars together.   90·855D.

39. Subtract 5D. 3d. 5c. and 9m. from 10D.
4·641D.

40. What is the difference between 151·397 and 478.9 dollars?   327.503D.

41. Multiply 41D. 9d. by 178.   7458·2D.

42. Multiply 1·49D. by 7, 52, and 365.
By 7=10.43D. by 52=77·48D. by 365=543·85D.

43. Divide 1571D. by 52.   30·211.

44. Divide 130728D. among a certain number of people, and give each 41·9D. How many people will share it?   312.

PROPOSITION

THE
FEDERAL
ARITHMETICIAN.

PART THE *EIGHTH.*

SECTION THE FIRST.
THE INTRODUCTION.

EXCHANGE Defined—Extracts from the ACTS of CONGRESS for establishing the MINT, and regulating the COINS of the UNITED STATES —Substance of the Reports of the COMMITTEES of the SENATE respecting WEIGHTS and MEASURES—Some Particulars of the ACT of CONGRESS for regulating FOREIGN COINS—On the UNIVERSAL MEASURE— Table of the intended FEDERAL COINS— their Value in the American Currencies, and in Foreign Money—their relative Value, as compared with each other.

DEFINITION.

(ARTICLE 257.) EXCHANGE is the Reduction of the *Money, Measures* and *Weights* of one Nation to their equivalent in *another.*

EX-

EXTRACT from the Act of Congress *of April* 2, 1792, *for establishing a* MINT, *and regulating the* COINS *of the* UNITED STATES.

I.

(258.) That there shall be from time to time struck and coined at the said Mint, Coins of Gold, Silver, and Copper of the following Denominations, Values, and Descriptions, *viz..*

II.

252

(259.) EAGLES—each to be of the Value of Ten Dollars or Units, and to contain two hundred and forty-seven grains, and four-eighths of a grain of pure, or two hundred and seventy grains of Standard Gold.

III.

(260.) HALF EAGLES—each to be of the Value of Five Dollars, and to contain one hundred and twenty three grains, and six-eighths of a grain of pure, or one hundred and thirty-five grains of Standard Gold.

IV.

(261) QUARTER EAGLES—each to be of the Value of Two Dollars and an half Dollar, and to contain sixty-one grains and seven-eighths of a grain of pure, or sixty-seven grains and four-eighths of a grain of Standard Gold.

V.

(262.) DOLLARS or UNITS—each to be of the Value of a Spanish milled Dollar as the same is now current, and to contain three hundred and seventy-one grains, and four-sixteenths of a grain of pure, or four hundred and sixteen grains of Standard Silver.

VI.

VI.

(263.) HALF DOLLARS—each to be of half the Value of the Dollar or Unit, and to contain one hundred and eighty-five grains, and ten-sixteenths of a grain of pure, or two hundred and eight grains of Standard Silver.

VII.

(264.) QUARTER DOLLARS—each to be of one fourth of the Dollar or Unit, and to contain ninety-two grains and thirteen-sixteenth parts of a grain of pure, or one hundred and four grains of Standard Silver.

253

VIII.

(265.) DISMES—each to be of the Value of one tenth of a Dollar or Unit, and to contain thirty-seven grains and two-sixteenths of a grain of pure, or forty-one grains and three-fifth parts of a grain of Standard Silver.

IX.

(266.) HALF DISMES—each to be of the Value of one-twentieth of a Dollar, and to contain eighteen grains, and nine-sixteenth parts of a grain of pure, or twenty grains and four-fifth parts of a grain of Standard Silver.

X.

(267.) CENTS—each to be of the Value of one-hundredth part of a Dollar, and to contain eleven pennyweights of Copper.

XI.

(268.) HALF CENTS—each to be of the Value of Half a Cent, and to contain five pennyweights and half a pennyweight of Copper.

XII.

XII.

(269.) On one fide of each of the faid Coins, there fhall be an emblematical Reprefentation of Liberty, with an Infcription of the Word LIBERTY, and the Year of the Coinage ; and upon the Reverfe of each of the Gold and Silver Coins, there fhall be the Figure or Reprefentation of an Eagle, with this Infcription UNITED STATES OF AMERICA, and upon the reverfe of each of the Copper Coins, there fhall be an Infcription which fhall exprefs the Denomination of the Piece, namely Cent, or Half Cent, as the cafe may require.

XIII.

254

(270.) The proportional Value of Gold to Silver, in all Coins, which fhall by Law be current in the United States fhall be as *fifteen* to *one*, according to Quantity in Weight of pure Gold or pure Silver ; that is to fay, every fifteen Pounds Weight of pure Silver fhall be of equal Value in all Payments, with one Pound Weight of pure Gold, and fo in Proportion.

XIV.

(271.) The Standard of all *Gold* Coins of the United States, fhall be eleven parts fine to one part of Alloy ; and accordingly that eleven parts in twelve of the entire Weight of the faid Coins, fhall confift of pure Gold, and the remaining one-twelfth part of of Alloy ; and the faid Alloy fhall be compofed of Silver and Copper, in fuch Proportions not exceeding one-half Silver, as fhall be found convenient ; to be regulated by the Director of the Mint, for the time being, with the approbation of the Prefident of the United States, until further Provifion fhall be made by Law.

XV.

(272.) The Standard for all *Silver* Coins of the United States fhall be one thoufand four hundred and eighty.

eighty-five parts fine, to one hundred and seventy-nine parts Alloy ; and accordingly, that one thousand four hundred and eighty-five parts, in one thousand six hundred and sixty-four parts of the entire Weight of each of the said Coins shall consist of pure Silver, and the remaining one hundred and seventy-nine parts of Alloy, which Alloy shall be wholly of Copper.

XVI.

(273.) The MONEY OF ACCOUNT of the United States, shall be expressed in DOLLARS or UNITS, DISMES or TENTHS, CENTS or HUNDREDTHS, and MILLS or THOUSANDTHS ; a Disme being the tenth part of a Dollar, a Cent the hundredth part of a Dollar, a Mill the Thousandth part of a Dollar; and that all Accounts in the Public Offices, and all Proceedings in the Courts of the United States, shall be kept and had in Conformity to this Regulation.

XVII.

(274.) By an Act of Congress of January 14, 1793, so much of the preceding Act as respects the Weight of Cents and Half Cents (contained in *Art.* 267 and 268) is repealed ; and it is enacted, that a Cent shall weigh 208 grains, and the Half Cent 104 grains of Copper.

The Substance of the REPORT *of the* COMMITTEE *of the* SENATE *of the* UNITED STATES *on the Subject of* WEIGHTS *and* MEASURES, *the Consideration of which was postponed until the next Session of Congress.*

255

Some Particulars of the Act of Congress, of February 9, 1793, for Regulating FOREIGN COINS.

I.

(286.) After the First Day of July next, and during three Years next enfuing, Foreign Gold and Silver Coins fhall pafs as Money, and be a legal Tender, at the following Rates.

II.

(287.) Gold Coins of Great Britain, and Portugal, at the rate of one Federal Dollar for every twenty-feven grains weight.—Thofe of France and Spain, at twenty-feven and two fifths of a grain in weight.

III.

(288.) Spanifh Milled Dollars of 17 pennyweights 7 grains, at a Federal Dollar; and in the fame proportion for parts of Dollars.

Crowns of France, weighing 18 pennyweights 17 grains, at 1 Dollar 1 Dime.—Parts in the fame proportion.

IV.

(289.) An Affay is to be made at the Mint of the the United States on the fecond Monday in February annually, in order to afcertain whether any Coins, newly iffued, are conformable to the above Standard.

SEC.

SECTION THE SECOND.

CONTINENTAL EXCHANGE.

————

*Value of the FEDERAL DOLLAR in each of the States—
the Currencies changed to Federal Money——Federal
Money changed into the Currencies——The Currencies
changed into each other——General Table and Direction——Table of the FEDERAL Value of any Number of Pounds, Shillings, Pence, and Farthings.*

257

————

DEFINITIONS and *PRINCIPLES.*

I.

(ARTICLE 291.) CONTINENTAL EXCHANGE is
the Conversion of the Federal
Dollar, with its inferior Denominations ; and the various Currencies of the United States, into each
other.

II.

(292.) Calculations are formed upon the Value of
the Federal Dollar in each State.

III.

(293.) The Currencies of the States of New-Hamp-
shire, Massachussetts-Bay, Rhode-Island, Connecticut,
Vermont, Virginia, and Kentucky are the same ; and
the Dollar passes for *Six Shillings.*

IV.

(294.) The Currencies of New-York and North-
Carolina

Carolina are the fame ; and the Dollar is *Eight Shil-lings.*

V.

(295.) The Currencies of New-Jerfey, Pennfyl-vania, Delaware, and Maryland, are the fame ; and the Dollar is valued at *Seven Shillings and Sixpence.*

VI.

(296.) The Currencies of South-Carolina and Georgia are the fame ; and the Dollar paffes for only *Four Shillings and Eight-pence.*

258

PROPOSITION the FIFTIETH.

To change the CURRENCIES *to* FEDERAL MONEY.

DIRECTION.

(297) If the Value of a Dollar in the given State, and the given Sum, are not in one, and the fame De-nomination, reduce them fo ; then divide the latter by the former.

EXAMPLES.

Ex. 1.) Reduce £. 15 3, New-England, &c. Cur-rency to Federal Money.

$$\text{Sum} = £.15\ 3 = \frac{303\ Sh.}{6} = 50.5\ Doll.$$
$$Doll.\qquad 6 =$$

2.) Reduce £. 96 15, New-York, &c. Currency to Federal Money.

$$\text{Sum}\qquad £.96\ 15 = \frac{1935\ Sh.}{8} = 241.875\ Doll.$$
$$Doll.\qquad 8 =$$

2.)

3.) Reduce £. 49 4 4¼ New-Jersey, &c. Currency to Federal Money.

Sum £. 49 4 4¼ = 23625 *halfpence.*

$$\frac{}{180} = 131 \cdot 25 \ Doll.$$

Doll.   7 6   =   180

4.) Reduce £. 100 South-Carolina Currency, to Federal Money.

Sum £. 100 0 0 = 24000 *pence.*

$$\frac{}{56} = 428 \cdot 571 \ Doll.$$

Doll.   4 8   =   56

5.) Reduce £. 315 10 6 New-England Currency, to Federal Money.   1051·75 *Doll.*

6.) Reduce £. 522 5 New-York. &c. Currency, to Federal Money.   1305·625 *Doll.*

7.) Reduce £. 2548 9 0¾ New-Jersey, &c. Currency, to Federal Money.   6795·875 *Doll.*

8.) Reduce £. 4928, South-Carolina, &c. Currency to Federal Money.   21120 *Doll.*

——— ———

Proposition the Fifty-First.

To change FEDERAL MONEY *into the* CURRENCIES *of the different States.*

Direction.

(298.) Take the Value of a Dollar in the required Currency, by Aliquot Parts from the number of Dollars.

Examples.

9.) Reduce 50·5 Dollars to New-England, &c. Currency.

$$
\begin{array}{ll}
5 = \frac{1}{4} £. & 50 \cdot 5 \\
1 = \frac{1}{5} & 12 \cdot 625 \\
\hline
6 & 2 \cdot 525 \\
\hline
& 15 \cdot 15 \ \text{or} £. 15 \ 3 \\
\end{array}
$$

10.)

T

10.) Reduce 241·875 Dollars to New-York, &c. Currency.

$$
\begin{array}{rcl}
4 &=& \frac{1}{3} £. \\
4 &=& \frac{1}{3} \\
\hline
8 &&
\end{array}
\qquad
\begin{array}{r}
241·875 \\
\hline
48·375 \\
48·375 \\
\hline
96·75 \text{ or } £.\ 96\ 15
\end{array}
$$

11.) Reduce 131·25 Dollars to Pennsylvania Currency.

s. d.

$$
\begin{array}{rcl}
5 \ 0 &=& \frac{1}{4} £. \\
2 \ 6 &=& \frac{1}{8} \\
\hline
7 \ 6 &&
\end{array}
\qquad
\begin{array}{r}
131·25 \\
\hline
32·8125 \\
16·40625 \\
\hline
49·21875 \text{ or } £.\ 49\ 4\ 4\frac{1}{2}
\end{array}
$$

12.) Reduce 428·571 Dollars to South-Carolina Currency.

s. d.

$$
\begin{array}{rcl}
4 \ 0 &=& \frac{1}{5} £. \\
\ 8 &=& \frac{1}{30} \\
\hline
4 \ 8 &&
\end{array}
\qquad
\begin{array}{r}
428·571 \\
\hline
85·7142 \\
14·2857 \\
\hline
99·9999 \text{ or } £.100
\end{array}
$$

13.) Reduce 1051·75 Dollars to New-England, &c. Currency. £·315 10 6

14.) Reduce 1305·625 Dollars, to New-York, &c. Currency. £·522 5 0

15.) Reduce 6795·875 Dollars, to New-Jersey, &c. Currency. £·2548 9 0½

16:) Reduce 21120 Dollars to South-Carolina, &c. Currency. £·4928

PRO-

260

PROPOSITION the FIFTY-SECOND.

To change a Sum of Money in the Currency of ONE
STATE *to its equivalent Value in that of* ANOTHER.

DIRECTION.

(299.) As the Value of a Dollar in the State in
which the Sum of Money is given, is to its Value in
the State in which it is required; so is the given Sum
to the Sum required.

EXAMPLES.

17.) What is the Value of £.1700 8 6¾ New-
Hampshire Currency in North-Carolina?
6 *Sh* : 8 *Sh.* :: £.1700 8 6¾ : £.2267 4 9.

18.) What is the Value of £.900 10 4, Massachusetts-Bay Currency in Pennsylvania Currency?

6 *Sh.* : 7s. 6d. :: £.9000 10 14 : £.11250 12 11.

19.) Bring £.9004 14 6, Virginia Currency, to
South Carolina Currency.

6 *Sh.* : 4s. 8d. :: £.9004 14 6 :: £.7003 13 6.

20) Find the Value of £.2267 4 9, New-York
Currency, in Rhode-Island.   £.1700 8 6¾

21). Reduce the Sum of £.2000 North-Carolina
Currency to New-Jersey Currency.   £.1875.

22.) Reduce £.1575 19 6, New-York, to South-
Carolina Currency.   £.919 6 4¾

23.) Required the Amount of £.11250 12 11, of
Maryland Money in Connecticut.   £.9000 10 4.

24.) Required the Amount of £. 1875, Delaware
Currency, in New-York.   £.2000.

25.) What is the Worth of £.686 16 3, Pennsylvania Currency, in Georgia?   £.427 7
T 2   26.)

261

26.) Turn £. 7003 13 6, South-Carolina. Currency, to Maſſachuſetts-Bay Currency.

£.9004 14 6.

27.) What is the Value of £.919 6 4½, at Charleſton, (S. C.) in New-York Currency?

£. 1575 19 6.

23.) Turn £. 427 7, Georgia Currency into Pennſylvania Currency.   £.686 16 3.

————

T A B L E III.

262

(300.) *Numbers which taken as* FACTORS *or* DIVISORS *change the* FEDERAL MONEY *and the* CURRENCIES *into each other by a ſingle Operation.*

Explanation. The Tabular Number is found where the Perpendicular and Horizontal Rows meet as in a common Multiplication Table.

Federal DOLLAR.				
0·3	New-England, &c. POUND.			
0·4	1·3	New-York &c. POUND.		
0·375	1·25	0·9375	New-Jerſey, &c. POUND.	
0·23	0·7	0·533	0·62	South-Carolina,&c. POUND.

PRO.

PROPOSITION the FIFTY-THIRD.

To perform the work of any Example in the three last Propositions by the preceding Table.

DIRECTION.

(301.) *Multiply* the given Sum by the Tabular Number, if *descending*; or *divide* it, if *ascending*.

Thus 0·375 will be a *Factor* in reducing Federal Money to Pennsylvania Currency, and a *Divisor* in reducing Pennsylvania Currency to Federal Money.

EXAMPLES.

29). Find the Value of 1000 Federal Dollars in New-England Currency. $1000 \times \cdot 3 = 300 \pounds.$

30.) Find the Value of the same Number in New-York Currency. $1000 \times \cdot 4 = 400 \pounds.$

31.) Find the same Sum in New-Jersey, &c. Currency. $1000 \times \cdot 375 = 375 \pounds.$

32.) Find the same in South-Carolina, &c. Currency. $1000 \times \cdot 2\dot{3} = 233 \cdot \dot{3} \pounds.$

33.) Turn £205 10 New-England, &c. Currency, to North-Carolina. $\pounds 205 \cdot 5 \times 1 \cdot \dot{3} = \pounds. 274,$

34.) Turn £.195 10, New-England, &c. Currency, to New-Jersey, &c.
$$\pounds.195 \cdot 5 \times 1 \cdot 25 = \pounds. 244 \cdot 375$$

35.) Turn £.130 2 6, New-England, &c. Currency, to South-Carolina.
$$\pounds. 130 \cdot 125 \times \dot{7} = \pounds. 101 \cdot 2\dot{0}8\dot{3}.$$

36.) Turn £. 300 New-England, &c. Currency, to Federal Money.
$$\frac{300}{\cdot 3} = 1000 \, Doll.$$

T 3

37.)

37.) Reduce £.274, New-York, &c. Currency,
New-England, &c. Currency.

$$\frac{274}{1\cdot3} = £. \ 205\cdot5$$

(38.) Reduce £.336 16, New-York, &c. Currency, to New-Jersey, &c. Currency.

$$£. \ 336\cdot8 \times \cdot9375 = £.315\cdot$$

39.) Reduce £.166 0 3, New-York, &c. Currency to South-Carolina Currency.

$$£.166.0125 \times \cdot58\overset{.}{3} = £. \ 96\cdot840625.$$

40.) Reduce £.400, New-York, &c. to Federal Money.

$$\frac{400}{\cdot4} = 1000 \ Dol$$

41.) Change £.244 7 6, New-Jersey, &c. Money, to New-England.

$$\frac{244\cdot375}{1\cdot25} = £.195\cdot5$$

42.) Change £.315 15, New-Jersey, &c. Money to New-York.

$$\frac{315\cdot75}{\cdot9375} = £.336$$

43.) Change £.260 8 9, New-Jersey, &c. Currency, to South-Carolina Currency.

$$£.260\cdot4375 \times \cdot6\overset{.}{2} = £. \ 162\cdot0\overline{3}$$

44). Change £.375, New-Jersey, &c. Currency to Federal Money.   1000 *Doll.*

45.) Bring £.101 4 2, South-Carolina, &c. Currency, to New-England, &c. Currency.

$$£.130\cdot125.$$

46.) Bring £.96 16 9¾, South-Carolina Currency to New-York, &c. Currency.   £. 166·0125.

47.) Bring £.162 1, South-Carolina, &c. Currency, to New-Jersey, &c. Currency.   £.260·4375.

48.) Bring £. 233 6 8, South-Carolina Currency to Federal Money.   1000 *Doll.*

S c Al

SECTION THE THIRD.

FOREIGN EXCHANGE.

FOREIGN EXCHANGE defined—Value of the Money of Foreign Nations in FEDERAL Money, as stated by CONGRESS for the Valuation of the Impost—Of the Money of Account of Russia——Portugal——China——Spain——England and Ireland——France——United Netherlands——Hamburg——Bengal——India——Examples—Observations——Table shewing the Value of any Number of Dollars in the Money of various Nations.

265

DEFINITION.

(ARTICLE 302.) FOREIGN EXCHANGE is the Conversion of the Money of different Nations, &c. to Federal Money, agreeable to the Ordinance of Congress for estimating the Impost.

THE

(303.) *The* VALUATION *of* FOREIGN MONEY *in* FEDERAL.

FOREIGN MONEY.		FEDERAL.
Countries, &c.	Denominations.	Dol. d. c.m.
Ruffia -	Rouble -	1· 0 0 0
Portugal -	Mill Ree -	1· 2 4 0
China -	Tale - -	1· 4 8 0
Spain - {	Dollar -	1· 0 0 0
	Real Plate .	0· 1 0 0
Denmark -	Rix Dollar -	1. 0 0 0
Sweden -	Rix Dollar -	1· 0 0 0
England -	Pound Sterling	4. 4 4 0
Ireland -	Pound Irish -	4. 1 0 0
France -	Livre Tournois	1· 8 5 0
United Nether.	Guilder -	0· 3 9 0
Hamburgh -	Marc Banco -	0· 3 3 3
Bengal -	Rupee -	0· 5 5 5
India -	Pagoda -	1· 9 4 0

The INFERIOR DENOMINATIONS *of the* MONEY OF ACCOUNT *of* FOREIGN NATIONS, &c.

(304.) *RUSSIA.*

Accounts are kept in Ruffia in Roubles, Grieveners, and Copecs, decreasing in decuple Proportion, and exactly corresponding with the Dollars, Dimes, and Cents of the United States. They have also the Muscoque, which is the Federal Half Cent.

(305.) *PORTUGAL.*

Mill Ree.	Testoon.	Half Vintin.	Ree.
1	10	100	1000
	1	10	100
		1	10

CHINA.

(306.)   *C H I N A.*

Tale.	Mace.	Cadarene.	Cash.
1	10	100	1000
	1	10	100
		1	10

(307.)   *S P A I N.*

Dollar.	Real Plate.	Marvedie.
1	10	340
	1	34

The Dollar and Real Plate of Spain correspond to the Federal Dollar and Dime.

(308.)   *D E N M A R K.*

267

Rix Dollar.	Mark.	Schilling.
1	6	96
	1	16

(309.)   *S W E D E N.*

Rix Dollar.	Copper Doll.	Runflicks.
1	6	192
	1	32

(310.)   *E N G L A N D,   I R E L A N D, &c*

Accounts are kept in England, Ireland, &c. in Pounds, Shillings, Pence, and Farthings, as in the American Currencies.

(311.)   *F R A N C E.*

Livre Tournois.	Sols.	Deniers.
1	20	240
	1	12

(312.) *U N I T E D   N E T H E R L A N D S.*

Guilder.	Stivers.	Pennings.
1	20	320
	1	16

HAM-

(313.)   *H A M B U R G H.*

Marc Banco.	Schillings Lub.	Phennings.
1	16	192
	1	12

(314)   *B E N G A L.*

Rupee.	Anas.	Pices.
1	16	192
	1	12

(315.)   *I N D I A.*

Pagoda.	Fanams.	Pices.
1	36	288
	1	8

OBSERVATION.

(316.) The Portuguese make use of the Denominations Rees and Mill Rees only ; and they separate them by a Mark resembling the *Theta* of the Greeks; thus 37Θ456 denotes 37 Mill Rees and 456 Rees.

Pounds, Shillings, Pence and Farthings, are distinguished by the (£ .) prefixed to the superior Denomination, the Inferiors following in their regular order: and it is requisite, that the Federal Money should receive some such conspicuous distinction, as well as to contract the usual expression of *Doll. d. c. m.*

The Letter *D* or *d*, whether placed before, after, or as the Decimal Point in the Expression, does not appear sufficiently characteristic of *Dollar*, it being equally used for *Pence, Dimes, Degrees,* &c.

Perhaps the Greek *Delta*, placed as in Portuguese Money, between the superior and inferior Denominations, might answer the Purpose, or at least till
some

some more eligible Method, or character, shall be fixed upon.—Thus 37 Dollars, 4 Dimes, 5 Cents, and 6 Mills would be expressed 37ɗ456 :—and this distinction is adopted in the succeeding parts of this Treatise.

PROPOSITION the FIFTY-FOURTH.

To change FOREIGN *and* FEDERAL MONEY *into each other.*

DIRECTION I.

(317.) To bring Foreign Money to Federal, *multiply* the given Sum, decimally expressed, by the Federal Value in the preceding Table, *Art.* 303.

DIRECTION II.

(318.) To bring Federal Money to Foreign, *divide* the given Sum by the same Federal Value.

EXAMPLES.

RUSSIA.

Ex. 49.) Express 1157 Roubles, 6 Grieveners, and 8 Copecs of Russia in Federal Money.

Doll. 1157ɗ68.

50.) Express 4678ɗ365 Dollars in Russian Money.

4678 Roubles, 3 Griev. 6 Cop. 1 Moscoque.

PORTUGAL.

51.) What is the Federal Value of an Invoice from Oporto, of 2560 Mill Rees?

2560 × 1·24 (Tab. Num. Art. 303) = 3174ɗ3.

52.) Change 3174ɗ4 Dollars to Portuguese Money.

$$\frac{3174\cdot4}{1\cdot24} = 2560 \text{ Mill Rees.}$$

53.)

53.) How many Federal Dollars are in 35670425?

$$3567 \cdot 425 \times 1 \cdot 24 = 44238607.$$

54.) Turn 44238607 to Mill Rees.

$$\frac{4423 \cdot 607}{1 \cdot 24} = 35670425.$$

CHINA.

55.) To what Sum in Federal Money will 1000 Chinese Tales amount?

$$1000 \times 1 \cdot 48 \text{ (Tab. Num.)} = 1480 \text{ } doll.$$

56.) How many Chinese Tales are in 1480 Dollars?

$$\frac{1480}{1 \cdot 48} = 1000 \text{ Tales.}$$

57.) Goods bought at China to the Value of 3278 Tales, 4 Mace, 6 Cadarenes, and 3 Cash—What is their Amount in Federal Money?

$$3278 \cdot 463 \times 1 \cdot 48 = 4852812524.$$

58.) Turn 4852812524 Federal Dollars into Chinese Money. $\quad \dfrac{4852 \cdot 12524}{1 \cdot 48} = 3278 \cdot 463 \text{ Tales.}$

☞ *No Examples need be given respecting* Spain, Denmark, *and* Sweden, *as the Money Unit is the same.—The Comparison of the Inferior Denominations is easily attained from the* General Table, *facing the* Title.

ENGLAND.

59.) What is the Value of £. 1000 Sterling in the Federal Money? $\quad 1000 \times 4 \cdot 44 = 4440 \text{ } doll.$

60.) Find the Value of £. 326 15 9, Sterling, in Federal Money.

$$£. 326 \ 15 \ 9 \text{ or } 326 \cdot 7855 \times 4 \cdot 44 = 1450 \delta 9365.$$

61.) An Invoice of Goods from London, amounts to £. 7572 5.—Required the Sum in Federal Money?

$$7572 \cdot 25 \times 4 \cdot 44 = 33620 \delta 79.$$

62.)

62.) To what Sum Sterling Money will 4440 Dollars amount?

$$\frac{4440}{4\cdot44} = 1000 \pounds.$$

63.) Expreſs 1450ſ9365 in Sterling Money.

$$\frac{1450\cdot9365}{4\cdot44} = 326\cdot7875 \text{ or } \pounds.326\ 15\ 9.$$

64.) What Sterling Sum is equal to 33620ſ79?

$$\frac{33620\cdot79}{4\cdot44} = 7572\cdot25 \text{ or } \pounds.7572\ 5.$$

IRELAND.

65.) What is the Value of £. 1000 Iriſh, in Federal Money? $1000 \times 4\cdot1 = 4100$ doll.

271

66.) Find the Value of £. 326 15 9, Iriſh, in Federal Money.

$$326\cdot7875 \times 4\cdot1 = 1339ſ82875.$$

67.) An Invoice of Goods from Dublin amounts to £.7572 5:—Required the Sum in Federal Currency?

$$7572\cdot25 \times 4\cdot1 = 31046ſ225.$$

68.) To what ſum in Iriſh Money, will 4100 Federal Dollars amount? $\dfrac{4100}{4\cdot1} = 1000\ \pounds.$

69.) Expreſs 1339ſ82875 Dollars, in Iriſh Money.

$$\frac{1339\cdot82875}{4\cdot1} = 326\cdot7875\ \pounds.$$

70.) What ſum Iriſh, is equal to 31046ſ225?

$$\frac{31046\cdot225}{4\cdot1} = 7572\cdot25\ \pounds.$$

FRANCE.

71.) What ſum in Federal Money is equal to 1000 Livres Tournois? $1000 \times \cdot185 = 185$ doll.

II   73.)

72.) Turn an Invoice from Bourdeaux, of 5762 Liv. 15 Sol. 6 Den. to Federal Money?

$$5762 \cdot 775 \times \cdot 185 = 1066 \,\$\, 113375.$$

73.) How many Livres Tournois are equal to 185 Federal Dollars?

$$\frac{185}{\cdot 185} = 1000 \text{ Livres.}$$

74.) Turn 1066·113375 Dollars to Livres Tournois.

$$\frac{1066 \cdot 113375}{\cdot 185} = 5762 \cdot 775 \text{ Liv.}$$

UNITED NETHERLANDS.

272

75.) What is the Federal Value of an Invoice from Amsterdam of 3750 Guilders?

$$3750 \times \cdot 39 = 1462 \,\$\, 5.$$

76.) Turn 1462·5 Federal Dollars to Guilders.

$$\frac{1462 \cdot 5}{\cdot 39} = 3750$$

77.) Goods imported from Amsterdam, to the Amount of 97861 Guilders, 4 Stivers, and 8 Pennings—Their Federal Value is required?

$$97861 \cdot 2025 \times \cdot 39 = 38165 \,\$\, 869.$$

78.) Turn 38165·869 Federal Dollars to Guilders.

$$\frac{38165 \cdot 869}{\cdot 39} = 97861 \cdot 2025 \text{ nearly.}$$

HAMBURGH.

79.) What is the Value of 10000 Marcs Banco in the United States?

$$10000 \times \cdot \dot{3}\dot{3}\dot{3} = 3333 \,\$\, 333.$$

80.) What is 3333 $\$$ 333 Federal Money worth at Hamburgh?

$$\frac{3333 \cdot 333}{\cdot 333} = 10000 \text{ Marcs.}$$

81.)

81.) Turn 235 Marcs, 8 Schillings-Lub, to Federal Money.

$$1 \text{ Dol.} = 3 \text{ Marcs, so } \frac{235 \cdot 5}{3} = 78 \text{ } \text{\textdollar} 5.$$

82.) Change 78 \textdollar 5 to Marcs Banco of Hamburgh.
78.5 × 3 = 235·5 or 235 *Marcs, 8 Schillings.*

B E N G A L.

83.) What is the Federal Value of 1690 Rupees of Bengal? 1690 × ·555 = 937 \textdollar 95.

84.) How many Rupees are there in 937 \textdollar 95 Federal Money?

$$\frac{937 \cdot 95}{\cdot 555} = 1690 \text{ Rupees.}$$

85.) Bring 7000 Rupees, 12 Anas, to Dollars.
7000·75 × ·555 = 3885·41625.

86.) Reduce 3885 \textdollar 41625 Federal Money to Bengal Money.

$$\frac{3885 \cdot 41625}{\cdot 555} = 7000 \cdot 75 \text{ or } 7000 \text{ Rup. 12 An.}$$

I N D I A.

87.) What is the Value of 1792 Pagodas of India in Federal Money?

1792 × 1·94 = 3476 \textdollar 48.

88.) Turn 3476 \textdollar 48, to India Money.

$$\frac{3476 \cdot 48}{1 \cdot 94} = 1792 \text{ Pagodas.}$$

89.) Find the Value of 375 Pagodas, 18 Fanams, in the United States.

375·5 × 1·94 = 728 \textdollar 47.

90.) Turn 728 \textdollar 47 to India Money.

$$\frac{728 \cdot 47}{1 \cdot 94} = 375 \cdot 5 \text{ or } 375 \text{ Pagodas, 18 Fan.}$$

U 2

Ob.

OBSERVATIONS.

I.

319.) THE CONGRESS have repealed that Part of the Act which fixes the Value of the Rix Dollar of Denmark, the Rouble of Russia, and the Livre of France.

II.

(320.) The Pound Sterling is valued at 4·44 Dollars, which gives 4*s*. 6*d*. ·05̇4̇, or 4*s*. 6*d*. $\frac{4}{11}$, for the Value of the Federal Dollar in Sterling Money.— At this rate, £.1000 amounts to only 4440 Dollars, but at 4*s*. 6*d* to 4444·44̇4̇ Dollars. Had 4·4 Federal Dollars been the Pound Sterling, a Dollar would have been 4*s*. 6*d*. exactly, and would have been also of the same Value with the Pezzo of Genoa, and the Piaftre of Leghorn.

III.

(321.) The Portuguese neglect the advantage of the Decuple Subdivision of their Mill-Ree, by passing over the intermediate denominations of Teftoon, and half Vintin.—It may, perhaps, be more familiar in Conversation to say, (for inftance), 8 Mill-Rees and 5 Rees; but the Sum ought always to be expreffed 8·005, the place of Rees when compared with the Mill-Ree, as an Unit, is that of Thirds, and not Primes.

IV.

(322.) In the same manner, the Congrefs have diminished the Merit of their own valuable Improvement, by the Omiffion of Dimes and Mills, as obferved in *Art.* 140. Thus, 2½ Cents ought always to be written ·025, for Arithmetical Calculations; in the fame manner as in England, a Guinea is always written £. 1 1.—It can be no Improvement to turn the convenient

venient and elegant decimal Form, into a Fractional, or any other, expreſſion.   We ſeem to adopt the decuple Subdiviſion with Reluctance, and to be inſenſible of its Simplicity, its Beauties and its Advantages.

SECTION the FOURTH.

The PAR of EXCHANGE.

EXCHANGE AT PAR—Definitions and Principles— The Intrinſic Value of FOREIGN MONEY in STERLING—Calculations of EXCHANGE at PAR between LONDON and other NATIONS—Obſervations

275

DEFINITIONS AND PRINCIPLES.

I.

(*ARTICLE* 323.) THE PAR of EXCHANGE, (or *Par pro Pari*) denotes an Exchange at Equality ; that is, according to the *Intrinſic* Value of the Species to be exchanged.—So Public Securities, Bills of Exchange, &c. are ſaid to be at PAR, when they are worth their own nominal or ſpecific Value.

II.

(324.) If the Trade between two Nations is equal, that is, if their Purchaſes from each other exactly balance, a merchant who delivers Caſh or Bills in

U 3   the

the one, will receive their *Intrinfic* Value in the other, and the Exchange will be at PAR.

III.

(325.) The *Intrinfic* Value of the Coins of the various Commercial Nations, as compared with each other, is to be obtained from Affays, and other Attempts to afcertain their Value, publifhed by different Authors on the Subject; of which *Sir Ifaac Newton's* Table is generally efteemed the moft extensive and authentic, and has been the Foundation of Calculations on the Subject.

276

IV.

(326.) Soon after the Affay of Sir *Ifaac Newton,* Mr. *Caftaign,* one of the moft eminent Exchange Brokers of his time, publifhed a Table of the Par of Exchange between London and the principal trading Places in Europe. He has been fucceeded by a confiderable Number of Commercial Writers, who differ from each other only in fome fmall particulars; arifing principally from the inequality or difproportion of fome of fome of the principal Coins, and their Aggregates in the Intrinfic Values thereof.

V.

(327.) The following ftatement, is taken for the moft part, from Mr. *Thomas's* BRITISH NEGOCIATOR; a Work in high eftimation in the Mercantile World, and the moft accurate for practical Purpofes; as the Author, though favoured with original Accounts from many of the Principal Places of Exchange, feldom depended on a fingle Authority, however celebrated.

The

(328.) *The* INTRINSIC STERLING VALUE *of the* COINS *or* MONEY OF ACCOUNT *of different Commercial Places.*

Countries, &c.	Denominations.	Sterling Value.			
		£.	s.	d.	
Ireland,	Pound Irish		18	5·5384	=0·9230769
N. England, &c.	Pound Cur.		15	0	=0·75
New-York, &c.	Pound Cur.		11	3	=0·5625
N. Jersey, &c.	Pound Cur.		12	0	=0·6
S. Carolina, &c.	Pound Cur.		19	3·428	=0·9642857
Amsterdam &	Pound Flemish		10	9·6	=0·54
Rotterdam	Guilder		1	9·6	=0·09
Antwerp and Hamburgh	Pound Flemish		11	3	=0·5625
Hamburg	Marc Banco		1	6	=0·075
Sweden Denmark and Norway	Rix Dollar		4	6	=0·225
Russia -	Rouble		4	6	=0·225
Genoa - -	Pezzo		4	6	=0·225
Leghorn,	Piastre		4	6	=0·225
Spain -	Dollar		4	6	=0·225
	Piastre		3	7·2	=0·18
France -	Crown, or 3 Livres Tourn		2	7.0298	=0·12929
Portugal	Mill-Ree		5	7·5	=0·28125
Venice	Ducat Banco		4	2·22	=0·20925

PROPOSITION the FIFTY-FIFTH.

To calculate EXCHANGE AT PAR, *between* LONDON *and other* NATIONS.

DIRECTION.

(329.) Apply the Rule of Proportion Inverse.

Ex-

EXAMPLES.

Ex. 91.) Change £. 157 12 6, Iriſh Money to Sterling.

$$£. St. \quad s. \quad d. \qquad\qquad £. \quad s. \quad d. \qquad £. \quad s.$$
$$1 : 18\ 5\cdot5384 \ :: \ 157\ 12\ 6 \ : \ 145\ 10$$

or $\dfrac{157\ 12\ 6 \times 12}{13} = £.145\ 10.$

92.) Change £. 145 10. Sterling to Iriſh Money.

$$Sh. \quad d. \qquad £. \qquad £. \quad s. \qquad £. \quad s. \quad d.$$
$$18\ 5\cdot5384 \ : \ 1 \ :: \ 145\ 10 \ : \ 157\ 12\ 6$$

or $\dfrac{145\cdot5 \times 13}{12} = £.157\cdot625.$

93.) Reduce £. 500, New-England, &c. Currency to Sterling.

$$£. \qquad Sh. \qquad £. \qquad £.$$
$$1 \ : \ 15 \ :: \ 500 \ : \ 370.$$

94.) Reduce £.370 Sterling, to New-England, &c. Currency.

$$Sh. \qquad Sh \qquad £. \qquad £.$$
$$15 \ : \ 20 \ :: \ 373 \ : \ 500.$$

95.) Turn £. 750, New-York, &c. Currency, to Sterling.

$$£. \qquad Sh. \quad d. \qquad £. \qquad £. \quad s. \quad d.$$
$$1 \ : \ 11\ 3 \ :: \ 750 \ : \ 421\ 17\ 6.$$

96.) Turn £.421 17 6 Sterling, to New-York Currency.

$$Sh. \quad d. \qquad £. \qquad £. \quad s. \quad d. \qquad £.$$
$$11\ 3 \ : \ 1 \ :: \ 421\ 17\ 6 \ : \ 750.$$

97.) Bring £. 3147 15 10, New-Jerſey, &c. Currency to Sterling.

$$£. \qquad Sh. \qquad £. \quad s. \quad d. \qquad £. \quad d. \quad d.$$
$$1 \ : \ 12 \ :: \ 3147\ 15\ 10 \ : \ 1888\ 13\ 6.$$

98.)

278

98). Bring £.1888 13 6, Sterling, to New-Jersey, &c. Currency.

Sh.   £.   £. s. d.   £. s. d.
12 : 1 :: 1888 13 6 : 3147 15 10.

99.) Bring £. 1000, South-Carolina, &c. Currency, to Sterling.

£.   Sh. d.   £.   £. s. d.
1 : 19 3·428 :: 1000 : 964 5 8¼ ⅞.

100.) Bring £.964 5 8¼ ⅞ Sterling, to South-Carolina Currency.

Sh. d.   £.   £. s. d.   £.
19 3·428 : 1 :: 964 5 8¼ ⅞ : 1000.

279

101.) What is the Sterling Value of £.1562 10 Flemish, at Amsterdam?

£.   Sh. d.   £. d.   £. s.
1 : 10 9·6 :: 1562 10 : 843 15.

102.) What is the Value at Amsterdam in Pounds Flemish of £.843 15 Sterling?

Sh. d.   £.   £. s.   £. s.
10 9·6 : 1 :: 843 15 : 1562 10.

103.) Reduce 7560 Guilders of Amsterdam to Sterling.

Guil. Sh. d.   Guil.   £. s.
1 : 1 9·6 :: 7560 : 680 8

104.) Reduce £. 680 8 Sterling, to Guilders of Amsterdam.

Sh. d.   Guil.   £. d.   Guil.
1 9·6 : 1 :: 680 8 : 7560.

105.) Find the Value of £.1000 Flemish of Antwerp in Sterling.

£. F.   Sh. d.   £. F.   £. s.
1 : 11 3 :. 1000 : 562 10.

106.) Find the Value of £. 562 10 Sterling, at Antwerp. Sh. d.   £. F.   £. s.   £. F.
11 3 : 1 :: 562 10 : 1000.

107.)

107.) Turn 5780 Marcs Banco of Hamburg to Sterling.

$$M.B. \quad s. \quad d. \qquad M.B. \qquad \text{£.} \quad s.$$
$$1 \quad : \quad 1 \quad 6 \quad :: \quad 5780 \quad : \quad 433 \quad 10.$$

108.) Turn £.433 10 Sterling to Marcs Banco of Hamburgh.

$$Sh. \quad d. \quad M.B. \qquad \text{£.} \quad s. \qquad M.B.$$
$$1 \quad 6 \quad : \quad 1 \quad :: \quad 433 \quad 10 \quad : \quad 5780.$$

109.) To what Sum Sterling 4760 Rix Dollars, Roubles, &c. amount?

$$R.D. \quad Sh. \, d. \qquad R.D. \qquad \text{£.}$$
$$1 \quad : \quad 4 \, 6 \quad :: \quad 4760 \quad : \quad 1071.$$

110.) To what Number of Rix Dollars, &c. will £.1071 Sterling amount?

$$s. \, d. \quad R.D. \qquad \text{£.} \qquad R.D.$$
$$4 \, 6 \quad : \quad 1 \quad :: \quad 1071 \quad : \quad 4760.$$

111.) Find the Sterling Value of 9400 Spanish Piastres.

$$P. \quad Sh. \, d. \qquad P. \qquad \text{£.}$$
$$1 \quad : \quad 3 \, 7 \cdot 2 \quad :: \quad 9400 \quad : \quad 1692.$$

112.) Find the Number of Spanish Piastres in £. 1692 Sterling.

$$Sh. \, d. \qquad P. \qquad \text{£.} \qquad Piaſt.$$
$$3 \, 7 \cdot 2 \quad : \quad 1 \quad :: \quad 1692 \quad : \quad 9400.$$

113.) Bring 12250 Crowns, or 36750 Livres Tournois, of France, to Sterling.

$$Cr. \quad Sh. \, d. \qquad Cr. \qquad \text{£.} \quad s. \quad d.$$
$$1 \quad : \quad 2 \, 7 \cdot 029 \quad :: \quad 12250 \quad : \quad 1583 \quad 15 \quad 5\tfrac{1}{7}.$$

114.) Bring £.1583 15 5⅐ Sterling to French Livres.

$$Sh. \, d. \qquad Liv. \qquad \text{£.} \quad s. \quad d. \qquad Liv.$$
$$2 \, 7 \cdot 029 \quad : \quad 3 \quad :: \quad 1583 \quad 15 \quad 5\tfrac{1}{7} \quad : \quad 36750.$$

115.) Bring 15780 Mill Rees to Sterling.

$$M.R. \quad s. \quad d. \qquad M.R. \qquad \text{£.} \quad s. \quad d.$$
$$1 \quad : \quad 5 \, 7 \cdot 5 \quad :: \quad 15780 \quad : \quad 4438 \quad 2 \quad 6.$$

116.)

116.) Bring £.4438 2 6 Sterling, to Mill Rees.

Sh. d.   M. R.   £.   s. d.   M. R.
5 7·5 :   1   :: 4438 2 6 : 15780.

117.) Reduce 17560 Ducats Banco of Venice, to Sterling.

D. B. Sh. d.   D. B.   £.   s.   d.
  1   : 4 2·22 :: 17560 ; 3674 8 7·2.

118.) Reduce £. 3674 8 7·2 Sterling, to Ducats Banco of Venice.

Sh. d.   D. B.   £.   s. d.   D. B.
4 2·22 :   1   :: 3674 8 7·2 : 17560.

_____

Observation.

(330.) The PAR of EXCHANGE between any two other Places, or between those and a third, &c. may be found by two or more Statings of the Rule of Three, or the Rule of Arbitration of Exchanges, taught in most Books on the Subject. Or, might be easily reduced to the Form of the Tables in *Art*. 300, &c. &c.; but as Exchange is seldom at Par, and Sterling Money is generally the Medium of our Exchanges, it was not thought necessary farther to pursue the Subject.

SEC-

SECTION THE FIFTH.

THE COURSE OF EXCHANGE.

The COURSE OF EXCHANGE—Definitions—Observations—Inferences—Calculations of the COURSE of EXCHANGE——Examples.

282

DEFINITIONS AND PRINCIPLES.

I.

(*ARTICLE* 331.) The COURSE of EXCHANGE is that *uncertain* Quantity *above* or *below* PAR, of the Money of one Nation which is given in Exchange for a *certain* Sum of another.

II.

(332.) When one Nation supplies another with more Commodities, &c. than it takes in return, there will be a BALANCE of TRADE against the latter Nation; and in order to make Payment the Demand for Cash, or Bills of Exchange of the former Nation will, become greater in the latter, than the Quantity to supply the Demand, and then they will rise *above Par,* or their specific Value; while the Cash, Bills, &c. of the latter Nation will fail *below it,* and this Rise or Fall, constitutes the COURSE of EXCHANGE.

III.

(333.) The *Course of Exchange* continually fluctuates, and can only be ascertained by an extensive, Mercantile Correspondence;—It is affected principally

I

pally

pally by the Balance of Trade, but sometimes by other Circumstances; as an extraordinary or unexpected Surplus or Deficiency of Cash.

IV.

(334.) All Arts, Professions, and Mechanical Trades on Account of either brevity or secrecy, adopt variety of phrases peculiar to themselves, which are, for the most Part, unintelligible without Explanation.—Thus, among the Merchants of Philadelphia, a Bill of Exchange on London is said (for Instance) to sell for *Seventy*, meaning thereby that £.100 Sterling sells for £.170 Pennsylvania Currency; and they are also said to be *up* to *Seventy-two*, or *down* to *Sixty-five* as expressive of their Relation to £.166 13 4, the *Par of Exchange*.

283

INFERENCES.

I.

(335.) That a favourable *Balance of Trade* naturally "imports Specie, and renders Money at Home more valuable Abroad; whereas, on the other Hand, if the Balance is against a Nation, their Specie is exported, and becomes thereby less valued."

II.

(336.) " That the Nation which is indebted has the Disadvantage in Commerce and Money Transactions; and that the one which has the Balance in its Favour, hath in every Respect the Advantage."

III.

(337.) " That the regular *Course of Exchange* may be considered as an HERALD, who publicly proclaims the State of Commerce and Money Negociations betwixt the two Countries, and which is indebted to the other."

X   PRO-

PROPOSITION the FIFTY-SIXTH.

To find the Value of a Sum of Money of one Country in that of another, the Course of Exchange being given.

DIRECTION.

(338.) Apply the Rule of Proportion.

EXAMPLES.

119.) How may Federal Dollars muſt be given for a Bill on London, of £.1000 Sterling?—Exchange at 75¼, that is, at £.175 10 Pennſylvania Currency for £.100 Sterling.

Ster.	Pen. Cur.		Ster.		Pen. Cur.
100	:	175·5	:: 1000	:	1755.

Then (by Art. 301.) $\dfrac{1755}{0·375} = 4680\ Doll.$

120.) What Number of Dollars muſt be given for the ſame Bill, if the Exchange is down to 160?

Ster.		Pen. Cur.	Ster.		Pen. Cur.
100	:	160	: 1000	:	1600.

Then $\dfrac{1600}{0·375} = 4266\ \textit{s}\ 666$

121.) A Merchant at Philadelphia remits £.357 10 Iriſh Money to Dublin.—How many Federal Dollars muſt be given for the Bill of Exchange at 56?

Iriſh.		Pen. Cur.	Iriſh.		Pen. Cur.
100	:	156	:: 357·5	:	557·7.

Then $\dfrac{557·7}{0·375} = 1487\ \textit{s}\ 2$

122.) I purchaſe a Bill of Exchange on Amſterdam for 6000 Guilders.—To how many Federal Dollars does

does it amount if the Exchange is at 2*s*. 8*d*. Pennsylvania Currency, and also if at 35½ Cents a Guilder?

By Pennsylvania Currency.

Guild. *s. d.*   Guild. £.
1 : 2 8 Pen. Cur. :: 6000 : 800 Pen. Cur.

Then $\dfrac{800}{0\cdot375} = 2133\,s333$

By Federal Money.

Guil. Doll. Guil. Doll.
1 : 0·355 :: 6000 : 2131.

☞ *Examples respecting the other Currencies are superfluous, as those relating to Pennsylvania sufficiently explain the Method of Operation, and any Currency may be changed into another by Art. 299.*

The following Examples of Sterling Money with other European Nations are taken from THOMAS'S BRITISH NEGOCIATOR.

123.) What will 2474 Guilders, being a Bill of Exchange from Amsterdam, Exchange at 33*s*. 4½*d*. Flemish, for one Pound Sterling, amounts to in English Money?   £.247 1 9¾.

124.) Suppose a Merchant in England draws on his Correspondent at Amsterdam for, or remits to him £.255 17 6—Exchange at 35*s*. 8*d*. Flemish, for 1 Pound Sterling, how many Guilders will it amount to?   2844 Guild. 17 Stiv. 4 Pen.

125.) How much English Money, will a Bill of 3460 Marcs of Hamburgh amount to, at 7' Marcs the Pound Flemish, and 35*s*. 10*d*. Flemish for 1 Pound Sterling?   *Ans.* £. 257 9 9.

126.) Suppose a Merchant in France sends over Goods to England, to the Value of 5427 Liv. 12 Sols. 9 Den. Exchange at 32'*d*. Sterling for one French Crown or Ecu; how much English Money will the same Amount to?   *Ans.* £.245 18 9¼.

X 2   127.)

127.) How much French Money will £. 365 15 6 Sterling amount to, Exchange at 39¾ d. for a French Crown? *Anf.* 8010 Liv. 17 Sol. 9 Den.

128.) A Merchant of Oporto fends over to England a Cargo of Wine to the Value of 1654 Mill Rees and 220 Rees, Exchange at 5s. 3¼ d. a Mill Ree: how much does the fame amount to in Sterling Money? *Anf.* £. 436 16 10¼ d.

129.) Suppofe a Merchant of Cadiz fends over Goods to Hull to the Value of 4326 Piaftres, 6 Rials old Plate: Exchange at 38¾ a Piaftre; how much will the fame amount to in Sterling Money? *Anf.* £. 691 16 7.

286

130.) How much will 5640 Ducats, 9 Grofs Banco of Venice, amount to in Sterling Money: Exchange at 53¾ d. a Ducat? *Anf.* £. 1254 7 11.

131.) How much will a Bill of Parcels from Genoa, of 3390 Pezzos, 16 Soldi, amounts to; Exchange at 51¾ d. Sterling a Pezzo? *Anf.* £ 733 18 1¼.

132.) How much will a Bill of Parcels for Goods bought in Saxony, of 5676 Rix Dollars, and 18 Grofs, Exchange at 52¼ d. a Rix Dollar, amount to in Sterling Money? *Anf.* £. 1244 14 10¼.

133.) How much will a Quantity of Iron from Sweden, to the Value of 26462 Copper Dollars, amount to in Sterling Money, Exchange at 41¼ Dollars for a Pound? *Anf.* £. 899 19 9.

134.) How much will a Quantity of Corn fent from Dantzic, to the Value of 14726 Florins, and 16 Grofhen, amount to in Sterling Money, Exchange at 20¼ Florins for a Pound Sterling? *Anf.* £. 727 4 8¼.

135.) How much will a Parcel of Hemp, to the Value of 347½ Roubles, and 70 Copecks, amount to in England, Exchange at 52¼ d. a Rouble? [303] *Anf.* £. 762 2 4½.

136.)

136.) If a London Merchant remits to Dublin £. 1758 Sterling, Exchange at 9½ *per Cent*. How much will the same amount to there?

Ans. £.1927 4 1¾.

137.) How much will £. 1250 Irish Money, amount to in England, Exchange at 10¾ *per Cent*.?

Ans. £.1132 10 0¾.

287

[Editor's prefatory note. Table 3 appears within
article 300, and numbers 4 and 5 directly follow,
below, the characterization of nine tables and a
page of advertising. Six of the exhibits are
absent from the source copy, are not fully intact
therein, or have otherwise been omitted for
reprint purposes.

The abbreviations "d.," "c.," and "m." (in ital-
ics) within column headings of chapter 4 stand for
"di[s]mes," "cents," and "mills." In number 5 the
inserted handwritten letters represent the fractions, as identified or imputed, (a) 1/4, (b) 1/2,
and (c) 3/4.

288

EXPLANATION *of the* TABLES *in* PART *the* EIGHTH.

TABLE I.

(351.) *The Federal Coins, their Names, &c.* from
the Act of Congress in *Art.* 253, 274.

TABLE II.

(352.) *The Value of the Federal Coins, &c.* found
in the American Currencies, from the value of a
Dollar in the several States as in *Art.* 239, 296; and
in the other Nations, from the Act of Congress for
the Valuation of the Impost, as in *Art.* 303. Their
Denominations of Account are laid down in *Art.* 304
—315.

TABLE III.

(353.) *Table of Factors or Divisors, &c. Art.* 300. The
Tabular Numbers in the left-hand Row are found by
dividing the Value of the Federal Dollar in each Currency by 20, the Shillings in 1 Pound : Thus 6 Shillings, New-England Currency, divided by 20 gives
0.3.—in the other Columns by dividing the Currencies by each other in their order : thus 6 *Sh.* New-
England Currency divides 8 *Sh.* New-York, and gives
a Quotient, 1.3.

Y

TABL.

T A B L E IV.

(354) *The Value of any Number of Pounds,* &c.
The Currencies in this Table are founded on *Art.*
293, 296 ; and Sterling and Irish Money on *Art.* 303.
—The Tabular Numbers are calculated by the Direction in *Art.* 297, or the General Rule in *Art.* 301;
or by that at *Art.* 317.

T A B L E V.

355.) *The Value of any Number of Federal Dollars,* &c. The Tabular Numbers are calculated by
the Direction at *Art.* 298, or the General Rule
Art. 301; or by that at *Art.* 318.

The Marc Banco of Hamburg is valued by Congress at 0 *d* 333, though considered by all commercial
Nations as one-third of a Dollar, or 0 *d* 3.—At the
former Supposition 10000 Marcs amount to only 3330
Dollars.—At the latter to 3333 *d* 333.

The Rupee of Bengal is also valued by Congress at
0 *d* 555 but by all the other Nations at five-ninths of
a Dollar or 0 *d* 5 —This makes a Difference of 5 *d* 555
in 10000 Rupees.—As it was impossible to ascertain
the Intention of Congress precisely, the Columns under these Heads are calculated on the latter Supposition ; that of Sterling Money at 4 *d* 44 as observed in
Art. 320.

T A B L E VI.

(356.) *Sir* ISAAC NEWTONS'S *Assay Table, of the
Weights and Values of most Foreign Silver and Gold
Coins, actually made at the Mint, by Order of the Privy
Council,* &c. It is to be observed, that the English
Pound *Troy* contains 12 Ounces ; 1 Ounce, 20 Pennyweights ; 1 Pennyweight, 24 Grains ; and 1 Grain,
20 Mites.—The present English Standard for Gold
Coin is 22 carats of fine Gold, and 2 Carats or $\frac{1}{11}$ of
Alloy.—The Silver Coin contains 11 Ounces, 2 pennyweights fine Silver, and 18 Pennyweights of Alloy
in

289

in the Pound.—The firſt Column of the Table ex-
preſſes the fineneſs of the aſſayed Piece ; the Letters
B ſignifying *better*, and W *worſe* than the Engliſh Standard.—The ſecond Column, the abſolute Weight of
the Piece.—The third Column its Standard Weight,
or its Quantity of Standard Metal.—The fourth Column its Value in Engliſh Money.—For Example, in
the ſecond Article of Silver Coin, the new Seville
Piece of Eight is 1¼ Pennyweight in the Pound worſe
than the Engliſh Standard Weight, 13 Pennyweight,
21 Grains, and 15 Mites of Sterling Silver; and is in
Value 43.11*d.* of a Penny.

In the Royal Mint a Pound of Standard Gold is cut
or divided into 44¼ Parts, each a Guinea, at which
Rate a Guinea will will weigh 5 pennyweight, 9
Grains, ·4382 Parts.

TABLE VII.

357.) Dr. RITTENHOUSE's *Aſſay of Gold and
Silver Coins, &c.* This Aſſay of the Coins of France,
Spain, England, and Portugal, was made January
7, under the Care and Inſpection of the Director
of the Mint, agreeable to a Reſolution of Congreſs
of November 29, 1792.——On this Aſſay the Value
of Foreign Coins in *Art.* 287 and 288 is formed. It
is to be annually repeated, as obſerved in *Art.* 289.

TABLE VIII.

(358.) *Table of Factors or Diviſors, &c.* This
Table is arranged and calculated as Table III.—It is
formed upon the Authorities in *Art.* 339 and 340.—
And the Letters in each Table correſpond.—Thus
for, *Antwerp* or *Brabant* look to the Column under
C, and for *Portugal* under T.

TABLE IX.

(359.) *Table of Factors or Diviſors, &c.* This
Table is ſimilar to Table V. It is formed upon the
Authorities in *Art.* 345.

THE 'END.

BOOKS — *By the same Author.*

Sold by T. DOBSON, Philadelphia, and the principal Bookfellers in the United States.

I. GURNEY's BRACHYGRAPHY IMPROVED —— the *large* Edition—illuftrated with Thirteen Copperplates. Price *Half a Guinea*, bound.

II. Abridged Edition of the fame Work—with Ten Plates—Price *One Dollar*.

III. The ELEMENTARY PRINCIPLES OF ARITHMETIC; with their Application to the *Trade* and *Commerce* of the UNITED STATES OF AMERICA.

IV. An INTRODUCTION TO THE COUNTING-HOUSE; or a fhort Specimen of *Mercantile Precedents*, adapted to the prefent Situation of the Commerce of THESE STATES.

Preparing for the Prefs.

V. SELECT ARITHMETICAL EXERCISES; or the Application of the Elementary Principles of Arithmetic to the *Mathematical Sciences*, and to various branches of *Natural Philofophy*.

☞ *Tables the Firft, Fourth, and Fifth of the* FEDERAL ARITHMETICIAN, *may be had feparate at* One Sixteenth *of a* Dollar *each*.

8

THOMAS DILWORTH'S
BOOK-KEEPERS ASSISTANT,
1794

THE YOUNG
BOOK-KEEPER's ASSISTANT:

SHEWING HIM

In the most plain and easy Manner,

THE ITALIAN WAY OF STATING

DEBTOR and CREDITOR;

WITH

Proper and instructive Notes under every Entry in the WASTE-BOOK, where necessary, by which the Method of Journalizing is rendered more easy and intelligible; and also the like Notes in the JOURNAL and LEDGER, inserted by way of Information, how to post the JOURNAL, and correct Errors in the LEDGER: Wherein there is a great Variety of Examples, not only in the common and ordinary Way of buying and selling, but in that of trading beyond the Seas, both for a Merchant's Self and in Company. All which is contained in two Setts of Books, directing the Learner, not by Precept only, but by Example, how to draw out a new Inventory from the old Books, and insert it in the new ones; and the Trade continued as if it were in the real Shop or 'Compting House.

TO WHICH IS ANNEXED

A SYNOPSIS OR COMPENDIUM

OF THE

Whole Art of stating DEBTOR and CREDITOR,

In all the Circumstances of BOOK-KEEPING, both in Proper, Factorage and Company Accompts, Domestic and Foreign.

THE TWELFTH EDITION.

By THOMAS DILWORTH,

Author of the NEW GUIDE to the ENGLISH TONGUE
SCHOOLMASTERS ASSISTANT, &c. &c.

PHILADELPHIA:

PRINTED BY BENJAMIN JOHNSON,
No. 147, Market-Street.

To the WORTHY

MERCHANTS and TRADESMEN

OF THE

CITY OF LONDON:

GENTLEMEN!

AS the major Part of your Children, among other branches of Literature, are educated in the Principles of BOOK-KEEPING (a Science which all Men ought to be acquainted with, but highly worth the attention of every one concerned in Trade) permit me to put into your hands the following Treatiſe; which, as it is calculated in the moſt plain, and therefore eaſy manner, I flatter myſelf will not be unacceptable. Your Approbation of the ſame will very much encourage,

GENTLEMEN!

Your moſt humble,

And obedient Servant,

Thomas Dilworth.

P R E F A C E.

AMONG the feveral Writers on the Subject of Book-keeping, one would imagine that it was quite exhausted, and no more Room left for any thing elfe to be faid; but as I write not fo much for the Advancement of the Art itfelf (that being brought to a Degree of Perfection not eafily to be amended) as for the Eafe of the Teacher, and to fave him both Trouble and Time, as well as for the greater improvement of the learner, I hope this treatife will be the better accepted.

There is but one that I have feen, viz. Mr. *Webfter*, who has gone before me in the Method I have chofen, and to him I muft own myfelf indebted for the Plan : but as that Performance is by much too fhort, for that and fome other Reafons, it gave occafion for the Appearance of the following Sheets.

I have, in this Attempt of mine, very much enlarged on the Subject, and have taken in, if not all the common Cafes, at leaft the major Part of them, together with many others that are more curious, yet not lefs ufeful ; and have given fuch full Explanations on each Entry in the Wafte-Book, and in fome Places in the Journal and Ledger, that the Teacher has abundantly lefs Trouble than formerly, in attending his Pupils ; many Words faved ; and I think, but with Submiffion to better judges, the Whole made fo clear and intelligible, that any Tutor may venture to teach by this Book with all the pleafure that he can defire.

The Method of balancing the old-Ledger, and drawing an Inventory from the fame, in order to begin new books, is not here taught by Precept, but by example : and to make this appear the plainer to the Pupil, he is fhewed how this muft be done by doing it ; the whole Trade, for two Months being clofed, and properly balanced, and an Inventory drawn from thence, and the trading carried on for ten months more, without any interruption. He is alfo actually taught how to balance an Account full written, and to remove the fame to another Folium, as in the Cafh-Book, and likewife to correct an Error committed in the Ledger, by placing any Sum of Money, or parcel of Goods, to a contrary accompt ; I fay the Pupil is not told this barely by Precepts, but informed by Examples, he being obliged to do thofe Things himfelf; Errors being made on Purpofe to give him an Opportunity of properly correcting them. Yet, by the Way, I do not think every Error that may be committed by a good Book-keeper is to be corrected after this manner : For though to correct a whole entry in the Ledger, by erafing or obliterating it, is no way juftifiable, yet a wrong figure may be, by a light hand, and a good penknife, fo neatly altered, as that a good eye can fcarcely difcern it.

The feveral Journal entries, relating to the receiving and paying of Money, though ommitted by fome book-keepers are yet ufed by others, and therefore I have placed them in the journal as well as in the Cafh-Book, judging it moft convenient fo to do for the learner's fake, that he may underftand them the better.

Its bulk I think cannot reafonably be objected againft, fince a Repetition of examples rather ferve to give the learner a good idea of them, and eftablifh them in his memory, than hinder his progrefs ; while fingle ones are as foon forgot as learnt ; and a continual Succeffion of new Paffages is fo far from helping the Learner, that they only ferve to thruft out one another. Yet if any Teacher fhould think the whole too large, as it ftands divided into two parts, he may ufe which he pleafes, but for my own Part I fhall ufe both.

If any Merchant should object against it as not falling in with his particular Method; I would observe that the present Manner of treating the Subject was chose before any other as being the easiest and plainest for the pupil. Shorter ways, by experienced Book-keepers, may be used at pleasure; but to a person who is to begin with the first Rudiments, and in whom the foundation must be laid, before the superstructure can be raised, every difficult passage ought to be cleared up, and the whole suited to his understanding.

It is very certain that the Method of Book-keeping, by Double Entry, may be applied to every other particular Sort of Business, such as the Tradesman, Farmer, Army, Ship, &c. as well as the Merchant; yet because each Trade has always something peculiar to itself, it was thought more adviseable to follow that of the Merchant, rather than any other, as being the most general; a good Understanding of which, will enable any Tradesman, of what Denomination soever, to keep his Books, both according to Double Entry and his particular Calling.

The Letter *J*, being put at the Beginning of every Entry in the Waste-Book, signifies that *that* Entry is Journalized.—The several Figures at the Beginning of each Journal Entry, signifies their being posted; the Upper Figure denoting the Dr. Side, and the lower Figure the Cr. Side.— The Columns in the Ledger, next after the Day of the Month, both in the Dr. and Cr. Sides, shew the particular Pages in the Journal where those Entries were taken from.—And, in the same Columns, the Letter R signifies Rest or Remainder on the Balance of that particular Accompt where it is placed.—The Column in the Dr. Side next before the Money, shews the Page where that particular Entry stands on the Cr. Side, and the like Column on the Cr. Side, shews the Page where each particular Entry stands on the Dr. Side.

That a Treatise of this Kind is preferable to written Copies, is, I think, so clear, that it is beyond a Dispute, inasmuch as written Copies not only rob the Master of a great deal of his Time, but are so liable to be defaced, that it is very hard for him to supply his Scholars with a sufficient Number of them, especially in some of our Academies, where the Teaching runs pretty much his Way.

There is a small Difference between the two Ledgers, with regard to the balancing them: the first being only for two Months, every Accompt is kept open till the final closing; whereas in the second, every Accompt is balanced as soon as it is made even, and Lines of Separation are drawn to make it appear so at first Sight, after which it begins again afresh, and so on.

To speak fully of all the Books that are used in an Accompting-House in such a System as this, would be altogether useless, and therefore needless: yet, that the Learner may have such an Idea of them as is necessary here, I will give him a Definition of them all, which I presume will be a sufficient Introduction. And,

1. The Waste-Book is that wherein is wrote, whatever occurs in the Business of Merchandizing, whether buying, selling, exchanging, bargaining, shipping, &c. setting down first the Day of the Month, and the Year, and beneath that expressing all the Business done on that Day, together with the Mark, Weight, Measure, &c. of each Commodity bought, sold, received, delivered, or bargained for that Day; as also the Contract in buying and selling, be it for ready Money, Time, or Barter; drawing a Line between each particular Parcel for Distinction

298

fake. It always begins with the Inventory of a Merchant's Effects and Debts, and contains a compleat Record of every Transaction of his Affairs, with all the Circumstances, in a plain Narration of Matter of Fact ; every Transaction following another in the Order of the Dates.

Note, Any one may write in this Book that is of ordinary capacity, and therefore it ought to be always ready at hand for this purpose.

2. The Journal is in effect, the same with the Waste-Book, it being a compleat Transcript thereof, in the same order of time, but in a different style, with a line between each particular Parcel. And whereas the Waste-Book expresses every transaction in a simple narration of what is done, and according to the capacity of those who understand nothing at all of book-keeping or Accompts, the Journal distinguishes the Debtors and Creditors as a preparation for the Ledger. So that no one can post out of the Waste-book into the Journal but he who understands well the method of book-keeping.

Note, To an experienced Book-keeper, a Journal without a Waste-Book, or a Waste-Book without a Journal is sufficient.

3. The Ledger is a large volume, containing all the transactions of a Man's Affairs, in such order, as that those belonging to every different subject lie together in one place ; making so many distinct or several Accompts. In this book all the accompts dispersed in the Journal are drawn out and stated in Debtor and Creditor. To form each accompt two pages, are required, opposite to each other ; that on the left Hand serving for Debtor, the other for Creditor ; by which means, at any Time, whenever the merchant pleases, he may be satisfied how his estate is in general ; or how any particular Accompt of Men, Money, or Wares stand : and for the more readily turning to any particular Accompt, the Ledger has always an Alphabet prefixed to it.

Note, 1, The title of every Accompt ought to be entered in this book, in a text hand on the Dr. Side ; and on the Cr. side, in the same text-hand, per Contra Cr.

2. Turn to the Alphabet, and under such letter as the title begins with, write down the same title, with the number of the page or Folium, where that account is entered.

4. The Debt-Book ; in which is entered the day wherein all sums become due whether paid or received, by bills of exchange, merchandizes, or otherwise to the end, that by comparing receipts and payments, provision may be made in time for a fund for payment ; by receiving Bills &c. due or taking other precautions.

Note, Accompts in this book, like the Ledger must be on two opposite pages : the monies to be received to be placed on the left hand, and those to be paid, on the right hand.

5. The Cash-Book, in which is entered all the sums received and paid daily : it is called the Cash-Book, because it contains, in Debtor and Creditor, all the cash that comes in, and goes out of the merchant's stock ; and usually once in a month is transferred into the Ledger.

Note. By this Book, a merchant may know, at any time, what ready money he has by him, without the trouble of telling it over.

6. The Invoice-Book ; which contains an Accompt of all the Goods which a merchant ships off, either for his own Accompt, or for others in commission, according to the Bills of Lading, with the whole charges, till on board.

Note 1, The use of this book is to save the Journal from erasures, inevitable in taking accompts or invoices of the several goods received, sent, or sold ; where it is necessary to be very particular, and to render those invoices easier to be found, than they can be in the waste-book.

2. The Form of an Invoice of 100 qrs. of Wheat as mentioned *April* 1, in the second Waste-Book, will run thus ; viz

March 8, 1789.

Invoice of 100 qrs. of Wheat in Sacks, ship'd on board the good Ship *Swan, William Lyon*, Master, and consign'd to *Jacob Van-Horne* of *Amsterdam*, for the Accompt of *John*

Simmons, of *London*, Merchant: Mark'd and number'd as *per* Margin.

		l.	s.	d.
	100 qrs of Wheat, at 12s. *per* qr.	60	0	0
	200 Sacks —— at 1s. each	10	0	0
JVH	Meeterage	2	0	0
JS	Porterage —— at 1s. 6d. *per* qr.	7	10	0
No 1 to 100	Cartage	5	18	4
	Litherage	3	0	0
	Freight —— at 2s. *per* qr.	10	0	0
		98	8	4
	Commiffion on 98l. 8s. 4d: at 1 *per cent.*	0	19	8
		99	8	0

7 The Factorage-Book, which contains an account of what a merchant receives to fell in Commiffion for others, with all charges, and of the difpofal thereof.

Note 1, This is only a Copy of the employers accompt of goods, in the Ledger, in the Language of the Wafte-Book, but muft be number'd into Foliums like the Ledger.

2. The Form of a Factorage accompt of the receipt and difpofal of paper, Holland and Long Lawn, as mentioned *June* 2, 6, 8 and 12, will run thus; viz.

June 12, 1789.

Factory of 1000 reams of fine paper; 120 pieces of Holland; and 100 pieces of long lawn; received from on board the *Dolphin*, *Jacob Swaert* Mafter, for Accompt of *Abraham Van Shooten*	Dr.	l. s. d.	Per Contra 1789	Cr. l. s. d.
To Freight		22 6 8	June 5 By Sale of 1000 Rms. of paper at 6s *per* Rm.	300 0 0
Cuftom on 1000 Rms. at 2s. 2d.		108 6 8	8 By fale of 12 pieces of Holland at 3l. *per* piece	360 0 0
120 Ps. Holland. ea. 20 Ells, at 4d.		40 0 0		
100 Ps. Long Lawn, at 2s.		10 0 0	12 By fale of 100 pieces of long lawn at 2l. 10s. *per* piece	250 0 0
Litherage		3 0 0		
Waterage		4 12 6		
Cartage		3 17 4		
Porterage		3 14 4		
Warehoufe room		1 0 0		910 0 0
		196 17 6		
Commiffion on 910l. at 4 *per cent.*		36 8 0		
Neat proceed		676 14 6		
		910 0 0		

1. The Acquittance or Receipt-Book, in which, every one, to whom Money is paid, muft give his Receipt for the fame, expreffing for whofe Ufe, or upon what Accompt the fame is received.

9. The Book of Charges of Merchandize, wherein is entered the charges of every Commodity bought, received, fhipped or fold, whether for Proper, Factorage, or Company Accompt.

10. The Book of Houfe-Expenfes; wherein is inferted whatever is daily expended in Houfe-keeping, together with fome other Articles not occuring in Trade, as may be feen in the Book of Houfe-Expenfes following.

Note, This Book is neceffary for Merchants, Factors, and Tradefmen of all Kinds, to know their yearly Expenfes.

11. The Letter-Book, which contains the Copies of all fuch Letters as a Merchant fends, either Inland or Over fea, efpecially fuch as relate to Trade.

Note, 1, When an Anfwer is received, it will be convenient to exprefs, at the End of the foregoing Letter, the Date of that which came for an Anfwer.

2. When Letters are received they fhould be carefully folded up, and indorfed with the Perfon's Name it came from, the place where it was dated, with the Date, the time that you received it, and by what conveyance it came.

300

3. When an Anfwer is returned to any Letter received, note upon the Letter the time of anfwering it.

12. The Remembrancer or Note-Book, which, for the Help of the Memory, contains fuch Bufinefs as the Merchant is to go about.

Note. This is a fmall Pocket-Book ufed by fuch Merchants or Tradefmen as have a Multitude of Bufinefs to go through, and when fuch Bufinefs is performed as is therein mentioned it may be known by fome private Mark ther on, or by Obliteration.

Among the forementioned Books, the Wafte-Book, Journal and Ledger are held to be effentially neceffary; the reft are auxiliary, of which the Cafh-Book, Book of House-Expenfes, and of Charges of Merchandize, ferve to eafe the Ledger; the reft are kept fome by one Merchant or Trader, fome by another, according to the Nature and Circumftances of his Way of Dealing in the World.

It is generally agreed on, that it was the *Italians*, particularly thofe of *Venice*, *Genoa* and *Florence*, who firft introduced the Method of keeping Books double, or in two Parts: hence among us it is called the *Italian* Method.

And now having finifhed the Definitions and Detail of the Books ufed in the Accompting-Houfe, I fhall beg leave to make an Obfervation of another kind.

Some (few) Inftructors of Youth, propofe to teach Book-keeping in fix Weeks, fome in a Month, and fome in twenty-four hours, and all of them in their own propofed Times, engage to make their Pupils complete Mafters of the Art: But whatever their pretentions may be, this Treatife (though inferior to none of them) has none fuch; nor can it be done in fo fhort a time, the Reafon being very obvious. For,

Firft, Whofoever learns Book-keeping, is to fuppofe himfelf not at School, but in the Compting-Houfe, where Examples in Arithmetic are propofed out of the ordinary School way. Now if every fuch Example be wrought (as it ought to be) and not taken upon truft, this will oblige the Pupil to run over his Arithmetical rules in his mind, and there faften them fecurely. This is a work of time.

Secondly, The Method of ftating Debtor and Creditor confifts wholly of words and has no Connection at all with the Arithmetical part, being quite different from it, and confequently is a Work where found reafon and Judgment are called in to affift: and here it is neceffary for the Pupil fo to underftand this Part, as, upon fight of the Wafte-Book, to be able to journalize and poft any Paffage therein, which is alfo a Work of Time.

Thirdly, If to the two former be added the Time that muft neceffarily be taken up in writing out a fair Wafte-book, Journal and Ledger, I think it will very evidently appear, to any confiderate perfon, that all this can't be done in fix Weeks, much lefs in twenty-four hours. Such hafty performances in Book-keeping, or in any other branch of Literature, being more likely to produce a crazy and tottering Building, fubject to fall at every blaft, if not wholly undermine it, rather than make it firm and lafting. And

In order to render the following Treatife ftill more ufeful, as well to Merchants themfelves, in their Compting-Houfes, as to Pupils during the time of their Inftruction in this neceffary Science, I have placed at the end, a Synopfis or Compendium of the whole Art of Book-keeping, in which is comprifed particular Rules for ftating Dr. and Cr. in all the Cafes that can poffibly happen in the whole courfe of a Merchant's Dealing, whether by himfelf, or in Company, Foreign or Domeftic: Nothing of this kind, in fo full a Manner being any where extant that I know of.——Lefs than all this, in juftice to the fubject I could not fay; and more I think there is no occafion for in this place, fince the many ufeful and inftructive Notes, which are interfperfed in almoft every Page, fufficiently fpeak for themfelves and declare the Utility of the whole Work.

Upon the Whole as I was not willing to thruft it into the world without fubjecting it to a very impartial examination, I applied to my good and worthy friend Mr. *William Mountai*'s F. R. S. Teacher of the mathematicks, at *Shad Thames*, who being a very capable judge of the fubject, and whom I efteem *Inftar omnium*, or in other words, *Nulli fecundas*, very readily granted my requeft, and honoured me with his kind remarks, for which I beg leave here to return him my hearty Thanks.

One Word more. As my *Schoolmafters Affiftant* is made ufe of in many fchools, and increafes in its Sale; fo I am not out of Hope that this alfo will meet with the like approbation; it being compofed for the fame Reafons which that was, *viz.* for the eafe of the teacher, and the benefit of the learner. Alfo,

As fome errors crept in through inadvertancy and efcaped correction in the former Editions; I have been at the pains to go over the whole again, in the minuteft and moft circumftantial manner. However, if the kind Reader fhould meet with any Error in the following work, as it is not impoffible but he may, notwithftanding the greateft Care to the Contrary, he is defired to correct it with his Pen, and then all will be right.

301

The WASTE-BOOK.

LONDON, January 1, 1789.

		l.	s.	d.
	An INVENTORY of my whole Estate, confisting of Money, Goods and Debts, owing to and by me JOHN SIMMONS, taken this Day; and is as follows, viz.			

		l.	s.	d.
J.	Imprimis, I have in ready Money -	8000	0	0
J.I.C.	Item, 19 Hhds. of Tobacco, qt. 63 C. 1 qr. 14 lb. at 4 l. 14 s. per C.	297	17	3
J.	48 Bags of Pepper, qt. 1026 lb. at 16 d. per lb. - - -	68	8	0
J.I.L.	16 Pipes of Canary, at 25 l. per Pipe. - - - -	400	0	0
J.S.C.	30 Bags of Hops, qt. 109 C. 1 qr. 12 lb. at 2 l. per C. -	218	14	3¼
J.A.B.	10 Hhds. of French Wine, at 27 l. per Hhd. - - -	270	0	0
J.	20 Pieces of Holland, qt. 384 Ells, at 3 s. per Ell - -	57	12	0
J.	10 Pieces of Broad Cloth, qt. 180 Yards, at 10 s. per Yd.	90	0	0
J.	7 Pieces of Shalloon, qt. 100 Yds. at 2 s. 4 d. per Yd. -	11	13	4
J.	5 Pieces of Drugget, qt. 60 Yds. at 3 s. 6 d. per Yd. - -	10	10	0
J.	Thomas Preston, Esq; owes me on Demand - - - -	100	0	0
J.	Sir Robert Johnson owes me -	476	0	0
J.	John Herbert owes me - - -	250	0	0
J.	Capt. John Smith owes me (to pay the 18th instant) -	580	0	0

10830 | 14 | 10¼

	I am indebted as follows:	l.	s.	d.
J.	To Capt. William Andrews on Demand - - - - -	270	0	0
J.	To Sir Humphrey Parsons (to pay the 8th Instant) - -	100	0	0
J.	To William Baker, Esq; (to pay the 17th Instant) -	150	0	0
J.	To Mr. William Warner - - -	15	13	0

535 | 13 | ---

Note 1. The first Thing that a Merchant begins Trade with is his *Stock*: And the first Thing that he opens his Books with is the *Inventory* of that Stock, together with his ready *Money* and *Debts* owing to and by him.

B

303

LONDON, January 1, 1789.

2. This *Inventory* being first placed in the *Waste-Book*, as above, you must next open the *Journal* with the same, and there first make *Sundry Accompts* Drs. to *Stock* for the whole Sum (except what you owe) because each Particular, there mentioned, is a Part of *Stock*, and then mention the Particulars, as they are in the *Journal*.

3. Then for the several Sums, which you owe, make *Stock* Dr. to *Sundry Accompts* for the whole Sum: and then name each Man and the respective Sum due to him. This is *Journalizing*.

———— 2 ————

J. Sold 8 Pieces of Holland, qt. 132 Ells, at 3s. 4d. per Ell for ready Money - - - - - - - - - - | 22 | — | —

Note 1. As the *Holland* is disposed of, and the Money received for it at the same Time; it is not necessary to know to whom it was sold, but make the *Money* received, *i. e. Cash* Dr. to the *Holland* for the Value, and let the *Holland* be made Cr. by *Cash*, for the Quantity sold and the said Value.

2. Whatever is made Dr. belongs both to the *Journal* and *Ledger*, but whatever is made Cr. both in this Place and hereafter, belongs to the *Ledger* only, because there the Entry is double.

———— 3 ————

J.B.A. Sold *Brandon George* 2 Hhds. of *French* Wine, at 28l. 10s. per Hhd. to pay in one Month - - - | 57 | — | —

Note, As the *Wine* is sold, but not paid for, it is natural, in this Case, to make *Brandon George* Dr. for the same, and let *French Wine* be made Cr. by *Brandon George* for the Quantity sold, and the Value thereof.

———— 4 ————

J.T.P. Bought of *Thomas Preston*, Esq; 5 Hhds. of *Oporto* Wine, at 7l. per Hhd. - - - - - - - - | 35 | — | —

Note 1. As the *Wine* is bought, but not paid for, you necessarily become Dr. to *Thomas Preston* for the same: But as you are not to erect an Accompt of yourself, and because the *Wine* is now become a Part of your Stock; so you must make *Oporto* Wine Dr. to *Thomas Preston* for the Quantity bought and its Value, and *Thomas Preston* Cr. by *Oporto* Wine for the said Value.

2. As *Thomas Preston* stands indebted already to you in the Sum of 100l. it looks like a Contradiction to write yourself his *Debtor*, when the Goods you receive are not equal in Value to the Sum first due: But (in the Language of the Book-keeper) this is not to be regarded, since the Wine, which you receive of him is only in Part of Payment, and therefore lessens the Debt by so much as it is worth.

———— 5 ————

J. Sold *Samuel Fairman* 1 Hhd. of *French* Wine for - | 28 | — | —

Note, Here 'tis plain that as you have sold the *French Wine* to *Samuel Fairman*, he must be your Dr. Hence if you make *Samuel Fairman* Dr. to *French Wine* for the Worth of it; and *French Wine* Cr. by *Samuel Fairman* for the Quantity, as well as the Value, it will be right.

LONDON, January 6, 1789.

		l.	s.	d.

J.T.P. Sold *Elias Skinner* 3 Hhds. of *Oporto* Wine, at 9*l.* per Hhd. to pay the 12th Inftant - - - - — 27

Note, This Entry is of the fame Nature with the former, and therefore you muft make *Elias Skinner* Dr. to *Oporto Wine*, for the Value; and *Oporto Wine* Cr. by *Elias Skinner* for both Quantity and Value.

———— 7 ————

J. Received of Sir *Robert Johnfon* in Part - - - - 100

Note 1. By the Inventory, it appears that Sir *Robert Johnfon* owed you 476*l.* but as no Erafements are to be made in Mercantile Books; fo you have no other Way of reducing the Debt, but that of making *Cafh* Dr. to Sir *Robert Johnfon* for the Sum received, and Sir *Robert Johnfon* Cr. by *Cafh* for the fame Sum.

2. In all Receipts of Money you muft be careful to mention whether they be in full or in Part.

———— 8 ————

J. Paid Sir *Humphrey Parfons* in Full - - - - 100

Note 1. It appears in the Inventory that you ftood indebted to Sir *Humphrey Parfons* in the Sum of 100*l.* and confequently in your *Ledger* he is made Cr. by the faid Sum : Therefore to prevent any Erafement or croffing out, you have no other Way of difcharging the Debt in your Books, but by making Sir *Humphrey Parfons* Dr. to *Cafh* for the Money paid him; and *Cafh* Cr. by Sir *Humphrey Parfons* for the fame Sum.

2. In all Payments of Money you muft be careful to mention whether they be in full or in Part.

———— 9 ————

J.E.I Bought of *Elias Ingram*, 7 Hhds. of *Lifbon* Wine, at 7*l.* per Hhd. - - - - - - - - 49

J. Sold d° *Ingram* 5 Pieces of Broad Cloth, qt. 96 Yards, at 10*s.* 2*d.* ½ per Yard, amounting to the fame Sum, 49

Note, This Way of difpofing of *Goods* for *Goods* is properly called *Barter*; and when the Exchange happens to be fingle, that is, one particular Sort of *Goods* for another as above, and both amounting to the fame Value, you need only make the *Goods* received Dr. to the *Goods* delivered, i. e. *Lifbon Wine* Dr. to *Broad Cloth* for the Quantity of Wine received, and its Value; and *Broad Cloth* Cr. by *Lifbon Wine* for the Quantity of Cloth delivered, and its Value.

———— 10 ————

J.S.C. Sold *William Lowfield*, Efq; 10 Bags of Hops, qt. 31 C. 2 qr. at 2*l.* 2*s.* per C. on Demand - - - - 66 3

Note, As *William Lowfield* is the buying Man, he muft be made Dr. to *Hops* for the Value of the Purchafe; and as *Hops* are the Commodity by him purchafed, they muft be made Cr. by *William Lowfield*, for their Quantity and Value.

———— 11 ————

J.E.I. Sold Sir *Humphrey Parfons* 2 Hhds. of *Lifbon* Wine, at 8*l.* per Hhd. - - - - - - - - 16

Note, Notwithftanding that you ftand indebted in your Ledger, to Sir *Humphrey Parfons*, in the Sum of 100*l.* you muft make him Dr. to *Lifbon Wine* for its Value, and *Lifbon Wine* Cr. by

305

LONDON, January 11, 1789. | *l.* | *s.* | *d.*

Sir *Humphrey Parsons* for the said Quantity and Value, as if you had owed him nothing, and therefore as you stood indebted before in a larger Sum, this only helps to discharge the Debt.

———— 12 ————

J. | Received of *Elias Skinner* in Full - - - - - | 27 | — | —

Note, As *Elias Skinner* stands indebted to you in the Sum of 27*l.* so now he must be discharged of that Debt; to do which you must make *Cash* Dr. to *Elias Skinner* for the Sum received, and *Elias Skinner* Cr. by *Cash* for the same Sum.

———— 13 ————

J.E.I. | Sold 3 Hhds. of *Lisbon* Wine, at 8*l.* 10*s. per* Hhd. for present Money - - - - - - - - | 25 | 10 | —

Note, This is of the same Nature with that of the 2d Instant, and therefore you are to make *Cash* Dr. to *Lisbon* Wine for the Value, and *Lisbon Wine* Cr. by *Cash* for the Quantity and its Value.

———— 14 ————

J.J.H. | Bought of *John Harrison*, Esq; 20 Hhds. of Tobacco, qt. 74 C. 2 qrs. at 4*l. per* C. for present Money - | 298 | — | —

Note 1. The *Tobacco* being bought and the Money paid down, in this Case, you must make the *Tobacco* Dr. to *Cash* for the Quantity bought, and its Value, and *Cash* Cr. by *Tobacco* for the said Value

2. It is to be observed that you had some *Tobacco* before, which was a Part of your *Stock*, and yet remains unsold; and therefore when the same Sort of Goods happens to be bought of several Persons, and at different Prices, it is convenient to have some distinguishing *Mark*, to know them by, that when you come to balance the Accompt of such Goods, you may the more easily inform yourself of the *Prime Cost* of what may be left unsold.

———— 15 ————

J.I.H. | Sold *Thomas Johnson*, 10 Hhds. of the aforesaid Tobacco, qt. 37 C. 1 qr. 15*lb.* at 4*l.* 12*s. per* C. - - - } *l.* 171 *s.* 19 *d.* 3¾

J.B.A. | And 3 Hhds. of *French* Wine, at 22*l.* 5*s. per* Hhd. - - - - - - } 84 15 0 | 256 | 14 | 3¾

Note, This is much the same as if it had been but one Parcel, for either Way you must make *Thomas Johnson* Dr. but here he must be made Dr. to *Sundry Accompts* for the Value of the Whole; and each Parcel must be made Cr. by *Ditto Johnson* for its respective Quantity and Value.

———— 16 ————

J. | Received of Sir *Robert Johnson* in Part - - - - | 100 | — | —

Note, This Passage is exactly the same with that of the 7th Instant, and therefore needs no other Explication.

———— 17 ————

J. | Paid *William Baker*, Esq; in Full - - - - - | 150 | — | —

Note, This also is the same with that of the 8th Instant.

LONDON, January 18, 1789.

		l.	s.	d.

J. Received of Capt. *John Smith* in Full - - - - **580 — —**

Note, Here *Cash* must be made Dr. to Capt. *Smith* for the Sum received; and Capt. *Smith* Cr. by *Cash* for the same Sum.

19

J. Bought of *John Herbert*, 20 Pieces of Stuffs, qt. 240 Yards, at 20*d. per* Yard - - - - - - - **20 — —**

Note, As *John Herbert* is the selling man, you must make *Stuffs* Dr. to him for their Quantity and Value, and *John Herbert*, Cr. by *Stuffs* for the said Value.

20

J.I.H. Sold *John Hammond*, Esq. 10 Hhds. of Tobacco, qt. 37C. oqr. 13*lb.* at 4*l.* 10*s. per* C. he to pay as follows, viz.

	l.	s.	d.
On *February* the 9th next - - -	67	0	5
In three Months - - - - -	100	0	0

167 — 5

Note 1, This *Case* differs nothing from *Goods* sold upon *Time*, *Jan.* 3, in the stating of *Dr.* and *Cr.* for whether the payment be one or many (if no Money be paid down) *John Hammond* must be made Dr. to *Tobacco*, for the Value of the Quantity sold him; and *Tobacco* must be made Cr. by *John Hammond* for the Quantity sold and its Value; only in the *Journal* you must mention the several times of Payment.
2. By the Rule of Three the Money is a Farthing more, which is purposely omitted.

21

J. Sold Capt. *William Andrews*, 20 Pieces of Stuffs, qt. 240 Yards, at 2*s. per* Yard - - - - - - **24 — —**

Note, As Capt. *Andrews* is the buying man, he necessarily becomes Dr. to *Stuffs* for the Value: and as *Stuffs* are the Things sold, they as necessarily become Cr. by *William Andrews* for both quantity and Value.

22

J.I.C. Sold *Robert More*, the following Goods, viz.

	l.	s.	d.
19 Hhds of Tobacco, qt. 65 C. 1qr. 14*lb.* at 4*l.* 15*s. per* C. - - -	301	0	7½
48 Bags of Pepper, qt. 1026*lb.* at 17*d. per lb.*	72	13	6
J.S.C. 20 Bags of Hops, qt. 77C. 3qrs. 12*lb.* at 2*l.* 1*s. per* C.	159	12	1½

533 6 3

J.R.M. Bought of d° *Moore* 20 pipes of Canary at 25*l per* Pipe. **500**

Note, This sort of *Barter*, being partly simple, and partly compounded, *i. e.* several sorts of Goods given for one Sort, and their total Values being different, you must not (as at *Jan.* 9) make the *Goods* received Dr. to the *Goods* delivered; but you must
1. Make *Robert Moore* Dr. to *Sundry Accompts* for the whole Value of the *Goods* delivered to him; and each Sort of *Goods* must be made Cr. by *Robert Moore* for the Quantity delivered to him, and its respective Value. And
2. Make *Canary* Dr. to *Robert Moore*, for the Quantity you received of him, and its Value; and *Robert Moore* Cr. by *Canary* for the said Value.

307

LONDON, January 23, 1789.

		l.	*s.*	*d.*

JR.M. Sold *John Osborne,* 20 Pipes of Canary, at 28*l. per* Pipe   56c

Received in part - - - - 290
The rest upon Demand, viz. - 270
Note, This *Case* will admit of two ways of *Journalizing* it, viz.
1. Make *John Osborne* Dr. to *Canary* for the whole Value, and *Canary* Cr. by *John Osborne* for both Quantity and Value; then make *Cash* Dr. to *John Osborne* for the present Payment, and *John Osborne* Cr. by *Cash* for the same Sum.
      Or,
2. Make *Sundry Accompts* Drs. to *Canary,* viz. *Cash* for the Money received, and *John Osborne* for what remains due; then make *Canary* Cr. by *Sundry Accompts* for both Quantity and Value; This latter being more Clerk-like than the former, I have accordingly made choice of it.

--------------------- 24 -----------------

J.I.L. Sold *Richard Remnant* 16 Pipes of Canary, at 27*l.*   432
per Pipe, to pay in three Months - - - -
Note, Here *Richard Remnant* must be made Dr. to *Canary* for its Value; and *Canary* Cr. by *Richard Remnant* for both Quantity and Value.

308

--------------------- 25 -----------------

J. This day *Richard Remnant* offered to pay me for the 16 pipes of Canary sold to him Yesterday, if I would allow him 5 *per Cent.* Rebate for his early Payment, which I accordingly accepted of, and received in ready Money -   *l. s. d.* 426 13 4

J. Allowed Rebate on 432*l.* for 3 Months at 5 *per Cent* - - - - -   5 6 8

  432

Note 1, Though *Richard Remnant* did not pay the full Debt, yet he must have the same Discharge as if he had; therefore *Sundry Accompts* must be made Drs. to *Richard Remnant,* viz. *Cash* for the early Payment, and *Profit* and *Loss* for the Rebate; and *Richard Remnant* Cr. by both.
2. If the Rebate had been agreed upon, and the Money paid you by the buying Man, before he was made Dr. in your Books for the same, then there would be no need of any more than one *Journal* Entry; for in that Case you must value the Goods at no more than just what the buying Man paid for them upon Rebate, and enter them as is shewn in the Example of *Jan.* 2.

--------------------- 26 -----------------

J. Sold *William Lowfield,* Esq. 7 Pieces of Shalloon, qt.   12 10
100 Yards, at 2*s.* 6*d. per* Yard - - - -
Note, Here you must make *William Lowfield* Dr. to *Shalloon* for its Value; and *Shalloon* Cr. by *William Lowfield* for both Quantity and Value.

LONDON, January 27, 1789.

		l.	*s.*	*d.*

J. Bought of *Martin Unwin*, 1000 Reams of Paper, at 10s. *per* Ream   500

J. For which I am to pay as follows, *viz.* 100*l.* at 1 Month, 100*l.* at 2 Months, and 300*l.* at 3 Months after the date hereof.

> *Note*, This *Cafe* is juft the Reverfe of that of *John Hammond*, *Jan.* 21, and differs nothing from Goods bought upon *Time*, in the ftating of Dr. and Cr. as in the *Cafe* of *Thomas Prefton*, Efq. *Jan.* 5, for whether the Payment be one or many (if no Money be paid down) you, *i. e. Paper*, for you, muft be made Dr. to *Martin Unwin* for the Quantity bought of him, and the Value of it, and *Martin Unwin* muft be made Cr. by *Paper* for the faid Value; only in the *Journal* you muft mention the feveral times of Payment.

----------- 28 -----------

J. This Day I offered to pay *Martin Unwin* for the 1000 Reams of Paper bought of him Yefterday, if he would allow me 5 per cent. Rebate for my early Payment, which he accordingly accepted of, and received of me in ready Money   } *l. s. d.*   495 1 1½

J. Allowed me Rebate on 500*l.* at 5 per Cent.   } 4 18 10½

> *Note* 1. This *Cafe* is juft the reverfe of that in *Jan.* 25: And you muft obferve that although you did not pay the full Debt yet you muft have the fame Difcharge as if you had; therefore *Martin Unwin* muft be made Dr. to *Sundry Accompts*, viz. to *Cafh* for your early Payment, and to *Profit* and *Lofs* for the Rebate he allowed you; and each of them Cr. by *Martin Unwin* for their refpective Sums.
> 2. If the Rebate had been agreed on, and the Money paid to the felling Man, before the Goods had been entered in your Books, then there would have been no need of any more than one *Journal* Entry; for in that *Cafe* you muft Value the Goods at no more than juft what you paid for them upon Rebate, and enter them as is fhewn in the Example of *Jan.* 14.

----------- 29 -----------

J. Bought of *Robert Uxley*, 100 Pieces of *Norwich Crape*, qt. 1600 Yards, at 3s. 6d. *per* Yard   280

J. Sold d° *Uxley*, 500 Reams of Paper, at 10s. 6d. *per* Ream   262 10

> *Note*, Though this is but a fingle Cafe in *Barter*, *i. e.* only one Sort of Goods given for another, yet, becaufe they are unequal in their Value, and the Crape which you bought being worth more than the Paper, which you fold, you muft of courfe be indebted to *Uxley*; therefore (as at *Jan.* 22, in the *Cafe* of *Robert Morris*) you muft
> 1. Make *Norwich Crape* Dr. to *R. Uxley* for the Quantity bought of him, and its Value; and *R. Uxley* Cr. by *Norwich Crape* for the faid Value.
> 2. Make *R. Uxley* Dr. to *Paper* for its Value, and *Paper* Cr. by *Robert Uxley* for the Quantity fold him, and the Value thereof.

309

LONDON, January 30, 1789.

J. Sold *William Warner*, 40 Pieces of *Norwich* Crape.
qt. 640 Yards, at 4*s. per* Yard - - - - -   128 | —

J. For which I have received prefent Money £28 0 0

J. And by affignment on *William Lowfield* Efq; 50 0 0

J. The reft to ftand out 3 Months, viz. - 50 0 0

> *Note* 1. The *Norwich Crape* was fold to *William Warner* alone; but becaufe *Thomas Lowfield* was indebted to *William Warner*, in the Sum of 50l. and that Sum is now affigned or made over to you, *Thomas Lowfield* therefore becomes Dr. to *Norwich Crape*, i. e. to you, as well as *William Warner*; and in order to journalize this Cafe truly, you muft make *Sundry Accompts* Drs. to *Norwich Crape* for the whole Value. viz. *Cafh* for the Money received.
> *William Lowfield* Efq. for the Affignment on him; and *William Warner* for the remaining Sum due from him. Then make *Norwich Crape* Cr. by *Sundry Accompts* for the Quantity fold, and the Value thereof, and it will be right.
> 2. With regard to the Affignment on *William Lowfield*, Efq; which is a *Bill receivable*; fome would erect an Accompt of *Bills receivable*, on account of fuch *Bills* as they may have Occafion to receive, and it is not wrong fo to do, when Circumftances direct that way. However, I have not done it, principally becaufe the feveral *Bills receivable*, are for the moft part from Perfons, with whom the Merchant is fuppofed to correfpond, for which Reafon the Accompt of *Bills receivable* is ufelefs.

--- **31** ---

J. Paid fundry Charges this Month, as *per* Book of
House Expences . . . .   37 | 13

> *Note*, As a careful Merchant would be frugal in all his Expences; fo it is not amifs to keep a Book of his *Houfehold Expences* in particular, and once in the Month (or oftner if he thinks it proper) to transfer the fame into the *Ledger*, by opening an Account of *Houfe Expences*, and making it Dr. to *Cafh* for the Expences of that Month; and *Cafh* Cr. by *Houfe Expences* for the fame Sum, balancing the fame at laft by *Profit and Lofs*.

--- *February* 1. ---

Sold *Elias Skinner*, Efq; as follows,   *l.*   *s.*   *d*

J.E.I.   2 Hhds. of *Lifbon* Wine, at 8*l. per* Hhd. 16 0 0

J.T.P.   2 Hhds. of *Oporto* Wine, at 9*l. per* Hhd. 18 0 0

J.B.A.   4 Hhds. of *French* Wine, at 30*l. per* Hhd. 120 0 0   154 | —

For which I have received as follows, *viz.* *l.*   *s.*   *d*

Prefent Money 90 0 0

By Affignment on *Martin Urwin* . . 20 0 0

The reft to ftand until the 18th Inftant 44 0 0

> *Note*, This *Cafe* is a little complex, and cannot be ftated like the laft, becaufe here are feveral Sorts of Goods fold, whereas in the laft there was but one Sort fold; therefore, that Dr. and Cr. may be truly ftated, you muft
> 1. Make *Elias Skinner* Dr. to *Sundry Accompts*, viz. to *Lifbon*, *Oporto* and *French* Wine, for the Value of the Whole; and let each Sort of Goods be made Cr. by *Elias Skinner* for the Quantity fold, and its refpective Value.

310

LONDON, February 1, 1789.

		s.	*d.*

2. As you have received some Money, and also an Assignment in Part of Payment, you must discharge so much of the Accompt as these come to; to do which, you must make *Sundry Accompts* Drs. to *Elias Skinner*, viz. *Cash* for the Money which you have received, and *Martin Unwin* for *E. Skinner*'s Assignment on him, payable to you; and then make *E. Skinner* Cr. by *Sundry Accompts*, for the Value of them both. Thus will *E. Skinner* stand discharged by so much as the Cash and Assignment come to.

— 2 —

7. Bought of *Isaac Reynolds*, as follows, viz

	l.	*s.*	*d.*
40 Pieces of Duroy, qt. 600 Yards, at 6*s. per* Yard - - - - -	180	0	0
100 Pieces of Sagathee, qt. 1200 Yds. at 2*s.* 6*d. per* Yard - -	150	0	0

330

For which I have paid as follows,

	l.	*s.*	*d.*
Present Money - - - - -	100	0	0
Given do. *Reynolds, E. Skinner's* Note on *Martin Unwin* - - - -	20	0	0
The rest to stand out 4 Months - -	210	0	0

Note, This Case is just the reverse of the former, and to state it truly in your Journal, you must

1. Make *Sundry Accompts,* viz. *Duroy* and *Sagathee,* Drs. to *Isaac Reynolds* for the several Quantities and their respective Values; and *Isaac Reynolds* Cr. by *Sundry Accompts,* for the whole Value.

2. As you have given both *Money* and a *Note* in part of Payment, you must take care to discharge so much of the Debt as the *Note* and *Money* come to; to do which you must make *Isaac Reynolds* Dr. to *Sundry Accompts,* viz to *Cash* for the Money paid him, and to *Martin Unwin* for *Skinner's* Note on him, now payable to *Isaac Reynolds;* and *Cash* and *Martin Unwin* Crs. by *Isaac Reynolds* for the Money and Note paid to ditto *Reynolds.*

— 3 —

7. Received of *John James* for the use of *Thomas Shaw.* | 100 | — | —

Note, This Case is different from that in Jan. 8, because the Money which you received is not your own, but *Thomas Shaw's* to whom you are accountable for the same; therefore you must make *Cash* Dr. not to the Person of whom you received it, but to *Thomas Shaw,* to whom it was before and is now due; and *Thomas Shaw* Cr. by *Cash* for the sum so received.

— 4 —

7. Paid to *William Smith,* the Sum of 100*l.* which I Yesterday received for the Use of *Thomas Shaw,* by Order of do. *Shaw* - - - - | 100 | — | —

Note, This is the Converse of the former *Case,* and differs from that in *Jan.* 9, because the Money which you paid was not your own, nor did *William Smith* receive the same as due from you, but from *Thomas Shaw;* therefore you must not make the Person to whom you paid the Money, but *Thomas Shaw* Dr. to *Cash* for the Sum paid; and *Cash* Cr. by *Thomas Shaw* for the same Sum.

C

311

LONDON, February 5, 1789.

	l.	*s.*	*d.*

7. Received of *Brandon George* in full . . . . . .   57 | — |

Note, Here you must make *Cash* Dr. to *Brandon George* for the Sum received, and *Brandon George* Cr. by *Cash* for the same Sum.

——————— 6 ———————

7. Received of *Thomas Preston*, Esq; in full . . .   65 | — |

Note 1. Here you must make *Cash* Dr. and *Thomas Preston* Cr.
   2. Like *Cases* should always have like *Expressions*.

——————— 7 ———————

7.T.P. Bought of *Thomas Preston*, Esq; 10 Hhds. of *Oporto*
Wine, at 9*l.* per Hhd. to pay *May* 14 next . .   90 | — |

Note, *Oporto Wine* must here be made Dr. to *Thomas Preston*, for the Quantity and its Value, and *Thomas Preston* Cr. by *Oporto Wine* for the said Value.

——————— 8 ———————

7.T.L. Sold *Abraham Sims*, as follows,

	l.	*s.*	*d.*
5 Pieces of Drugget, containing 60 Yards, at 4*s.* 4*d.* per Yard . .	13	0	0
5 Pieces of Broad Cloth, qt. 85 Yards, at 11*s.* per Yard	46	15	0
12 Pieces of Holland, qt. 252 Ells, at 4*s.* per Ell	50	8	0

312

For which he paid me in Full.   100 | 3 | — |

Note 1. There is not a great deal of Difference between one Parcel of *Goods* sold for ready Money, and several Parcels: for *Cash* must be made Dr. to them all, each Parcel being made Cr. by *Cash* for itself; and therefore must be journalized after the following Manner, *viz.* *Cash* Dr. to *Sundry Accompts* for the whole Value received; and *Drugget, Broad Cloth* and *Holland* Crs. by *Cash* for the several Quantities sold, and their Values respectively.

   2. In the Account of *Broad Cloth*, the Learner should observe, that he has sold one Yard more than he bought; it must therefore be understood that he gained that Yard by the Difference of Measurement.

——————— 9 ———————

7. Received of *John Hammond* in Part .   £67 | 0 | 0 |
         Abated . . . . | 0 | 0 | 5 | 67 | — | 5 |

Note, By looking back to the 20th Day of the last Month, you will find that *John Hammond* was to pay 67*l.* 0*s.* 5*d.* and the Abatement of the *Five-Pence* being but a Trifle, the young Book-keeper may, perhaps, think it not worth taking Notice of; but as exactness is always required (or your Books will not balance) so it must by no Means be omitted; and therefore, to state the Case truly, you must make *Sundry Accompts* Drs. to *John Hammond* for the whole Payment that should be made, *viz.*

Cash for the Money you have received of him, and
Profit and Loss for the Money abated him;
Then make *John Hammond* Cr. by *Sundry Accompts* for both Money and Abatement.

LONDON, February 10, 1789.

J. | Bought of *William Baker*, Efq. 100 Pieces of Serge, qt, 1400 Yards, at 1*s.* per Yard.

For which I paid prefent Money . . £20 0 0

The reft to be paid the 20th Inftant . £50 0 0

> *Note,* This *Cafe* admits of two ways of journalizing, and is the Reverfe of that mentioned *Jan.* 23.
> 1. Make *Serge* Dr. to *William Baker* for the whole Quantity bought, and its Value, and *William Baker* Cr. by *Serge* for the faid Value; then, becaufe you have paid 20*l.* in Part, make *William Baker* Dr. to *Cafh* for the Money paid him, and *Cafh* Cr. by *William Baker* for the fame Sum. Or,
> 2. Make *Serge* Dr. to *Sundry Accompts*, expreffing the Quantity and its Value; then make Cafh Cr. by *Serge* for the Money paid, and *William Baker* Cr. by *Serge* for the 50*l.* remaining due to him. But as this latter looks more like a good *Book-keeper* than the former: fo I have made choice of it accordingly.

70

————— 11 —————

J.R.M. | Bought of *Robert Moore*, 40 Hhds. of *Lifbon* Wine, at 7*l.* per Hhd. . . . .

Given *Robert Moore* in Part of Payment, as follows,

J. | 200 Reams of Paper, at 11*s.* per Ream £ 110 0 0

In prefent Money 70 0 0

The reft on Demand 100 0 0

280

> *Note,* This *Cafe* will admit of two ways of journalizing, viz.
> 1. Make *Lifbon* Wine Dr. to *Robert Moore* for the whole Quantity of Wine bought, and its Value, and *Robert Moore* Cr. by *Lifbon* Wine for its Value; then make *Robert Moore* Dr. to *Sundry Accompts* for the Value of what he has received, and *Paper* Cr. by *Robert Moore* for the Quantity fold and its Value; alfo Cafh Cr. by *Robert Moore* for the Sum paid him, the Balance of which is the 100*l.* due to him. Or,
> 2. Make *Lifbon* Wine Dr. to *Sundry Accompts* for the whole Quantity bought, and its Value; then make *Paper* Cr. by *Lifbon* Wine for the Quantity fold, and its Value; Cafh Cr. by *Lifbon* Wine for the Sum of Money paid *Robert Moore*, and *Robert Moore* Cr. by *Lifbon* Wine for the Sum remaining due to him.— Either of thefe ways will do, but the expert *Book-keeper* will, I believe, make choice of the latter, as the better of the two.
> 3. As *Robert Moore* flood indebted to you 33*l.* 6*s.* 8*d.* before the Accompt was entered, it may feem fomething odd, that you fhould be made Debtor to him 100*l.* in the above affair, when in reality you owe him no more than 66*l.* 13*s.* 4*d.* but this difficulty will vanifh with a little confideration. For as the feveral parts of the whole taken together muft be equal to that Whole; fo in the above Quantity of *Lifbon* Wine amounting to 280*l.* that particular Accompt muft be ballanced by your being made Dr. to *Robert Moore* 100*l.* though in reality you owe him no more than 66*l.* 13*s.* 4*d.* as before, which Sum only muft be paid on Demand.

————— 12 —————

J. | Sold *Brandon George* 4 Hhds. of *Lifbon* Wine, at 8*l.* per Hhd. . . . .

32

> *Note, Brandon George* muft be made Dr. to *Lifbon* Wine, and *Lifbon* Wine Cr. by *Brandon George* for its Quantity and Value.

313

LONDON February 13, 1789.

	l.	*s.*	*d.*

J. Sold *Robert Uxley*, 10 Pieces of Serge, qt. 140 Yards, at 15*d. per* Yard . . . .   8 | 15 | —

Note, Here you must make *Robert Uxley* Dr. to *Serge* for its Value, and *Serge* Cr, by *R. Uxley* for its Quantity and Value.

--------------------- 14 ---------------------

Sold *Samuel Grainger*, as follows,   *l.*   *s.*   *d.*

J. 4 Pieces of *Norwich* Crape, qt. 64 Yards, at 4*s. per* Yard . . . . } 12 16 0

J. 10 Pieces of Duroy, qt. 150 Yards, at 6*s.* 6*d. per* Yard . . . . . } 48 15 0

J. 10 Pieces of Sagathee, qt. 120 Yards, at 2*s.* 10*d. per* Yard . . . . . . } 17 0 0

     Received prefent Money . . 28 11 0   78 | 11 | —

     The reft to pay *March* 1ft. next 50 0 0

Note, This differs very little from only one Sort of *Goods* fold in like manner: for either way the Buyer muft be made Dr. but here the Buyer, *i. e. Samuel Grainger* muft be made Dr. to *Sundry Accompts* for the whole Value of the *Goods* fold to him, and the feveral Sorts of *Goods*, viz. *Norwich* Crape, *Duroy*, and *Sagathee*, muft be made Crs. by *Samuel Grainger* for their feveral Quantities fold to him, and their refpective Values: Then *Cafh* muft be made Dr. to *Samuel Grainger* for the Money received, and *Samuel Grainger* Cr. by *Cafh* for the fame Sum.

--------------------- 15 ---------------------

Bought of *Robert Uxley*, as follows, *viz. l.*   *s.*   *d.*

J. R.U.   10 Hhds. of *French* Wine, 30*l. per* Hhd. 300 0 0

J. R.U.   10 Pipes of Canary, at 25*l. per* Pipe 250 0 0

J. R.U.   10 Hhds. of *Lifbon* Wine, at 7*l. per* Hhd. 70 0 0   620 | — | —

J. For which I paid prefent Money . . 100 0 0

   300 Reams of paper, at 10*s.* 6*d. per Ream* 157 10 0

The reft payable, as *per* Note, in 2 Months 362 10 0

Note, This Cafe appears fomething like that in the 11th Inftant, but is confined to only one Way of ftating Dr. and Cr. becaufe here are feveral Sorts of *Goods* bought. And although here is *Barter* in this Cafe, as in that, yet the Goods not being Value for Value, you muft make *Sundry Accompts*, viz. *French Wine, Canary,* and *Lifbon Wine* Drs. to *R. Uxley* for the feveral Quantities bought, and their refpective Values, and *R. Uxley,* Cr. by *Sundry Accompts* for the whole Value: Then make *R. Uxley,* Dr. to *Sundry Accompts* for the Value of what he has received, and *Cafh* Cr. by *R. Uxley* for the Sum paid him, and *Paper* Cr. by *R. Uxley,* for the Quantity fold and its Value.

2. What was faid of *Bills receivable* p. 8, *Jan.* 30, may here be obferved concerning *Bills payable.*

314

LONDON, February 16, 1789.

			l.	*s.*	*d.*

J.J.H. Bought of *John Herbert*, 20 Hhds. of Tobacco, qt. 76C. 1qr. 14lb. at 4l. 10s. per C. . . . . .   343 | 13 |

	l.	*s.*	*d.*

Which I have received in lieu of a Debt of 230 0 0
And return'd the Overplus, which was   113 13 9

Note, This *Case* may be journalized two Ways, *viz.*
1. Make *Tobacco* Dr. to *John Herbert* for the Quantity bought and its Value, and *John Herbert* Cr. by *Tobacco* for the said Value: then make *John Herbert* Dr. to Cash for the Overplus paid him, and Cash Cr. by *John Herbert* for the said Overplus.   Or,
2. Make *Tobacco* Dr. to *Sundry Accompts*, *viz.* to Cash and to *John Herbert* for the whole Sum that the *Tobacco* amounts to, and its Quantity, and *John Herbert* Cr. by *Tobacco* for so much as the Debt amounted to, and Cash Cr. by *Tobacco* for the Overplus paid to *John Herbert*. Either of these is right, but the ingenius *Book-keeper* will, I believe, prefer the latter, if he examines them carefully.

-------- 17 --------

J.J.H. Sold *Martin Unwin*, 20 Hhds. of Tobacco, qt. 76C. 1qr. 14lb. at 5l. per C. . . . .   381 | 17 | 6

Note, It is very plain that *Martin Unwin* (he being the buying Man) must be made Dr. to *Tobacco* for its Value, and that *Tobacco* must be made Cr. by *Martin Unwin* for both Quantity and value.

-------- 18 --------

J. Received of *Elias Skinner* in Full . . . . . .   44 | — | —

Note, As you receive the Money, you must necessarily make Cash Dr. to *Elias Skinner* for the same, and *Elias Skinner* Cr. by Cash for the like Sum.

-------- 19 --------

Sold *Isaac Reynolds*, as follows, *viz.*   *l.*   *s.*   *d.*

J.R.M. 14 Hhds. of *Lisbon* Wine, at 8l. per Hhd.   112   0   0

J.R.U. 5 Pipes of Canary, at 28l. per Pipe   140   0   0   252 | — |

The Balance of our Accompt to be paid in 6 Months

Note, Whatever Dealings there may be between yourself and *Isaac Reynolds*, as often as he receives Goods he must be made Dr. for the same: And as here are several Sorts of Goods sold to him; so you must make him Dr. to *Sundry Accompts* for the whole Value, and each of them Cr. by *Isaac Reynolds*, for its respective Quantity and Value.

-------- 20 --------

J. Paid *William Baker*, Esq; in full . . . . . .   50 | — | —

Note, As you have paid *William Baker*, he must be made Dr. to Cash, for that Sum, and Cash must be made Cr. by *William Baker* for the same Sum.

315

LONDON, February 21, 1789.

		l.	*s.*	*d.*		*l.*	*s.*	*d.*
	Bought of *Thomas Shaw*, as follows, *viz.*							
J.T.S.	44 Bags of Hops, wt. 132C. 2qrs. at 28s. *per* C.	185	10	0				
J.T.S.	20 Pieces of Drugget, qt. 280 Yds. at 3s. 4d. *per* Yard	46	13	4				
						232	3	4
	Sold to *Thomas Shaw*, as follows, *viz.*	*l.*	*s.*	*d.*				
J.T.P.	10 Hhds. of *Oporto* Wine, at 11*l.* per Hhd.	110	0	0				
J.R.M	7 Hhds. of *Lisbon* Wine, at 8*l.* per Hhd.	56	0	0				
	And returned him the Overplus, which was	66	3	4				
						232	3	4

Note, This is a Case in *Barter*, that is compound on both Sides; wherein several Sorts of Goods are given in Exchange for several other Sorts, and the difference of their whole Values paid by you to *Thomas Shaw*; and therefore to book all these Circumstances rightly, you must

1. Make *Sundry Accompts* Drs. to *Thomas Shaw* for what you bought of him, viz. Hops and *Drugget*, for their respective Quantities and Values; and *Thomas Shaw* Cr. by *Sundry Accompts* for their whole Value.
2. Make *Thomas Shaw* Dr. to *Sundry Accompts* for what he has received: and make *Oporto Wine*, *Lisbon Wine* and Cash Crs. by *Thomas Shaw* for their respective Quantities and Values.

--------------------- 22 ---------------------

		l.	*s.*	*d.*
J.	My good Friend *William Baker* Esq; having Occasion for some Money, has desired me to lend him the Sum of 500*l.* upon Bond, for 6 Months, at 5 *per Cent*. which I have agreed to, and he has received the said Sum accordingly	500	—	

Note, Most Writers on this Subject make the Borrower Dr. to *Sundry Accompts*, that is, to Cash for the Sum lent him, and to *Interest Reckoning*, or else to *Profit and Loss* for the Interest; but as the Borrower may pay the Principal either before or after the limited time in the Bond: so the *Interest* cannot be known at first, and therefore it is best to omit it, and only make the Borrower Dr. to Cash for the *Principal* by him received, and Cash Cr. by the Borrower for the same Sum, letting the *Interest* alone till it shall be paid.

--------------------- 23 ---------------------

		l.	*s.*	*d.*
J.	*John Osborne* being indebted to me in the Sum of 270*l.* has given me an Assignment on *James Jenkins* for the same Sum, which I have this Day received	270	—	

Note, As *John Osborne* stands indebted to you in your *Ledger*, in the above named Sum; so he only must be cleared, though you have received the Money of *Jenkins*; for by *Jenkins* paying you the Money by *Osborne*'s Order, it is that *Osborne* stands clear of the Debt, and therefore you must make Cash Dr. to *John Osborne* for the aforesaid Sum, and *John Osborne* Cr. by Cash for the same Sum; *Jenkins* being out of the Question.

LONDON, February 24, 1789.

J. I am indebted to Capt. *William Andrews*, in the Sum of 246*l*. which he has called on me for; I have therefore given him an Assignment on Sir *Robert Johnson* for the like Sum, which he has this Day received . . . . **246 —**

Note, This Entry differs from that next before, in as much as you stand indebted to Capt. *William Andrews,* and at the same Time Sir *Robert Johnson* stands indebted to you in a greater Sum: Therefore as Sir *Robert Johnson* has answered the Assignment, you must make Capt. *William Andrews* Dr. to Sir *Robert Johnson* for the Sum mentioned in the Assignment, and Sir *Robert Johnson* Cr. by Capt. *William Andrews* for the same sum.

—— 25 ——

J. I am indebted to *Robert Moore* 66*l*. 13*s*. 9*d*. he therefore has given *John Ash* a Draft on me for the like Sum, which I have this Day paid . . **66 13 9**

Note, This Case is just the reverse of that of the 23d Instant, therefore when you paid *John Ash,* it was for *Robert Moore's* Use: Hence you have nothing more to do, but to make *Robert Moore* Dr. to *Cash* for the Money paid on the Draft, and *Cash* Cr. by *Robert Moore* for the like Sum.

—— 26 ——

J. *Samuel Grainger,* who stands indebted to me 50*l*. has compounded with his Creditors to pay them 2*s*. 6*d*. in the Pound; I have therefore received of him 6*l*. 5*s*. and given him a general Discharge . . **6 5 —**

Note, Notwithstanding that *Samuel Grainger* has paid you no more than 6*l*. 5*s*. yet you must give him Credit for the whole 50*l*. and in Order to do this you must
1. Make *Sundry Accompts* Drs. to *Samuel Grainger* in the whole Sum, that is,
Cash for the Money that you have received, and
Profit and *Loss* for the Sum abated him: and then
2. Make *Samuel Grainger,* Cr. by *Sundry Accompts* for the same Sum.

—— 27 ——

J. Sold 10 Pieces of Duroy, qt. 150 Yards, at 6*s*. 6*d*. per Yard, to *Robert Uxley* . . . . **48 15 —**

Note, As *Robert Uxley* has bought the *Duroy,* but not paid for it, he, in course, must be your Dr. for the same; and therefore if you make *Robert Uxley* Dr. to *Duroy* for the Value of it, and *Duroy* Cr. by *Robert Uxley* for both the Quantity and Value, the Accompt will be rightly stated.

—— 28 ——

J. Paid sundry Charges this Month, as *per* Book of House Expenses . . . **70 12 —**

Note, This Entry is exactly the same with that of *Jan. 31. last,* and therefore you are only to make *Houshold Expenses* Dr. to *Cash* for the Money expended this Month, and *Cash* Cr. by *Houshold Expenses* for the same Sum.

The end of the first Waste Book.

317

The JOURNAL.

LONDON, January 1, 1789.

318

		l.	*s.*	*d.*	*l.*	*s.*	*d.*
	Sundry Accompts Drs. to Stock . . .	10830	14	10¼			
1	Cash in ready Money	8000	0	0			
1	Tobacco, for 19 Hhds. qt. 63C. 1qr. 14*lb.* at 4*l.* 14*s. per* C. . . . . . }	297	17	3			
1	Pepper, for 48 Bags, qt. 1026*lb.* at 16*d. per lb.* . . . . . . }	68	8	0			
2	Canary, for 16 Pipes, at 25*l. per* Pipe, .	400	0	0			
2	Hops, for 30 Bags, qt. 109C. 1qr. 12*lb.* at 2*l. per* C. . . . . . . }	218	14	3¼			
2	French Wine, for 10 Hhds. at 27*l. per* Hhd.	270	0	0			
2	Holland, for 20 Pieces, qt. 384 Ells, at 3*s.* *per* Ell . . . . . . }	57	12	0			
2	Broad Cloth, for 10 Pieces, qt. 180 Yards, at 10*s. per* Yard . . . . . }	90	0	0			
3	Shalloon, for 7 Pieces, qt. 100 Yards, at 2*s.* 4*d. per* Yard . . . . }	11	13	4			
3	Drugget, for 5 Pieces, qt. 60 Yards, at 3*s.* 6*d. per* Yard . . . . }	10	10	0			
3	*Thomas Preston,* Esq; on Demand . .	100	0	0			
3	Sir *Robert Johnson*	476	0	0			
3	*John Herbert*	250	0	0			
4	Capt. *John Smith* (to pay the 18th Instant)	580	0	0			
1	Stock Dr. to Sundry Accompts . . .	535	13	0	10830	14	10¼
4	To Capt. *William Andrews* on Demand .	270	0	0			
4	To Sir *Humphrey Parsons* (to pay the 8th Instant) . . . . }	100	0	0			
4	To *William Baker,* Esq; (to pay the 17th Instant) . . . . }	150	0	0			
4	To *William Warner*	15	13	0	535	13	—

Note, The *Inventory* being journalized, as above, you must next turn to your *Ledger,* and therein erect an Accompt for each of these Particulars, in the following Manner :

(1.) You must begin with *Stock,* and in a good round Text-Hand, on the left Folium of the Book, write *Stock Dr.* and on the right Folium, in the same Hand, write *Per Contra Cr.*

(2.) Because Sundry Accompts are Drs. to *Stock,* you must, in your *Ledger,* make Stock Cr. by Sundry Accompts, expressing the whole Value.

(3.) Make every particular Part Dr. to *Stock* for its Quantity (which mention in your inner Columns) and Value respectively.
(4.) Beginning these Particulars with *Cash,* you must, as in *Stock,* make *Cash Dr. per Contra Cr,* and then beneath, in small Hand,

LONDON, January 1, 1789.

on the Debtor Side, put the Year and Day of the Month, and the Folium of the *Journal*, and then write, To *Stock* in Ready Money, expreſſing the Sum. The like do with *Tobacco*, *Pepper*, &c.

(5.) After this is done, you muſt next (becauſe you ſtand indebted to ſeveral Perſons) make *Stock* Dr. to *Sundry Accompts*, for the Sum of all your Debts.

(6.) Make each particular Man **Cr.** by *Stock* (on the Creditor Side) for the Sum which you owe him; obſerving alſo, the *Date* and *Folium*. This is poſting.

2. The left Hand Page of the *Ledger* is always the Debtor Side, and the right Hand Page is always the Creditor Side.

3. No Merchant erects an Accompt of himſelf in the *Ledger*, becauſe his own *Stock* ſtands for him.

		l.	s.	d.
	— 2 —			
1 / 2	Caſh Dr. to Holland . . . . . . £22 0 0 For 8 Pieces, qt. 132 Ells, at 3s. 4d. per Ell, for ready Money.	22	—	—
	— 3 —			
5 / 2	*Brandon George*, Dr. to *French* Wine . . £57 0 0 For 2 Hhds. at 28l. 10s. per Hhd. to pay in one Month	57	—	—
	— 4 —			
5 / 3	*Oporto* Wine Dr. to *Thomas Preſton*, Eſq; £35 0 0 For 5 Hhds. at 7l. per Hhd.	35	—	—
	— 5 —			
5 / 2	*Samuel Fairman* Dr. to *French* Wine . . £28 0 0 For 1 Hhd. at 28l. per Hhd.	28	—	—
	— 6 —			
5 / 5	*Elias Skinner*, Dr. to *Oporto* Wine . . . £27 0 0 For 3 Hhds. at 9l. per Hhd. to pay the 12th Inſtant	27	—	—
	— 7 —			
1 / 3	Caſh Dr. to Sir *Robert Johnſon* . . . . £100 0 0 Received in Part	100		
	— 8 —			
4 / 1	Sir *Humphrey Parſons* Dr. to Caſh . . £100 0 0 Paid in full	100	—	—
	— 9 —			
6 / 2	*Liſbon* Wine Dr. to Broad Cloth . . . £49 0 0 For 7 Hhds. at 7l. per Hhd. bought of *Elias Ingram*, for which I ſold him 5 Pieces of Broad Cloth, qt. 96 Yards, at 10s. 2d.¼ per Yard, amounting to the ſame Sum	49	—	—
	— 10 —			
6 / 2	*William Lowfield*, Eſq; Dr. to Hops . . £66 3 0 For 10 Bags, qt. 31C. 2qrs. at 2l. 2s. per C. . . .	66	3	—
	— 11 —			
4 / 5	Sir *Humphrey Parſons* Dr. to *Liſbon* Wine £16 0 0 For 2 Hhds. at 8l. per Hhd.	16	—	—
	— 12 —			
1 / 5	Caſh Dr. to *Elias Skinner* . . . . . £27 0 0 Received in Full	27	—	—

D

319

LONDON, January 13, 1789.

			£.	s.	d.
1	Cash Dr. to *Lisbon* Wine	£ 25 10 0			
6	For 3 Hhds. at 8*l.* 10*s.* per Hhd.		25	10	
	———— 14 ————				
1	Tobacco Dr. to Cash	£298 0 0			
1	For 20 Hhds. qt. 74*C.* 2*qrs.* at 4*l.* per *C.* .		298	—	
	———— 15 ————				
6	*Thomas Johnson* Dr. to Sundry Accompts	£256 14 3¼			
1	To Tobacco, for 10 Hhds. qt. 37*C* 1*qr.* 15*lb.* at 4*l.* 12*s.* per *C.* }	171 19 3¾			
2	To *French* Wine for 3 Hhds. at 28*l.* 5*s.* per Hhd. 84 15 0				
	———— 16 ————		256	14	3¾
1	Cash Dr. to Sir *Robert Johnson* . . .	£100 0 0			
3	Received in Part		100	—	
	———— 17 ————				
4	*William Baker*, Esq; Dr. to Cash . .	£150 0 0			
1	Paid in Full		150	—	
	———— 18 ————				
1	Cash Dr. to Capt. *John Smith* . . .	£580 0 0			
4	Received in full		580	—	
	———— 19 ————				
6	Stuffs Dr. to *John Herbert* . . .	£20 0 0			
3	For 20 Pieces, qt. 240 Yards, at 20*d.* per Yard .		20	—	
	———— 20 ————				
6	*John Hammond*, Esq; Dr. to Tobacco .	£167 0 5			
1	For 10 Hhds. qt. 37*C.* 0*qrs.* 13*lb.* at 4*l.* 10*s.* per *C.* he to pay as follows, viz.				
	On *February* the 9th next . . . £67 0 5				
	In three Months 100 0 0				
	———— 21 ————		167	—	5
4	Capt. *William Andrews* Dr. to Stuffs, . £ 24 0 0				
6	For 20 Pieces, qt. 240 Yards, at 2*s.* per Yard . .		24	—	
	———— 22 ————				
7	*Robert Moore* Dr. to Sundry Accompts . £533 6 3				
1	To Tobacco, for 19 Hhds. qt. 63*C.* 1*qr.* 14*lb.* at 4*l.* 15*s.* per *C.* }	301 0 7½			
1	To Pepper, for 48 Bags, qt. 1026*lb.* at 17*d.* per *lb.* }	72 13 6			
2	To Hops, for 20 Bags, qt. 77*C.* 2*qrs.* 12*lb.* at 2*l.* 1*s.* per *C.* }	159 12 1½			
2	Canary Dr. to *Robert Moore* £500 0 0		533	6	3
7	For 20 Pipes, at 25*l.* per Pipe		500	—	

320

LONDON, January 23, 1789.

		l.	s.	d.
	Sundry Accompts Drs. to Canary, for 20 Pipes, at 28l. per Pipe, sold *John Osborne* } 560 0 0			
1	Cash received in Part 290 0 0			
7	*John Osborne* for the Remainder 270 0 0			
2	———— 24 ————	560	—	—
7	*Richard Remnant*, Dr. to Canary . . . £432 0 0			
2	For 16 Pipes, at 27l. per Pipe, to pay in 3 Months . .			
	———— 25 ————	432	—	—
	Sundry Accompts Dr. to *Richard Remnant* £432 0 0			
1	*viz.* Cash received for early Payment . . 426 13 4			
9	Profit and Loss, for the Rebate on 432l. } for 3 Months, at 5 per Cent. . . } 5 6 8			
7	———— 26 ————	432	—	—
6	*William Lowfield*, Esq; Dr. to Shalloon . £12 10 0			
3	For 7 Pieces, qt. 100 Yards, at 2s. 6d. per Yard . .	12	10	—
	———— 27 ————			
7	Paper Dr. to *Martin Unwin* . . . £500 0 0			
7	For 1000 Reams, at 10s. per Ream, for which I am to pay as follows,			
	Within 1 Month . . 100 0 0			
	2 Months . . 100 0 0			
	3 Months . . 300 0 0			
	———— 28 ————	500	—	—
7	*Martin Unwin* Dr. to Sundry Accompts . £500 0 0			
1	*viz.* To Cash 495 1 1½			
9	To Profit and Loss, for the Rebate, on } 500l. at 5 per Cent. . . . . . } 4 18 10½			
	———— 29 ————	500	—	—
8	*Norwich* Crape Dr. to *Robert Uxley* . . 280 0 0			
8	For 100 Pieces, qt. 1600 Yards, at 3s. 6d. per Yard .	280	—	—
8	*Robert Uxley* Dr. to Paper 262 10 0			
7	For 500 Reams, at 10s. 6d. per Ream	262	10	—
	———— 30 ————			
	Sundry Accompts Drs to *Norwich* Crape, for } 40 Pieces, qt. 640 Yards, at 4s. per Yard } 128 0 0			
1	*viz.* Cash received in Part 28 0 0			
6	*William Lowfield*, Esq; for *William* } *Warner*'s Assignment on him } 50 0 0			
4	*William Warner* for the Remainder, to } stand 3 Months . . . . } 50 0 0			
8		128	—	—

321

LONDON, January 31, 1789.

		l.	s.	d.
5	House Expenses Dr. to Cash 37 13 3			
1	For sundry Charges paid this Month, as *per* Book of House-Expenses	37	13	3

―――――――――――― February 1 ――――――――――――

		l.	s.	d.
5	*Elias Skinner* Dr. to Sundry Accompts . 154 0 0			
6	*viz.* To *Lisbon* Wine, for 2 Hhds. at 8*l per* Hhd. 16 0 0			
5	To *Oporto* Wine, for 2 Hhds. at 9*l per* Hhd. 18 0 0			
2	To *French* Wine, for 4 Hhds. at 30*l per* Hhd. 120 0 0	154	—	—
	Sundry Accompts Drs. to *Elias Skinner* . £110 0 0			
1	*viz.* Cash received in Part 90 0 0			
7	*Martin Unwin*, for d° *Skinner's* Assign-} 20 0 0			
5	ment on him, payable to me . . }			

―――――― 2 ――――――

		l.	s.	d.
		110	—	—
	Sundry Accompts Drs. to *Isaac Reynolds* . £330 0 0			
8	*viz.* Duroy, for 40 Pieces, qt. 600 Yards, } 180 0 0			
	at 6 *s* per Yard . . . . . }			
8	Sagathee, for 100 Pieces, qt. 1200 } 150 0 0			
8	Yards, at 2*s.* 6*d. per* Yard . . }			
	Isaac Reynolds Dr. to Sundry Accompts . 120 0 0	330	—	—
1	*viz.* To Cash paid him in Part for the above } 100 0 0			
	mentioned Goods . . . . }			
7	To *Martin Unwin*, for *Skinner's* Note } 120 0 0			
	on him, payable to *Reynolds* . . }			

―――――― 3 ――――――

		l.	s.	d.
		120	—	—
1	Cash Dr. to *Thomas Shaw* £100 0 0			
9	Received of *John James* for the Use of d° *Shaw* .	100	—	—

―――――― 4 ――――――

		l.	s.	d.
9	*Thomas Shaw* Dr. to Cash £100 0 0			
1	Paid to *William Smith*, by Order of do. *Shaw* . . .	100	—	—

―――――― 5 ――――――

		l.	s.	d.
1	Cash Dr. to *Brandon George* £57 0 0			
5	Received in Full	57	—	—

―――――― 6 ――――――

		l.	s.	d.
1	Cash Dr. to *Thomas Preston*, Esq; . . . £65 0 0			
3	Received in Full	65	—	—

―――――― 7 ――――――

		l.	s.	d.
5	*Oporto* Wine Dr. to *Thomas Preston*, Esq; £90 0 0			
3	For 10 Hhds. at 9*l. per* Hhd. to pay *May* 14 next . .	90	—	—

322

LONDON, February 8, 1789.

		l.	s.	d.
1	Cash Dr. to Sundry Accompts £110	3	0	
3	viz, To Drugget, for 5 pieces, qt. 60 Yards, at 4s. 4d. per Yard	13	0	0
2	To Broad Cloth, for 5 Pieces, qt. 85 Yards, at 11s. per Yard .	46	15	3
2	To Holland, for 12 Pieces, qt. 252 Ells, at 4s. per Ell .	50	8	0
	9	110	3	
	Sundry Accompts Drs. to John Hammond, Esq. £67	0	0	
1	viz. Cash received in part 67	0	0	
9	Profit and loss abated him . . . 0	0	5	
6	10	67		5
9	Serge Dr. to Sundry Accompts, for 100 Pieces qt. 1400 Yards, at 1s. per Yard .	70	0	0
1	viz. To Cash paid in Part 20	0	0	
4	To William Baker, Esq; for the rest to be paid the 20th Instant .	50	0	0
	11	70		
5	Lisbon Wine Dr. to Sundry Accompts, for 40 Hhds. at 7l. per Hhd. .	280	0	0
7	viz. To paper, for 200 Reams, at 11s. per Ream .	110	0	0
1	To Cash paid in part 70	0	0	
7	To Robert Moore for the rest, to be paid on Demand .	100	0	0
5	12	280		
6	Brandon George, Dr. to Lisbon Wine . £32	0	0	
	For 4 Hhds. at 8l. per Hhd.	32		
8	13			
9	Robert Uxley Dr. to Serge . . . £8	15	0	
	For 10 Pieces, qt. 140 Yards, at 15d per Yd.	8	15	
0	14			
	Samuel Grainger, Dr. to Sundry Accompts . £78	11	0	
8	viz. To Norwich Crape, for 4 Pieces qt. 64 Yards, at 4s. per Yard .	12	16	0
8	To Duroy, for 10 Pieces, qt. 150 Yds. at 6s. 6d. per Yard	48	15	0
8	To Sagathee, for 10 Pieces, qt. 120 Yards, at 2s. 10d. per Yard .	17	0	0
		78	11	
1	Cash Dr. to Samuel Grainger . . . 28	11	0	
0	Received in Part for the above Goods .	28	11	

323

LONDON, February 15, 1789.

		£		
Sundry Accompts Drs. to *Robert Uxley*		620	0	0
viz. *French* Wine, for 10 Hhds. at 30*l.* per Hhd.	}	300	0	0
Canary, for 10 Pipes, at 25*l.* per Pipe		250	0	0
Lisbon Wine, for 10 Hhds. at 7*l.* per Hhd.	}	70	0	0

———— 16 ————

		£		
Robert Uxley Dr. to Sundry Accompts		257	10	0
viz. To Cash paid him in Part		100	0	0
To Paper, for 300 Reams, at 10*s.* 6*d.* per Ream	}	157	10	0

———— 16 ————

		£		
Tobacco Dr. to Sundry Accompts, for 20 Hhds. qt. 76 *C.* 3 qr. 14*lb.* at 4*l.* 10*s.* per *C.*	}	343	13	9
viz. To Cash, paid in Part		113	13	9
To *John Herbert*, for the Clearing of a Debt of	}	230	0	0

———— 17 ————

		£		
Martin Unwin Dr. to Tobacco		381	17	6
For 20 Hhds. qt. 76 *C.* 1 qr. 14*lb.* at 5*l.* per *C.*				

———— 18 ————

		£		
Cash Dr. to *Elias Skinner*		44	0	0
Received in Full				

———— 19 ————

Isaac Reynolds Dr. to Sundry Accompts		252	0	0
viz. Lisbon Wine, for 14 Hhds. at 8*l.* per Hhd.	}	112	0	0
To Canary, for 5 Pipes, at 28*l.* per Pipe	}	140	0	0

The balance of our Accounts, to be paid in 6 Months.

———— 20 ————

		£		
William Baker, Esq; Dr. to Cash		50	0	0
Paid him in Full				

324

LONDON, February 21, 1789.

		l.	s.	d.
	Sundry Accompts Drs. to *Thomas Shaw* . £232 3 4			
2	*viz.* Hops, for 44 Bags, wt. 132 C. 2qrs. 0lb. at 28s. *per* C. 185 10 0			
3 9	Drugget, for 20 Pieces, qt. 280 Yards at 3s. 4d. *per* Yard 46 13 4	232	3	4
9	*Thomas Shaw* Dr. to Sundry Accompts . £232 3 4			
5	*viz.* To *Oporto* Wine, for 10 Hhds. at 11l. *per* Hhd. 110 0 0			
6	To *Lisbon* Wine, for 7 Hhds. at 8l. *per* Hhd 56 0 0			
1	To Cash for the Overplus paid him . 66 3 4	232	3	4

Note, In the *Cash Book* there is an *Error* made by the placing of the above mentioned 66l. 3s. 4d. on the Dr. Side instead of the Cr. Side. And therefore, as no Erasements are to be made in your Books of Accompts, this *Error* can be corrected no other Way than by making another *Error* of the same Sum to balance it on the Cr. Side. This *Error* was made on Purpose to shew the Learner how he must correct an *Error* made in the like Case.

	22			
4 1	*William Baker*, Esq; Dr. to Cash . . . £500 0 0 For so much lent him upon Bond, for 6 Months, at 5 *per* Cent.	500	—	—
	23			
1 7	Cash Dr. to *John Osborne* . . . . £270 0 0 Which Sum I have received this Day, of *James Jenkins*, by an Assignment on d° *Jenkins*, by d° *Osborne* . . .	270	—	—
	24			
4 3	Capt. *William Andrews* Dr. to Sir *Rob. Johnson*£246 0 0 For my Assignment on d° Sir *Robert*, payable to d° *Andrews*	246	—	—
	25			
7 1	*Robert Moore* Dr. to Cash . . . . £66 13 9 For a Draft on me by d° *Moore*, payable to *John Ash*, or Order	66	13	9
	26			
	Sundry Accompts Drs. to *Samuel Grainger* £50 0 0			
1 9	*viz.* Cash received of d° *Grainger* . . . 6 5 0			
10	Profit and Loss abated in Composition . 43 15 0	50	—	—
	27			
8 9	*Robert Uxley* Dr. to Duroy . . . £48 15 0 For 10 Pieces, qt. 150 Yards, at 6s. 6d. *per* Yard . .	48	15	—
	28			
5 1	House-Expenses Dr. to Cash . . . . £70 12 11 For sundry Charges paid this Month, as *per* Book of House-Expenses	70	12	11

The End of the first Journal.

The Alphabet to the LEDGER.

A.	E.	I.
Andrews Capt. William 4		Johnson Sir Robert Johnson Thomas

B.	F.	K.
Broad Cloth — — 2 Baker William, Esq; 4 Balance — — — 10	French Wine — — 2 Fairman Samuel — 5	

C.	G.	L.
Cash — — — 1 Canary — — — 2 Cloth Broad — — 2 Crape Norwich — 8	George Brandon — 5 Grainger Samuel — 10	Lisbon Wine — Lowfield William

D.	H.	M.
Drugget — — — 2 Duroy — — — 8	Hops — — — 2 Holland — — — 2 Herbert John — 3 House-Expenses — 5 Hammond John, Esq; 6	Moore Robert — 7

The LEDGER.

The Alphabet to the LEDGER.

N.		R.		W.	
Norwich Crape - - -	8	Remnant Richard -	7	Wine Canary - - -	2
		Reynolds Isaac - -	8	Wine French - - -	2
				Warner William - -	4
				Wine Oporto - -	5
				Wine Lisbon - - -	6

O.		S.		X.	
Oporto Wine - -	5	Stock - - - -	1		
Oborne John - -	7	Shalloon - - -	3		
		Smith Capt. John -	4		
		Skinner Elias - -	5		
		Stuffs - - - -	6		
		Sagathee - - -	8		
		Shaw Thomas - -	9		
		Serge - - - -	9		

P.		T.		Y.	
Pepper - - - -	1	Tobacco - - - -	1		
Peston Thomas, Esq;	3				
Parsons Sir Humphrey	4				
Paper - - - -	7				
Profit and Loss - -	9				

Q.		U.		Z.	
		Unwin Martin - -	7		
		Uxley Robert - -	8		

1789		Stock						Dr.		l.	s.	d.
Jan. 1	—	To Sundry Accompts										
Feb. 28	R	To Balance, for the neat Proceed of my whole Estate							10	1051	5	4
										1104	13	4

Note 1, The first Line on this Side, contains the whole of what you owed at your first setting out in Trade;
2, The Balance contains the whole of your Estate, in Goods, Cash and Debts, due to you at the closing of your Books.
3, Every Entry in the Ledger must contain so much of the Transaction as may be wrote in one Line, and no more; though for Necessity's Sake, two Lines are often used here.

1789		Cash		Dr.		l.	s.	d.
Jan. 1	1	To Stock			1	8000		
31	—	To Sundry Accompts, received this Month .				1599	3	4
Feb. 8	—	To Sundry Accompts, received this Month .				837	19	
						10437	2	4

1789		Tobacco		Dr.				
			Hhds.	C.	qr.	lb.	Mark	
Jan. 1	1	To Stock, at 4l. 14s. per C.	19	63	1	14	I C	1
14	3	To Cash, at 4l. per C.	20	74	2	0	I H	1
Feb. 16	7	To Sundry Accompts, at 4l. 10s. per C.	20	76	1	14	I H	1
28	R	To Profit and Loss gain'd by this Account . . .						9
			59	214	1	0		

l.	s.	d.
29	17	3
298		
24	13	0
5	6	10
1021	1	10

Note, All Accompts of Goods are balanced either by Profit and Loss for the Gain or Loss on the Sale thereof; or by Balance for what remains unsold; or by both: In the present Case, the Tobacco is all sold, and therefore balanced only by Profit and Loss for the Gain, which is very easily obtained; for as the Dr. Side contains the prime Cost of the Goods, that is,

1789		Pepper		Dr.			l.	s.	d.
					Bags	lb.			
Jan. 1	1	To Stock, at 16d. per lb. for . .			48	1026	1	68	8
Feb. 28	R	To Profit and Loss gain'd by this Accompt					9	4	5	6
								72	13	6

1789		Per Contra	Cr.		l.	s.	d.
Jan. 2	1	By Sundry Accompts			10830	14	10¼
Feb. 28	R	By Profit and Loss gain'd by two Month's trading	9		218	3	6

Note 1, The first Line on this Side contains the Whole
of your Estate, viz. Goods, Cash and Debts, due to
you at your first setting out in Trade.

2, The Profit and Loss contains the whole of your Gain
at the closing of your Books.

					11048	18	4¼

1789		Per Contra	Cr.				
Jan. 31		By Sundry Accompts, paid this Month . . .			1080	14	4¼
Feb. 28		By Sundry Accompts, paid this Month . .			1257	3	9
	R	By Balance remaining in Hand, carried to the next Ledger	10		8099	4	2½

Note, The Balance of this Accompt (if any) is always
placed on the Cr. Side, and shews what Money is remaining in your Hands; and the Reason is very obvious, because no Man can pay more than he receives.

					10437	2	4

1789		Per Contra				Cr.					
			Hhds.	C.	qr.	lb.	Mark				
Jan. 15	3	By Thomas Johnson, at 4l. 12s. per C. for . . .	10	37	1	15	I H	6	171	19	3¾
20	3	By John Hammond, Esq; at 4l. 10s. per C. for .	10	37	0	13	I H	6	167	—	5
22	3	By Robert Moore, at 4l. 15s. per C. for . .	19	63	1	14	I C	7	301	—	7½
Feb. 17	7	By Martin Unwin, at 5l. per C. for	20	76	1	14	I H	7	381	17	6
			59	214	1	c			1021	17	10¼

what you gave for them, and the Cr. Side what they
were sold for; so, if the Cr. Side be the greater, the
Difference between them is the Gain; but if it should
happen that the Dr. Side is the greater (as it does
sometimes, through Decay of Goods, or the Market
Price falling) then the Difference is the Loss, and
will always fall on the Cr. Side.

1789		Per Contra		Cr.			
			Bags	lb.			
Jan. 23	3	By Robert Moore, at 17d. per lb. for	48	1026	7	72	13	6

329

Canary		Dr.		*l.*	*s.*	*d*
		Pipes	Mark			
1789 Jan. 1	1 To Stock, at 25*l.* *per* Pipe . .	16	L	1	400	—	—
22	5 To *Robert Moore*, at 25*l.* *per* Pipe .	20	R M	7	500	—	—
Feb.15	7 To *Robert Uxley*, at 25*l.* *per* Pipe .	10	R U	8	250	—	—
28	R To Profit & lofs, gain'd by this Accompt			9	710	—	—
		41			1257	—	—

Note, Here it appears that the Goods are not all fold ;
and therefore before you can tell the *Gain* or *Lofs*,
you muft firft find the Value of the Goods that are
untold, at prime Coft, and add to it the Value of the

Hops		Dr.						*l.*	*s.*	*d*
		Bags	C.	qr.	lb.	Mark				
1789 Jan. 1	1 To Stock, at 2*l.* *per* C. for	30	109	1	12	S C	1	218	14	3¼
Feb.21	8 To *Thomas Shaw*, at 1*l.* 8*s.* *per* C. for . .	44	132	2	0	T S	9	185	10	—
28	R To Profit and Lofs, gained by this Accompt . .						9	7	—	10¼
		74	241	3	12			411	5	1½

Note, Hence appears the Ufefulnefs of having Goods
marked, when they have been purchafed of feveral

French Wine		Dr.			*l.*	*s.*	*d*
		Hhds.	Mark				
1789 Jan. 1	1 To Stock at 27*l.* *per* Hhd. for . .	10	B A	1	270	—	—
Feb.15	7 To *Robert Uxley*, at 30*l.* *per* Hhd. for	10	R U	8	300	—	—
28	R To Profit & Lofs, gain'd by this Accompt			9	19	15	—
		20			589	15	—

Holland		Dr.			*l.*	*s.*	*d*
		Pcs.	Ells.				
1789 Jan. 1	1 To Stock at 3*s.* *per* Ell	20	384	1	57	12	—
Feb.28	R To Profit & Lofs, gain'd by this Accompt			9	14	16	—
		20	384		72	8	—

Broad Cloth		Dr.			*l.*	*s.*	*d*
		Pcs.	Yds.				
1789 Jan. 1	1 To Stock, at 10*s.* *per* Yard . .	10	180	1	90	—	—
Feb.2?	R To Profit & Lofs gain'd by this Accompt			9	5	15	—
		10	180		95	15	—

330

1789	Per Contra		Cr.	Pipes	Mark		l.	s.	d.
Jan. 23	4	By Sundry Accompts, at 28l. per Pipe, for		20	RM	—	560	—	—
24	4	By Richard Remnant, at 27l. per Pipe, to pay in three Months		16	I L	7	432	—	—
Feb. 19	7	By Isaac Reynolds, at 28l. per Pipe, for		5	R U	8	140	—	—
28	R	By Balance, remaining unsold, at 25l. per Pipe, for		5	R U	10	125	—	—
		Goods that have been sold (for the whole Quantity must stand on both Sides, be the Value less or more) then the Difference, as before, will be the Gain or Loss on the Sale of those Goods.		46			1257	—	

1789	Per Contra		Cr.	Bags	C.	qr.	lb.	Mark		l.	s.	d.
Jan. 10	2	By William Lowfield, Esq; at 2l. 2s. per C. for . . .		10	31	2	0	S C	6	66	3	—
22	4	By Robert Moore, at 2l. 1s. per C. for		20	77	3	12	S C	7	159	12	1½
Feb. 28	R	By Balance unsold, at 1l. 8s. per C. for		44	132	2	0	T S	10	185	10	—
		Persons at different Times and Prices.		74	241	3	12			411	5	1¼

1789	Per Contra		Cr.	Hhds.	Mark		l.	s.	d.
Jan. 3	2	By Brandon George, at 28l. 10s. per Hhd. for		2	B A	5	57	—	—
5	2	By Samuel Fairman, at 28l. per Hhd. for		1	B A	5	28	—	—
15	3	By Thomas Johnson, at 28l. 5s. per Hhd. for		3	B A	6	84	15	—
Feb. 1	5	By Elias Skinner, at 30l. per Hhd. for .		4	B A	5	120	—	—
28	R	By Balance unsold, at 30l. per Hhd. . .		10	R U	10	300	—	—
				20			589	15	—

1789	Per Contra		Cr.	Pcs.	Ells		l.	s.	d.
Jan. 2	2	By Cash, at 3s. 4d. per Ell, for		8	122	1	22	—	—
Feb. 8	6	By Cash, at 4s. per Ell, for		12	252	1	50	8	—
				20	334		72	8	—

1789	Per Contra		Cr.	Pcs.	Yds.		l.	s.	d.
Jan. 9	2	By Lisbon Wine, at 10s. 2d. ½ per Yard		5	96	6	49	—	—
Feb. 8	4	By Cash, at 11s. per Yard . . .		5	85	1	46	15	—
		Note, Here is a Yard gain'd by the Difference of Measurement.		10	181		95	15	—

331

Shalloon · Dr.

1789				Pcs.	Yds.	fol.	£	s.	d.
Jan. 1	1	To Stock, 2s. 4d. per Yard, for . .		7	100	1	11	13	4
Feb. 28	R	To Profit & Loss, gain'd by this Accompt				9	—	16	8
							12	10	—

Drugget · Dr.

1789				Pcs.	Yds.	Mark	fol.	£	s.	d.
Jan. 1	1	To Stock, at 3s. 6d. per Yard, for		5	60	T L	1	10	10	—
Feb. 21	8	To Thomas Shaw, at 3s. 4d. per Yard, for		30	280	T S	9	46	13	4
	2	R	To Profit and Loss, gain'd by this Accompt				9	2	10	—
				25	340			59	13	4

332

Thomas Preston, Esq; · Dr.

1789				fol.	£	s.	d.
Jan. 1	1	To Stock		1	100	—	—
Feb. 28	R	To Balance due to him, to pay May 14 next .		10	90		
					190		

Note 1, The Dr. Side of any Man's Accompt shews what he stands indebted to you; and the Cr. Side shews what you stand indebted to him; and when the Cr. Side exceeds the Dr. (as in this Case) the Balance of the Accompt must be placed on the Dr. Side, and

Sir Robert Johnson · Dr.

1789				fol.	£	s.	d.
Jan. 1	1	To Stock		1	476	—	—
Error	R	To Balance due to him		10	30	—	—
					506	—	—

Note 1, This Error was designedly made, to shew the young Book-keeper how to correct it; which see on the Cr. Side.

John Herbert · Dr.

1789				fol.	£	s.	d.
Jan. 1	1	To Stock		1	250	—	—

		Per Contra	Cr.	Pcs. Yds.		*l.*	*s.*	*d.*
1789								
Jan. 26	4	By *William Lowfield*, Esq. at 2s. 6d. per Yard, for		7 100	6	12	10	—

		Per Contra	Cr.	Pcs. Yds. Mark				
1789								
Feb. 8	6	By Cash, at 4s. 4d. per Yard, for		5 60 T L	1	13	—	—
28	R	By Balance, unsold, at 3s. 4d. per Yard, for		20 280 T S	10	46	13	4
				25 340		56	13	4

		Per Contra	Cr.					
1789								
Jan. 4	2	By *Oporto* Wine			5	35	—	—
Feb. 6	5	By Cash, received in full			1	65	—	—
7	5	By *Oporto* Wine, to pay *May* 14 next . .			5	90	—	—
						190	—	—

shews what you are really indebted to him.
2, The Price per *Hhd. Piece, Yard, Ell, &c.* and the *Quantity* of any Sort of Goods, are never put under any Man's Name in the Ledger.

		Per Contra	Cr.					
1789								
Jan. 7	2	By Cash, received in Part			1	100	—	—
16	3	By Cash, received in Part			1	100	.	—
Feb. 24	8	By Capt. *William Andrews*, for my Draft on Sir *Robert*, payable to d° *Andrews* . .			4	246	—	—
27	R	By Error on the Dr. Side				30	—	—
28	R	By Balance due to me			10	30	—	—
						506	—	—

2, The last Line but one, having the *Index* to it, shews that it was inserted, in Order to balance the *Error* committed on the Dr. Side of this Account.

		Per Contra	Cr.					
1789								
Jan. 10	2	By Stuffs			6	20	—	—
Feb. 16	7	By Tobacco			1	230	—	—
						250	—	—

1789		Capt. John Smith	Dr.		l.	s.	d.
Jan. 1	1	To Stock, to pay the 18th Inftant		1	580	—	—

1789		Capt. William Andrews	Dr.		l.	s.	d.
Jan.21	3	To Stuffs		6	42	—	—
Feb.24	8	To Sir *Robert Johnfton*, for my Draft on him, payable to do. *Andrews*		3	246	—	—
					270	—	—

334

1789		Sir Humphrey Parfons	Dr.		l.	s.	d.
Jan. 8	2	To Cafh, paid in full		1	100	—	—
11	2	To *Lisbon* Wine		6	16	—	—
					116	—	—

Note, When the Dr. Side of any Man's Accompt exceeds the Cr. Side, the *Balance* thereof muft be placed on the Cr. Side, and fhews what he is indebted to you.

1789		William Baker, Efq ;	Dr.		l.	s.	d.
Jan.17	3	To Cafh, paid in full		1	150	—	—
Feb.20	7	To Cafh, paid in full		1	50	—	—
22	8	To Cafh, for 500*l.* lent him on Bond, for 6 Months, at 5 *per Cent.*		1	500	—	—
					700	—	—

1789		William Warner	Dr.		l.	s.	d.
Jan.30	4	To *Norwich* Crape, to pay in 3 Months		8	50	—	—

				l.	*s.*	*d.*
1789	Per Contra	Cr.				
Jan. 1	By Cash received in full . . .	1	530	—	—

				l.	*s.*	*d.*
1789	Per Contra	Cr.				
Jan. 1	1 By Stock	1	270	—	—

				l.	*s.*	*d.*
1789	Per Contra	Cr.				
Jan. 1	1 By Stock to pay the 8th Inftant . .	1	100	—	—
Feb. 23	R By Balance, due to me . .	10	16	—	—
			116		

				l.	*s.*	*d.*
1789	Per Contra	Cr.				
Jan. 1	1 By Stock to pay the 17th Inftant .	1	150	—	—
Feb. 10	6 By Serge, to pay the 20th Inftant .	9	50	—	—
28	R By Balance, due to me on Bond .	10	500	—	—
			700		

				l.	*s.*	*d.*
1789	Per Contra	Cr.				
Jan. 1	1 By Stock	1	15	12	—
Feb. 2	R By Balance, due to me, to be paid *April* 30, next	10	24	7	—

335

1789			Per Contra	Cr.		*l.*	*s.*	
Feb. 5	5		By Cash, received in full . . .	1		57		
28	R		By Balance due to me . . .	10		32		
						89		

1789			Per Contra	Cr.		*l.*	*s.*	
Feb. 28	R		By Profit and Loss . . .	9		108	6	2

Note, This *Accompt* must not be balanced by any thing else but *Profit* and *Loss,* because the several things that are made *Drs.* to Cash, are of no estimation in the Mercantile Way, but are an entire *Loss.*

1789			Per Contra	Cr.	Hhds.	Mark		
Jan. 6	2		By *Elias Skinner,* at 9*l. per* Hhd. for	2	TP	5	27	
Feb. 1	5		By *Elias Skinner,* at 9*l. per* Hhd. for	2	TP	5	18	
21	8		By *Thomas Shaw,* 11*l. per* Hhd. for	10	TP	9	110	
				15			155	

1789			Per Contra	Cr.		*l.*		
Feb. 28	R		By Balance due to me . . .	10		28		

1789			Per Contra	Cr.		*l.*		
Jan. 12	3		By Cash, received in full . . .	1		27		
Feb. 1	5		By Sundry Accompts . . .			110		
15	7		By Cash, received in full . . .	1		44		
						181		

336

1739		Brandon George	Dr.		*l.*	*s.*	*d.*
Jan. 3	2	To *French*-Wine to pay in one Month		2	57	—	
Feb. 12	6	To *Lisbon*-Wine		6	32		
					89	—	

1789		House-Expenses	Dr.		*l.*	*s.*	*d.*
Jan. 31	5	To Cash for sundry Charges this Month		1	37	13	3
Feb. 2ᵒ	8	To cash for sundry Charges this Month		1	70	12	11
					108	6	2

337

1789		Oporto-Wine	Dr.			Hhds. Mark			*l.*	*s.*	*d.*
Jan. 4	2	To *Thomas Preston*, Esq; at 7*l. per* Hhd.		5	TP	3		35	—	—
Feb. 7	5	To *Thomas Preston*, Esq; at 9*l. per* Hhd.		10	TP	3		90	—	—
2ᵉ	R	To Profit & Loss, gain'd by this Accompt				9		3ᵒ	—	—
				15				155	—	—

1739		Samuel Fairman	Dr.		*l.*	*s.*	*d.*
Jan. 5	2	To *French* Wine		2	28	—	

1789		Elias Skinner	Dr.		*l.*	*s.*	*d.*
Jan. 6	2	To *Oporto* Wine, to pay the 12th Instant		5	27	—	
Feb. 1	5	To Sundry Accompts			154	—	
					181	—	

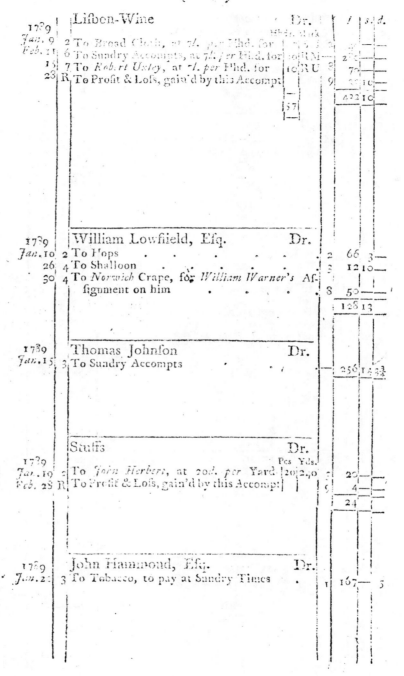

338

		Lisbon-Wine	Dr.			l	s	d
1739						Hhds. Vack		
Jan. 9	2	To Broad Cloth, at 7l. per Hhd. for						
Feb. 11	6	To Sundry Accompts, at 7l. per Hhd. for		M		2		
15	7	To Robert Uxley, at 7l. per Hhd. for		R U		7		
23	R	To Profit & Loss, gain'd by this Accompt			9		10	
						422	10	
					57			

		William Lowfield, Esq.	Dr.		l	s	d
1739							
Jan. 10	2	To Hops		2	66	3	—
26	4	To Shalloon		3	12	10	—
30	4	To Norwich Crape, for William Warner's Assignment on him		8	50	—	—
					128	13	

		Thomas Johnson	Dr.		l	s	d
1739							
Jan. 15	3	To Sundry Accompts			256	14	—

		Stuffs	Dr.		Pcs	Yds.		
1739								
Jan. 19	2	To John Herbert, at 20d. per Yard	20	2,0	2	20		
Feb. 28	R	To Profit & Loss, gain'd by this Accompt			9	4		
						24		

		John Hammond, Esq.	Dr.		l	s	d
1739							
Jan. 21	3	To Tobacco, to pay at Sundry Times		1	167	—	5

1789	Per Contra	Hhds.	Mark.	Cr.	l.	s.	d.
Jan. 11	2 By Sir *Humphrey Parsons* at 8*l.* per Hhd. for	2	E I	4	16	—	—
13	3 By Cath, at 8*l.* 10*s.* per Hhd. for	3	E I	1	25	10	—
Feb. 1	5 By *Filas Skinner*, at 8*l.* per Hhd. for	2	E I	5	16	—	—
12	6 By *Brandon George*, at 8*l.* per Hhd. for	4	R M	5	32	—	—
15	7 By *Isaac Reynolds*, at 8*l.* per Hhd. for	14	R M	8	112	—	—
21	8 By *Thomas Shaw*, at 8*l.* per Hhd. for	7	R M	9	56	—	—
28	R By Balance, unsold, at 7*l.* per Hhd. for	25	{RM 15}{RU 10}	10	175	—	—
		57			422	10	

1789	Per Contra			Cr.			
Feb. 28	R By Balance due to me			10	123	13	—

1789	Per Contra			Cr.			
Feb. 29	R By Balance due to me			10	256	14	3¼

1789	Per Contra	Pcs.	Yds.	Cr.			
Oct. 21	2 By Capt. *William Andrews*, at 2*s.* per Yard, for	10	240	6	24	—	—

1789	Per Contra			Cr.			
Feb. 9	6 By Sundry Accompts				67	—	5
28	1 By Balance, due to me, payable *April* 20th next			10	102	—	—
					169	—	5

339

1789	Robert Moore	Dr.		*l.*	*s.*	*d.*
Jan. 22	3 To Sundry Accompts		—	533	6	3
Feb. 25	8 To Cash for his Draft on me, paid to *John Aſh*		1	66		9
				600	—	—

1789	John Oſborne	Dr.				
Jan. 23	4 To Canary		2	270		

340

1789	Richard Remnant	Dr.				
Jan. 24	4 To Canary, to pay in three Months . . .		2	432	—	

	Paper	Dr.	Reams			
1789						
Jan. 27	4 To *Martin Unwin*, at 10s. *per* Ream, to pay at ſundry Times, for		1000	7	500	— —
Feb. 28	8 To Profit and Loſs, gain'd by this Accompt			9	30	— —
			1000		530	— —

1789	Martin Unwin	Dr.				
Jan. 28	4 To Sundry Accompts		—	500		
Feb. 1	5 To *Elias Skinner*, for d° *Skinner*'s Aſſignment on *Unwin*, payable to me		5	20		
17	7 To Tobacco			381	7	6
				901	7	6

1789		Per Contra			Cr.			l.	s.	d.
Jan. 22	3	By Canary				2		500	—	—
Feb. 11	6	By Lisbon Wine, on Demand				6		100	—	—
								600	—	—

1789		Per Contra			Cr.					
Feb. 23	8	By Cash, received in Full, by an Assignment								
		on James Jenkins				1		270	—	

1789		Per Contra			Cr.					
Jan. 25	4	By Sundry Accompts						422	—	

1789		Per Contra			Cr.					
					Reams					
Jan. 29	4	By Robert Uxley, at 10s. 6d. per Ream, for	500	8		262	10	—	
Feb. 11	6	By Lisbon Wine, at 11s. - per Ream, for	200	6		110	—	—	
15	7	By Robert Uxley, at 10s. 6d. per Ream, for	300	8		157	10	—	
			1000			530	—	—	

1789		Per Contra			Cr.					
Jan. 27	4	By Paper				7		500	—	—
Feb. 2	9	By Isaac Reynolds, for E. Skinner's Note on								
		dᵒ Unwin, now given to I. Reynolds .				8		20	—	—
28	K	By Balance, due to me				10		381	17	6
								901	17	6

341

Norwich Crape   Dr.

1739				Pcs.	Yards	£	s	d
Jan. 29	4	To *Robert Uxley* at 3s. 6d. per Yard for		100	650	8	280	—
Feb. 28	R	To Profit and Loss gain'd by this Accompt				9	17	12
							297	12

Robert Uxley   Dr.

1739			£	s	d
Jan. 29	4	To Paper	7	262	10
Feb. 15	6	To Serge	9	31	—
25	7	To Sundry Accompts		257	10
27		To Duroy	8	48	15
28	R	To Balance, due to him	10	322	10
				980	—

Isaac Reynolds   Dr.

1739			£	s	d
Feb. 2	5	To Sundry Accompts		120	—
19	7	To Sundry Accompts		252	—
				372	—

Duroy   Dr.

1739			Pcs.	Yards	£	s	d
Feb. 2	5	To *Isaac Reynolds*, at 6s. per Yard, for		600	9	180	—
28	R	To Profit and loss gain'd by his Accompt			9	7	10
						187	—

Sagathee   Dr.

1739			Pcs.	Yards	£	s	d
Feb. 2	5	To *Isaac Reynolds*, at 2s. 6d. per Yard for	100	1200	8	150	—
28	R	To Profit and Loss, gain'd by this Accompt			9	2	—
						152	—

[Editor's note. The debit of 10 shillings should be footed for the Duroy account, and a credit total should be entered of 187 pounds, 10 shillings. The "Balance" credit for the

		Per Contra	Cr.	Pcs.	Yds.		£	s.	d.
1789									
Jan. 30	5	By Sundry Accompts, at 4s. per Yard for		40	640	—	128	—	—
Feb. 14	7	By *Samuel Grainger*, at 4s. per Yard for		4	64	10	12	16	—
29	R	By Balance, unfold, at 3s. 6d. per Yard for		56	896	10	156	16	—
				100	1600		297	12	—

		Per Contra	Cr.		£	s.	d.
1789							
Jan. 29	4	By *Norwich* Crape			280	—	—
Feb. 15	7	By Sundry Accompts			620	—	—
					900	—	—

		Per Contra	Cr.		£	s.	d.
1789							
Feb. 2	5	By Sundry Accompts			330	—	—
29	R	By Balance due to me			42	—	—
					372	—	—

		Per Contra	Cr.	Pcs.	Yds.		£	s.	d.
1789									
Feb. 14	6	By *Samuel Grainger*, at 6s. 6d. per Yard		10	150	0	48	15	—
27	8	By *Robert Uxley*, at 6s. 6d. per Yard		10	150	0	48	15	—
28	R	By Balance, unfold, at 6s. 0d. per Yard		20	300	0	90	—	—
				40	600				

		Per Contra	Cr.	Pcs.	Yds.		£	s.	d.
1789									
Feb. 14		By *Samuel Grainger*, at 2s. 10d. per Yard		10	120	0	17	—	—
28		By Balance, unfold, at 2s. 6d. per Yard		90	1080	0	1	0	—
				100	1200				

for the Sagathee account should be 135 pounds,
yielding a total of 152 pounds. Dilworth seems
inadvertantly to have matched, as it were, the
debit to Duroy with the credit to Sagathee.]

343

		Thomas Shaw	Dr.	l.	s.	d.
1789						
Feb. 4	5	T Shaw, paid *William Smith*, by order of				
		To ditto		100		
21	8	To Sundry Accompts		232	3	4
				332	3	4

		Serge	Dr	Pcs.	Yd.				
1789									
Feb. 10	6	To Sundry Accompts, at 1s. per Yard	1	50	1400		70		
80	R	To Profit and Lofs gain'd by this Accompt				9	1	15	
							71	15	

344

		Profit and Lofs	Dr.	l.	s.	d.
1789						
Jan. 5	4	To *Richard Remnant*, loft by the Rebate of 432*l*. for 3 Months, at 5 *per Cent.* . .			5	8
Feb. 9		*John Hammond*, Efq; loft by an Abatement.			6	5
2		To *Samuel Grainger*, abated in Compofition		4	15	
2	R	To Houfe Expenfes		108	6	2
	R	To Stock gain'd by two Months trading . .		218	3	6
				37	1	9

Note, This Accompt is always made Dr. to *Stock* for the Balance thereof, if there be a Gain in the Trade, and Cr. by *Stock* if there be a *Lofs*: and the Reafon is obvious enough; For if there be a *Gain*, it is evident that the Goods were fold for more than they were bought for, and therefore *Stock* muft be Cr by *Profit and Lofs* for the fame: the contrary, if there be a *Lofs*, which feldom happens to a careful Trader.

Admit, therefore, a Man's whole *Stock* to confift of but one Sort of Goods; hence as that is his *Stock*, the *prime Coft* thereof, and the *Gain* muft go together to balance the Cr. Side, which will confift of what was fold at an advantageous Price: For the Difference between the Prices of Goods bought, and fold out advantageoufly, muft be the *Profit* arifing from the fale of thofe *Goods*: and as that muft be placed on the Cr fide of *Stock*, fo *Profit and Lofs* muft be Dr. to *Stock*, for the fame Balance or Gain, and not to any thing elfe.

For Example.

1. Suppofe the Merchant's whole *Stock* fhould confift of *Pepper*, which is worth 68*l*. 8*s*. Page 1, then it muft be

Pepper	Dr.	Stock	Cr.
To Stock - - - 68*l*. 8*s*.		By Pepper - - - 68*l*. 8*s*.	

2. Suppofe the *Pepper* to be all fold upon Truft to *Robert Moore* for 72*l*. 13*s*. 6*d*. then is

Robert Moore	Dr.	Pepper	Cr.
To Pepper 72*l*. 13*s* 6*d*.		By Robert Moore 72*l*. 13*s* 6*d*.	

3. To balance this Accompt; as there is a *Gain* upon the Sale of the faid *Pepper*: fo for that *Gain* you muft make

Pepper	Dr.	Profit and Lofs	Cr.
To profit and Lofs 4*l*. 5*s*. 6*d*.		By Pepper - - 4*l*. 5*s*. 6*d*.	

						l.	s.	d.
1789		Per Contra			Cr.			
Feb. 3	5	By Cash received of *John James*, for *Shaw's* use			1	100	—	—
21	8	By Sundry Accompts				232	3	4
						332	3	4

			Pcs.	Yds.		l.	s.	d.
1789		Per Contra			Cr.			
Feb. 13	6	By *Robert Uxley*, at 15*d. per* Yard .	10	140	8	8	15	—
	R	By Balance unsold, at 1*s. per* Yard .	90	1260	0	63	—	—
			100	1400		71	15	—

						l.	s.	d.
1789		Per Contra			Cr.			
Jan. 28	4	By *Martin Unwin*, gain'd by the Rebate of 500*l.* at 5 *per Cent.*			7	4	18	10¼
Feb. 28	R	By Tobacco			1	82	6	10¼
—	R	By Pepper			1	4	5	6¼
—	R	By Canary			2	107	—	—
—	R	By Hops			2	7	—	10¼
—	R	By *French* Wine			2	19	15	—
—	R	By Holland			2	14	16	—
—	R	By Broad Cloth			2	5	15	—
—	R	By Shalloon			3	—	16	8
—	R	By Drugget			3	2	10	—
—	R	By *Oporto* Wine			5	30	—	—
—	R	By *Lisbon* Wine			6	33	10	—
—	R	By Stuffs			6	4	—	—
—	R	By Paper			7	30	—	—
—	R	By *Norwich* Crape			8	17	12	—
—	R	By Duroy			8	7	10	—
—	R	By Sagathee			8	2	—	—
—	R	By Serge			9	1	15	—
						375	11	9

4. To balance the Accompt of *Profit* and *Loss*, you must make

Profit and Loss	Dr.	Stock	Cr.
To Stock - - 4*l.* 5*s.* 6*d.*		By Profit and Loss 4*l.* 5*s.* 6*d.*	

5. Then because Robert Moore has not paid for the *Pepper*, to balance his Accompt, you must make

Balance	Dr.	Robert Moore	Cr.
To Robert Moore 72*l.* 13*s.* 6*d.*		By Balance - 72*l.* 13*s.* 6*d.*	

Lastly, To balance the whole Accompt, you must make

Stock,	Dr.	Balance	Cr.
To balance 72*l.* 13*s.* 6*d.*		By Stock - 72*l.* 13*s.* 6*d.*	

Hence it appears, by taking a survey of these Statings, that *Stock* stands Cr. both by *Pepper* for the prime Cost, and by *Profit* and *Loss* for the Gain thereon; and that *Stock* is Dr. to *Balance* for the whole Value of the said *Pepper* sold to Advantage, which is equal to the *Prime Cost* and the *Profit* taken together.

G 2

1789 Feb. 14	Samuel Grainger To Sundry Accompts	Dr.	Mark.		l.	s.	d.
					78	11	—

1789 Feb. 28	Balance	Dr.	Mark.		l.	s.	d.
	To Cash remaining in Hand, carried to the next Ledger			1	8099	4	2½
— R	To Canary, unfold, 5 Pipes, at 25l. per Pipe		R U	2	125	—	
— R	To Hops, unfold, 44 Bags, wt. 132C. 2qrs. at 28s. per C. .		T S	2	185	10	
— R	To French Wine, unfold, 10 Hhds. at 30l. per Hhd. . . .		R U	2	300	—	
— R	To Drugget, unfold, 20 Pieces, qt. 280 Yards, at 3s. 4d. per Yard		T S	3	46	13	4
— R	To Sir Robert Johnson, due to me			3	30	—	
— R	To Sir Humphrey Parsons, due to me			4	16	—	
— R	To William Baker Esq; due to me on Bond			4	500	—	
— R	To William Warner, due to me, to be paid April 20th next .			4	34	7	
— R	To Brandon George, due to me			4	32	—	
— R	To Samuel Fairman, due to me			5	28	—	
— R	To Lisbon Wine, unfold, 25 Hhds. at 7l. per Hhd. . . .		{R M 15} {R U 10}	6	175	—	
— R	To William Lawfield Esq; due to me			6	128	13	
— R	To Thomas Johnson, due to me			6	256	14	3½
— R	To John Hammond, Esq; due to me, to be paid April 20th next			6	160	—	
— R	To Martin Unwin, due to me .			7	381	17	6
— R	To Norwich Crape, unfold, 5 Pcs. qt. 896 Yds. at 3s. 6d. per Yard		R U	8	156	16	
— R	To Isaac Reynolds, due to me .			8	42	—	
— R	To Duroy, unfold, 20 Pieces, qt. 300 Yards, at 6s. per Yard .		I R	8	90	—	
— R	To Sagathee, unfold, 90 Pieces, qt. 1080 Yards, at 2s. 6d. per Yard		I R	8	135	—	
— R	To Serge, unfold, 100 Pieces, qt. 1260 Yards, at 1s. per Yard		W B	9	63	—	
					10925	15	4¼

Note 1 Every *Article* under the head of *Balance*, on the *Dr.* fide, is derived or brought from the *Cr.* Side of that particular *Accompt*, which is made *Cr.* by *Balance.*

2. These *Articles* taken together, make up the Whole of your prefent *Eftate* in *Money, Goods*, and *Debts* due to you; and in your next *Books*, that is, in your *Journal* and *Ledger*, they muft each of them be made *Dr.* to *Stock*, becaufe each Particular is a Part thereof.

[Editor's note. A typescript of the Balance entry, debit side, along with the two notes, appears at the close of this chapter.

1739		Per Contra	Cr.		*l.*	*s.*	*d.*
Feb. 14	6	By Cash received in Part	1		28	11	—
26	8	By Sundry Accompts			50	—	—
					78	11	—

1739		Per Contra	Cr.				
Feb. 28	R	By *Thomas Preston*, Esq; due to him, to be paid *May* 14th next			90	—	—
	R	By *Robert Uxley*, due to him	3		90	—	—
	R	By Stock, for the neat Proceed of my whole Estate	8		322	10	—
					10513	5	4¼
					10925	5	4¼

Note 1, every *Article* under the head of *Balance* on the the Cr. Side (the last only excepted) is derived or brought from the *Dr.* side of that particular Accompt which is *Dr.* to *Balance*.

2. These *Articles* taken together make up the whole of what you owe or stand indebted to others: And as your *Stock* is obliged to make good those *Debts*; so, in your next *Journal* and *Ledger*, your *Stock* must be made *Dr.* to every one of them, the being so many *Crs.* to whom you are *obliged*.

3. The last *Article* only, where *Balance* is made Cr. by *Stock*, shews the *neat Produce* of your whole *Estate*, and what you are really worth, when all your *Debts* are paid.

4. This *Balance* is always placed on the Cr. Side (except your *Debts* should exceed) and in your next Books *Stock* must be credited with the same, for the whole Quantity and value, because each particular is *Dr.* to *Stock* for its respective Quantity and Value.

Lastly, If what you owe should at any time exceed your *Cash, Goods* unsold, and *Debts* due to you, it will then look very bad; and the *Balance*, which then must be placed on the *Dr.* side, shews that you are so much worse than nothing, which Sum if it should be pretty large, will oblige you to call your *Creditors* to a Composition, in order to enable you to carry on business again.

347

l.	s.	d.			l.	s.	d.
535	1	—	Stock	1	10350	14	10¼
10437	2	4	Cash	1	2337	18	1½
939	1	—	Tobacco	1	1021	17	10¼
68		—	Pepper	1	72	13	6
1150	—	—	Canary	2	1122		
404	4	3¼	Hops	2	225	15	1½
570	—	—	French Wine	2	239	15	—
57	12	—	Holland	2	72	8	
90	—	—	Broad Cloth	2	95	15	
11	13	4	Shalloon	3	12	10	
57	3	4	Drugget	3	13		
100	—	—	Thomas Preston, Esq; . . .	3	190		
476	—	—	Sir Robert Johnson . . .	3	446		
250	—	—	John Herbert	3	250		
580	—	—	Capt. John Smith . . .	4	580		
270	—	—	Capt. William Andrews . . .	4	270		
116	—	—	Sir Humphrey Parsons . . .	4	100		
700	—	—	William Baker, Esq; . . .	4	200		
50	—	—	William Warner . . .	4	15	13	
89	—	—	Brandon George . . .	5	57		
103	6	2	House Expenses . . .	5			
325	—	—	Oporto Wine	5	155		
23	—	—	Samuel Fairman . . .	5			
131	—	—	Elias Skinner . . .	5	181		
399	—	—	Lisbon Wine . . .	6	257	10	
128	13	—	William Lowfield, Esq. . . .	6			
256	14	3¾	Thomas Johnson . . .	6			
20	—	—	Stuffs	6	24		
167		5	John Hammond, Esq. . . .	6	67		5
600	—	—	Robert Moore . . .	7	600		
270	—	—	John Osborne . . .	7	270		
432	—	—	Richard Remnant . . .	7	432		
500	—	—	Paper	7	530		
90	17	6	Martin Unwin . . .	7	520		
28	—	—	Norwich Crape . . .	8	140	16	
577	10	—	Robert Uxley . . .	8	900		
372	—	—	Isaac Reynolds . . .	8	330		
130	—	—	Duroy	8	97	10	
110	—	—	Sagathee	8	17		
332	3	4	Thomas Shaw, . . .	9	332	3	4
70	—	—	Serge	9	8	15	
40	2	1	Profit and Loss . . .	9	4	18	10½
70	11	—	Samuel Grainger . . .	10	78	11	
23159	5	1	End of the first Ledger.		21530	5	1

348

THE

CASH-BOOK.

1789			Cafh.	Dr.	*l.*	*s.*	*d.*
Jan. 1	1		To Stock	1	800	—	
2	2		To Holland, received in full . .	2	2	—	
7	2		To Sir *Robert Johnfon*, received in Part .	3	100	—	
12	2		To *Elias Skinner*, received in full . .	5	27	—	
13	3		To *Lifbon* Wine, received in full . .	6	25	10	
15	3		To Sir *Robert Johnfon*, received in Part .	3	100	—	
18	3		To Capt. *John Smith*, received in full .	4	530	—	
23	4		To *Canary*, received in part . .	1	290	—	
25	4		To *Richard Remnant*, received in full for his early Payment	7	420	13	4
30	4		To *Norwich* Crape, received in Part of *William Warner*	8	28	—	
					9599	3	4

1789			Cafh	Dr.	*l.*	*s.*	*d.*
Feb, 1.	5		To Balance brought from the laft Month . .	—	8518	8	11¼
	5		To *Elias Skinner*, received in Part . .	5	90	—	
3	5		To *Thomas Shaw*, received of *John James*, for *Shaw's* Ufe	9	100	—	
5	5		To *Brandon George*, received in full . .	5	57	—	
6	5		To *Thomas Prefton*, Efq. received in full .	3	65	—	
8	6		To Sundry Accompts received in full . .		110	3	
9	6		To *John Hammond*, Efq. received in Part .	6	67	—	
14	6		To *Samuel Grainger*, received in Part .	10	28	11	
18	7		To *Elias Skinner*, received in full . .	5	44	—	
Err. 21	8		To *Thomas Shaw*, received in full . .	9	66	3	4
25	8		To *John Ofborne*, received in full of *James Jenkins*	7	270	—	
26	8		To *Samuel Grainger*, received in full of a Compofition	10	6	5	
					9422	11	2½

Note 1. The laft Line but three, marked with *Error* in the Margin, was done on Purpofe to fhew the Learner how to balance it in the Like Cafe; which fee on the Cr. Side.

2, The Error muft not be added with the reft of the Money when it is carried to the Ledger, becaufe it was never received.

The end of the

1789		Per Contra	Cr.	l.	s.	d.
Jan. 8	2	By Sir *Humphrey Parsons'* paid in full . . .	4	100		
14	3	By Tobacco, paid in full	1	298		
17	3	By *William Baker*, Esq. paid in full. . . .	4	150		
25	4	By *Martin Unwin*, paid in full . . .	7	495	1	1½
31	5	By House-Expenses, for Sundry Charges this Month	5	37	13	3
—	R	By Balance, remaining in Hand, carried to the next Month		8518	8	11
				9599	3	4

1789		Per Contra	Cr.	l.	s.	d.
Feb. 2	5	By *Isaac Reynolds*, paid in part . . .	8	100		
4	5	By *Thomas Shaw*, paid *William Smith*, by order of do. *Shaw* . . .	9	100		
10	6	By Serge, paid in Part	9	20		
11	6	By *Lisbon* Wine paid in Part . . .	6	70		
15	7	By *Robert Uxley*, paid in Part . . .	8	100		
16	7	By Tobacco, paid in Part . . .	1	112	13	9
20	7	By *William Baker*, Esq. paid in full . . .	4	50		
21	8	By *Error* on the Dr. Side . . .	—	66	3	4
	8	By *Thomas Shaw*, paid in full . . .	9	66	3	4
22	8	By *William Baker*, Esq. lent him on bond for 6 Months, at 5 per Cent. . . .	4	500		
25	8	By *Robert Moore*, for his Draft on me, payable to *John Ash*, or Oder . . .	7	66	13	9
28	8	By House-Expenses, for sundry Charges this Month	5	70	12	11
—	R	By Balance, remaining in Hand, carried to the next Month	10	8099	4	2½
				9422	11	3½

Note 1. The last Line but nine, having the *Index* prefixt to it in the Margin, shews that it was inserted to balance the Error committed on the Dr. Side of this accompt.

2. The Error must not be added with the rest of the Money, when it is carried to the *Ledger*, because it was never paid.

first Cash-Book.

H

351

THE
BOOK of HOUSE-EXPENCES

Houfe-Expences Dr. to Cafh.	l.	s.	d.	l.	s.	d.
1789						
Jan. 1 Paid for 2 Rabits	0	2	6			
2 a load of Hay . . .	1	16	0			
3 a *Chefhire* Cheefe, wt. 57 *lb*, at 4*d.* per *lb.* . . .	0	19	0			
4 a Firkin of Butter, wt. 56 *lb.* at 8*d.* per *lb.* . . .	1	17	4			
5 a Load of Straw . . .	1	7	0			
6 the Baker's Bill . . .	0	17	0			
7 a Suit of Apparel . . .	8	0	0	14	18	10
8 6 Mahogany Chairs . . .	6	0	0			
9 the Coachman's Bill . . .	0	17	7			
10 the Butcher's Bill . . .	0	19	0			
11 2 *lb.* Saufages . . .	0	1	0			
12 Turnips and Potatoes . . .	0	0	9			
13 Endive and Celery . . .	0	0	4			
14 ¼ lb. Flour of muftard . . .	0	0	6			
15 the Brewer's Bill . . .	0	10	0	8	9	9
16 the Smith's Bill . . .	0	10	8			
17 3 Quarters of oats, at 15*s.* per Quarter . . .	2	5	0			
18 1 Quarter's Wages for the Cook . .	2	0	0			
19 a Goofe . . .	0	3	6			
20 a Sett of China Ware . . .	0	5	0			
21 a Grofs of beft Corks . . .	0	5	0			
22 a Turkey . . .	0	5	0			
23 2 Fowls . . .	0	3	0	9	7	8
24 1 Quarter's Salary to the Coachman	2	15	0			
25 1 *Gloucefterfhir* Cheefe, wt. 21 lb at 3*d.* per lb . . .	0	5	3			
26 the Baker's Bill . . .	0	19	0			
27 2 Hair Brooms . . .	0	2	0			
28 3 Hearth Brufhes . . .	0	1	0			
29 a Gammon of Bacon . . .	0	4	0			
30 2 Quarts of Peafe . . .	0	0	0			
31 the Butcher's Bill . . .	1	0	0	5	3	0
				37	3	3

352

House-Expences Dr. to Cash.	l.	s.	d.	l.	s.	d.
1739						
Feb. 1 Paid for a load of Sand	0	6	0			
2 the House maid, for a Quarter's Wages	1	5	0			
3 the Brewer for a Barrel of Beer	0	10	0			
4 for Potatoes	0	0	3			
5 The Smith, for mending the Poker, Tongs, and Fire shovel.	0	2	6			
6 for mending the Jack and Spits	0	2	6			
7 the Carpenter, for mending the Shelves in the kitchen . . .	0	7	6			
				2	13	9
8 the Butcher's Bill	1	19	2			
9 the Baker's Bill	0	19	10			
10 for 6 Chaldron of Coals . . .	9	0	0			
11 the Mason for mending the Kitchen Floor	0	12	6			
12 the Footman, 1 Quarter's Wages	2	0	0			
13 the Cook's Bill for Greens, &c.	0	7	8			
14 the Chambermaid, a Quarter's Wages	1	0	0			
				16	9	2
15 for a new Stove in the Parlour	4	10	0			
16 ditto . . . . Dining-room	6	0	0			
17 the Rack maker for some Brewing Vessels	7	8	0			
18 the Cooper for six new Barrels	2	7	6			
19 the Copper-smith for 2 new coppers	9	14	6			
20 the Bricklayer for setting the said Coppers	5	3	0			
21 the Smith for Iron work to the same	3	17	0			
				39	0	6
22 for a Mill to grind the Malt . .	1	16	0			
23 for a Quarter of Malt and 10lb. of Hops	3	4	0			
24 for a Load of Hay . .	1	16	0			
25 ditto . of Straw .	0	18	0			
26 the Baker's Bill	1	12	0			
27 the Butcher's Bill	2	16	0			
28 for 1 Dozen of Candles . . .	0	7	0			
				1	9	6
				72	12	11

The End of the first Book of House Expenses.

353

The WASTE-BOOK.

London, March 1, 1789.

An INVENTORY of my whole Estate, confisting of Money, Goods and Debts, owing to and by me JOHN SIMMONS, taken this Day; and is as follows, viz.

354

		l.	*s.*	*d.*
J.	*Imprimis,* I have in ready money	8099	4	2½
J. R U	*Item,* 5 Pipes of Canary, at 25*l.* per Pipe	125	0	0
J. T S	44 Bags of Hops, wt. 132 C. 2 qrs. at 28*s.* per C.	185	10	0
J. R U	10 Hhds. of *French* Wine, at 30*l.* per Hhd.	300	0	0
J. T S	20 Pieces of Drugget, qt. 280 Yards, at 2*s.* 4*d.* per Yd.	46	13	4
J {RM 15 {RU 10	25 Hhds. of *Lisbon* Wine, at 7 *l.* per Hhd.	175	0	0
J. R U	56 Pieces of *Norwich* Crape, qt. 896 Yards, at 3*s.* 6*d.* per Yd.	156	16	0
J. I R	20 Pieces of Duroy, qt. 300 Yds. at 6*s.* per Yard	90	0	0
J. I R	90 Pieces of Sagathee, qt. 1080 Yards, at 2*s.* 6*d.* per Yard	135	0	0
J. W B	90 Pieces of Serge. qt. 1260 Yds. at 1*s.* per Yard	63	0	0
J.	Sir *Robert Johnson* owes me	30	0	0
J.	Sir *Humphrey Parsons*	16	0	0
J.	*William Baker,* Esq. on bond	500	0	0
J.	*William Warner,* to be paid *April* 30 next	54	0	0
J.	*Brandon George*	32	0	0
J.	*Samuel Fairman*	28	0	0
J.	*William Lowfield,* Esq.	123	13	0
J.	*Thomas Johnson*	256	14	3½
J.	*John Hammond,* Esq. to be paid *April* 20 next	100	0	0
J.	*Martin Unwin*	381	17	6
J.	*Isaac Reynolds*	42	0	0
				10925

I am indebted as follows: viz.

J.	To *Thomas Preston,* Esq. to pay *May* 14 next	90	0	0
J.	To *Robert Unwin*	522	10	0
				412

(2)

LONDON, March 2, 1789.

	l.	*s.*	*d.*

3. Sir *Robert Johnson* has paid me in full 30

Note, This being a very plain Case, the Learner, I presume, by this time, can tell that *Cash* must be made Dr. Sir *Robert Johnson* for the sum received, and Sir *Robert Johnson*, Cr. by *Cash* for the same Sum; and therefore for the future, in all such single Cases of paying and receiving Money, and of buying and selling wares, either upon trust or present Payment, I shall omit any further instructions concerning them, imagining what has been already said to be sufficient.

———— 4 ————

3. Bought of *James Allen*, at *Garraway's* Coffee-House, the good Ship *James*, Burthen 500 Tons, or thereabout, for 1500*l.* . . . . *l. s. c.*

Paid 5 *per Cent.* down 75 0 0

And the rest in 5 Days 1425 0 0

I have also ordered her to be repaired and fitted out 1500 with all speed, for a Privateer against the *French*.

Note, This may be journalized two ways, viz.
1. Make Ship *James* Dr. to *James Allen* for the whole Sum, and *James Allen* Cr. by Ship *James*, for the same Sum. Next make *James Allen* Dr. to *Cash* for the Sum paid him, and *Cash* Cr. by *James Allen* for the same Sum. Or,
2. Ship *James*, Dr. to *Sundry Accompts* for the whole Value; then make *Cash* Cr. by Ship *James* for the Money paid down, and *James Allen* Cr. by the said Ship for what remains due. I have made choice of this latter Way.

———— 6 ————

3. Sold to *John Herbert*, 1/15 Part of the abovesaid Ship *James*, and received present Money 125

Note, The Part of the Ship *James*, in this Case, is to be esteemed as Goods, and then it will be easy to conceive, that *Cash* must be Dr. to Ship *James* for the Sum received, and Ship *James* Cr. be *Cash* for the same Sum.

———— 8 ————

3. Sold to Capt. *John Smith* 1/16 Part of the Ship *James*, and received present Money 125

I have also agreed to his going master of the said Ship

———— 9 ————

3. Paid *James Allen* in full for the Ship *James* . . . 142

———— 10 ————

3. Sold to *William Baker*, Esq, 1/15 part of the abovesaid Ship, for which he is to pay in 7 Days 125

355

LONDON, March 12, 1789.

	l.	s.	d.

J. By an unlucky Accident laſt Night, 3 Iron Hoops broke off from one of the Hhds. of *Liſbon* Wine, in conſequence of which, one of the Staves gave way, whereby about 6 Gallons only were ſaved, which I ordered to be bottled off; the reſt was entirely loſt. The Prime Coſt of the ſaid Hhd. was . . . . .

> *Note,* Notwithſtanding that ſome of the Wine was ſaved, yet as it was not intended for ſale, the whole Hogſhead muſt go to the Accompt of *Profit* and *Loſs,* which muſt be made Dr. to *Liſbon* Wine for the prime Coſt of the ſaid Hogſhead, and *Liſbon* Wine muſt be made Cr. by *Profit* and *Loſs* for the ſaid Hogſhead and its Value as aforeſaid.

7 |

——————— 14 ———————

J. Sold to *Robert Uxley* $\frac{1}{10}$ part of the Ship *James,* for . . . . . . 125 |

——————— 17 ———————

William Baker, Eſq. has paid me for his $\frac{1}{10}$ Part of the Ship *James* . . . . 125 |

——————— 20 ———————

J. Sold a Pipe of Canary to *William Dello,* for which he paid me in full . . . . 30 |

——————— 21 ———————

J. Sold to Sir *Robert Johnſon* 20 Pieces of Drugget, qt. 280 Yards, at 3s. 6d. *per* Yard . . . . . 49 |

——————— 23 ———————

	l.	s.	d.
J. Paid *Thomas Preſſon,* Eſq. in Part . .	89	7	$0\frac{3}{4}$
Abated me for my early Payment at 5 *per Cent*	0	12	$11\frac{1}{4}$

> *Note,* This Caſe is the ſame with that of *Jan.* 28, which ſee.

90 |

——————— 25 ———————

	£		
J. Sold to Sir *Robert Johnſon* $\frac{1}{10}$ Part of the Ship *James,* for which he has paid me in full . .	125	0	0
He has alſo paid me in full of a Debt . .	49	0	0

> *Note,* The Caſh here received is on a double Accompt, viz. 125l. for the Ship *James,* and 49l. more for a debt formerly due, and therefore you muſt, in this Caſe, make *Caſh* Dr. to *Sundry Accompts* for the whole Sum, and then you muſt make Ship *James* Cr. by *Caſh* for the 125l. paid you on her Accompt, and Sir *Robert Johnſon* Cr. by *Caſh* for the reſt.

174 |

——————— 26 ———————

J. Paid *Thomas Young,* Joiner, for Work done in the Ship *James* . . .

> *Note,* In this Caſe you are not to make *Thomas Young,* but Ship *James* Dr. to *Caſh* for the Joiner's Work, and *Caſh* Cr. by Ship *James* for the ſame, it being another Expenſe on the ſaid Ship.

20 17 |

	l.	*s.*	*d.*

LONDON, March 27, 1789.

J. Paid *Thomas Pearce* Rigger, for rigging the Ship *James* — 25 | 2 | 6

—————— 28 ——————

J. Paid *Dryden Smith*, Builder, for his repairing the Ship *James* . . . . — 40 | 8 | —

—————— 30 ——————

J. Paid *Nathaniel Weftall*, Painter, for Painting the Ship *James* . . . . — 7 | 4 | 6

—————— 31 ——————

J. Paid fundry Charges this Month, as *per* Book of Houfe-Expences . . . . — 33 | 4 | 6

—————— *April* 1 ——————

Richard Lamb of *Harwich*, fends me Word that he has bought for my Accompt, purfuant to an Order fent him the 4th of laft Month, 100 Quarters of Wheat, and fhip'd it on board the good Ship *Swan*, *William Lyon*, Mafter, and confign'd it to *Jacob Van Hoove* of *Amfterdam*, to fell for my Accompt. That he alfo paid fundry Charges on fhipping it, as *per* Invoice, all which, with his Commiffion, at 1 *per Cent.* comes to . . . . — 99 | 8 | —

> *Note*, In this Cafe there is no occafion to defcend to Particulars, but make Voyage to *Amfterdam*, confign'd to *Jacob Van Hoove*, Dr. to *Richard Lamb* of *Harwich*, for the whole Coft of the faid *Wheat*, and *Richard Lamb* Cr. by Voyage to *Amfterdam*, for the fame Sum.

—————— 2 ——————

J. *Richard Lamb*, of *Harwich*, has drawn a Bill on me for 99*l*.8*s* payable to *William Angel*, or Order, the 30th Inftant, which Bill I have this day accepted, and becomes due *May* 3 next, including the three days of Grace . . . . — 99 | 8 | —

> *Note*, This is not only transferring the Accompt from *Lamb* to *Angel* and by your Acceptance of the Note *Lamb* is paid, therefore make *Lamb* Dr. to *Angel*, and *Angel* Cr. by *Lamb*, both for the Value of the faid Note. Or the whole Entry might be omitted till the Day of Payment, and then make *Lamb* Dr. to *Cafh*, and *Cafh* Cr. by *Lamb*; though I have ufed the former.

—————— 3 ——————

J. Paid the Blockmaker's Bill, for the *Ship James* . . — 19 | 17 | 6

—————— 5 ——————

J. Sold 10 Bags of Hops, weighing together 20*C.* 1*qr.* at 33*s.* per *C.* to *Robert Uxley* . . . . . — 49 | 8 | 3

—————— 7 ——————

J. Paid the Ship Chandler's Bill, for feveral Guns, fmall Arms, Powder, Shot, and other Stores, for the Ship *James* . . . . — 705 | 13 | —

357

LONDON, April 10, 1789.

		l.	s.	d.
J.	Sold to *William Evans*, ⅕ part of the Ship *James*; and received present Money	125	—	—
	——————— 12 ———————			
J.	Sold to *James Jackson*, ⅕ Part of the Ship *James*, and received present Money	125	—	—
	——————— 14 ———————			
J.	Sold to *Thomas Jones*, 1/16 part of the Ship *James*, and received present Money	125	—	—
	——————— 20 ———————			
J.	*John Hammond* has paid me in full	100	—	—
	——————— 24 ———————			

J.	Bought of *James Gray*, 100 Bags of Pepper, containing 3252lb. at 10d. per lb. $\left.\begin{array}{c}l.\quad s.\quad d.\\135\ 10\ 0\end{array}\right.$ and paid present Money			
	Which Pepper I have shipped on board the good Ship *Mary*, *James Hilder*, Master, and consign'd the same to *Jacob Van Hoove* of *Amsterdam*, to sell for my Accompt.			
	Paid Charges on shipping the said Pepper $\left.\right\}$ 4 17 10 as per Book of Charges of Merchandize			
	Note, As the Pepper is consign'd to *J. Van Hoove* to sell for your Accompt, you must make Voyage to *Amsterdam*, consign'd to *J. Van Hoove* Dr. to Cash for the whole Expense, and Cash Cr. by Voyage to *Amsterdam*, &c. for the same Sum.	140	7	10
	——————— 25 ———————			

J.	*John Adams* has insured my aforesaid Adventure of Pepper, at the Rate of 5 per Cent which I have paid him			
	Note, This being an Additional Charge on the above Voyage, you must make the said Voyage Dr. to Cash for the Money laid out, and Cash Cr. by the same. Voyage for the same Sum.	7	—	—
	——————— 27 ———————			

J.	Paid *John Jones*, Butcher, his Bill on the Ship *James*	109	10	6
	——————— 30 ———————			
J.	*William Warner*, has paid me in full	34	7	—
J.	Paid Sundry Charges this Month, as per Book of House-Expenses . . . . / .	39	16	10
	——————— May 1 ———————			
J.	Paid *James Thatcher*, Baker, his Bill on the Ship *James*	86	18	6
	——————— 2 ———————			
J.	Paid *John Prestwick*, Rope-maker, his Bill on the Ship *James*	46	17	—

358

LONDON, May 3, 1789.

	l.	s.	d.
Paid *Richard Lamb's* Draft on me to *William Angel,* which became due this Day, including the three Days of Grace	99	8	—

Note, By looking back to *April* 2, the Time that you accepted the Bill, there was a Direction to make *R. Lamb* Dr. to *William Angel,* which discharged the Accompt of *Lamb*; and now, as you have paid the same, whether to *W. Angel* himself, or any other person that may have received it of him; it matters not: so you must make *William Angel* Dr. to Cash for the money paid, and Cash Cr. by *William Angel* for the same sum.

————— 6 —————

	l.	s.	d.
Paid *John Pepwell,* Anchorsmith, his Bill on the Ship *James*	73	11	6

————— 7 —————

This day the several Proprietors of the Ship *James* gave me a Meeting, and paid me their several and respective Parts of the foregoing Bills, except *Robert Uxley,* viz.

	l.	s.	d.
John Herbert	70	17	0
John Smith	70	17	0
William Baker Esq. . . .	70	17	0
[not paid] *Robert Uxley*	70	17	0
Sir *Robert Johnson* . . .	70	17	0
William Evans	70	17	0
James Jackson	70	17	0
Thomas Jones	70	17	0
	566	16	—

Note, As these several Payments were made upon the Accompt of the Ship *James*; so Cash must be made Dr. to the said Ship for the same, and Ship *James* Cr. by Cash for the like Sum.

2. *Robert Uxley,* being one of the Proprietors, has not paid his part nor is there any occasion for it, because you stand largely indebted to him already; and therefore you must make *R. Uxley,* Dr. to Ship *James* for his Part, and Ship *James* Cr. Or, you may make *Sundry Accompts* Dr. to Ship *James*, viz. Cash for the Sum received, and *R. Uxley* for his part, and Ship *James* Cr. by *Sundry Accompts* for the whole Sum. I have followed this last Method.

————— 10 —————

	l.	s.	d.
Paid *Robert Uxley* in full	76	14	9

————— 12 —————

	l.	s.	d.
Received Advice from *Jack Van Hoeve,* that the Ship *Mary,* in which I had ten Bags of Pepper, was unhappily lost on the Coast of *Holland,* and no part of her Cargo saved. The Value was	140	—	10

Note, By looking back to *April* 25, you will find that the said Pepper was insured by *John Adams,* who now becomes your Dr. for the same, by virtue of that Insurance; therefore you must make *John Adams* Dr. to Voyage to *Amsterdam,* for the said Sum, and Voyage to *Amsterdam* Cr. by *John Adams* for the same Sum.

I

359

LONDON, May 14, 1789.

		l.	*s.*	*d.*

J. Jacob Van Hoove of Amsterdam, writes to me in his Letter of the 5th Instant, that he had disposed of my 100 Quarters of Wheat, consigned to him at 16 *Guilders*, 12 *Stivers per* Quarter, amounting in the whole to 1650 *Guilders*: That he had also paid for Custom, and other necessary Charges, which, with his Commission, came to 43 *Guilders*, 17 *Stivers*, to be deducted. And that the neat Proceed was 1611 *Guilders*, 3 *Stivers*, which at 33s. 4d. per *l.* Sterling amounts to   **161** | **2** | **2¼**

Note 1, A *Stiver* is 2d. *Flem.* and a *Guilder* is 40d. See *Scheelm. Aff.* p. 82. 33s. 4d.: 1l. :: 1611G. 3 St : 161l. 2s. 3d.½

2. As the above *Wheat* was consign'd to *Jacob Van Hoove*, for your own Accompt, so he becomes your Dr. whenever he disposes of it, and therefore you must make *Jacob Van Hoove's* Accompt Current Dr to Voyage to *Amsterdam* for the neat proceed of the same; and Voyage to *Amsterdam* Cr. by *Jacob Van Hoove* for the Sum.

3. The Cr. Side, exceeding the Dr. that Difference will be the Gain by this Voyage.

— 17 —

360

J. Sold 1 Pipe of Canary to *William Coles*, and received of him for the same . . . . | **30** | — | —

— 20 —

J. Ship *James* having been out upon a Cruise, has taken a *French* Merchant Ship richly laden, homeward bound, which was ransomed for 40.00l. Half of which, viz 20000l. belongs to the Master and Men, and the other half to the Owners; my half of which I have received and deposited in the Bank of *England*, and comes to | **10000** | — | —

Note, As the Money which you have received was upon the Accompt of Ship *James*: so Cash must be made Dr. to the said Ship for the Sum received, and Ship *James* Cr. by Cash for the same Sum.

— 22 —

J. This Day had 10000l. Bank Annuity, bearing Interest at 3l. per Cent. transferred to me at 94l. per Cent.

	l.	*s.*	*d.*
Bank Annuity .	9400	0	0
Brokage . . .	12	10	0

| **9412** | **10** | — |

The rest of the Money I have taken home.

Note, In this Case you must make *Bank Annuity* Dr. to Cash for the whole sum expended, and Cash Cr. by *Bank Annuity* for the same Sum. The remaining part being taken home, there need nothing be said about it, because it was understood to be in your own Possession before. Or, you may make *Sundry Accompts* Drs. to Cash, viz.

Bank Annuity for the Sum paid for the Stock bought, and Profit and Loss for the Brokage: then make Cash Cr. by *Sundry Accompts* for the whole expence. Either way will be right, though I have used the former.

LONDON, May 25, 1789.

		l.	*s.*	*d.*

J. My prefent Dwelling-Houfe being out of Repair, I have, by Order of *Thomas Prefton*, Efq. (my Land-lord) employed *James Hart*, Joiner, and have paid him in full . . . .   17 | 9 | 6

> Note, As you are not to be at the Charge of repairing your Houfe yourfelf; fo you muft make your Landlord Dr. to Cafh for the Money you have laid out on it, and Cafh Cr. by your Landlord for the fame Sum.

———— 28 ————

J. I have infured to *James Allen*, 200*l.* on the *Golden Fleece*, *John Abney*, Mafter, bound to *Jamaica*, at 4*l.* per Cent. Premium . . . .   8 | — | —

> Note, As you are the Underwriter in this Policy of Infurance, for the fum of 200*l.* at 4*l.* per Cent the faid *James Allen* becomes your Dr. for that Sum, he not having paid the Money down: Hence if *James Allen* be made Dr. to Infurance Accompt for the aforefaid Premium, and Infurance Accompt Cr. by *James Allen* for the fame fum, the Accompt will be rightly ftated.

———— 31 ————

J. Paid Sundry Charges this Month, as per Book of Houfe-Expenfes . . . .   43 | 11 | 2

———— June 2 ————

J. Received from on Board the *Dolphin*, *Jacob Swaert*, Mafter, the following Goods, viz.
1000 Reams of fine Paper,
120 Pieces of Holland Cloth, and
100 Pieces of Long Lawn.

J. Which were configned to me from *Abraham Van Schoo-ten*, Merchant, at *Roan*, to fell for his Accompt, for which I am to have 2 per Cent for Sale, and 2 per Cent for Employment, and am to make Returns in *Norwich* Crape, Duroy, and Broad Cloth, as per Advice. Paid Freight, Cuftom, and other incident Charges on Receipt of the fame . . . . . .   196 | 17 | 6

> Note. As you have received the Goods for the Accompt of *Van-Schooten*, and not for yourfelf, and having the Security in your own hands, for the Money that you have laid out for him; fo you muft make *Goods for the Accompt of Abraham Van Schooten* Dr. to Cafh for the Charges, and Cafh Cr. by the faid Goods for the fame Sum.

———— 5 ————

J. Sold to *James Eaton* the 1000 Reams of Paper, for the Accompt of *Abraham Van Schooten*, at 6*s.* per Ream, for which he has paid me in full . . . .   300 | — | —

> Note, As *James Eaton* has paid for the Paper, fo you muft make Cafh Dr. to Goods for the Accompt of Abraham Van Schooten, for the Quantity of Paper and its Value, and *Goods for the Accompt of Abraham Van Schooten* Cr. by Cafh for the fame.

361

I 2

LONDON, June 8, 1789.

	l.	*s.*	*d.*

J. Sold to Sir *Robert Johnson*, 120 Pieces of Holland, for
the Accompt of *Abraham Van Schooten*, at 3*l.* per
Piece. for which he is to pay in 10 Days . . . . | 360 | — | —

> Note, As Sir *Robert* has not paid for the Holland, you must make
> him Dr. to *Goods for the Accompt of Abraham Van Schooten* for the
> Value of the Holland, and *Goods for the Accompt of A. V. Schooten*
> Cr. by Sir *Robert* for both Quantity and Value.

——————————— 12 ———————————

J. Sold to the above Sir *Robert Johnson* 100 Pieces of Long
Lawn, for the Accompt of *Abraham Van Schooten*,
at 2*l.* 10*s. per* Piece . . . . | 250 | — | —

> Received present Money . . . *l.*100 0 0
> The Rest in 12 Days 150 0 0
> Note 1, This may be Journalized two Ways, as at Jan. 23, but
> take this method, viz. make *Sundry Accompts* Dr. to *Goods for the*
> *Accompt of Abraham Van Schooten* for the Value of the *Long Lawn,*
> viz.
>
> Cash for the Money received, and
> Sir *Robert Johnson* for the Rest.
> Then make *Goods for the Accompt of A. V. Schooten* Cr. by *Sundry*
> *Accompts* for both Quantity and value.
> 2, The *Goods* being all fold, you may close the Accompt by making
> the said *Goods* Dr. to *Sundry Accompts*, viz. to *Profit and Loss* for
> the advantage you received by your Commission, and to *Abra-*
> *Van Schooten's Accompt Current* for the neat Produce : then make
> each of them Cr by *Goods for the Accompt of Abraham Van Schooten*
> for their respective values, and 'tis done.

——————————— 16 ———————————

J. *Samuel Fairman* has paid me in full . . . . . | 25 | — | —

——————————— 17 ———————————

J. Sir *Robert Johnson* has paid me in Part . . . . | 360 | — | —

——————————— 19 ———————————

J. Sold to *Samuel Fairman* 10 Hhds. of *Lisbon* Wine, at
10*l. per* Hhd. . . . . | 100 | — | —

——————————— 23 ———————————

J. *William Lowsfield*, Esq. has paid me in full . . . | 128 | 1 | —

——————————— 24 ———————————

J. Sir *Robert Johnson* has paid me in full . . . . | 150 | | —

J. Due to me Half a Years Dividend on 10000*l.* Bank An-
nuity . . . . ; . | 150 | — | —

362

LONDON, June 27, 1789.

		l.	s.	d.
J.	sold to *James Hicks* 10 Hhds. *Lisbon* Wine, at 10*l.* 10*s.* per Hhd. and received present Money	105	—	—

—————————— 29 ——————————

J. Shipped on board the *Goodwill*, *William Higgins*, Master,

		l.	s.	d.
56 Pieces of *Norwich* Crape, qt. 896 Yards, at 4*s.* per Yard . .	179	4	0
20 Pieces of Duroy, qt. 300 Yards at 6*s.* 6*d.* per Yard . .	97	10	0
22 Pieces of Broad Cloth, at 18*l.* per Piece, (paid for) . . .	396	0	0
Charges thereon as *per* Invoice .	10	7	6
My Commission on 683*l.* 1*s.* 6*d.* at 2 per Cent.	13	13	3

696 14 9

All which go consign'd to *Abraham Van Schooten*, Merchant at *Roan*, for his own Accompt and Risque.

Note 1. As the foregoing Goods are consign'd to *Van Schooten*, for his own Accompt, and not for yours, so whether they ever come to his Hands or not, you must make *Van Schooten's Accompt Current* Dr. to *Sundry Accompts* for the whole Charge, viz.

To *Norwich* Crape for its Quantity and Value.

To *Duroy* for the same;

To *Cash* for the *Broad Cloth*, because you have bought it, and paid for it, but not entered it in your Books, and also for the Charges on Shipping; and

To *Profit and Loss* for your Commission.

☞ The Commission comes to but 13*l.* 13*s.* 2*d.* 2qrs. though put down 13*l.* 13*s.* 3*d.* which thing is often done, not by mistake but for the purpose.

2. Then make each of them Cr. by *Van Schooten's* Accompt Current, for its respective Quantity and Value, and the whole will be right.

3. The Difference between the Dr. and Cr. Sides in *Van Schooten's* Accompt Current will shew what he owes you, or you owe him, which must be brought to Accompt the next time you are employed by him; or it may be done by Draft.

—————————— 30 ——————————

		l.	s.	d.
J.	Paid sundry Charges this Month, as *per* Book of House Expences	40	8	10

363

LONDON, July 4, 1789.

		£	s.	d.	£	s.	d.
J.	Shipped on board the *Goldfinch, William Davis* Master						
Cafe JJ	1 Cafe, containing 100 Silver Watches at 3*l.* each, bought of *William Warner*	300	0	0			
Bale JJ	1 Bale of Scarlet Cloth, containing 20 Pieces, at 20*l. per* Piece, bought of *William Lowfield,* Efq.	400	0	0			
Hhds. 1 to 30 each JJ	30 Hhds. of Tobacco, containing 170 *C.* Weight, bought of *Thomas Johnſon* at 4*l.* 6*s.* 4*d. per C.*	733	6	8			
	Paid Cuſtom, Freight, and other Charges on ſhipping the ſame	29	13	0			
					1462	9	8
	The Drawback on the ſaid Tobacco, at 2*l.* 11*s.* 4*d. per C.* amounts to				426	6	—

All which are conſign'd to *Jaques Joliffe,* Merchant, at *Copenhagen,* to ſell for the joint Accompt of *Samuel Smith* and myſelf, each Half, and are numbered and marked as per Margin.

Note 1. In order to Journalize this Accompt rightly, you muſt make *Voyage to Copenhagen* in Comp. between *Samuel Smith* and ſelf, each half, conſign'd to *Jaques Joliffe* Dr. to *Sundry Accompts,* viz

To *Wiliikm Warner,* for the Watches, and their Value;
To *William Lowfie'd,* Efq. for the Scarlet Cloth and its Value;
To *Thomas Jackſon,* for the Tobacco, and its Value; and
To *Cafh* for the Charges.

2. Then each of them muſt be made Cr. by the ſaid Voyage for the Goods, and their Values reſpectively.

3. As you are concerned in Partnerſhip, your Partner's *Accompt Current* muſt be made Dr. to his *Accompt in Company* for his half of the ſaid Goods and Charges.

4. For the Drawback on the Tobacco, you muſt make the *Commiſſioners* of the *Cuſtoms* Dr. to the ſaid *Voyage in Company* for the Value of the Drawback, becauſe the Tobacco is to be exported.

5. As you are ſuppoſed to be the principal Actor in this Caſe, you muſt alſo make your Partner's *Accompt in Company* Dr. to his *Accompt Current* for his half part of the Drawback now, or let it alone till the *Commiſſioners* pay you; however I have done it now.

6 The young Book keeper, perhaps, may be at a Loſs for the Meaning of the Word Drawback, and therefore I give him this ſhort Explanation.

When Goods are imported, they pay a Duty to the King; and when thoſe Goods, or any part of them are exported again, the *Commiſſioners of the Cuſtoms* pay back again ſo much of the Money they had received, as is in Proportion to the Quantity of Goods exported; and the Money ſo repaid is called the *Drawback.*

364

London, July 9, 1789.

	l.	*s.*	*d.*

7. Ship *James*, after a smart Engagement with a *French* Merchant-man, took her, but afterwards she was ransomed for 5000*l.* the Half Part coming to the Owners is 25000*l.* my Half whereof as being Half Owner, (which I have received) comes to . . .   **12500 —**

Note, This must be Journalized exactly as p. 7, *May* 20.

——— 12 ———

7. This Day had 12000*l. Old South Sea* Annuity transferred to me at 91½ *per Cent.*

                      l.   *s.*   *d.*

   Old South Sea Annuity   .   .   10930   0   0

   Paid Brokerage 13   14   6   **10993 14 6**

Note, Here you must make *Old South Sea Annuity* Dr. to *Cash* for the Money that you have laid out; and *Cash* Cr. by *Old South Sea Annuity* for the same Sum. *Vide May* 22, p. 7.

——— 14 ———

7. I have insured 200*l* on the Scarlet Cloth that Sir *Humphrey Parsons* has shipp'd on board the *Falcon* from *London* to *Smyrna,* at 1 *per Cent.* to be paid upon News of her safe Arrival there   **16 —**

Note, As you have not received the *Premium* therefore you must make Sir *Humphrey* Dr. to *Insurance* for it, and *Insurance* Cr. by Sir *Humphrey* for the same Sum.

——— 17 ———

7. Bought of *John Marsh,* of *Manchester,* 5628*lb.* of superfine Thread at 14*s.* 10*d.* ½ *per lb.* **4185 16 6**

To pay at three two Months as follows, as *per* 3 Bills delivered, *viz.*

The first of 2185*l.* 16*s.* 6*d.* to pay 17 *September* next;

The second of 1000*l.* to pay 17 *November* next; and

The third of 1000*l.* to pay 17 *January* next.

Which Thread is for the Accompt of *James Severn* and Self, each Half, myself having the Disposal of the same.

Note 1. As the *Thread* is in Comp. you must make *Thread in Comp.* between *James Severn* and Self, each Half, Dr. to *John Marsh,* for the Quantity and its Value; then make *John Marsh* Cr. by *Thread in Comp.* &c. for the same Sum.

     2. Because you have a Partner, you must make his *Accompt Current* Dr. to his *Accompt in Comp.* for his Half of the said *Thread;* and your Partner's *Accompt in Comp.* Cr. by his *Accompt Current* for the same Sum.

——— 20 ———

7. *Jaques Joliffe* of *Copenhagen,* writes me word in his Letter of the 10th Instant, that he had received the Goods consigned to him, for the joint Accompt of *Samuel Smith* and Self; and the Commissioners of the Customs being made Dr. to that Voyage for a Drawback on 30 Hhds. of Tobacco, Part of the Goods consigned to the said *Jaques Joliffe,* I have received the said Drawback, which is **436 6 9**

365

LONDON, July 20, 1789.

	l.	*s.*	*d.*

Note, 1 In this cafe you are only to clear the *Commiffioners,* and therefore you muſt make *Caſh* Dr. to them for the Money received, and *Commiffioners* of the *Cuſtoms* Cr. by *Caſh* for the ſame Sum.

2. This *Tranſaction,* to ſome, may ſeem a little too haſty; but as ſome Perſons are more ſucceſsful in *Trade* then others, the whole of this *Voyage,* in all its following Circumſtances, may be looked upon as happy in its quick Return.

― 23 ―

J. Paid ſundry Charges in bringing the Thread in Comp. between *James Severn* and ſelf, into my Warehouſe   17   14   6

Note 1, This being an additional Charge on the ſaid *Thread,* you muſt make that Dr. to Caſh for the Money paid, and Caſh Cr. by the ſaid *Thread* for the ſame ſum.

2. Then, becauſe your Partner is concerned in the ſaid Charges by you paid, you muſt make his *Accompt Current* Dr. to his *Accompt in Comp.* for his Half; and your Partner's *Accompt in Comp.* Cr. by his Accompt Current for the ſame Sum.

― 24 ―

J. This Day *John Adams* came to pay me his Inſurance on my 100 Bags of Pepper loſt, which was done as follows, *viz.*   *l. s. d.*

Drawback on 140*l.* 7*s.* 10*d.* at 8 *per* Cent   11 . 4 . 7

Received in Caſh   129 . 3 . 3

    140   7   10

Note 1. On the Payment of Inſurance, it is cuſtomary for the paying Man to receive a Drawback of 6 7, or more per cent Hence *Profit and Loſs,* and Caſh muſt be made Drs. to *Adams* for their reſpective Sums, and *Adams* Cr. by *Sundry Accompts* for the whole Sum.

2. The Drawback is 11*l.* 4*s.* 7*d.* ¼, but the 1-2 is purpoſely omitted.

― 26 ―

J. Received of Sir *Humphrey Parſons* in Part   1 ſ

― 23 ―

J. Sold *Timothy Hart,* and Comp. 1000*lb.* of Thread, in Comp between *James Severn* and Self, at 18*s. per lb.*   900

For which they are to pay in 6 Months, that is to ſay, on *September* 28, *November* 28, and *January* 28, at 30*l.* each Payment, as *per* 3 Notes received.

Note 1. It is evident enough that *T. Hart* and Comp. muſt be made Dr. to *Thread in Comp.* between *James Severn* and Self for the Value; and that the ſaid *Thread* muſt be made Cr. by *T. Hart* and Comp. for both Quantity and Value.

2. As you have a Partner, you muſt alſo make his *Accompt in Comp.* Dr. to his *Accompt Current* for his Half of the ſaid *Thread* ſold as above, *viz.* 45*l.* and then make your Partner's *Accompt Current* Cr. by his *Accompt in Comp.* for the ſame ſum.

☞ I find a Difference of Opinions with regard to the making a Partner's *Accompt in Comp.* Dr. to his *Accompt Current* for Goods ſold but not paid for Some chuſing to do it as ſoon as the Goods are ſold, though upon Credit, while others omit

LONDON, July 28, 1789.

the Entry till the Money is paid. But I really think that the former way is the most eligible: because when the Goods are all sold, and the Accompt closed, each *Partner's Accompt Current* shews what is due to him, and consequently, what that Partner who keeps the Accompt has to pay him.

————— 31 —————

J. Paid sundry Charges this Month, as *per* Book of House-Expenses . . . .   21 18 —

————— *August* 3 —————

J. Sold to *Abraham Sanders* 1000 *lb.* of Thread in Comp. between *James Severn* and self, at 18s. *per lb.* for which I have received present Money   900

Note, This Entry differs so very little from that of the 28th ult. in the manner of journalizing, that it can scarcely be called a Difference, only making *Cash* Dr. to *Thread in Comp.* instead of the Person; the other Part of making your Partner's *Accompt in Comp.* Dr. for his half is the same as in that.

————— 6 —————

J. Paid sundry Charges in refitting the Ship *James,* as *per* Bills . . . .   207 5 —

Note 1. As the Money was paid on the Accompt of Ship *James* she must be made Dr. to Cash for the same, and Cash Cr. by the said Ship for the like Sum.

2. Make each Partner Dr. to the said Ship for his $\frac{1}{16}$ Part of the said Charges, viz. 12*l.* 19*s.* 0*d.* 3 *qrs.* and Ship *James* Cr. by *Sundry Accompts* for their several Sums taken together, viz. 103*l.* 12*s.* 6*d.*

————— 8 —————

J. *Jaques Joliffe* of *Copenhagen,* by his Letter of the 2d Instant, writes me Word, that he had the good Fortune to dispose of all the Effects consign'd to him for the joint Accompt of *Samuel Smith* and self, soon after he received them; the neat proceed whereof, deducting all Charges and his commission thereon, as *per* his Accompt of Sale, amounts to 10040 Rix Dollars, Exchange at 5s. per Dollar   2510 — —

Note 1, *Jaques Joliffe* having disposed of all the Effects, you must now clear Voyage to *Copenhagen,* by making *Joliffe's* Accompt Current Dr. to the *Voyage* for the neat Produce of the same; and the said Voyage Cr. by *J. Joliffe's* Accompt Current for the same Sum.

2. Your Partner's Accompt in Comp. must be made Dr. to his Accompt Current, and his Accompt Current Cr by his Accompt in Comp. for his half of the said neat Produce.

————— 12 —————

J. *Johannes Scheelhase* having occasion to go to *Copenhagen,* has desired me to draw a Bill on *Jaques Joliffe* for the aforesaid 10040 Rix Dollars, payable to the said *Scheelhase,* which I have accordingly done, he paying me 5s. 0d. $\frac{1}{4}$ per Dollar, which comes to 2520 0 2

K

LONDON, August 12, 1789.

Note 1. This is called buying a Bill, and is much safer to travel with than so much Money.

2. As you have received the Money, and as it concerns, in this Case, *Jaques Joliffe* more than *Johannes Scheelhase*, you must make Cash Dr. to Sundry Accompts for the whole Sum, viz.

To *Jaques Joliffe's* Accompt Current for the Money due from him to you, viz. 251*ol*.

To *Profit and Loss* for your Half of the Gain on the said *Dollars*, viz. 5*l*. 4. 7*d*. and to *Samuel Smith's* Accompt Current for his Half, this being an additional Gain on the said *Voyage*, then make each of them Cr. by Cash for their respective Sums.

Thus will the Balance of your Partner's Accompt in Comp. shew what he has gain'd by Trade; and likewise the Balance of his Accompt Current shew what you are to pay him.

3. The Balance of your Partner's Accompt in Comp: must be carried to *Voyage* to Copenhagen, by making it Cr. by Voyage to Copenhagen for his half Share of the gain thereof, and *Voyage* to Copenhagen Dr. to Partner's Accompt in Comp. for the same Gain.

4. The *Balance* of the said Voyage will be your own clear Gain, which will also be the same with your Partner's; and therefore you must make Voyage to Copenhagen Dr. to *Profit and Loss* for your own half Share of the Gain, and *Profit and Loss*, Cr. by *Voyage* to Copenhagen for the same Sum : thus will this Accompt be closed.

—————————— 14 ——————————

J. Upon examining the List at *Lloyd's* Coffee-House, I found the good Ship *Falcon* was lost on the Rocks of *Scilly*, and very little of her Cargo saved, but none of the Scarlet Cloth on which I had insured to Sir *Humphrey Parsons* 200

Note, As you have not yet paid the Money, you must make *Insurance* Dr. to Sir *Humphrey Parsons*, for the Sum insured, and Sir *Humphrey Parsons* Cr. by *Insurance* for the same Sum.

—————————— 15 ——————————

J. My Brother-in-law *Christopher Verax* being dead, there is due to me from his Executor Mr. *William Warner* 1000

Note, Your Brother-in-Law, *Verax* being dead, you have now a Claim for the above-mentioned Sum, by Virtue of his last Will, which you could not have while he was living. Hence as *William Warner* is his Executor, he becomes your Dr. of Course, and accordingly must be made so in your Books, and *Profit and Loss* must be made Cr. by *William Warner* for the same Sum.

—————————— 17 ——————————

	l.	*s.*	*d.*
J. *William Simpson*, Cooper, has by my Order bottled off 1 Hhd of *French Wine*, Value	30	0	0
Do *Lisbon Wine*	7	0	0

for the Use of the Family.

Note, As the French and Lisbon Wines were bottled off for the Use of the House, and not to be sold, you must here make House-Expenses or *Profit and Loss* Dr. to Sundry Accompts for the two Hhds thus set aside out of trade at their prime Cost; then make each of them Cr. by House-Expenses or by *Profit and Loss* for their Quantities and Values respectively. I have used House-Expenses.

LONDON, August 20, 1789.

	l.	*s.*	*d.*

J. This Day received the unfortunate News, that Ship *James* was taken by a *French* Privateer of superior Force and carried into *Brest*.

> *Note*, This Passage being a Matter of Information, more than any thing else; and as the said Ship has already made a sufficient Gain, no journalizing need be made, but the whole Accompt of the said Ship may be balanced, and thereby the clear Gain be known.

------------ 22 ------------

J. *William Baker*, Esq. has paid me Half a Years Interest, which is due this Day on the 500*l.* lent him *Feb.* 22 last . . . . **12 | 10 | —**

> *Note*, In this Case you are to make *Cash* Dr. to *Profit and Loss*, or to *Interest Accompt* (I have made it *Profit and Loss*) and not to the Man that you received it of, for the Sum so received, and *Profit and Loss* Cr. by *Cash* for the same Sum.

------------ 23 ------------

J. This Day the several Proprietors of the Ship *James* met, and paid me their several Parts of the Charges by me paid the 6th Instant, belonging to the said Ship, viz.

	l.	*s.*	*d.*
John Herbert	12	19	0¾
John Smith	12	19	0¾
William Baker, Esq.	12	19	0¾
Robert Uxley	12	19	0¾
Sir *Robert Johnson*	12	19	0¾
William Evans	12	19	0¾
James Jackson	12	19	0¾
Thomas Jones	12	19	0¾

103 | 12 | 6

> *Note*, In this Case you are only to make *Cash* Dr. to *Sundry Accompts* for the Money received, and each Man, Cr. by *Cash* for his respective Sum by him paid.

------------ 26 ------------

J. The three Bills given by me to *John Marsh*, of *Manchester*, for Thread in Comp. between *James Severn* and myself, were this Day brought to me for Acceptance by the following Persons, which I have accordingly accepted, viz.

Thomas Preston for 2185*l.* 16*s.* 6*d.* payable 17. *Sept.* next.
Sir *R. Johnson* for 1000 0 0 do.   17 *Nov.* next.
Robert Uxley for 1000 0 0 do.   17 *Jan.* next.

4185 | 16 | 6

> *Note*, This is no more than transferring the Accompt from *Marsh* to the several Possessors of those Bills; and by your Acceptance of them *Marsh* is paid, and therefore must be discharged; consequently you must make *John Marsh* Dr. to *Sundry Accompts* for the whole Sum due from you, and each Man Cr. by the Sum of that particular Bill which is in his Possession.

K 2

369

London, August 28, 1789.

		l.	s.	n.
J.	Bought of *Andrew Collins*, the Ship *Hopewell*, Burthen 300 Tons, *John Hill*, Master, for which I have paid down . . . . . , ... r .	1200		

------------------------------ 31 ------------------------------

		l.	s.	n.
J.	Paid sundry Charges this Month, as *per* Book of House Expenses . . . . , , .	21	17	6

------------------------------ *September* 3 ------------------------------

		l.	s.	n.
J.	Sent to Mr. *William Warner*, Executor to the last Will and Testament of my late Brother-in-law, *Christopher Verax*, 1 Hhd. of *French* Wine as a Present; the prime Cost whereof is	30		

> *Note,* The Wine thus given, must here be looked on as lost, because not sold, nor any Value received thereon ; therefore you must make *Profit* and *Loss* Dr. to *French* Wine, for the Value of the said Hhd. and *French* Wine, Cr. by *Profit* and *Loss* for the same Sum.

------------------------------ 5 ------------------------------

		l.	s.	n.
J.	Paid Sir *Humphrey Parsons* the Balance of our Accompt, which was	184		
	viz. In Cash . . . . , . . . 172 0 0			
	Drawback on 200*l.* at 6 *per Cent.* 12 0 0			
		184		

> *Note,* It is customary on the Payment of *Insurance.* to have a *Drawback* of 4, 5. 6, or more per cent. and as Sir *Humphrey* has not paid the Premium of 16*l.* there remains on the Balance of the Accompt but 184*l.* to be paid by you ; but as you demand a *Drawback* of 6 per cent. you are to pay him, in reality no more than 172*l.* Hence, to state the Accompt right, you must make Sir *Humphrey* Dr. to Sundry Accompts for the 184*l.* then make Cash Cr. by Sir *Humphrey* for the Sum paid him, and *Profit* and *Loss* Cr. for the *Drawback*.

------------------------------ 7 ------------------------------

		l.	s.	d.
J.	Sold the Ship *Hopewell* to *Abraham Sanders* and received of him two Bank Notes for }	1500	0	0
	One Warrant to be paid by the Treasurer of the South Sea Company, for . . }	100	0	0
		1600		

> *Note,* In this Case the *Bank Notes* and the *Warrant* may be esteemed as Cash, and as such made Dr. to the said *Ship*, and the said *Ship* Cr. by Cash, both of t em for the Value of the said Notes and Warrants.

370

London, September 9, 1789.

	l.	s.	d.

7. Received Advice from *Timothy Sutton*, of *Barbadoes*, that he hath according to my Order, shipped on board the *Whale*, *John Miller*, Master, 45 Chests of Sugar, qt. neat 223C. 2qrs. 7lb. Avoirdupois, at 15s. Sterling per C. including the charges of shipping   1671   5¼

Which Sugar, although consigned to me, is for the Account of *John Parrot*, *George Hale*, and Self, each 1-3 my two Partners having agreed to allow me 2 *per cent.* on their own Parts for Warehouse-Room, and my Care on the Sale thereof.

> Note 1, After *Sutton* had received your Order, and taken Care to ship the Sugar, it was then no longer his, but yours, and you are obliged to stand the chance of the Seas, and become Dr. to him, whether it ever comes to your Hands or not. Hence,
>
> 2. You must make Voyage from *Barbadoes* Dr. to *Timothy Sutton*, for the whole charge of the Sugar, and *Timothy Sutton* Cr. by Voyage from *Barbadoes* for the same Sum.
>
> 3. As you have Partners, you must make each Man's Accompt Current Dr. to his Accompt in Comp. for the third of the said charge, and each Man's Accompt in Comp. Cr. by his Accompt Current for the like Sum.

371

———————— I I ————————

2. Received from *Nathaniel Keeble*, of *Hull*, 150 Pieces of *Yorkshire* Cloth, which he bought for my Accompt, pursuant to my Order of the 24th. ult. at 7l. 10s. *per* Piece   } 1125   0   0

Paid Charges on bringing the same into my Warehouse   } 27   4   6   1152   4   6

7. Received also from Do *Keeble*, 50 Pieces of the same Cloth, which he desires me to dispose of for his Accompt.

7. Paid Charges on bringing the same into my Warehouse.   11   4   8

> Note 1, The first 150 Pieces of *Yorkshire* Cloth, are for your own Accompt, and therefore you must make *Yorkshire* Cloth Dr. to *Sundry Accompts*, viz.
> To *Nathaniel Keeble* for the Quantity you have received of him, and its Value; and
> To Cash for the Charges by you paid in bringing the same Home; Then make each of them Cr. by *Yorkshire* Cloth for their respective Sums.
>
> 2. The other 50 Pieces are for the Accompt of ditto *Keeble*, and therefore as you have the Cloth in your own Hands, you need only make *Yorkshire* Cloth for the Accompt of *Nathaniel Keeble* of *Hull* Dr. to *Cash* for the charges that you have been at in bringing it into your Warehouse, naming the Quantity; and *Cash* Cr. by ditto Cloth, &c. for the same Expense.

London, September 15, 1789.

		l.	s.	d.

J. Received the 45 Chests of Sugar from on board the *Whale*, consigned to me by *Timothy Sutton* of *Barbadoes*. . . . . 167 | 13 | 5¼

	l.	s.	d.

Paid Custom thereon, at 4s. 9l. $\frac{90}{100}$ per C. on 223 C. 2 qrs. 7lb. 53 18 8¼

Freight at 4s. *per* Chest 9 0 0

Litherage 1 7 3

Cartage 2 10 7

66 | 16 | 6¼

C. D. C. qrs. lb. l. s. d.

Note 1. 1 : 57-9 : : 223 2 7 : 53 18 8 1-4

2. As you have received the Sugar, you must 1st make *Sugar in Comp.* with *John Parrot, George Hale* and self, each one third Dr to *Sundry Accompts* for the whole charge, viz. to *Voyage* from *Barbadoes* for the Quantity and its Value, and to *Cash* for the charges in bringing the same home; then make each of them Cr. by *Sugar in Comp. &c.* for its respective Value.

3. Your Partners also must each of them have his *Accompt Current* made Dr. to his *Accompt in Comp.* for the third of the said charges, and his *Accompt in Comp.* Cr. by his *Accompt Current* for the same. The like for the first Value was done before.

—— 20 ——

J. Paid *Thomas Preston*, Esq. my Note given to *John Marsh*, of *Manchester*, and by him assigned to do. *Preston*.

	l.	s.	d.

Paid 2185 16 0

Abated me 0 0 6

2185 | 16 | 6

Note, In this case you must make *T. Preston* Dr. to *Sundry Accompts*, viz. To *Cash* for the Money paid, and to *Profit and Loss* for the Gain made by the Abatement of the 6d. then make each of them Cr. by their respective Sums.

—— 22 ——

J. Sold to *James Jackson* the 45 Chests of Sugar in Comp. with *John Parrot, George Hale* and self, containing neat 223 C. 2 qrs. 7lb. at 4l. per C. together with my own 8 Hhds. of *French* Wine, at 35l. per Hhd.

	l.	s.	d.

Sugar in Comp. 894 5 0

French Wine of my own . . . 280 0 0

1147 | 5 |

For all which I have received

In Cash 200 0 0

By a Draft on *William Harrison* . . 400 0 0

The rest to stand out 6 Months . . 574 5 0

1174 | 5 |

Note 1, That this Accompt may be journalized, and then posted right, you are to consider that although *Jackson* has bought the *Sugar* in Comp. and your own *French* Wine, and paid for them in Part, yet you must first make him Dr. for the whole; and then make him Cr. by what Part he has paid, in the following Manner, viz. *James Jackson* Dr. to *Sundry Accompts*

l. s. d.

372

LONDON, September 22, 1789.

l. | s. | d.

for the whole Value of the Goods bought, that is, to *Sugar in Comp.* for the whole Value thereof, and also to *French* Wine (for your own proper Accompt) for its Value; then make each of them Cr. by *James Jackson* for its respective Quantity and Value.

2. Because *Jackson* has paid part in Cash, and a Draft on *Harman*, they, i. e. *Cash* and *Harman*, or Sundry Accompts must be made Drs. to *James Jackson* for their respective sums, and *Jackson* Cr. by Sundry Accompts for the whole that he has paid.

3. The Sugar in Comp. being disposed of, you must next make each Partner's Accompt in Comp. Dr. to his Accompt Current for his third Share of the Sugar sold as aforesaid, and each Partner's Accompt Current Cr. by his Accompt in Comp. for the same Sum.

4. Because you are to be allowed 2 per Cent on the sale &c. of the said Sugar by way of Commission, it will be necessary to observe that the whole was sold for 894*l*. 5*s*. which Sum at 2 per Cent. amounts to 17*l*. 17*s*. 8*d*. 1-4 : one third of which comes to 5*l*.19 2*d*. 3-4 for each Partner to pay : and in this case you must make each Partner's Accompt Current Dr. to Profit and Loss in the Sum of 5*l*. 19*s*. 2*d*.3-4 for his third on the sale &c. as aforesaid, and Profit and Loss Cr. by each Partner's Accompt for the same Sum.

Thus will the Balance of each Partner's Accompt in Comp. shew what he has gain'd by Trade, and likewise the Balance of his Accompt Current shew what you are to pay him.

373

———— 24 ————

J. | Sold to *William Evans* 1000lb. of Thread in Comp. between *James Severn* and self, at 18*s*. per *lb*. . . | 900 | — |

	l.	s.	d.
Received in Cash	200	0	0
————a Draft on *Thomas Jones* for	300	0	0
The rest in 6 Months	400	0	0

900

Note 1, Here you must make Sundry Accompts Drs. to *Thread in Comp.* for the whole Value, viz. Cash for the Money that you have received :

Thomas Jones for the Draft on him ; and

William Evans for the Remainder :

Then make Thread in Comp. Cr. by Sundry Accompts for the whole Quantity sold, and its Value.

2. Make your Partner's Accompt in Comp. Dr. to his Accompt Current for his half part of the said *Thread*, and your Partner's Accompt Current Cr. by his Accompt in Comp. for the same Value.

———— 27 ————

J. | Sold to *Thomas Jones* 50 Pieces of my own *Yorkshire* Cloth, at 8*l*. 10*s*. per Piece . ; . . . . | 425 | — |

———— 29 ————

J. | Due to me Half a Year's Dividend on 12000*l*. Stock, Old South Sea Annuity . . . . | 180 | — |

LONDON, September 30, 1789.

		l.	*s.*	*d.*
J.	Paid Sundry Charges this Month, as per Book of House-Expences	22	12	6

——— October 1 ———

| J. | Received of *Timothy Hart* and Comp. . . . . . . | 300 | — | — |

——— 3 ———

| J. | Sold to *Adam Hewitt* 50 Pieces of my own *Yorkshire* Cloth, at 8*l*. 10*s*. *per* Piece for present Money. . | 425 | — | — |

——— 6 ———

| J. | Received of Mr. *William Warner*, the Legacy due to me by the last Will of my late Brother *Christopher Verax* . . . . | 1000 | — | — |
| | At which Time I also paid him my Debt of . . . . | 300 | — | — |

——— 10 ———

| J. | Received Half a Year's Interest on my 12000*l*. Old South Sea Annuity, due at Michaelmas last . . . | 180 | — | — |

——— 14 ———

| J. | Received Half a Year's Interest on my 10000*l*. Bank Annuity, due at Midsummer last . . . . | 150 | — | — |

——— 18 ———

| J. | Received of *William Harman*, by Virtue of a Draft on him by *James Jackson* . . . . | 400 | — | — |

——— 22 ———

| J. | Received of *Thomas Jones*, by Virtue of a Draft on him by *William Evans* . , ... | 300 | — | — |

——— 24 ———

| J. | Sold 1 Pipe of Canary to *John Hammond*, Esq. for . | 30 | — | — |

——— 26 ———

| J. | Received of *Martin Unwin* in Part . . . . . , | 100 | — | — |

——— 28 ———

| J. | Shipped on Board the *Whale*, *John Miller* Master. | | | |

		l.	*s.*	*d.*			
	30 Bags of Hops, qt. 90C. 1qr. at 28*s*. *per* C. . . , ...	126	7	0			
	20 Pieces of Sagathee, qt. 240 Yards, at 2*s*. 6*l*. *per* Yard	30	0	0			
	20 Pieces of Serge, qt. 280 Yards, at 1*s*. *per* Yard	14	0	0			
	Paid Charges on shipping the same . .	19	17	6	190	4	6

All which go consign'd to *Timothy Sutton*, Merchant at *Barbadoes*, for my own Accompt and Risque.

Note 1. In this Case the young Book-keeper might ask, Why Commission is not charged here, as well as at June 28? To which I answer, that as the Goods are to be disposed of for

LONDON, October 28, 1789.

		l.	*s.*	*d.*

your own Accompt, and not for *Sutten's* it would be abfurd for you to charge Commiffion on your own Goods, which are to be fold for your own Ufe: and therefore when *Sutten* has difpofed of the Goods, he muft charge Commiffion according for what he can fell them.

2. As the goods are confign'd to *Sutten* for your own Accompt, *Sutten* is not to run the Rifque of the Seas; and therefore if the Ship fhould be loft, you muft ftand to the Lofs, and not *Sutten.*

3. You muft make *Voyage to Barbadoes* Dr. to *Sundry Accompts* for the whole Charge, and each of them Cr. by the faid *Voyage* for its refpective Value, fubmitting the reft to the chance of the Market, which, if Goods of this Nature fhould happen to be plenty, will occafion the Price to run low; but if fcarce will enhance the Price in Proportion.

4. The Goods thus fent, muft be charged at the prime Coft, becaufe it is only removing them from one Place to another.

— 29 —

7. *Brandon George* has infured the aforementioned Goods, confign'd to *Timothy Sutton*, at 6 *per cent.* for which I am to be credited. — 11 | 9 | 3

Note, This cafe being a further Expence on the juft mentioned Voyage, you muft make that Dr. to *Brandon George* for the Sum infured, and *Brandon George* Cr. by the faid *Voyage* for the fame Sum.

— 30 —

7. Sold to *Brandon George*   *l. s. d.*
1 Pipe of Canary 30 0 0
1 Hhd. of *Lifbon* Wine . . . . 10 0 0   40 | — | —

— 31 —

7. Paid Sundry Charges this Month, as *per* Book of Houfe Expenfes . . . . — 26 | 13 | 8

— November 1 —

7. Paid *William Lowfield*, Efq. in full . . . . . 400 | — | —

— 4 —

7. Received of *Samuel Fairman* in full . . . . . 100 | — | —

— 7 —

7. Paid *Thomas Johnfon* in Part . . . . . . 100 | — | —

— 10 —

7. Sold *John Adams*   *l. s. d.*
1 Bag of Hops, wt. 3C. at 36s. per C. . 5 8 0
1 Pipe of Canary 33 0 0
for which I have received in full . . . . 38 | 8 | —

L

375

London, November 15 1789.

		l.	s.	d.

J. Received a Bill of Exchange from *Jacob Van Hoove of Amsterdam*, of 1611 *Guil.* 3 *Sti.* drawn upon *Jaques Van-Brook*, for the Value received there, by ditto *Van-Hoove*, Exchange at 33s. 4d. *Flem. per l. Ster.* payable at 10 Days after Sight, which *Van-Brook* has accepted . . . . **161 | 2 | 3½**

Note 1. The laſt Accompt that you received from *Van-Hoove* was on *May* 10 laſt, which is a long Time, to the preſent Day. It may therefore be ſuppoſed, that in all this Time there was no ſuch thing as bringing him to Accompt; and that Letters were wrote and Perſons employed to accommodate the Affair, which at laſt was obtained by receiving a Bill of Exchange as above.

2. This is the Reverſe of *Aug.* 26, though it is transferring the Accompt from one Man to another as that is, and therefore you muſt make *Van-Brook* Dr. to *Van-Hoove* for the Value of the Bill, and *Van-Hoove* Cr. by *Van-Brook* for the ſame Sum.

———— 18 ————

J. Sold to *William Baker*, Eſq.   *l.*   *s.*   *d.*
20 Pieces of Sagathee, qt. 240 Yards, at 3s. *per* Yard 36   0   0
20 Pieces of Serge, qt. 280 Yards, at 14d. *per* Yard 16   0   0

for which I have received in Part . . . 16   6   8   **52 | 6 | 8**

Note, As *Baker* has paid for the *Serge*, you muſt make *Caſh* Dr. to it for the worth of it, and *Serge* Cr. by Caſh for the ſame Sum; And as the *Sagathee* is not paid for, make *Baker* Dr. to it for its Value, and *Sagathee* Cr. by *Baker* for the like Sum.

———— 20 ————

J. Paid Sir *Robert Johnſon* one of the promiſſary Notes given by me to *John Marſh* of *Manchester*, which was due this Day, including the three days of Grace   **1000 | |**

———— 24 ————

J. *Thomas Johnſon* having freighted the *John* and *Hannah*, *James Tickner*, Maſter, for a Voyage to *Spain*, I have underwrote his Policy for 300*l.* at 6 *per Cent.* giving him Credit for the ſame, viz. . . . . .   **18 | |**

Note, Here you muſt make *Thomas Johnſon* Dr. to *Inſurance* for the Sum credited, and *Inſurance* Cr. by *Thomas Johnſon* for the ſame Sum.

———— 27 ————

J. Received of *Martin Unwin* in Part . . . . . .   **100 | |**

———— 28 ————

J. Received of *Jaques Van-Brook* in full . . . . .   **161 | 2 | 3½**

———— 30 ————

J. Paid ſundry Charges this Month, as *per* Book of Houſe-Expenſes . . . .   **2 | 13 | 6**

376

LONDON, December 1, 1789.

	l.	s.	d.
7. Received of *Timothy Hart* and Comp. in Part . . .	300		

—————— 3 ——————

7. This Day I was informed at *Lloyd's*, that the *John* and *Hannah* was unfortunately loft in the *Downs*, by a fevere Gale of Wind. I had infured on her Freight
Note, In this Cafe you muft make *Infurance* Dr. to *Thomas Johnfon* for the Sum by you infured, and *Thomas Johnfon* Cr. by *Infurance* for the like Sum·

300

—————— 6 ——————

7. Received of *John Hammond*, Efq. in full . . . . .

30

—————— 9 ——————

	l.	s.	d.
7. *William Baker*, Efq. has taken up his Bond and paid me	500	0	0
He has also paid me the Intereft of it, which from *Aug.* 22, being 3 M. 17 D. at 5 *per Cent.* is	7	8	4
	507	8	4

Note 1. Though you receive all the Money of *William Baker*, yet you muft make *Cafh* Dr. to *Sundry Accompts* for the whole Sum, and then make *William Baker* Cr. by *Cafh* for the 500*l* and *Profit and Lofs* Cr. by the fame for the Intereft.
2. The Intereft for 3 Months is 6*l.* 5*s.* and the Intereft for 17 Days is 1*l.* 3*s.* 3*d.* 1 *qr.* making 7*l.* 8*s.* 3*d.* 1*qr.* which here is pupofely augmented to 4*d.*

—————— 1 0 ——————

7. This Day *Thomas Johnfon* came to demand my Infurance on a Voyage to *Spain*, the Ship being loft in the *Downs*. The Sum infured was . . . .

300

	l.	s.	d.
Paid in Cafh	276	0	0
Drawback on 300*l.* at 8 *per Cent.* .	24	0	0
	300	0	0

Note, the Ship being loft, you neceffarily become Dr. to *Thomas Johnfon* for the Sum infured, as aforementioned; and now that you have paid that Infurance, including the Drawback, *Thomas Johnfon* becomes Dr. to *Sundry Accompts* for the whole Sum, and *Cafh* Cr. by ditto *Johnfon* for the Sum paid him and *Profit and Lofs* Cr. for the Drawback. See *Sept.* 5, p. 17,

—————— 1 2 ——————

	l.	s.	d.
7. Sold to *John Hammond*, Efq. my 50 Pieces of *Yorkfhire* Cloth, at 8*l.* 10*s per* Piece	425	0	0
Alfo 50 Pieces for the Accompt of *Nathaniel Keeble* of *Hull*, at the fame Rate	425	0	0
	850		

Note 1. In this Cafe *Hammond* muft be made Dr. to *Sundry Accompts* for the whole Sum, then make each of them Cr. by ditto *Hammond* for their refpective Values.

377

LONDON, December 12, 1789.

<table>
<tr><td></td><td>l.</td><td>s.</td><td>d.</td></tr>
</table>

2. *Keeble's* Cloth being all fold, you have acted by Commiffion (which fuppofe at 2 *per cent.* on the above Sum) and therefore muft charge that to him : Hence to cloſe the Accompt, you muft make the faid Cloth Dr. to *Sundry Accompts,* viz. to *Profit and Loſs* for the faid Commiffion, and to ditto *Keeble's Accompt Current* for the neat proceed; then make each of them Cr. by the faid Cloth for their refpective Sums, and the Accompt will be cloſed.

----- 13 -----

J. My Landlord *Thomas Preſton*, Efq. has paid me for the Repairs done to my prefent dwelling Houfe, by *James Hart*, Joiner. 17 9 6

----- 14 -----

J. Received Advice from *Joram Gonderil* of *Cadiz*, that he hath fhipped for my Accomqt and Rifque, in the *Pidgeon, William Pidgeon*, Mafter,

50 Chefts of Limons
50 do. *China* Oranges } at 8 Rials *per* Cheft, including all Charges.
50 do. *Seville* do.

Which amounts to 1200 Rials, Exchatge at 4*s.* 6*d. per* piece of Eight, and its Sterling . . . . . .   33 15 —

Note 1. Eight Rials make a Piece of Eight.
2. See the firft and fecond Notes on *Sep.* 9, p. 18, for the reft, that Entry being of the fame Nature with this, fetting afide the Partnerfhip.

----- 17 -----

J. I have this Day accepted a Draft on me by *Nathaniel Keeble* of *Hull,* payable to *Timothy Hart* and Comp. at 20 Days after Sight, for . . . .   1125 — —
But they having Occaſion for prefent Money, have agreed to allow me Rebate for the faid 20 Days, and no more, after the Rate of 8 per cent. on the faid Sum.

                                                    l.   s.   d.
I have therefore paid them   1120   2   0
Abated me on prompt payment . . . .   4 18   0   1125 — —

Note 1. The Sum of 1125*l.* being trasferred from *Keeble* to *Hart & Comp.* your Acceptance of the fame pays *Keeble* and makes you accountable to *Hart & Comp.* for the fame; therefore you muft firft make *Nathaniel Keeble* Dr. to *Timothy Hart and Comp.* for the fame Sum, and *Timothy Hart and Comp.* Crs. by ditto *Keeble* for the like Sum.
Then, as you have paid *Hart and Comp.* you muft make him Dr. to *Sundry Accompts* for the whole, and *Cafh* and *Profit & Loſs* Crs. by ditto *Hart* for their Sums refpectively.
2. The whole might be journalized fomewhat fhorter, by having Regard only to *Keeble*, the other being paid in truft for him; but as the former Method is more agreeable to the Nature of the tranſaction, I have accordingly made choice of it.

378

LONDON, December 18, 1789.

		l.	*s.*	*d.*

J. Received the 150 Chests of Oranges and Limons, from on board the *Pidgeon*, *William Pidgeon* Master, consign'd to me by *Joram Conderil*, of *Cadiz*.

	l.	*s.*	*d.*
Paid Custom thereon	12	6	6
Freight at 3s. *per* Chest	22	10	0
Waterage	1	10	0

36 6 6

Note, As you have now received the Goods, you must make *Oranges* and *Limons* Dr. to *Sundry Accompts* for the whole Charge, *viz.* to *Voyage to Cadiz* for the prime Cost thereof, and to *Cash* for the after–Charges in bringing the same home ; then make each of them Cr. by *Oranges* and *Limons* for its respective Value.

———— 20 ————

J. Received of *Martin Unwin* in Part **100**

———— 22 ————

J. *Joram Conderil*, of *Cadiz*, hath drawn upon me for the Fruit received of him payable to *John Hammond*, Esq. or Order, at Sight, 1200 Rials, Exchange at 4s. 6d. *per* Piece of Eight, which I have accepted, but not paid, because the same is to be placed to Accompt, as *per* Agreement between d° *Hammond* and myself   **33 15**

Note 1, Nothing more need be done than to make *Joram Coderil* Dr. to *John Hammond* for the Value of the Bill, and *Hammond* Cr. by *Conderil* for the same Sum.
2. Eight Rials are = 1 Piece of Eight. Vide *Sch. Aff.* p. 77.

———— 24 ————

J. Received of *Isaac Reynolds* in full **42**

———— 25 ————

J. Due to me Half a Year's Dividend on 10000l. Bank Annuity **150**

———— 26 ————

J. Sold to *Isaac Reynolds* 50 Chests of Limons, at 17s. *per* Chest **42 10**

———— 27 ————

J. Received of *James Allen* in full **8**

———— 28 ————

J. Sold to *James Allen*, 1000lb. of Thread in Comp. between *James Severn* and self, at 18s. *per lb.* for which he has given me a Draft on Mess. *Snell* and *Hartley*, Bankers, which I have received **900**

Note, This is nearly the same with July 28, p. 13, only make *Cash* Dr. for the Person, which see.

———— 29 ————

J. Sold to Sir *Humphrey Porters* 1000lb. of Thread in Comp. as above, at 18s. *per lb.* to pay in 6 Months   **900**

379

LONDON, December 30, 1789.

	l.	*s.*	*d.*

J. Sold to *William Baker*, Efq. the remaining 628 *lb.* of Thread, in Comp. as above, at 17*s. per lb.* . . . 533 16 —

For which he has given me my Note to *Marſh*, payable *January* 20 next, including the three Days of Grace, and transferred to *Robert Uxley*, I having paid him the reſt; *Baker* at the ſame time allowing me for my prompt payment for 23 Days 8 *per Cent.*

	l.	*s.*	*d.*
Promiſſary Note	1000	0	0
Thread in Comp.	533	16	0
Due *January* 20 next	466	4	0
Allow'd for prompt Payment for 23 Days	2	6	8
Return'd to d° *Baker*	463	17	4

Note, To Journalize this paſſage aright, and in the plaineſt manner, you muſt

1. Make *William Baker* Dr to *Thread in Comp.* for the Value thereof; and *Thread in Comp.* Cr. by *William Baker* for both Quantity and Value.
2. Becauſe *Baker* has paid for it by returning you one of your own Notes, by which *Uxley* was Cr. therefore *Uxley* by that means is paid, and you muſt make him Dr. to *William Baker* for the Value of that Note, and *Baker* Cr. by *Uxley* for the ſame.
3. Becauſe you have return'd *Baker* the Overplus, partly by *Caſh* and partly by his abatement on *prompt Payment*, therefore *Baker* muſt be made Dr. to *Sundry Accompts*, viz. to *Caſh* for the Money which he has received of you, and to *Profit and Loſs* for his Abatement; then make each of them Cr. by ditto *Baker* for their reſpective Sums.

☞ This might be done in a ſhorter manner, by making *Uxley* Dr. to *Sundry Accompts* for the Value of the Bill, viz.

	l.	*s.*	*d.*
To *Thread in Comp.* - - - - - - - -	533	16	0
To *Caſh* paid *William Baker* - - - - - -	463	17	4
To *Profit and Loſs* gain'd by prompt Payment -	2	6	8
	1000	0	0

The Teacher may uſe either way, though I have followed the former, as being moſt expreſſive of the whole Tranſaction.

4. Make your Partner's *Accompt in Comp.* Dr. to his Accompt Current for his Half, and your Partner's Accompt Current Cr. by his Accompt in Comp. for the ſame.
5. The *Thread* being all ſold you may cloſe the Accompt by the Directions given at *Aug.* 12, p. 15.

———————— 31 ————————

J. Paid Sundry Charges this Month as *per* Book of Houſe-Expenſes 22 8

The End of the Second Waſte-Book.

380

The J O U R N A L.

LONDON, March 1, 1789.

		l.	s.	d.	l.	s.	d.
	Sundry Accompts Drs. to Stock . . .	10925	15	4¼			
	viz.						
1	Cash in Ready Money	8099	4	2½			
1	Canary, for 5 Pipes, at 25 l. per Pipe .	125	0	0			
1	Hops, for 44 Bags, wt. 132C. 2 qrs. at ⎱ 28s. per C. . . . . ⎰	185	10	0			
2	French Wine, for 10 Hhds. at 30l. per Hhd.	300	0	0			
2	Drugget, for 20 Pieces, qt. 280 Yards, at ⎱ 3s. 4d. per Yard . . . . . ⎰	46	13	4			
2	Lisbon Wine, for 25 Hhds. at 7l. per Hhd.	175	0	0			
2	Norwich Crape, for 56 Pieces, qt. 896 ⎱ Yds. at 3s. 6d. per Yard . . . . ⎰	156	16	0			
2	Duroy, for 20 Pieces, qt. 300 Yards, at ⎱ 6s per Yard . . . . ⎰	90	0	0			
3	Sagathee, for 90 Pieces, qt. 1080 Yards, ⎱ at 2s. 6d. per Yard. . . . . . ⎰	135	0	0			
3	Serge, for 90 Pieces, qt. 1260 Yards, at ⎱ 1s. per Yard . . . . ⎰	63	0	0			
3	Sir Robert Johnson	30	0	0			
3	Sir Humphrey Parsons	16	0	0			
4	William Baker, Esq. on Bond . . .	500	0	0			
4	William Warner, to be paid April 30 next	34	7	0			
4	Brandon George	32	0	0			
4	Samuel Fairman	28	0	0			
4	William Lowfield, Esq;	128	13	0			
5	Thomas Johnson	256	14	3¾			
5	John Hammond, Esq. to be paid April 20 next	100	0	0			
5	Martin Unwin	381	17	6			
5	Isaac Reynolds	42	0	0			
1	Stock Dr. to Sundry Accompts . . .	412	10	0	10925	15	4¼
1	viz.						
5	To Thomas Preston, Esq. to pay May 14 next	90	0	0			
5	To Robert Uxley	322	10	0			
	2				412	10	—
1	Cash Dr. to Sir Robert Johnson . . .	30	0	0			
3	Received in full				30		—
6	4						
1	Ship James Dr. to Sundry Accompts .	1500	0	0			
6	viz. To Cash paid down at 5 per Cent. .	75	0	0			
	To James Allen, to pay in 5 Days	1425	0	0	1500		—

		l.	s.	d.

LONDON, March 6, 1789.

1	Cash Dr. to Ship *James* *l.*125 0 0			
6	Received of Capt. *John Smith* for $\frac{1}{16}$ Part of the said Ship	125	—	
	——————— 8 ———————			
1	Cash Dr. to Ship *James* *l.*125 0 0			
6	Rec'd. of Capt. *John Herbert* for $\frac{1}{16}$ part of the said Ship	125	—	
	——————— 9 ———————			
6	*James Allen* Dr. to Cash *l.*1425 0 0			
1	Paid him in full for Ship *James*	1425	—	
	——————— 10 ———————			
4	*William Baker*, Esq; Dr. to Ship *James l.*125 0 0			
6	For $\frac{1}{16}$ Part sold him, for which he is to pay in 7 Days	125	—	
	——————— 12 ———————			
7	Profit and Loss Dr. to *Lisbon* Wine . . *l.*7 0 0			
2	For 1 Hhd. lost except 6 Gallons by 3 Iron Hoops break-ing off	7	—	
	——————— 14 ———————			
6	*Robert Uxley* Dr. to Ship *James* . . . *l.*125 0 0			
6	For $\frac{1}{16}$ sold him	125	—	
	——————— 17 ———————			
1	Cash Dr. to *William Baker* Esq. . . . *l.*125 0 0			
4	Received his $\frac{1}{16}$ Part of Ship *James*	125	—	
	——————— 20 ———————			
1	Cash Dr. to Canary *l.*30 0 0			
1	For 1 Pipe sold *William Dello* for which he paid me in full	30	—	
	——————— 21 ———————			
3	Sir *Robert Johnson* Dr. to Drugget . . *l.*49 0 0			
2	For 20 Pieces, qt 280 Yards, at 3s. 6d. *per* Yard .	49	—	
	——————— 23 ———————			
5	*Thomas Preston*, Esq. Dr to Sundry Accompts *l.*90 0 0			
1	*viz.* To Cash paid him in Part . . . *l.*89 7 0¾			
7	To Profit and Loss abated me for my early Payment . . . . . . } 0 12 11¼	90	—	
	——————— 25 ———————			
1	Cash Dr. to Sundry Accompts . . . *l.*174 0 0			
6	*viz.* To Ship *James*, receiv'd of Sir *Robert Johnson*, for $\frac{1}{16}$ . . } 125 0 0			
3	To Sir *Robert Johnson*, received in full 49 0 0	174	—	
	——————— 26 ———————			
6	Ship *James* Dr. to Cash *l.*20 17 0			
1	Paid *Thomas Young* in full for Joiner's Work done in the said Ship	20	17	—
	——————— 27 ———————			
6	Ship *James* Dr. to Cash *l.*27 14 6			
1	Paid *Thomas Pierce* in full for Rigging Work done in the said Ship	27	14	6
	——————— 28 ———————			
6	Ship *James* Dr. to Cash *l.*40 8 0			
1	Paid *Dryden Smith* in full for repairs done in the said Ship	40	8	—

LONDON, March 30, 1789.

		l.	s.	d.
6	Ship James Dr. to Cash *l*7 4 6			
1	Paid *Nathaniel Westall* in full for painting the said ship	7	4	6

_____ 31 _____

		l.	s.	d.
7	House-Expences Dr. to Cash *l*33 4 6			
1	Paid sundry Charges this Month, as *per* Book of House-Expenses	33	4	6

_____ April 1 _____

		l.	s.	d.
8	Voyage to *Amsterdam* consign'd to *Jacob Van Hoove* Dr.			
8	to *Richard Lamb*, of *Harwich* . . . *l*99 8 0			
	For 100 Quarters of Wheat, shipped on board the good Ship *Swan*, *William Lyon*, Master, consign'd to *Jacob Van Hoove*, of *Amsterdam*, to sell for my Accompt which with his Commission at 1 *per Cent.* and other Charges, come to	99	8	—

_____ 2 _____

		l.	s.	d.
8	*Richard Lamb*, of *Harwich*, Dr. to *Wm. Angel l*99 8 0			
8	For this Draft on me, payable to d° *Angel*, or Order, the 30th Instant, which will become due *May* 3 next, including the 3 Days of Grace	99	8	—

_____ 3 _____

		l.	s.	d.
6	Ship *James*, Dr. to Cash *l*19 17 6			
1	Paid the Blockmaker's Bill in full	19	17	6

_____ 5 _____

		l.	s.	d.
6	*Robert Uxley* Dr. to Hops *l*49 18 3			
1	For 10 Bags, weighing together 30*C.* 1*qr.* at 33*s. per C.*	49	18	3

_____ 7 _____

		l.	s.	d.
6	Ship *James* Dr. to Cash. *l*700 13 0			
1	Paid the Ship Chandler's Bill for Guns, Small-Arms, Powder, Shot, and other Stores for the said Ship	700	13	—

_____ 10 _____

		l.	s.	d.
1	Cash Dr. to Ship *James* *l*125 0 0			
6	For $\frac{1}{16}$ Part of the said Ship sold to *William Evans* .	125	—	—

_____ 12 _____

		l.	s.	d.
1	Cash Dr. to Ship *James* *l*125 0 0			
6	For $\frac{1}{16}$ Part of the said Ship sold to *James Jackson* .	125	—	—

_____ 14 _____

		l.	s.	d.
1	Cash Dr. to Ship *James* *l*125 0 0			
6	For $\frac{1}{16}$ Part of the said Ship sold to *Thomas Jones* .	125	—	—

_____ 20 _____

		l.	s.	d.
1	Cash Dr. to *John Hammond*, Esq. . . . *l*100 0 0			
3	Received in full	100	—	—

M

383

LONDON, April 24, 1789.

		£	s.	d.
8	Voyage to *Amsterdam*, consign'd to *Jacob Van Hoove*,			
1	Dr to Cash *l.*140 7 10			
	For 100 Bags of Pepper, *qt.* 3252*lb.* at 10*d.* ⎫			
	per *lb.* bought of *James Gray*, for which ⎬ 135 10 0			
	I paid present Money . . . . . . ⎭			
	Which Pepper I have shipped on board the			
	good Ship *Mary*, *James Hilder*, Master			
	and consign'd the same to *Jacob Van*			
	Hoove of *Amsterdam*, to sell for my Acct.			
	Paid Charges on shipping the same, as *per* ⎱ 4 17 10			
	Book of Charges of Merchandize . . ⎰	140	7	10
	———— 25 ————			
8	Voyage to *Amsterdam*, consign'd to *Jacob Van Hoove*, Dr.			
1	to Cash *l.*7 0 4½			
	For Insurance Money paid to *John Adams*, for his insu-			
	ring the aforesaid Sum on my Adventure, at 5 *per Cent.*	7	—	4½
	———— 27 ————			
6	Ship *James* Dr. to Cash *l*109 10 6			
1	Paid *John Jones* in full, for Beef and Pork	109	10	6
	———— 30 ————			
1	Cash Dr. to to *William Warner* . . . *l*34 7 0			
4	Received in full	34	7	—
7	House-Expenses Dr. to Cash . . . *l*39 16 10			
1	Paid sundry Charges this Month, as *per* Book of House-			
	Expenses	39	16	10
	———— May 1 ————			
6	Ship *James* Dr. to Cash *l*86 18 6			
1	Paid *James Thatcher* in full for Bread, Flour, and Pease	86	18	6
	———— 2 ————			
6	Ship *James* Dr. to Cash *l.*46 17 0			
1	Paid *John Prestwick* in full for Cordage, &c. . . .	46	17	—
	———— 3 ————			
8	*William Angel* Dr. to Cash *l*99 8 0			
1	Paid *Richard Lamb's* Draft on me to *William Angel* .	99	8	—
	———— 6 ————			
6	Ship *James* Dr. to Cash *l*73 11 6			
1	Paid *John Pepwell* in full for Smith's Work . . .	73	11	6

384

LONDON, May 7, 1789.

		l.	s.	d.
Sundry Accompts Drs. to Ship *James* . *l*566 16 0				
1	*viz.* Cash for the following Sums paid by			
	John Herbert 70 17 0			
	John Smith 70 17 0			
	William Baker, Esq. . 70 17 0			
	Sir Robert Johnson . . 70 17 0			
	William Evans - . . 70 17 0			
	James Jackson . . . 70 17 0			
	Thomas Jones 70 17 0			
	495 19 0			
6/6	*Robert Uxley* for his part unpaid . . . 70 17 0	566	16	—
	—— 10 ——			
6/1	*Robert Uxley* Dr. to Cash *l.*76 14 9	76	14	9
	—— 12 —— Paid him in full			
8/8	*John Adams* Dr. to Voyage to *Amsterdam l.*140 7 10	140	7	10
	Being so much insured on 100 Bags of Pepper, consign'd			
	—— 14 —— to *Jacob Van Hoove,* of *Amsterdam*			
8/8	*Jacob Van Hoove's* Accompt Current Dr. to Voyage to			
	Amsterdam . - *l.*161 2 3½	161	2	3½
	For 100 Quarters of Wheat consign'd to him, which he			
	has sold at 16 *Guil.* 12 *Sti. per* Quarter, amounting			
	to 1660 Guilders, deducting for his Commission, Cus-			
	tom, and other necessary Charges, 48 *Guil.* 17 *Sti.*			
	the neat Proceed of which amounts to 1611 *Guil.* 3			
	Sti. which at 33*s.* 4*d. Flem. per l.* Sterl. comes to			
	—— 17 ——			
1/1	Cash Dr. to Canary *l.*30 0 0	30	—	
	For a Pipe sold to *William Coles*			
	—— 20 ——			
1/6	Cash Dr. to Ship *James* . . . . . *l.* 10000 0 0	10000	—	
	For my half of 20000*l.* belonging to the Owners of the			
	said Ship ; the whole Prize taken by the said Ship			
	being ransomed for 40000*l.* one half of which belongs			
	to the Master and Men, the other half is due to the			
	Owners ; my Half of which is			
	—— 22 ——			
9/1	Bank Annuity Dr. to Cash *l.*9412 10 0	9412	10	
	For 10000*l.* Bank Annuity, at 3 *per Cent* Interest, trans-			
	ferred to me at 94*l. per Cent.*			
	Bank Annuity . . 9400 0 0			
	Brokerage 12 10 0			
	—— 25 ——			
5/1	*Thomas Preston,* Esq. Dr. to Cash . . *l.*17 9 6	17	9	6
	For Repairs done to my Dwelling-house, by Order of			
	my Landlord, *Thomas Preston,* Esq. by *James Dart,*			
	Joiner, for which I have paid him in full . . .			

385

LONDON, May 28, 1789.

			l.	s.	d.
6	*James Allen* Dr. to Insurance 18 0 0				
9	For my insuring 200*l.* in the *Golden Fleece*, *John Abney* Master, bound to *Jamaica*, at 4 *per Cent.* Premium		8	—	—

———— 31 ————

			l.	s.	d.
7	House-Expenses Dr. to Cash *l.*43 11 2				
1	Paid Sundry Charges this Month, as *per* Book of House Expenses		43	11	2

———— *June* 2 ————

			l.	s.	d.
9 2	Goods for the Accompt of *Abraham Van Schooten* Dr. to Cash . . . . *l.*196 17 6 Paid Freight, Custom, and other incident Charges on the Receipt of				
	1000 Reams of fine Paper,				
	120 Pieces of Holland Cloth, and				
	100 Pieces of Long Lawn				
	Which were consign'd to me from *Abraham Van Schooten*, Merchant, at *Roan*, to sell for his Accompt, for which I am to have 2 *per Cent.* for Sale, and 2 *per Cent.* for Employment, and am to make Returns in *Notwich* Crape, Duroy, and Broad Cloth		196	17	6

———— 5 ————

			l.	s.	d.
2 9	Cash Dr. to Goods for the Accompt of *Abraham Van Schooten,* . . . . *l.*300 0 0 For 1000 Reams of Paper, at 6*s. per* Ream, sold to *James Eaton* for which I have received		300	—	—

———— 8 ————

			l.	s.	d.
3 9	Sir *Robert Johnson* Dr. to Goods for the Accompt of *Abraham Van Schooten* . . . . . . *l.*360 0 0 For 120 Pieces of Holland, at 3*l. per* Piece, for which he is to pay in ten Days		360	—	—

———— 12 ————

			l.	s.	d.
	Sundry Accompts Drs. to Goods for the Accompt of *Abraham Van Schooten* *l.*250 0 0				
2	*viz.* Cash received in Part for 100 Pieces of ⎱ Long Lawn . . . . ⎰ 100 0 0				
3 9	Sir *Robert Johnson* [to be paid in 12 Days] 150 0 0		250	—	—
	Goods for the Accompt of *Abraham Van Schooten* Dr. to Sundry Accompts for the Close . *l.*713 2 6				
7	*viz.* To Profit and Loss for my Commission ⎱ on 910*l.* at 4 *per Cent.* . . . . ⎰ 36 8 0				
9	To *Abraham Van Schooten's* Accompt ⎱ Current for the neat Produce . ⎰ 676 14 6		713	—	6

London, June 16, 1789.

		l.	s.	d.
2	Cash Dr. to *Samuel Fairman* *l*.28 0 0	28	—	
4	Received in full			

——— 18 ———

		l.	s.	d.
2	Cash Dr. to Sir *Robert Johnson* . . . *l*.360 0 0	360	—	
3	Received in Part			

——— 19 ———

		l.	s.	d.
4	*Samuel Fairman* Dr. to *Lisbon* Wine . . *l*.100 0 0	100	—	
3	For 10 Hhds. at 10*l*. per Hhd.			

——— 23 ———

		l.	s.	d.
2	Cash Dr. to *William Lowfield* Esq. . . *l*.28 13 0	128	13	—
4	Received in full			

——— 24 ———

		l.	s.	d.
2	Cash Dr. to Sir *Robert Johnson* . . . *l*.150 0 0	150	—	
3	Received of him in full			

387

		l.	s.	d.
9	Bank Annuity Dr. to Profit and Loss . *l*.150 0 0	150	—	
7	For Half a Year's Dividend due on 10000*l*.			

——— 27 ———

		l.	s.	d.
2	Cash Dr. to *Lisbon* Wine *l*.105 0 0	10	—	
2	For 10 Hhds. sold to *James Hicks*, at 10*l*. 10*s*. per Hhd. for present Money			

——— 28 ———

		l.	s.	d.
9	*Abraham Van Schooten* his Accompt Current Dr. to Sundry Accompts *l*.696 14 9			
2	viz. To *Norwich* Crape, for 56 Pieces, qt. 896 Yards, at 4*s*. per Yard . . . }179 4 0			
3	To Duroy, for 20 Pieces, qt. 300 Yards, at 6*s*. 6*d*. per Yard . . . . }97 10 0			
2	To Cash, for 22 Pieces of Broad Cloth, at 18*l*. per Piece . . . . . }396 0 0			
	To do for Charges on the whole . 10 7 6			
7	To Profit and Loss for my Commission on 683*l*. 1*s*. 6*d*. at 2 per Cent. . . }12 13 3	696	14	9

——— 30 ———

		l.	s.	d.
7	House-Expenses Dr. to Cash *l*.40 8 10			
2	Paid sundry Charges this Month, as *per* Book of House-Expenses	40	8	10

London, July 4, 1789.

		l.	s.	d.

10	Voyage to *Copenhagen* in Comp. between *Samuel Smith* and felf, each Half, confign'd to *Jaques Jolliffe*, Dr. to fundry Accompts £1463 9 8			
4	viz. To *William Warner*, for 1 Cafe, containing 100 Silver Watches, at 3l. each 300 0 0			
4	To *William Lowfield*, Efq. for 1 Bale of Scarlet Cloth, containing 20 Pieces, at 20l. per Piece 400 0 0			
5	To *Thomas Johnfon*, for 30 Hhds of Tobacco, containing 170 C. weight, at 4l. 6s. 4d. per C. 733 16 8			
2	To Cafh, Paid Cuftom, Freight, and other charges on fhipping the fame 29 13 0			
		1463	9	8
10 10	*Samuel Smith's* Accompt Current Dr. to his Accompt in Comp. . . . . £731 14 10 For his Half of the abovefaid Goods	731	14	10
10 10	Commiffioners of the Cuftoms Dr. to Voyage to *Copenhagen* in Comp. between *Samuel Smith* and felf, each Half, . . . £436 6 8 For the Drawback on the above faid 170 C. weight of Tobacco	436	6	8
10 10	*Samuel Smith's* Accompt in Comp. Dr. to his Accompt Current . . . . £218 3 4 For his Half of the Drawback above mentioned due to him	218	3	4
	———— 9 ————			
2 6	Cafh Dr. to Ship *James* . . . . £12500 0 0 For my Half Part of 25000l. belonging to the Owners of the faid Ship, the whole Prize taken by the faid Ship from the *French*, being ranfomed for 50000l. one Half of which belongs to the Mafter and Men, and the other Half is due to the Owners; my Half of which is	12500	—	—
	———— 12 ————			
10	Old *South Sea* Annuity Dr. to Cafh . £10993 14 6			
2	For 12000l at 91½ per Cent. transferred to me viz. Old *South Sea* Annuity . . . £10980 0 0 Brokerage 13 14 6	10993	14	6
	———— 14 ————			
3 9	Sir *Humphrey Parfons* Dr. to Infurance . £16 0 0 for my infuring 200l. on the Scarlet Cloth that Sir *Humphrey* has fhipped on board the *Falcon* from *London* to *Smyrna* at 8l. per Cent. to be paid upon News of her fafe Arrival there	16	—	—

388

LONDON, July 17 1789.

		l.	s.	d.
11 11	Thread in Comp. between *James Severn* and felf, each Half, Dr. to *John Marſh* of *Mancheſter*, for 5628*lb*, at 14*s*. 10*d*. ½ *per lb*.	4185	16	6
	The whole to be paid at three two months, as *per* three Bills delivered, viz.			
	The 1ſt of 2185*l*. 16*s*. 6*d*. to pay 17 *Sept*. next.			
	2d of 1000 0 0 do 17 *Nov*. next.			
	3d of 1000 0 0 do 17 *Jan*. next.			
	Myſelf to have the diſpoſal of the whole.			
11 11	*James Severn's* Accompt Current Dr. to his Accompt in Com. . . . . .2092*l*. 18*s*. 3*d*.			
	For his Half of the aboveſaid Thread	2092	18	3
	———————— 20 ————————			
2 10	Caſh Dr. to the Honourable Commiſſioners of the Cuſtoms *l*436 6 8			
	Received in full	436	6	8
	———————— 23 ————————			
11 2	Thread in Comp. between *James Severn* and felf, each Half, Dr. to Caſh *l*17 14 6			
	For ſundry Charges paid for bringing the ſame into my Warehouſe	17	14	6
11 11	*James Severn's* Account Current Dr. to his Accompt in Comp. *l*8 17 3			
	For his Half of the Charges above mentioned . . .	8	17	3
	———————— 24 ————————			
7	Sundry Accompts Drs. to *John Adams* . *l*140 7 10			
2 8	*viz.* Profit and Loſs for a Drawback on 140*l*. 7*s*. 10*d*. at 8 *per Cent*. . . . } 11 4 7			
	Caſh received in full 129 3 3	140	7	10
	———————— 26 ————————			
2 3	Caſh Dr. to Sir *Humphrey Parſons* . *l*16 0 0			
	Received in Part	16	—	
	———————— 28 ————————			
12 11	*Timothy Hart* and Comp. Dr. to Thread in Comp. between *James Severn* and felf . . . *l*900 0 0			
	For 1000*lb*. at 18*s*. *per lb*. to pay in 3 two months.			
	viz. On *September* 28, *November* 28, and *January* 28, at 300*l*. each Payment, as *per* 3 Notes received . .	900	—	
11 11	*James Severn's* Accompt in Comp. Dr. to his Account Current *l*450 0 0			
	For his Half of the above ſaid Thread	450	—	
	———————— 31 ————————			
7 2	Houſe-Expences Dr. to Caſh *l*21 13 0			
	For ſundry Charges paid this Month	21	13	—

389

LONDON, August 3, 1789.

		l.	s.	
2	Cash Dr. to Thread in Comp. between *James Severn* and self *l*900 0 0			
11	For 1000*lb.* at 18*s. per lb.* sold *Abraham Saunders* for present Money	900	—	—
11	*James Severn's* Accompt in Comp. Dr. to his Accompt			
11	Current *l*450 0 0			
	For his half of the abovesaid Thread	450	—	—

———— 6 ————

2	Ship *James* Dr. to Cash *l*207 5 0			
	Paid Sundry Charges in refitting her, as per Bills .	207	5	—
12	Sundry Accompts Dr. to Ship *James* . *l*103 12 6			

12	*viz. John Herbert* 12 19 0¾			
4	*John Smith* 12 19 0¾			
6	*William Baker*, Esq. . 12 19 0¾			
3	*Robert Uxley* 12 19 0¾			
12	Sir *Robert Johnson* . . 12 19 0¾			
12	*William Evans* 12 19 0¾			
13	*James Jackson* 12 19 0¾			
6	*Thomas Jones* 12 19 0¾			

———— 8 ————

13		103	12	6
10	*Jaques Jolliffe's* Accompt Current Dr. to Voyage to *Copenhagen* . . . . *£*2510 0 0			
	He having disposed of all the Effects consign'd to him for the joint Accompt of *Samuel Smith* and self, the neat Produce of which, as *per* his Accompt, amounts to 10040 Rix Dollars, which at 5*s. per* Dollar, comes to	2510	—	—
10	*Samuel Smith's* Accompt in Comp. Dr. to his Accompt			
10	Current *l*1255 0 0			
	For his Half of the abovesaid Effects sold as above .	1255	—	—

———— 12 ————

2	Cash Dr. to sundry Accompts *l*2520 9 2			
13				
	viz. To *Jaques Jolliffe's* Accompt Current received of *Johannes Schesthase* . } 2510 0 0			
10	To Profit and Loss for my Half of the Gain on said Dollars . . . } 5 4 7			
	To *Samuel Smith's* Accompt Current, for his Half of the said Gain . . } 5 4 7	2520	9	2

———— 14 ————

9	Insurance Dr. to Sir *Humphrey Parsons* . *l*200 0 0			
	Occasioned by the Ship *Falcon* being lost on the Rocks of Scilly, wherein very little of her cargo was saved, but none of the Scarlet Cloth, on which I had insured to Sir *Humphrey*	200	—	—

———— 15 ————

	William Warner, Executor to the last Will of my late Brother-in-law *Christopher Verax*, Dr. to Profit and Loss *l*1000 0 0			
	Being so much left me by my said late Brother, as a Legacy in his said last Will	100	—	—

390

LONDON, August 17, 1789.

		l.	s.	d.
7	House-Expenses Dr. to Sundry Accompts /37 0 0			
2	viz. To *French* Wine, for 1 Hhd. . . . 30 0 0			
2	To *Lisbon* Wine, for 1 Hhd. . . . 7 0 0			
	Both which were bottled off, by my order, for the Use of the Family	37	—	—

———— 22 ————

| 2 | Cash Dr. to Profit and Loss . . . . /12 10 0 | | | |
| 7 | For Half a Year's Interest on 500*l*. paid me by *William Baker*, Esq. . . . . | 12 | 10 | — |

———— 23 ————

2	Cash Dr. to Sundry Accompts . . . /103 12 6			
12	viz. To *John Herbert* . . 12 19 0¾			
12	— *John Smith* . . 12 19 0¾			
4	— *William Baker*, Esq. 12 19 0¾			
6	— *Robert Uxley*, . . 12 19 0¾			
3	— *Sir Robert Johnson*, . 12 19 0¾			
12	— *William Evans*, . 12 19 0¾			
12	— *James Jackson*, . . 12 19 0¾			
13	— *Thomas Jones* . . 12 19 0¾			
	They, as Proprietors of the Ship *James* (lately taken by the *French*) having paid me their several parts of the Charges by me paid the sixth Instant, belonging to the said Ship	103	12	6

———— 26 ————

11	*John Marsh* Dr. to Sundry Accompts . /4185 16 6			
5	viz. To *Thomas Preston*, for 2185 16 6			
3	Sir *Robert Johnson*, for . . . 1000 0 0			
6	*Robert Uxley*, for 1000 0 0			
	Occasioned by the three Bills given by me to do *Marsh*, and by him given to the above Gentlemen, which were by them brought to me for Acceptance, and I have accordingly accepted them	4185	16	6

———— 28 ————

| 13 | Ship *Hopewell* Dr. to Cash . . . . /1200 0 0 | | | |
| 2 | Which said Ship I bought of *Andrew Collins*, and paid him | 1200 | — | — |

———— 31 ————

| 7 | House Expenses Dr. to Cash . . . . /21 17 6 | | | |
| 2 | Paid Sundry Charges this Month, as *per* Book of House-Expenses . . . . | 21 | 17 | 6 |

N

391

London, September 3, 1789.

		l.	s.	d.

7 | Profit and Lofs Dr. to *French* Wine . . *l*30 0 0
2 | Por 1 Hhd. given as a Prefent to *William Warner*, Executor to the laft Will and Teftament of my late brother *Chriftopher Verax* . . . . | 30 | |

———— 5 ————

3 | Sir *Humphrey Parfons* Dr. to fundry accompts *l*184 0 0
2 | *viz.* To Cafh paid him 172 0 0
7 | To Profit and Lofs for the Drawback } on 200*l*. at 6 *per Cent.* . . . . . } 12 0 0 | 184 | |

———— 7 ————

2 | Cafh Dr. to Ship *Hopewell* *l*1600 0 0
13 | Which faid Ship I fold to *Abraham Saunders*, for which I have received of him
| 2 Bank Notes for 1500 0 0
| 1 Warrant to be paid by the Treafurer of the South-Sea Company, for } 100 0 0 | 1600 | |

———— 9 ————

13 | Voyage from *Barbadoes* in Comp. with *John Parrot,*
15 | *George Hale* and Self, each ⅓ Dr. to *Timothy Sutton,* *l*67 13 5¾
| For 45 Chefts of Sugar, qt. neat 223*C.* 2*qrs.* 7*lb.* Avoirdupois, at 15*s.* Sterling, *per C.* fhipped on board the *Whale, John Miller,* Mafter, and is confign'd to me by faid *Sutton,* my faid Partners having agreed to allow me 2 *per Cent* for Warehoufe-Room, and my Care in the fale thereof . . . . . | 167 | 13 | 5¾

14 | *John Parrot*'s Accompt Current Dr. to his Accompt in
14 | Comp. *l*55 17 9¾
| For his ⅓ of the above-mentioned Sugar . . . . | 55 | 17 | 9¾
14 | *George Hale*'s Accompt Current Dr. to his Accompt in
14 | Comp. *l*55 17 9¾
| For his ⅓ of the above-mentioned Sugar . . . . | 55 | 17 | 9¾

———— 11 ————

15 | *Yorkfhire* Cloth Dr. to Sundry Accompts *l*1152 4 6
15 | *viz.* To *Nathaniel Keeble,* for 150 Pieces, } at 7*l.* 10*s.* per Piece . . . } *l*125 0 0
2 | To Cafh, for bringing the fame into } my Warehoufe . . . . } 27 4 6 | 1152 | 4 | 6

15 | *Yorkfhire* Cloth, for the Accompt of *Nathaniel Keeble,*
2 | Dr. to Cafh *l*11 4 8
| For charges paid on bringing his 50ps. into my warehoufe | 11 | 4 | 8

392

LONDON, September 15, 1789.

		l.	s.	d.
15	Sugar in Comp. with *John Parrot, George Hale,* and felf, each ⅓ Dr. to Sundry Accompts *l*234 9 11½			
13	*viz.* To Voyage from *Barbadoes* for 45 Chefts, qt. 223*C.* 2*qrs.* 7*lb.* Avoir-dupois, at 15*s.* Sterling *per C.* } 167 13 5¼			
2	Cuftom thereon at 4*s.* 9*d.* 90⁄100 *per Cent.* } 53 18 8¼ Freight at 4*s. per* Cheft 9 0 0 Lighterage . . . . 1 7 3 Cartage 2 10 7 66 16 6¼			
		234	9	11¼
14 / 14	*John Parrot's* Accompt Current Dr. to his Accompt in Comp. *l*22 5 6			
	For his ⅓ of the abovefaid after Charges	22	5	6
14 / 14	*George Hale's* Accompt Current Dr. to his Accompt in Comp. *l*22 5 6			
	For his ⅓ of the aforefaid after Charges	22	5	6
	—— 20 ——			
5	*Thomas Prefton,* Efq. Dr to Sundry Accompts *l*2185 16 6			
2	*viz.* To Cafh paid him . . . . *l*2185 16 0 To Profit and Lofs abated me . . 0 0 6			
		2185	16	6
	—— 22 ——			
12	*James Jackfon* Dr. to Sundry Accompts *l*1174 5 0			
15 2	*viz.* To Sugar in Comp. for 45 Chefts . 894 5 0 To *French* Wine, for 8 Hhds. at 35*l. per* Hhd. . . . . } 280 0 0			
		1174	5	—
	Sundry Accompts Drs. to *James Jackfon* *l*600 0 0			
2 15 12	*viz.* Cafh received of him . . . . 200 0 0 *William Harman,* for a Draft on him by d° *Jackfon* . . . . . . } 400 0 0			
		600	—	—
	The reft to ftand out 6 Months.			
14 / 14	*John Parrot's* Accompt in Comp. Dr. to his Accompt Current *l*298 1 8			
	For his ⅓ of Sugar in Comp. fold to *James Jackfon* .	298	1	8
14 / 14	*George Hale's* Accompt in Comp Dr. to his Accompt Current *l*298 1 8			
	For his ⅓ of Sugar in Comp. fold to do *Jackfon* . .	298	1	8

N 2

393

LONDON, September 24, 1789.

		£.	s.	d.

Sundry Accompts Drs. to Thread in Comp. fold to *William Evans*, at 18*s. per lb.* *l.*900 0 0

2 *viz.* Cafh received of d° *Evans* 200 0 0
13   *Thomas Jones*, for a Draft on him re-⎫
12   ceived of d° *Evans* . . . . ⎬ 300 0 0
11   *William Evans*, payable in 6 Months 400 0 0

                                                          900

11 *James Severn's* Accompt in Comp. Dr. to his Accompt
11 Current *l.*450 0 0
   For his ½ Part of the Thread fold as above   450

————————— 27 —————————
13 *Thomas Jones* Dr. to *Yorkshire* Cloth . *l.*425 0 0
15 For 50 Pieces, at 8*l.* 10*s. per* Piece . . .   425

————————— 29 —————————
10 Old *South-Sea* Annuity Dr. to Profit and Lofs *l.*180 0 0
7 For half a Year's Dividend on 12000*l.*   180

————————— 30 —————————
7 House-Expenfes Dr. to Cafh *l.*22 12 6
2 Paid fundry Charges this Month, as *per* Book of Houfe-
   Expenfes 22 12 6

—————————— *October* 1 ——————————
3 Cafh Dr. to *Timothy Hart* and Comp. . *l.*300 0 0
12 Received in Part   300

————————— 3 —————————
3 Cafh Dr. to *Yorkshire* Cloth . . . *l.*425 0 0
15 For 50 Pieces, at 8*l.* 10*s. per* Piece   425

————————— 6 —————————
3 Cafh Dr. to *William Warner* . . . *l.*1000 0 0
4 Received of him in full for a Legacy, left me by my
   Brother *Chriftopher Verax*   1000

4 *William Warner* Dr. to Cafh . . . *l.*300 0 0
3 Paid him in full   300

————————— 10 —————————
3 Cafh Dr. to Old *South-Sea* Annuity . . *l.*180 0 0
10 Received ½ a Year's Dividend on 12000*l.* due at *Michaelmas* laft   180

————————— 14 —————————
3 Cafh Dr. to Bank Annuity *l.*150 0 0
9 Received ½ a Year's Dividend on 10000*l.* due at *Midfummer* laft   150

————————— 18 —————————
3 Cafh Dr. to *William Harman* . . . *l.*400 0 0
15 Received of him in full   400

————————— 22 —————————
3 Cafh Dr. to *Thomas Jones* . . . *l.*300 0 0
13 Received of him   300

————————— 24 —————————
5 *John Hammond*, Efq. Dr. to Canary . . *l.*30 0 0
1 For 1 Pipe fold him   30

394

LONDON, October 26, 1789.

		£	s.	d.
3	Cash Dr. to *Martin Unwin* £100 0 0			
5	Received of him in Part	100	—	—

———————— 28 ————————

		£	s.	d.
16	Voyage to *Barbadoes* Dr. to Sundry Accompts £190 4 6			
1	*viz.* To Hops, for 30 Bags, qt. 90C. 1qr. } at 28s. *per* C. . . . . } 126 7 0			
3	To Sagathee, for 20 Pieces, qt. 240 } Yards, at 2s. 6d. *per* Yard . . . } 30 0 0			
3	To Serge, for 20 Pieces, qt. 280 } Yards, at 1s. *per* Yard . . . . } 14 0 0			
3	To Cash for the Charges paid on } shipping the same . . . . } 19 17 6			
		190	4	6

All which are shipped on board the *Whale, John Miller,* Master, and go consign'd to *Timothy Sutton*, Mercht. at *Barbadoes*, for my own Accompt and Risque.

———————— 29 ————————

		£	s.	d.
16	Voyage to *Barbadoes* Dr. to *Brandon George* £11 8 3			
4	He having insured my whole Adventure on that Voyage, at 6 *per* Cent.	11	8	3

———————— 30 ————————

		£	s.	d.
4	*Brandon George* Dr. to Sundry Accompts £40 0 0			
1	*viz.* To Canary for 1 Pipe £30 0 0			
2	To *Lisbon* Wine, for 1 Hhd. . . . 10 0 0			
		40		

———————— 31 ————————

		£	s.	d.
7	House-Expenses Dr. to Cash £26 13 8			
3	Paid sundry Charges this Month, as *per* Book of House-Expenses	26	13	8

———————— November 1 ————————

		£	s.	d.
4	*William Lowfield*, Esq. Dr. to Cash . . £400 0 0			
3	Paid him in Full	400	—	—

———————— 4 ————————

		£	s.	d.
3	Cash Dr. to *Samuel Fairman* £100 0 0			
4	Received in Full	100	—	—

———————— 7 ————————

		£	s.	d.
5	*Thomas Johnson* Dr. to Cash £100 0 0			
3	Paid him in Part	100	—	—

395

LONDON, November 10, 1789.

		l.	*s.*	*d.*

		l.	*s.*	*d.*
3	Cash Dr. to Sundry Accompts £38 8 0			
1	*viz.* To Hops, for 1 Bag. wt. 3 C. at 36*s.* ⎱ per C. . . . . ⎰ 5 8 0			
1	To Canary for 1 Pipe £33 0 0	38	8	
	———— 15 ————			
15	*Jaques Van-Brook* Dr. to *Jacob Van Hoove* £161 2 3½			
8	For a Bill of Exchange drawn by do *Van-Hoove* on do *Van-Brook* for 1611 *Guil.* 3 *Sti.* Exchange at 33*s.* 4*d.* Flemish *per l.* Sterling, payable at 10 Days after Sight, which do *Van-Brook* has accepted . . .	161	2	3½
	———— 18 ————			
3	Cash Dr. to Serge £16 6 8			
3	For 20 Pieces, qt. 230 Yards, at 14*d.* per Yard, sold to *William Baker* Esq.	16	6	8
4	*William Baker,* Esq. Dr. to Sagathee . . £36 0 0			
3	For 20 Pieces, qt. 240 Yards, at 3*s.* per Yard . . .	36		
	———— 20 ————			
3	Sir *Robert Johnson* Dr. to Cash . . . £1000 0 0			
3	Paid him one of the Notes given by me to *John Marsh*	1000		
	———— 24 ————			
5	*Thomas Johnson* Dr. to Insurance . . £18 0 0			
9	For my underwriting his Policy for 300*l.* at 6 per Cent. on a Freight for a Voyage to *Spain,* in the *John* and *Hannah, James Tickner,* Master		18	
	———— 27 ————			
3	Cash Dr. to *Martin Unwin* *l.*100 0 0			
5	Received of him in Part	100		
	———— 28 ————			
3	Cash Dr. to *Jaques Van Brook* . . . *l.*161 2 3½			
16	Received in full	161	2	3½
	———— 30 ————			
7	House-Expenses Dr. to Cash 27 13 6			
3	Paid Sundry Charges this Month, as *per* Book of House-Expenses	27	13	6
	———— *Dec.* 1 ————			
3	Cash Dr. to *Timothy Hart* and Comp. . *l.*300 0 0			
12	Received in Part	300		
	———— 3 ————			
9	Insurance Dr. to *Thomas Johnson* . . *l.*300 0 0			
5	For my insuring 300*l.* on a Freight in the *John & Hannah,* bound to *Spain;* that Ship being lost in the *Downs*	300		
	———— 6 ————			
3	Cash Dr. to *John Hammond,* Esq. . . . *l.*30 0 0			
5	Received in full	30		

396

LONDON, December 9, 1789.

	l.	*s.*	*d.*

Cash Dr to Sundry Accompts £507 8 4

viz. To *William Baker*, Esq. for the ⎱
  Principal received . . . . ⎰ 500 0 0
To Profit and Loss for the Interest . 7 8 4

  507 8 4

———————————— 10 ————————————

Thomas Johnson Dr. to Sundry Accompts £300 0 0

viz. To Profit and Loss for a Drawback ⎱
  on 300*l.* at 8 *per Cent* . . . . ⎰ 24 0 0
Cash paid him 276 0 0

  300 —

———————————— 12 ————————————

John Hammond, Esq. Dr. to Sundry Accompts £850 0 0

viz. To *Yorkshire* Cloth, for 50 Pieces, at ⎱
  8*l.* 10*s.* per Piece . . . . ⎰ 425 0 0
To *Yorkshire* Cloth, for the Accompt ⎱
  of *Nathaniel Keeble*, of *Hull*, for ⎰ 425 0 0
  50 Pieces at 8*l.* 10*s.* per Piece .

  850 —

Yorkshire Cloth for the Accompt of *Nathaniel Keeble*,
Dr. to Sundry Accompts for the Close £413 15 4

viz. To Profit and Loss for my Commission ⎱
  at 2 *per Cent.* on 425*l.* for the Sale ⎰ 8 10 0
  thereof . . . .
To do *Keeble's* Accompt Current for ⎱
  the neat Proceed . . . . . ⎰ 405 5 4

  413 15 4

———————————— 13 ————————————

Cash Dr. to *Thomas Preston*, Esq. . . . £17 9 6
for the Repairs done to my present Dwelling-House .

  17 9 6

———————————— 14 ————————————

Voyage from *Cadiz* Dr. to *Joram Condril* £33 15 0

for 50 Chests of Limons .⎫
  50 do of *China* Oranges ⎬ at 8 Rials *per* Chest
  50 do of *Seville* do ⎭ including all charges.

Which were shipped on Board the *Pidgeon*, *William
Pidgeon*, Master, for my Accompt and Risque, amounting in the Whole to 1200 Rials, Exchange at 4*s.* 6*d.*
per Piece of Eight, which is Sterling . . . . .

  33 15 —

LONDON, December 17, 1789.

				£	s.
15 12	*Nathaniel Keeble*, of Hull, Dr. to *Timothy Hart* and Comp. £1125 0 0				
	For his Draft on me, payable to do *Hart* and Comp. at 20 Days after Sight, for . . .			1125	
12	*Timothy Hart*, and Comp. Drs. to Sundry Accompts £1125 0 0				
3	*viz.* To Cash paid him 1120 2 0				
7	To Profit and Lofs gain'd by prompt Payment . . . . } 4 18 0			1125	

— 13 —

16	Oranges and Limons Dr. to Sundry Accompts £70 1 6				
16	*viz.* To Voyage from *Cadiz*, for				
	50 Chests of Limons				
	50 do China Oranges } At 8 Rials per Chest.				
	50 do Seville do				
	Exchange at 4s. 6d. per Piece of Eight } amounting to Sterling . . . . } 33 15 0				
3	To Cash paid Custom, Freight, and Waterage 36 6 6			70	1 6

— 20 —

2	Cash Dr. to *Martin Unwin* £100 0 0				
5	Received in Part			100	

— 22 —

16 5	*Joram Conderill*, of *Cadiz*, Dr. to *John Hammond*, Esq. £33 15 0				
	For *Conderill's* Draft on me, payable to do *Hammond*, or Order, for 1700 Rials, Exchange at 4s. 6d. per Piece of Eight, which I have accepted, but not paid, because the fame is to be placed to Accompt, as per Agreement			33	15

— 24 —

3	Cash Dr. to *Isaac Reynolds* £42 0 0				
5	Received in full			42	

— 25 —

9	Bank Annuity Dr. to Profit and Lofs . £150 0 0				
7	For Half a Year's Dividend due on 10000l.			150	

— 26 —

5	*Isaac Reynolds* Dr. to Oranges and Limons £ 42 10 0				
16	For 50 Chests of Limons, at 17s. per Chest			42	10

398

London, December 27, 1789.

	l.	s.	d.

3 Cash Dr. to *James Allen* £8 0 0

6 Received in full . . . . : . . . . 8 | —

———————— 28 ————————

3 Cash Dr. to Thread in Comp. between *James Severn*

11 and self £900 0 0

For 1000 *lb.* sold to *James Allen*, at 18*s. per lb.* . . . 900 | —

11 *James Severn's* Accompt in Comp. Dr. to his Accompt

11 Current £450 0 0

For his Half of the above Thread . . . . 450 | —

———————— 29 ————————

3 Sir *Humphrey Parfons* Dr. to Thread in Comp. between

11 *James Severn* and self £900 0 0

For 1000 *lb.* at 18*s. per lb.* to pay in 6 Months . . : 900 | —

11 *James Severn's* Accompt in Comp. Dr. to his Accompt

11 Current £450 0 0

For his Half of the above Thread . . . . 450 | —

———————— 30 ————————

4 *William Baker*, Efq. Dr. to Thread in Comp. between

11 *James Severn* and self £533 16 0

For 628 *lb.* at 17*s. per lb.* . . . . 533 16 —

6 *Robert Uxley*, Efq. Dr. to *William Baker*, Efq.

£1000 0 0

For my Note given to *Uxley*, and by him to do. *Baker*,

payable *January* 20 next, including the three Days

of Grace . . . . 1000 | —

4 *William Baker*, Efq. Dr. to Sundry Accompts £466 4 0

3 viz. To Cafh paid him 463 17 0

7 To Profit and Lofs gain'd by ⎱ 2 6 8

prompt Payment . . . . ⎰

466 4 —

11 *James Severn's* Accompt in Comp. Dr. to his Accompt

11 Current 266 18 0

For his Half of the abovefaid Thread . . . . . 266 18 —

———————— 31 ————————

7 Houfe-Expenfes Dr. to Cafh £22 8 4

3 Paid fundry Charges this Month, as *per* Book of Houfe-

Expenfes 22 8 4

The End of the fecond Journal.

O

399

The LEDGER.

The Alphabet to the Ledger.

A	E	I
Allen James . . . 6	*Evans William* . 12	I
Angel William . . 8		*Johnson Sir Robert* .
Adams John . . . 8		*Johnson Thomas* . . 3
Annuity *Bank* . . 9		*James* Ship . . . 6
Annuity *Old South*		Infurance . . . 9
Sea . 10		*Jackson James* . . 12
		Jones Thomas . . 13
		Jolliffe's Jaques Ac-
		compt Current . . 15

B	F	K
Baker William, Efq. 4	*French* Wine . . . 2	*Keeble Nat.* of Hull 15
Bank Annuity . . 9	*Fairman Samuel* . 4	
Barbadoes Voyage from		
13		
Barbadoes Voyage to 16		
Balance . . . 17		

400

C	G	L
Cafh 1	*George Brandon* . . 4	*Lifbon* Wine . . 2
Canary . . . 1	Goods for the Accompt	*Lowfield William*, Efq. 4
Crape *Norwich* . . 2	of *Abraham Van-*	Lofs and Profit . 7
Commiffioners of the	*Schooten* . . 9	*Lamb Richard of Harwich*
Cuftoms . . 10		S
Cloth *Yorkfhire* . 15		Limons & Oranges 16
Cloth *Yorkfhire*, for the		
Accompt of *Nathani-*		
el *Keeble* . . 15		
Cadiz, Voyage from 16		
Conderil Joram . . 16		

D	H	M
Drugget 2	Hops 1	M
Duroy 2	*Hammond John*, Efq. 5	*Marfh John* . . . 11
	Houfe-Expenfes . 7	
	Hart Tim. & Comp. 12	
	Herbert John . . 12	
	Hopewell, Ship . . 13	
	Hale's George Accompt	
	Current . . 14	
	Ditto in Comp. 14	
	Harman William . 15	

The Alphabet to the Ledger,

N.		R.		V.	
Norwich Crape	2	Reynolds Isaac	5	Wine Canary	1
				Wine French	2
				Wine Lisbon	2
				Warner William	4

O.		S.		X.	
Old S. Sea Annuity	10	Stock	1		
Oranges & Limons	16	Sagathee	3		
		Serge	3		
		Ship James	6		
		Smith's Samuel Accompt Current	10		
		Do in Comp.	10		
		S. Sea Annuity old	10		
		Severn's James Accompt Current	11		
		Do in Comp.	11		
		Smith John	12		
		Ship Hopewell	13		
		Sutton Tim. at Barb.	13		
		Sugar in Comp.	15		

P.		T.		Y.	
Parsons Sir Humph.	5	Thread in Comp.	11	Yorkshire Cloth	15
Preston Thomas Esq.	5			Yorkshire Cloth for the Accompt of Nat. Keeble	15
Profit and Loss	7				
Parrot's John Accompt Current	14				
Do in Comp.	14				

Q.	V.		Z.
	Unwin Martin	5	
	Uxley Robert	6	
	Voyage to Amsterdam	8	
	Van Hoove's Jacob Accompt Current	8	
	Van Schooten's Abraham Acct. Curr.	9	
	Voyage to Copenhagen	10	
	Voyage from Barba.	13	
	Voyage to Barba.	16	
	Van Brook Jaques	16	
	Voyage from Cadiz	16	

1789		Stock	Dr.		l.	s.	d.
Mar. 1	1	To Sundry Accompts		—	412	10	—
	R	To Balance for my neat Estate		17	34658	11	10
					35071	1	10

1789		Cash	Dr.				
Mar. 1	1	To Stock		1	8099	4	2
31	—	To Sundry Accompts received this Month .		—	609	—	—
Apr 30	—	To ditto . . . ditto		—	509	7	—
May 31	—	To ditto . . . ditto		—	10525	19	—
Jun. 30	—	To ditto . . . ditto		—	1171	13	—
Jul. 31	—	To ditto . . . ditto		—	15081	9	11
Aug 31	—	To ditto . . . ditto		—	3536	11	8
Sep. 30	—	To ditto . . . ditto		—	2000	—	—
Oct. 31	—	To ditto . . . ditto		—	2855	—	—
Nov 30	—	To ditto . . . ditto		—	415	16	11
Dec. 31	—	To ditto . . . ditto		—	1904	17	10
					44708	19	7

402

1789		Canary	Dr. Pipes				
Mar. 1	1	To Stock at 25l. per Pipe, for . . .	5	1	125	—	—
Nov 10	R	To Profit and Loss gain'd by this Accompt		7	28	—	—
					153	—	—

1789		Hops	Dr. Bags C. qrs. lb.				
Mar. 1	1	To Stock, at 28s. per C. for . 44|132 2 0		1	185	10	—
Dec. 31	R	To Profit and Loss gain'd by this Accompt .		7	8	15	3
					194	5	3

1789		Per Contra	Cr.	l.	s.	d.
Mar. 1	1	By Sundry Accompts	—	10928	15	4¼
	R	By Profit and Loss, gain'd by 10 Months trading	7	24145	6	6
				35071	1	10¼

1789		Per Contra	Cr.	l.	s.	d.
Mar 31		By Sundry Accompts paid away this Month	—	1718	15	6¾
Apr. 30		By ditto .... ditto	—	1017	6	½
May 31		By ditto .... ditto	—	9857	—	5
Ju. 30		By ditto .... ditto	—	643	13	10
July 31		By ditto .... ditto	—	11063	—	—
Aug 31		By ditto .... ditto	—	1429	2	6
Sep. 30		By ditto .... ditto	—	2485	14	2¼
Oct. 31		By ditto .... ditto	—	346	11	2
Nov 30		By ditto .... ditto	—	1527	13	6
Dec. 31		By ditto .... ditto	—	1918	14	2
	R	By Balance remaining in Hand, carried to the next Books	17	12701	8	2½
				44708	19	7

1789		Per Contra	Cr.	Pipes		l.	s.	d.
Mar 20	2	By Cash, sold *William Dello*		1	1	30		
May 17	5	By Cash, sold *William Coles*		1	1	30		
Oct. 24	14	By *John Hammond*, Esq. for		1	5	30		
30	15	By *Brandon George*, for		1	4	30		
Nov 10	16	By Cash, for		1	1	33		
				5		153		

1789		Per Contra	Cr.	Bags	C.	qr.	lb.	l.	s.	d.
Apr. 5	2	By *Robert Uxley*, at 33s. per C. for	10	30	1	0	6	49	18	3
Oct. 28	15	By Voyage to *Barbadoes*, at 28s. per C. for	30	90	1	0	16	126	7	—
Nov 10	16	By Cash, at 36s. per C. for	1	3	0	0	1	5	8	—
Dec. 31	R	By Balance, remaining unsold, at 28s. per C. for	3	9	0	0	17	12	12	
			44	132	2	0		1	9	3

403

French Wine   Dr.

1789				Hhds.		£.	s.	d.
Mar. 1	1	To Stock, at 30l. per Hhd. for		10	1	300	—	—
Sep. 22	R	To Profit and Loss, gain'd by this Accompt			7	40		
						340		

Drugget   Dr.

1789	1			Pcs.	Yds.		£.	s.	d.
Mar. 1	R	To Stock at 3s. 4d. per Yard, for		20	280	1	46	13	
21		To Profit and Loss, gain'd by this Accompt				7	2	6	8

Note, The Drugget being all sold, there is no necessity of staying till the general *Balance* shall be made, but this or any other particular Accompt of Goods

| | | | | | | 49 | — | |

Lisbon Wine   Dr.

1789				Hhds.		£.	s.	d.
Mar. 1	1	To Stock, at 7l. per Hhd. for		25	1	175	—	
	R	To Profit and Loss, gain'd by this Accompt			7	68	—	
						243	—	

Norwich Crape   Dr.

1789				Pcs.	Yds.		£.	s.	d.
Mar. 1	1	To Stock, at 3s. 6d. per Yard, for		56	896	1	156	16	
Ju. 28	R	To Profit and Loss, gain'd by this Accompt				7	22	8	
							179	4	

Duroy   Dr.

1789				Pcs.	Yds.		£.	s.	d.
Mar. 1	1	To Stock, at 6s. per Yard, for		20	300	1	90	—	
Ju. 28	R	To Profit and Loss, gain'd by this Accompt				7	7	10	
							97	10	

404

1789		Per Contra		**Cr.**			*l.*	*s.*	*d.*
				Hhds.					
Aug 17	11	By House-Expenses, bottled off . .		1	7		30	—	
Sept. 5	12	By Profit and Loss, given to *W. Warner*		1	7		30	—	
22	13	By *James Jackson*, at 35*l.* per Hhd. for		8	12		280	—	
				10			340	—	

1789		Per Contra		**Cr.**			*l.*	*s.*	*d.*
				Pcs.	Yds.				
Mar 21	2	By *Sir R. Johnfon*, at 3*s.* 6*d.* per Yard for	20	280	3		49	—	

may be balanced at any time after they are all difpofed of.

1789		Per Contra		**Cr.**			*l.*	*s.*	*d.*
				Hhds.					
Mar 12	2	By Profit & Lofs, loft by the burfting of		1	7		7		
Jun 19	7	By *Samuel Fairman*, at 10*l.* per Hhd. for	10	4			100		
27	7	By Cafh, at 10*l.* 10*s.* per Hhd. for		10	2		105		
Aug 17	11	By Houfe-Expenfes, bottled off . .		1	1		7		
Oct. 30	15	By *Brandon George*, for		1	4		10		
	R	By Balance unfold, at 7*l.* per Hhd. for		2	17		14		
				25			243	—	

1789		Per Contra		**Cr.**			*l.*	*s.*	*d.*
				Pcs.	Yds.				
Jun. 28	7	By *Abraham Van Schooten's* Accompt Current, at 4*s.* per Yard, for . . .	56	896	9		179	4	—

1789		Per Contra		**Cr.**			*l.*	*s.*	*d.*
				Pcs.	Yds.				
Jun. 23	7	By *Abraham Van Schooten's* Accompt Current, at 6*s.* 6*d.* per Yard, for .	20	300	9		97	10	—

405

			Sagathee	Dr.		l.	s.	d.
1789					Pcs. Yds.			
Mar. 1	1	To Stock, at 2s. 6d. per Yard, for . .	90	1080	1	135		
	R	To Profit and Lofs gain'd by this Ac-compt			7	6		
						141		

			Serge	Dr.				
1789					Pcs. Yds.			
Mar. 1	1	To Stock, at 1s. per Yard, for . .	90	1260	1	63		
	R	To Profit and Lofs, gain'd by this Ac-compt			7	2	6	8
						65	6	8

406

			Sir Robert Johnson	Dr.				
1789								
Mar. 1	1	To Stock		1	30			
21	2	To Drugget		2	49			
June 8	6	To Goods for the Accompt of Abraham Van-Schooten, for 120 Pieces of Holland .		9	360			
12	6	To do. in part for 100 Pieces of Long Lawn		9	150			
Aug. 6	10	To Ship James		6	12	19	3/4	
Nov 20	6	To Cafh paid him in full . . .		1	1000			

			Sir Humphrey Parfons	Dr.				
1783								
Mar. 1	1	To Stock		1	16			
July 14	8	To Infurance, for my infuring 200l. on his Scarlet Cloth		9	16			
Sept. 5	12	To Sundry Accompts, paid him in full . .		2	184			
						216		
Dec. 29	19	To Thread in Comp. between J. Severn and felf, to pay in 6 Months		11	900			

		Per Contra	Cr.	Pcs.	Yds.		*l.*	*s.*	*d.*
1789									
Oct. 28	15	By Voyage to *Barbadoes*, at 2*s.* 6*d. per* Yard, for		20	240	16	30	—	—
Nov 18	16	By *William Baker*, Efq. at 3*s. per* Yard for		20	240	4	36	—	—
	R	By Balance unfold, at 2*s.* 6*d. per* Yard		50	600	17	75	—	—
				90	1080		141	—	—

		Per Contra	Cr.	Pcs.	Yds.		*l.*	*s.*	*d.*
1789									
Oct. 28	15	By Voyage to *Barbadoes*, at 1*s. per* Yard, for		20	280	16	14	—	—
Nov 18	16	By *Cafh*, at 14*d. per* Yard, for . .		20	280	1	16	6	8
	R	By Balance, unfold, at 1*s. per* Yard for		50	700	17	35	—	—
				90	1260		65	6	8

		Per Contra	Cr.		*l.*	*s.*	*d.*
1789							
Mar. 2	1	By Cafh, received in full	1		30		
25	2	By ditto, received in full	1		49	—	—
Jun. 18	7	By ditto, received in Part	1		360		
24	7	By ditto, received in full	1		150		
Aug. 23	11	By ditto, received in full	1		12	19	3/4
26	11	By *John Marfh*, for a Bill payable by me to d° *Johnfon*, *November* 17 next . . .	11		1000	—	—

		Per Contra	Cr.		*l.*	*s.*	*d.*
1789							
July 26	9	By Cafh, received in Part	1		16	—	—
Aug. 14	10	By infurance, for his Scarlet Cloth, loft in the *Falcon*	9		200	—	—
					216	—	—
	R	By Balance, due to me, to pay *June* 29 next	17		900	—	—

P

1789		William Baker, Efq;	Dr.		l.	s.	d
Mar. 1	1	To Stock		1	500	—	—
10	2	To Ship James, for 1/16 Part to pay in 7 Days		6	125	—	—
Aug. 6	10	To ditto		6	12	19	3
Nov 18	16	To Sagathee		3	36	—	—
Dec. 30	19	To Thread in Comp. between James Severn and felf		11	533	16	—
—	19	To Sundry Accompts			466	4	—
					1672	19	3

1789		William Warner	Dr.				
Mar. 1	1	To Stock, to pay April 30 next . . .		1	34	7	—
Aug. 15	10	To Profit and Lofs, for a Legacy left me by my Brother C. Verax		7	1000	—	—
Oct. 6	14	To Cafh, paid him in full		1	300	—	—
					1300	—	—

1789		Brandon George	Dr.				
Mar. 1	1	To Stock		1	32	—	—
Oct. 30	15	To Sundry Accompts			40	—	—
					72	—	—

1789		Samuel Fairman	Dr.				
Mar. 1	1	To Stock		1	28	—	—
Jun. 19	9	To Lifbon Wine		2	100	—	—

1789		William Lowfield, Efq.	Dr.				
Mar. 1	1	To Stock		1	128	13	—
Nov. 1	1	To Cafh, paid in full		1	400	—	—

408

1789		Per Contra Cr.		l.	s.	d.
Mar 17	2	By Cash received in Part	1	125		
Aug 25	11	By ditto, received his Part of the last Charges on the Ship *James*	1	12	19	3/4
Dec. 9	17	By ditto, received the Principal which he borrowed	1	500	—	—
30	19	By *Robert Uxley*, for my Note given to *Uxley*, and by him to *Baker*	6	1000	—	—
—	R	By Balance, due to me	17	36	—	—
				1673	19	3/4

1789		Per Contra Cr.				
Apr. 30	4	By Cash received in full	1	34	7	—
July 4	8	By Voyage to *Copenhagen* in Comp. between S. Smith and self	10	300	—	—
Oct. 6	14	By Cash, received my Legacy in full . . .	1	1000	—	—
				1300	—	—

409

1789		Per Contra Cr.				
Oct. 29	15	By Voyage to *Barbadoes*, for Insurance at 6 per Cent.	16	11	8	3
	R	By Balance due to me	17	60	11	9
				72	—	—

1789		Per Contra Cr.				
Jun. 16	7	By Cash received in full	1	28	—	—
Nov. 4	20	By ditto, ditto	1	100	—	—

1789		Per Contra Cr.				
Jun. 23	7	By Cash, received in full	1	128	13	—
July 4	9	By Voyage to *Copenhagen* in Comp. between S. Smith and self	10	400	—	—

1789		Thomas Johnson	Dr.		*l.*	*s.*	*d.*
Mar. 1	1	To Stock		1	256	14	5
Nov. 7	15	To Cash, paid in Part		1	100	—	—
24	16	To Insurance, for my insuring 300*l.* at 6 *per* Cent.		9	18	—	—
Dec. 10	17	To Sundry Accompts, paid my Insurance on a Freight lost			300	—	—
	R	To Balance due to him		17	359	2	4¼
					1033	16	8

1789		John Hammond, Esq.	Dr.				
Mar. 1	1	To Stock, to pay *April* 20 next		1	100	—	—
Oct. 24	14	To Canary		1	30	—	—
Dec. 12	17	To Sundry Accompts		—	850	—	—

410

1789		Martin Unwin	Dr.				
Mar. 1	1	To Stock		1	38	17	6

1789		Isaac Reynolds	Dr.				
Mar. 1	1	To Stock		1	42	—	—
Dec. 26	18	To Oranges and Limons		16	42	10	—

1789		Thomas Preston, Esq.	Dr.				
Mar. 23	2	To Sundry Accompts		—	90	—	—
May 25	5	To Cash paid *James Hart* for repairing my Dwelling-House		1	17	9	6
Sept. 20	13	To Sundry Accompts			2185	16	6
					2293	6	—

1789	Per Contra	Cr.		l.	s.	d.
July 4	8 By Voyage to *Copenhagen* in Comp. between					
	S. Smith and self	10	733	16	8
Dec. 3	16 By Insurance, on a Freight, in the *John* and					
	Hannah, loft	9	300		
				1033	16	8

1789	Per Contra	Cr.				
Apr. 20	3 By Cash, received in full	1	100		
Dec. 6	16 By ditto, ditto	1	30		
22	15 By *Joram Conderil*, of *Cadiz*, for do *Conderil's*					
	Draft on me, payable to do *Hammond* . . .	16	33	15	
	R By Balance due to me	17	816	5	
				850		

1789	Per Contra	Cr.				
Oct. 26	15 By Cash, received in Part	1	100		
Nov 27	16 By ditto, ditto	1	100		
Dec. 20	18 By ditto, ditto	1	100		
	R By Balance, due me	17		17	6
				381	17	6

1789	Per Contra	Cr.				
Dec. 24	18 By Cash, received in full	1	42		
	R By Balance, due to me	17	42	10	

1789	Per Contra	Cr.				
Mar. 1	1 By Stock, to be paid *May* 14 next . . .	1	90		
Aug 26	11 By *John Marsh*, for a Bill payable by me to					
	do *Preston*, *September* 17 next	11	2185	16	6
Dec. 13	17 By Cash received for the Repairs of my present					
	Dwelling-House	1	17	9	6
				2203	6	

411

1789		Robert Uxley Dr.		l.	s.	d.
Mar. 14	2	To Ship *James*, for $\frac{1}{16}$ Part	6	125		
Apr. 5	3	To Hops	1	49	18	3
May 7	5	To Ship *James*, for his $\frac{1}{16}$ Part of Disbursements, on the said Ship	6	70	17	
10	5	To Cash, paid in full	1	76	14	9
Aug. 6	10	To Ship *James*	6	322	10	
				12	19	$\frac{3}{4}$
Dec. 30	19	To *William Baker*, Esq; for my Note given to *Uxley*, and by him to *Baker* . .	4	1000		

1789		Ship James Dr.				
Mar. 4	1	To Sundry Accompts		1500		
26	2	To cash paid *T. Young*, for Joiner's work in full	1	20	17	—
27	2	To ditto, paid *Tho. Pierce* for Rigging ditto	1	27	14	6
28	2	To ditto, paid *Dryden Smith* for Repairs ditto	1	40	8	—
20	3	To ditto, paid *Nat. Westall* for Painting ditto	1	7	4	6
Apr. 3	3	To ditto, paid the Blockmaker's Bill ditto	1	19	7	6
7	3	To ditto, paid the Ship Chandler's Bill ditto	1	700	13	—
27	4	To ditto, paid *John Jones* for beef and pork ditto	1	109	10	6
May 1	4	To ditto, paid *James Thatcher* for Bread, Flour and Pease . . . . ditto	1	86	18	6
2	4	To ditto, paid *J. Prestwick* for cordage &c. ditto	1	46	17	—
6	4	To ditto, paid *John Pepwell* for Smith's work ditto	1	73	11	6
Aug. 6	10	To ditto, paid sundry charges in refitting her ditto	2	207	5	—
20	R	To Profit and Loss, gain'd by the said Ship	7	21329	11	6
				24170	8	6

1789		James Allen Dr.				
Mar. 9	2	To Cash paid in full	1	1425		
May 28	6	To Insurance on 200*l.* in the *Golden Fleece*, at 4 *per Cent.*	9	8		

1789		Per Contra	Cr.		l.	s.	d.
Mar. 1	1	By Stock		1	322	10	—
Aug 23	11	By Cash, received in full		1	12	19	.
26	11	By John Marsh, for a Bill by me payable to d° Uxley. January 17 next		11	1000	—	—

1789		Per Contra	Cr.		l.	s.	d.
Mar. 6	1	By Cash, received of J. Herbert for $\frac{1}{16}$ part in full		1	125	—	—
8	2	By ditto, received of capt. J. Smith $\frac{1}{16}$ part ditto		1	125	—	—
10	2	By William Baker, Esq; . . . for ditto .		4	125	—	—
14	2	By Robert Uxley . . . . for ditto .		6	125	—	—
25	2	By Cash recd. of Sir R. Johnson for ditto .		1	125	—	—
Apr. 10	3	By ditto recd. of William Evans for ditto .		1	125	—	—
12	3	By ditto, recd. of James Jackson for ditto .		1	125	—	—
14	3	By ditto, recd. of Thomas Jones for ditto .		1	125	—	—
May 7	5	By Sundry Accompts		—	566	16	—
20	5	By Cash for my $\frac{1}{2}$ Part of a French Prize recd. in full		1	10000	—	—
July 9	8	By ditto for my ditto of a 2d ditto ditto .		1	12500	—	—
Aug. 6	10	By Sundry Accompts		—	103	12	6
					24170	8	6

1789		Per Contra	Cr.		l.	s.	d.
Mar. 4	1	By Ship James		6	1425	—	—
Dec. 27	9	By Cash received in full		1	8	—	—

413

1739		Profit and Loss	Dr.		l.	s.	d.
Mar 12	2	To *Lisbon Wine*, for 1 Hhd. except 6 Gallons, lost		2	7	—
July 24	9	To *John Adams*, for a Drawback on 140*l*. 7*s*. 10*d*. at 8 per Cent.		8	11	4	7
Sept. 3	12	To *French* Wine, for 1 Hhd. given to *William Warner*		2	30
	R	To House-Expenses		7	337	4	10
	R	To Bank Annuity. lost on the Abatement of its Price, with the Brokerage		9	75
	R	To Insurance		9	458	—
	R	To Old S. S. Annuity, lost by the Abatement of its Price, with the Brokerage		10	43	14	—
	R	To Stock, gain'd by 10 Months trading		1	24145	6	6

Note, This extraordinary Gain, made in so short a Time, may, perhaps, amaze some Readers; but if they consider that 21329*l*. 11*s*. 6*d*. of that Money arose by the success of the ~~ship~~ *James*, the remaining Part of the Gain will appear to be no more than what many Merchants make in the like Time.

| | | | | | 25107 | 10 | 5 |

1739		House-Expenses	Dr.				
Mar 31	3	To Cash, paid Sundry Charges this Month		1	33	4	6
Apr 30	4	To ditto . . . ditto		1	39	16	10
May 31	6	To ditto . . . ditto		1	43	11	2
Jun 30	7	To ditto . . . ditto		1	40	8	10
July 31	9	To ditto . . . ditto		1	21	18	—
Aug 17	11	To Sundry Accompts			37	—
31	11	To Cash, paid sundry Charges this Month		1	21	17	6
Sep. 30	1	To ditto . . . ditto		1	22	12	4
Oct. 31	15	To ditto . . . ditto		1	26	13	10
Nov. 30	16	To ditto . . . ditto		1	27	13	0
Dec. 31	19	To ditto . . . ditto		1	22	8	0

| | | | | | 337 | 4 | 10 |

414

1789		Per Contra			Cr.		*l.*	*s.*	*d.*
Mar 21	R	By Drugget				2	2	6	8
23	2	By *T. Preston*, Esq. abated for my early Payment of 90*l.*				5	—	12	11¼
May 14	R	By Voyage to *Amst.* consign'd to *J. Van Hoove*				8	54	13	11
Jun. 12	6	By Goods for the Accompt of *A. Van Schooten*				9	36	8	—
24	7	By Bank Ann. for ½ a Year's Divid. on 10000*l.*				9	150	—	—
28	7	By *Abr. Van Schooten's* Acc. Cur. for Commission				9	13	13	3
—	R	By Duroy				2	7	10	—
—	R	By *Norwich* Crape				2	22	8	—
Aug 12	R	By Voyage to *Copen.* for my ½ of the Gain thereof				10	741	8	6
—	10	By Cash, gain'd by *Johannes Scheelhase*				1	5	4	7
15	10	By *W. Warner*, for a Legacy left me by my Brother *Verax*				4	1000	—	—
20	R	By Ship *James*				6	21329	11	6
22	11	By Cash recd. of *W. Baker*, Esq. ½ Yrs Int. on 500*l.*				1	12	10	—
Sept. 5	12	By Sir *H. Parsons*, for a Drawback on 200*l.* at 6 per Cent.				3	12	—	—
7	R	By Ship *Hopewell*, gain'd on the sale thereof				13	400	—	—
20	13	By *Thomas Preston*, abated on my Payment of 2185*l.* 16*s.* 6*d.*				5	—	—	6
22	R	By *French* Wine				2	40	—	—
—	R	By *John Parrot's* Accompt Current				14	5	19	2¾
—	R	By *George Hale's* Accompt Current				14	5	19	2¾
—	R	By Sugar in Co. for my ⅓ part gained				15	219	18	4¼
29	14	By Old *S. S.* Ann. for ½ a Yrs. Div. on 12000*l.*				10	180	—	—
Nov 10	R	By Canary				1	28	—	—
Dec. 9	17	By Cash recd. of *W. Baker*, Esq. the Int of 500*l.*				1	7	8	4
10	17	By *T. Johnson*, for a Drawback on 300*l.* at 8 per Cent.				5	24	—	—
12	R	By *Yorkshire* Cloth				15	122	15	6
—	17	By ditto, for the Accompt of *Nat. Keeble*				15	8	10	—
17	18	By *Tim. Hart* and Co. gain'd by prompt paymt.				12	4	18	—
25	18	By Bank Ann. for ½ a Year's Div. on 10000*l.*				9	150	—	—
30	19	By *W. Baker*, Esq. gain'd by prompt Payment				4	2	6	8
—	R	By Thread in Co. between *James Severn* and self				11	415	2	6
	R	By Hops				1	8	15	3
	R	By *Lisbon* Wine				2	68	—	—
	R	By Sagathee				3	6	—	—
	R	By Serge				2	2	6	8
	R	By Oranges and Limons				16	19	2	10
							25107	10	5

		Per Contra			Cr.				
1789	R	By Profit and Loss				7	337	4	10

Q

415

416

		Voyage to Amsterdam, consign'd to Jacob Van-Hoove **Dr.**		l.	s.	d.
1789 Apr. 1	3	To *Richard Lamb*, of *Harwich*, for 100 qrs. of Wheat	8	9	8	-
24	4	To Cash, for 100 Bags of Pepper, with Charges	1	140	7	10
25	4	To ditto, paid *John Adams*, for insuring the aforesaid Pepper	8	7	-	
May 14	R	To Profit and Loss, gain'd by the said Voyage	7	54	15	11
				301	10	

[Editor's note. The first
entry should be 99 pounds, 8
shillings.]

		Richard Lamb of Harwich **Dr.**				
1789 April 2	3	To *William Angel*, for a Draft on me, payable to do *Angel*, or Order, *May* 3 next . .	8	99	8	-

		William Angel **Dr.**				
1789 May 3	4	To Cash, paid in full	1	99	8	-

		John Adams **Dr.**				
1789 May 12	6	To Voyage to *Amsterdam*, consign'd to *J. Van Hoove*, for 100 Bags of Pepper lost . .	8	140	7	

		Jacob Van-Hoove's Acct. Curt. **Dr.** Guil. Stiv.				
1789 Mar 14	5	To Voyage to *Amsterdam*, Exch. at 33s. 4d. Flemish per £ Sterling, for 1611 3 8		161	2	

				l.	s.	d.
1789		Per Contra	Cr.			
May 12	5	By John Adams, for 100 Bags of Pepper, by him insured and lost	8	140	7	10
14	5	By Jacob Van Hoove's Accompt Current, on the Sale of 100 qrs. of Wheat		161	2	3½
				301	10	1½
1789		Per Contra	Cr.			
April 1	3	By Voyage to Amsterdam, consign'd to Jacob Van Hoove	8	99	8	—
1789		Per Contra	Cr.			
April 2		By Richard Lamb, of Harwich, for a Draft on me payable to do Angel, or Order, May 3 next	8	99	8	—
789		Per Contra	Cr.			
uly 24	9	By Sundry Accompts		140	7	10
		Per Contra	Cr. Guil. Stiv.			
789		By Jaques Van Brook, Exch. at 33s.				
ov 15 16		4d. Flemish per £ Sterling . . . 1611 3 16		161	2	3½

Q 2

417

			Bank-Annuity	Dr.		*l.*	*s.*	*d.*
1789				*l.*				
May 22	5	To Cash, at 4*l. per Cent.* and Brokerage on	10000		1	9412	10	
Jun. 24	7	To Profit and Loss, for ½ a Year's Divid.			7	150		
Dec. 25	18	To ditto . . . . for ditto . . .			7	150		
						9712	10	

			Insurance	Dr.				
1789								
Aug 14	10	To Sir *Humphrey Parsons,* for his scarlet Cloth lost in the *Falcon*			3	200		
Dec. 3	16	To *Thomas Johnson,* for a Freight in the *John* and *Hannah,* lost			5	300		
						500		

Note, When you insure on other Men's Goods, and receive the *Premium,* or give Credit for it, you must make *Cash,* or the *Person* indebted, Dr to *Insurance,* and *Insurance* Cr. by *Cash,* or the Person indebted : But when others insure on your Goods, and you pay

Goods for the Accompt of Abraham Van Schooten Dr.

				Rms. Paper	Ps. Holl	Ps. Lo. Lawn.				
1789										
June 2	6	To Cash, paid Freight, Custom, and other Charges on . .	1000	120	100	1	196	17	6
12	6	To Sundry Accompts for the Close					713	2	6
								910		

			A. Van Schooten's Acct. Curt.	Dr.				
1789								
Jun. 28	7	To Sundry Accompts			696	14	9

Note, The Balance of this Accompt may seem something odd to the young Book-keeper, and he, perhaps, may wonder how the Merchant must come by his Money, when *A. Van Schooten* lives so far off, and the Balance so small ; but it is to be observed in this *Case* that *Van Schooten* is the Employer ; and therefore as the Merchant at *London* sells Goods for

		Per Contra	Cr.		*l.*		*l*	*s*	*d*
1789			*l.*						
Oct. 14	14	By Cash, received ½ a Year's Dividend			I		150	—	—
Dec. 31	R	By Balance, at 93 ¾ per Cent . . .	10000	17			9337	10	—
	R	By do for ½ a Year's Dividend, due thereon		17			150		
	R	By Profit and Lofs, loft by the Abatement of its price and the Brokerage		7			75	—	—
							9712	10	—

		Per Contra	Cr.		*l*	*s*	*d*
1789							
May 28	6	By *James Allen*, on 200*l.* at 4 *per Cent.* in the *Golden Fleece*		6	8		
July 14	7	By Sir *Humphrey Parsons*, on 200*l.* at 8 *per Cent* on Scarlet Cloth		3	16		
Nov 24	16	By *Thomas Johnson*, on 300*l.* at 6 *per Cent.* on the *John* and *Hannah*		5	18		
		By Profit and Lofs, loft by this Accompt . .		7	458		
					500		

the Premium, then you muft be governed by the circumftances; and make fuch Perfon or Thing Dr. to *Cafh*, as the Nature of the Affair requires. See *Voyage to Amfterdam*, Fol. 8.

		Per Contra	Cr.				*l*	*s*	*d*
			R.	Pcs.	Pcs. Lo.				
1789			Paper.	Holl.	Lawn.				
June 5	6	By Cafh, at 6*s.* per Ream, for	1000			I	300		
8	6	By Sir *Robert Johnson*, at 3*l.* per Piece, for		120		3	360	—	—
12	6	By Sundry Accompts, at 2*l.* 10*s.* per Piece, for			100		250		
							910		

		Per Contra	Cr.		*l*	*s*	*d*
1789							
Jun. 12	6	By Goods for the Accompt of *A. Van-Schooten*, for the neat Produce		9	676	14	6
	R	By Balance due to me		17	20		3
					696	14	9

him, and makes Returns to him by *Commiffion*; So whatever is defective or redundant at one Time, will eafily be brought to Accompt by the Sale of the next Quantity of Goods received from, or Returns made to the faid *Van Schooten*: and fo on from Time to Time, as Occafion fhall happen.

419

			Voyage to Copenhagen, in Co. between Sam. Smith and self, each Half **Dr.**		*l.*	*s.*	*d.*
1789							
July 4	8	To Sundry Accompts	—	1463	9	8
Aug 12	—	To *Samuel Smith's* Accompt in Comp. for his Half of the Gain thereof	10	741	8	6
12	R	To Profit and Loſs, for my Half of the Gain thereof	7	741	8	6
					2946	6	8

			Sam. Smith's Accompt Currt. **Dr.**		*l.*	*s.*	*d.*
1789							
July 4	8	To his Accompt in Comp. for his Half of the Voyage to *Copenhagen*	10	731	14	10
Aug 12	R	By Balance due to him	—	746	13	1
					1478	7	11

420

			Sam. Smith's Acct. in Co. **Dr.**		*l.*	*s.*	*d.*
1789							
July 4	8	To his Accompt Current, for his Half of the Drawback on 30 Hhds. of Tobacco . . .	10	218	3	4
Aug. 8	13	To ditto, for his Half of the Goods ſold at *Copenhagen*	10	125	—	
					1473	3	4

			Hon. Commiſſrs. of the Cuſtoms **Dr.**		*l.*	*s.*	*d.*
1789							
July 4	8	To Voyage to *Copenhagen* in Comp. between *S. Smith* and ſelf	10	436	6	8

			Old South Sea Annuity **Dr.** *l.*		*l.*	*s.*	*d.*
1789							
July 12	8	To Caſh, at 91¼ *per Cent.* transfer'd to me	12000	1	10993	14	6
Sept 29	14	To Profit and Loſs, for Half a Year's Dividend	7	180	—	
					11173	14	6

1789	Per Contra	Cr.		l.	s.	d.
July 4	8 By Commiffioners of the Cuftoms, for a Draw-back on Tobacco exported	10	436	6	8
Aug. 8	10 By Jaques Joliffe's Accompt	13	2510		—
				2946	6	8

1789	Per Contra	Cr.		l.	s.	d.
July 4	8 By his Accompt in Comp. for his Half of the Drawback on 30 Hhds. of Tobacco . . .	10	218	3	4
Aug. 8	10 By ditto, for his half of the Goods fold at Co-penhagen	10	1255		—
	12	10 By Cafh, for his half of the Gain on the Ex-change of 10040 Rix Dollars	1	5	4	7
				1478	7	11

1789	Per Contra	Cr.		l.	s.	d.
July 4	8 By his Accompt Current, for his Half of the Voyage to Copenhagen	10	731	14	10
Aug 12	R By Voyage to Copenhagen, for his Share of the Gain thereof	10	741	8	6
				1473	3	4

1789	Per Contra	Cr.		l.	s.	d.
July 20	9 By Cafh, received in full	1	436	6	8

1789	Per Contra	Cr.		l.	s.	d.
Oct. 10	14 By Cafh, received Half a Year's Dividend due laft Michaelmas	1	180		—
Dec. 31	R By Balance, at 91½ per Cent . . .	12000	17	10950		—
	R By Profit and Lofs, loft by the Abatement of its Price, and the Brokerage .	7	43	14	6
				11173	14	6

421

						l.	*s.*	*d*
			Thread in Co. between J. Severn and self, each half	**Dr.**				
1789					lb.			
July 17	9	To *John Marsh*, at 14s. 10*d.* ½ per *lb.* for			5628	11	4185	16	6
23	9	To Cash, paid Charges on bringing the said Thread Home				1	17	14	6
Dec. 30	R	To *James Severn's* Accompt in Comp. for his Share of the Gain				11	415	2	6
—	R	To Profit and Loss for my Share of ditto				7	415	2	6
							5033	16	—

1789			**John Marsh, of Manchester,**	**Dr.**				
Aug 26	11	To Sundry Accompts			—	4185	16	6

1789			**James Severn's Acct. Currt.**	**Dr.**				
July 17	9	To his Accompt in Comp. for his Half of Thread bought of *J. Marsh*			11	2092	18	3
23	9	To ditto, for his Half of Charges on the said Thread			11	8	17	3
	R	To Balance due to him			17	415	2	6
							2516	18	—

Note, Observe the *Index* under *Note* 2, July 28. p. 13. in the Waste-Book, concerning any Partner's Accompt *Current* giving Credit for his Part of Goods fold, but not paid for.

1789			**James Severn's Acct. in Co.**	**Dr.**				
July 28	14	To his Accompt Current, for his Half of Thread fold *T. Hart* and Comp.			11	450	—	—
Aug. 3	14	To ditto, for ditto fold for ready Money			11	450	—	—
Sept. 24	14	To ditto, for ditto, ——*William Evans*			11	450	—	—
Dec. 28	19	To ditto, for ditto, ——*James Allen*			11	450	—	—
29	19	To ditto, for ditto, ——*Sir H. Parfons*			11	450	—	—
31	19	To ditto, for ditto, ——*William Baker,* Esq			11	266	18	—
							2516	18	—

422

		Per Contra	Cr.		l.	s.	d.
			lb				
1789							
July 28	9	By Tim. Hart and Comp. at 18s. per lb for	1000	12	900	—	—
Aug. 3	10	By Cash, sold A. Sanders at 18s. . for	1000	1	900	—	—
Sept. 24	14	By Sundry Accompts at 18s. . for	1000	—	900	—	—
Dec. 28	19	By Cash, . . . at 18s. . . for	1000	1	900	—	—
29	19	By Sir Humphrey Parsons, at 18s. . for	10 0	3	900	—	—
30	19	By William Baker, Esq; at 17s. . . for	628	4	533	16	—
			5628		5033	16	—

		Per Contra	Cr.				
1789							
July 17	9	By Thread in Comp. between James Severn and					
		self each half		11	4185	16	6

		Per Contra	Cr.				
1789							
July 28	9	By his Accompt in Comp. for his half of Thread					
		sold T. Hart and Comp.		11	450	—	—
Aug. 3	10	By ditto for ditto sold for ready Money .		11	450	—	—
Sept. 24	14	By ditto for ditto sold William Evans, . .		11	450	—	—
Dec. 28	19	By ditto for ditto sold James Allen, . .		11	450	—	—
29	19	By ditto for ditto sold Sir H. Parsons, .		11	450	—	—
30	19	By ditto for ditto sold William Baker Esq; .		11	266	18	—
					2516	18	—

		Per Contra	Cr.				
1789							
July 17	9	By his Accompt Current for his half of Thread					
		bought of John Marsh		11	2092	18	3
23	9	By ditto for his half of the Charges on the said					
		Thread		11	8	17	3
Dec. 30	2	By Thread in Comp. for his share of the Gain					
		thereof		11	415	2	6
					2516	18	—

P.

1789		Timothy Hart and Comp. Drs.		l.	s.	d.
July 28	9	To Thread in Comp. between J. Severn and self	11	900		
Dec. 17	18	To Sundry Accompts		1125		
				202		

1789		John Herbert Dr.				
Aug. 6	10	To Ship James	6	12	19	4¼

424

1789		John Smith Dr.				
Aug. 6	10	To Ship James	6	12	19	4¼

1789		William Evans Dr.				
Aug. 6	14	To Ship James	6	12	19	4¼
Sept 24	10	To Thread in Comp. payable in 6 Months	11	400		

1789		James Jackson Dr.				
Aug. 6	12	To Ship James	6	12	19	4¼
Sep. 22	13	To Sundry Accompts		1174	5	

1789			Per Contra		Cr.	*l.*	*s.*	*d.*
Oct.	1	14	By Cash, received in Part	1		300	—	—
Dec.	1	16	By ditto, ditto	1		300	—	—
	17	18	By *Nathaniel Keeble*, of *Hull*, for *Keeble's* draft on me payable to do *Hart* and Comp. . .	15		1125	—	—
		R	By Balance, due to me	17		300	—	—
						2025	—	—

1789			Per Contra		Cr.			
Aug 23		11	By Cash, received in full	1		12	19	—¾

1789			Per Contra		Cr.			
Aug 23		11	By Cash received in full	1		12	19	—¾

1789			Per Contra		Cr.			
Aug 23		11	By Cash received in full	1		12	19	—¾
		R	By Balance due to me *March* 24 next . .	17		400	—	—

1789			Per Contra		Cr.			
Aug 23		11	By Cash, received in full	1		12	19	—¾
Sept 22		13	By Sundry Accompts			600	—	—
		R	By Balance due to me	17		574	5	—
						1174	5	—

425

1789		Thomas Jones	Dr.		l.	s.	d.
Aug. 6	10	To Ship James	6	12	19	$\frac{3}{4}$	
Sept 24	14	To Thread in Comp. for a Draft on him, receiv- ed of *William Evans*	11	300	—	—
27	14	To Yorkshire Cloth	15	425	—	—
				725	—	—

1789		Jaques Jolliffe's Acct. Currt.	Dr.				
Aug. 8	10	To Voyage to *Copenhagen*	10	2510	—	—

426

1789		Ship Hopewell	Dr.				
Aug 23	11	To Cash paid in full to *Andrew Collins*	1	1200		
Sept. 7	R	To Profit and loss gain'd by the said Ship .	7	400		
				1600		

		Voyage from Barbadoes, in Comp. with J. Parrot, George Hale, and self, each One Third.					
1789							
Sept. 9	12	To *Timothy Sutton*, for 45 chests of Sugar .	13	167	13	$5\frac{1}{4}$

1789		Tim. Sutton at Barbadoes	Dr.				
	R	To Balance, due to him	17	167	13	$5\frac{1}{4}$

1789			Per Contra	Cr.		l.	s.	d.
Aug 23	17	By Cash, received in full			1	12	19	3/4
Oct. 22	14	By Cash, received in Part			1	300		
	R	By Balance, due to me			17	42		
						72		

1789			Per Contra	Cr.				
Aug 12	10	By Cash, received of *Johannes Scheelhase* .			1	2510		

1789			Per Contra	Cr.				
Sep. 7	12	By Cash, received of *Abraham Sanders*, in full			1	1660		

1789			Per Contra	Cr.				
Sept 15	13	By Sugar, in Comp. with *Parrot*, *Hale*, and self, for 45 Chests			15	167	13	1/4

1789			Per Contra	Cr.				
Sept. 9	13	By Voyage from Barbadoes, in Comp. with *Parrot*, *Hale*, and self, for 45 Chests of Sugar			13	167	13	1/2

427

1789		John Parrot's Acct. Currt.	Dr.		l.	s.	d.
Sept. 9	12	To his Accompt in Comp. for his ⅓ of Sugar from Barbadoes	14		55	17	9¾
15	13	To ditto, for his ⅓ of after-Charges on the above said Sugar	14		22	5	6
22	R	To Profit and Loss, for his ⅓ on the Sale of Sugar in Comp. at 2 per Cent.	7		5	19	2⅔
—	R	To Balance due to him	17	2	13	19	1½
					293	1	8

1789		John Parrot's Acct. in Co.	Dr.				
Sept 22	13	To his Accompt Current, for his ⅓ of Sugar in Comp. sold	14		298	1	8

428

1789		George Hale's Acct. Currt.	Dr.				
Sept. 9	12	To his Accompt in Comp. for his ⅓ of Sugar from Barbadoes	14		55	17	9¾
15	13	To ditto for his ⅓ of after-Charges on ditto Sugar	14		22	5	6
22	R	To Profit and Loss, for his ⅓ on the Sale of ditto Sugar, at 2 per Cent.	7		5	19	2¾
—	R	To Balance, due to him	17	2	13	19	1½
					298	1	8

1789		George Hale's Acct. in Co.	Dr.				
Sept 22	13	To his Accompt Current, for his ⅓ of Sugar in Comp. sold	14		298	1	8

1789		Per Contra	Cr.		l.	s.	d.
Sept.22	13	By his Accompt in Comp. for his ⅓ of Sugar in Comp. fold	14		298	1	8

1789		Per Contra	Cr.				
Sept. 9	12	By his Accompt Current, for his ⅓ of Sugar from Barbadoes	14		55	17	9¾
15	12	By ditto, for his ⅓ of after-Charges on ditto Sugar	14		22	5	6
22	R	By Sugar in Comp. for his ⅓ of the gain thereof	15		219	18	4¼
					298	1	8

1789		Per Contra	Cr.				
Sept.22	12	By his Accompt in Comp. for his ⅓ of Sugar in Comp. fold.	14		298	1	8

1789		Per Contra	Cr.				
Sept 9	12	By his Accompt Current, for his ⅓ of Sugar from Barbadoes	14		55	17	9¾
15	13	By ditto, for his ⅓ of after-Charges on ditto Sugar	14		22	5	6
22	R	By Sugar in Comp. for his ⅓ of the Gain thereof	15		219	18	4¼
					298	1	8

429

								l.	*s.*	*d.*
		Yorkfhire Cloth				Dr.				
1789							Pcs.			
*Sept.*1	12	To Sundry Accompts, at 7*l.* 10*s.* per Piece								
		for				150		1152	4	6
*Dec.*12	R	To Profit and Lofs, gain'd by this Accompt					7	122	15	6
								1275	—	

								l.	*s.*	*d.*
1789		Nathaniel Keeble, of Hull				Dr.				
*Dec.*17	13	To *Timothy Hart* and Comp. for *Keeble's* Draft								
		on me, payable to d° *Hart* and Comp. . . .					12	1125		
	R	To Balance, due to him					17	405	5	4
								1530	5	4

430

								l.	*s.*	*d.*
		Yorkfhire Cloth for the Acct. of N. Keeble				Dr.				
1789							Pcs.			
*Sept.*1	12	To Cafh, paid Charges in bringing home	50	1				11	4	8
*Dec.*12	17	To Sundry Accompts, for the clofe . .						413	15	4
								425	—	

								l.	*s.*	*d.*
		Sugar in Co. with Parrot, Hale, and felf, each one Third				Dr.				
1789				Ch.	C.	qr.	lb.			
*Sept.*1	13	To Sundry Accompts, at 15*s.* Ster-								
		ling *per C.* with Charges for	45	223	2	7		234	9	11
	22	R	To ditto for my two Partner's							
		Shares of the Gain						439	16	8
	—	R	To Profit and Lofs, for my ⅓ of the							
		Gain					7	219	18	4
								894	5	—

								l.	*s.*	*d.*
1789		William Harman				Dr.				
*Sept.*22	13	To *James Jackson*, for a Draught on d° *Har-*								
		man by d° *Jackson*					2	400	—	

1789		Per Contra	Cr.	Pcs.		l.	s.	d.
Sept 27	14	By *Thomas Jones*, at 8l. 10s. per Piece, for		50	5	425		
Oct. 3	14	By Cash, . . . 8l. 10s. per Piece, for		50	1	425		
Dec 12	17	By *J. Hammond*, Esq; 8l. 10s. per Piece, for		50	5	425		
				150		1275		

1789		Per Contra	Cr.			l.	s.	d.
Sept 11	12	By *Yorkshire* Cloth, for 150 Pieces .		15		1125		
Dec 12	17	By ditto, for his own Accompt for the neat Proceed		15		405	5	4
						1530	5	4

		Per Contra	Cr.	Pcs.		l.	s.	d.
1789								
Dec. 12	17	By *John Hammond*, Esq; at 8l. 10s. per Piece for		50	5	425		

1789		Per Contra	Cr.	Ch. C. qrs. lb.		l.	s.	d.
Sept 22	13	By *James Jackson*, at 4l. per C. for	45	223 2 7	12	894	5	
	13	By Balance, for the defect . .			17			-¼
						894	5	-¼

Note 1, The great Gain made by this *Sugar* may be supposed to arise from some Accident that enhanced the price of Sugars in general.
2. The Defect of 1-4 arises from the Gain, the exact 1-3 of which is not reducible to Money.

1789		Per Contra	Cr.			l.	s.	d.
Oct. 18	14	By Cash, received in full		1		400		

S

431

			£.	s.	d.
1789	**Voyage to Barbadoes** Dr.				
Oct. 28	15	To Sundry Accompts	190	4	6
29	15	To *Brandon George*, for Insurance, at 6 *per Cent*	4	11	8	3
			201	12	9

Note, At Page 13, *Timothy Sutton* at *Barbadoes*, ftands Dr. to Balance in the Sum of 167*l.* 13*s.* 5*d.* 1-4 *i. e.* the Merchant ftands indebted to him fo much, and therefore the young Book-keeper may imagine, that as the Goods in the above Voyage are confign'd to him, the Debt is now paid; But it is to be obferved, that the faid Goods, though confign'd to *Sutton*, are not for his own Accompt and Rifque but for the Accompt and rifque of the Merchant

			£.	s.	d.
1789	**Jaques Van Broek** Dr.				
Nov. 15	16	To *Jacob Van Hoove*, Exch. at 33*s.* 4*d per £* Sterling, for 1611 *Guil.* 3 *Sti.*	8	161	2	3½

				Rials	£.	s.	d.
1782	**Voyage from Cadiz** Dr.						
Dec. 14	17	To *Joram Conderil*, Exchange, at 4s 6*d.* *per* Piece of Eight, for	1200	16	33	15	—

			£.	s.	d.
1789	**Joram Conderil, of Cadiz** Dr.				
Dec. 22	18	To *John Hammond*, Efq; for do *Conderil's* Draft, payable to do *Hammond*	5	33	15	—

		Chefts of Ch. Or.	**Chefts of Sev. Or.**	**Chefts of Limons**		£.	s.	d.
		Oranges and Limons Cr.						
1789								
Dec. 18	18	To Sundry Accompts	50	50	50	—	70	1	6
		To profit and lofs gain'd by this Accompt .				7	19	2	10
							89	4	4

432

1789		Per Contra	Cr.		*l.*	*s.*	*d.*
	R	By Balance, not difpofed of . . r . . .	17		201	12	9

that fent them; and in this Cafe, *Sutton*, when he receives the Goods, is only to fell them to the beft advantage that he can, and repay himfelf : And when he fends an Accompt of Sale, 'tis then, and not till then, that you muft place that to his Accompt, and make him Dr. for the Overplus, or Cr. by fo much as that fale falls fhort of what you owe him before.

1789 Nov 28	16	Per Contra : : Cr. By Cafh, received in full		1	161	2	3½

433

1789 Dec. 18	18	Per Contra Cr. Rials. By Oranges and Limons, for 150 Chefts | 1200	16	33	15	—

1789 Dec. 14	17	Per Contra Cr. By Voyage from Cadiz, for 150 Chefts of Oranges and Limons	16	33	15	—

		Per Contra			Cr.

			Chefts of Ch. Or.	Chefts of Sev. Or.	Chefts of Limons		*l.*	*s.*	*d.*
1719 Dec. 26	18	By *Ifaac Reynolds*, at 17s. *per* Cheft for .	—	—	50	5	42	10	—
		By Balance, unfold .	50	50	—	17	46	14	4
							89	4	4

S 2

1739		Balance Dr.		£	s	d
June 28	R	To *Abraham Van Schooten's* Accompt Current	9	20		3
Sept.22	R	To Sugar in Comp. for a Defect	5			¼
☞	R	To Error on the Cr. side	17	130 1	8	2½
	R	To Cash remaining in Hand, carried to the next Books	1	12701	8	2½
	R	To Hops unfold, at 28s. per C. 3 Bags, wt. 9C.	1	12 12	12	
	R	To *Lisbon* Wine, unfold, at 7l. per Hhd. 2 Hhds.	32	14		
	R	To Sagathee, unfold, at 2s. 6d. per Yard, 50 Pieces, qt. 600 Yards	3	75		
	R	To Serge, unfold, at 1s. per Yard, 50 Pieces, qt. 700 Yards	3	35		
	R	To Sir *Humphrey Parsons,* due to me *June* 29 next	3	900		
	R	To *William Baker,* Esq. due to me	4	36		
	R	To *Brandon George* . due to me	4	60	11	9
	R	To *John Hammond,* Esq; due to me	5	816	5	
	R	To *Martin Unwin,* due to me	5	81	17	6
	R	To *Isaac Reynolds,* due to me	5	42	10	
	K	To Bank Annuity, at 93⅜ per Cent. 10000l.	9	9337	10	
	R	To ditto, for Half a Year's Interest due thereon	9	150		
	R	To Old S. S. Annuity, at 91½ per Cent. 12000l.	10	10950		
	R	To *Timothy Hart* and Comp. due to me	12	300		
	R	To *Williams Evans,* due to me	12	400		
	R	To *James Jackson,* due to me	12	574	5	
	R	To *Thomas Jones,* due to me	13	425		
	R	To Voyage to *Barbadoes* not yet disposed of	16	201	12	9
	R	To Oranges and Limons, unsold, 50 Chests of *Ch.* Oranges, and 50 Chests of *Sev.* Oranges	16	46	14	4
				50211	15	.¼

Note, The third Line from the Top having the Index prefixt to it in the Margin, shews that it was inserted to balance the *Error* committed on the Cr. side of this Accompt.

434

1789		Per Contra	Cr.		*l.*	*s.*	*l.*
Aug 12	R	By *Samuel Smith's* Accompt Current due to him	10		746	13	1
Sep. 22	R	By *John Parrot's* Accompt Current, due to him	14		213	19	1½
—	R	By *George Hale's* Accompt Current, due to him	14		213	19	1½
Error	R	By Cash, remaining in Hand, carried to the next Books	1		13031	8	2½
	R	By *Thomas Johnson*, ... due to him	5		359	2	4½
	R	By *James Severn's* Accompt current, due to him	11		415	2	6
	R	By *Timothy Sutton*, at *Barbadoes*, due to him	13		167	13	5¼
	R	By *Nathaniel Keeble*, of *Hull*, . due to him	15		405	5	4
	R	By Stock, for my neat Estate	1		34658	11	10¼

Note, The fourth line from the Top, marked with *Error* in the Margin, was done on Purpose to shew the Learner how to balance it, which see on the Dr. side

50211 | 15 | ¾

435

Dr. The TRIAL BALANCE. Cr.

l.	*s.*	*d.*		P.	*l.*	*s.*	*d.*
412	10	—	Stock	1	10925	15	4¼
44708	19	7	Cash	1	32007	11	4½
153	—	—	Canary	1	153	—	—
185	10	—	Hops	1	181	13	3
340	—	—	*French* Wine	2	340	—	—
49	—	—	Drugget	2	49	—	—
175	—	—	*Lisbon* Wine	2	229	—	—
179	4	—	*Norwich* Crape	2	179	4	—
97	10	—	Duroy	2	97	10	—
135	—	—	Sagathee	3	66	—	—
63	—	—	Serge	3	30	6	8
1601	19	¾	Sir *Robert Johnson*	3	1601	19	¾
1116	—	—	Sir *Humphrey Parsons*	3	216	—	—
1673	19	¾	*William Baker* Esq;	4	1637	19	¾
1334	7	—	*William Warner*	4	1334	7	—
72	—	—	*Brandon George*	4	11	8	3
128	—	—	*Samuel Fairman*	4	128	—	—
528	13	—	*William Lowfield,* Esq;	4	528	13	—
674	14	3¾	*Thomas Johnson*	5	1033	16	8
980	—	—	*John Hammond,* Esq;	5	163	15	—
381	17	6	*Martin Unwin*	5	300	—	—
84	10	—	*Isaac Reynolds*	5	42	—	—
2293	6	—	*Thomas Preston* Esq;	5	2293	6	—
1335	9	¾	*Robert Uxley*	6	1335	9	¾
24170	8	6	Ship *James*	6	24170	8	6
1433	—	—	*James Allen*	6	1433	—	—
48	4	7	Profit and Loss	7	25003	5	8
337	4	10	House-Expenses	7	—	—	—
301	10	1½	Voyage to *Amsterdam*	8	301	10	1½
99	8	—	*Richard Lamb* of *Harwich*	8	99	8	—
99	8	—	*William Angel*	8	99	8	—
140	7	10	*John Adams*	8	140	7	10
161	2	3½	*J Van Hoove's* Accompt Current	8	161	2	3½
9712	10	—	Bank Annuity	9	150	—	—
500	—	—	Insurance	9	42	—	—
910	—	—	Goods for the Accompt of *A. Van Schooten*	9	910	—	—
96616	12	9	Carried over		107396	4	2

The End of the

Dr. The TRIAL-BALANCE continued. Cr.

l.	s.	d.		P.	l.	s.	d.
96616	12	9	. . . . . . Brought over	—	107396	4	2
696	14	9	*Abraham Van Schooten's* Accompt Current	9	696	14	9
2946	6	8	Voyage to *Copenhagen* in Co. bet. *S. S.* & self	10	2946	6	8
1478	7	11	*Samuel Smith's* Accompt Current	10	1478	7	11
1473	3	4	Ditto . . . . . . in Comp.	10	1473	3	4
436	6	8	Honourable Commiſſioners of the Cuſtoms	10	436	6	8
11173	14	6	Old South-Sea Annuity	10	180	—	—
5033	16	—	Thread in Co.	11	5033	16	—
4185	16	6	*John Marſh*	11	4185	16	6
2101	15	6	*James Severn's* Accompt Current . . .	11	2516	18	—
2516	18	—	Ditto . . . . in Comp. . . .	11	2516	18	—
2025	—	—	*Timothy Hart* and Co.	12	1725	—	—
12	19	¾	*John Herbert*	12	12	19	¾
12	19	¾	*John Smith*	12	12	19	¾
412	19	¾	*William Evans*	12	12	19	¾
1187	4	¾	*James Jackſon*	12	612	19	¾
737	19	¾	*Thomas Jones*	13	312	19	¾
2510	—	—	*Jaques Joliffe's* Accompt Current . .	13	2510	—	—
1600	—	—	Ship *Hopewell*	13	1600	—	—
167	13	5¼	Voyage from *Barbadoes*	13	167	13	5¼
—	—	—	*Timothy Sutton* of *Barbadoes*	13	167	13	5¼
298	1	8	*John Parrot's* Accompt Current	14	298	1	8
298	1	8	Ditto . . . . . . in Comp.	14	298	1	8
298	1	8	*George Hale's* Accompt Current	14	298	1	8
298	1	8	Ditto , ... in Comp.	14	298	1	8
1275	—	—	*Yorkſhire* Cloth	15	1275	—	—
1125	—	—	*Nathaniel Keeble,* of *Hull*	15	1530	5	4
425	—	—	*Yorkſhire* Cloth for the Accompt of *N. Keeble*	15	425	—	—
894	5	¼	Sugar in Comp.	15	894	5	¼
400	—	—	*William Harman*	15	400	—	—
201	12	9	Voyage to *Barbadoes*	16	—	—	—
161	2	3½	*Jaques Van Broek*	16	161	2	3½
33	15	—	Voyage from *Cadiz*	16	33	15	—
33	15	—	*Joram Conderii*	16	33	15	—
70	1	6	Oranges and Limons	16	42	10	—
20	—	¼	Balance	17	1174	11	4
143158	4	10			143158	4	10

ſecond Ledger.

1789	Cash	Dr.		l.	s.	d.
Mar. 1	1 To Stock brought from the last Month	1	8099	4	$2\frac{1}{2}$
2	1 To Sir *Robert Johnson*, received in full	3	30		
6	2 To Ship *James*, received in full of *John Herbert* for $\frac{1}{15}$	6	125		
8	2 To Ship *James*, received of Capt. *John Smith* in full for $\frac{1}{16}$	6	125		
17	2 To *William Baker* Esq; received in Part	4	125		
20	2 To Canary, for 1 Pipe sold to *William Delo*	1	30		
25	2 To Sundry Accompts		174	—	
			8708	4	$2\frac{1}{2}$

1789	Cash	Dr.		l.	s.	d.
April 1	To Balance brought from the last Month		6989	8	$7\frac{3}{4}$
10	3 To Ship *James*, received of *William Evans*, in full for $\frac{1}{16}$	6	125		
12	3 To Ship *James*, received of *James Jackson*, in full for $\frac{1}{16}$	6	125		
14	3 To Ship *James* received of *Thomas Jones*, in full for $\frac{1}{16}$	6	125		
20	3 To *John Hammond*, Esq; received in full	5	100		
30	4 To *William Warner*, received in full	4	34	7	
			7498	15	$7\frac{3}{4}$

1789	Cash	Dr.		l.	s.	d.
May 1	To Balance brought from the last Month		6481	9	$7\frac{1}{2}$
7	5 To Ship *James*, received of 7 Owners, their $\frac{7}{16}$ of Disbursements for the said Ship	6	495	19	—
17	5 To Canary, received of *William Coles*, in full for 1 Pipe	1	30		
20	5 To Ship *James*, received in full for my Half Part of a *French* Prize	6	10000		
			17007	8	$7\frac{1}{2}$

438

1789			Per Contra Cr.		*l.*	*s.*	*d.*
Mar.	4	1	By Ship *James*, paid in Part	6	75	—	
	9	2	By *James Allen*, paid in full . . .	6	1425	—	
	23	2	By *Thomas Preston*, Esq; paid in Part .	5	89	7	4¼
	26	2	By Ship *James*, paid *Thomas Young*, in full for Joiner's Work	6	20	17	
	27	2	By Ship *James*, paid *T. Pierce*, in full for Rigg.	6	27	14	6
	28	2	By Ship *James*, paid *Dryden Smith*, in full for Repairs	6	40	8	—
	30	3	By Ship *James*, paid *Nathaniel Westall*, in full for Painting	6	7	4	6
	31	3	By House-Expenses, paid sundry Charges this Month	7	32	4	6
		R	By Balance remaining in Hand, carried to the next Month	—	6990	8	7¾
					9708	4	2¼
1789			Per Contra Cr.				
Apr.	3	3	By Ship *James*, paid the Block-maker in full	6	19	17	6
	7	3	By Ship *James*, paid the Ship-chandler in full	6	700	13	—
	24	4	By Voyage to *Amsterdam*, consign'd to *Jacob Van-Hoove*	8	140	7	10
	25	4	By Voyage to *Amsterdam*, paid *J. Adams*, for insuring 100 Bags of Pepper	8	7	—	4½
	27	4	By Ship *James*, paid *John Jones*, in full for Beef and Pork	6	109	10	6
	30	4	By House-Expenses, paid sundry Charges this Month	7	32	16	10
		R	By Balance remaining in Hand, carried to the next Month	—	6481	9	7¼
					7498	15	7¾
1789			Per Contra Cr.				
May	1	4	By Ship *James*, paid *James Thaicher*, in full for Bread, Flour, and Pease . . .	6	86	18	6
	2	4	By Ship *James*, paid *John Prestwick*, in full for Cordage, &c.	6	46	17	—
	5	4	By *William Angel*, for *Lamb's* Draft on me, payable to d° *Angel*	8	99	8	—
	6	4	By Ship *James*, paid *John Pepwell*, in full for Smith's Work	6	73	11	6
	10	5	By *Robert Uxley*, paid him in full . . .	6	76	14	9
	22	5	By Bank Ann. at 94*l.* per Cent. with Brokerage	9	9412	10	—
	24	5	By *Thomas Preston*, Esq. paid *James Hart*, in full for repairing my Dwelling House . .	5	17	9	6
	31	6	By House-Expenses, paid sundry Charges this Month	7	43	11	2
		R	By Balance remaining in Hand, carried to the next Month	—	7150	8	2¼
					17007	8	7¼

T

1789		Cash	Dr.		l.	s.	
June	1	—	To Balance brought from the laſt Month .		7150	8	2¼
	5	6	To Goods for the Accompt of *A. Van-Schooten*, for 1000 Reams of Paper, received in full	9	300	—	—
	12	6	To Goods for the Accompt of *A. Van-Schooten*, for 120 Pieces of Holland, received in Part	9	100	—	—
	16	7	To *Samuel Fairman*, received in full . .	4	28	—	—
	18	7	To Sir *Robert Johnſon*, received in Part .	3	360	—	—
	23	7	To *William Lowfield* Eſq. received in full . .	4	128	13	—
	24	7	To Sir *Robert Johnſon*, received in full .	3	150	—	—
	27	7	To *Liſbon* Wine, ſold *J. Hicks*, received in full	2	105	—	—
					8322	1	2¼

1789		Cash	Dr.				
July	1	—	To Balance brought from the laſt Month		7678	7	4¼
	9	8	To Ship *James*, received in full for my Half Part of a *French* Prize	6	12500	—	—
	20	9	To Commiſſioners of the Cuſtoms, received in full	10	436	6	8
	24	9	To *John Adams*, received in full . .	8	129	3	3
	26	9	To Sir *Humphrey Parſons*, received in Part	3	16	—	—
					20759	17	3¼

1789		Cash	Dr.				
Aug.	1	—	To Balance brought from the laſt Month .		9696	17	3¾
	3	10	To Thread in Comp. between *J. Severn* and ſelf, for 100 lb. ſold for preſent Money	11	900	—	—
	12	10	To Sundry Accompts		2520	9	2
	22	11	To Profit and Loſs, received Half a Year's Intereſt on 500 l. of *William Baker* .	7	12	10	—
	25	11	To Sundry Accompts		103	12	6
					13233	8	11¾

1789		Cash	Dr.				
Sept.	1	—	To Balance brought from the laſt Month .		11804	6	5¼
	7	12	To Ship *Hopewell*, received of *Abraham Saunders* in full	13	1600	—	—
	22	13	To *James Jackſon*, received in Part . .	12	200	—	—
	24	14	To Thread in Comp. received of *William Evans* in Part	11	200	—	—
					13804	6	5¼

1789		Per Contra Cr.		*l.*	*s.*	*d.*
June 2	8	By Goods for the Accompt of *A. V. Schooten*, paid Freight &c.	9	196	17	6
28	7	By *A. Van Schooten's* Accompt Current for sundry Accompts	9	406	7	6
30	7	By House-Expenses, paid sundry Charges this Month	7	40	8	10
	R	By Balance, remaining in Hand, carried to the next Month	—	7678	7	4¼
				8322	1	2¼

1789		Per Contra Cr.				
July 4	8	By Voyage to *Copenhagen* in Comp. between *S. Smith* and self, each half	10	29	13	—
12	8	By Old S. S. Annuity, for 12000*l.* transferred to me at 91½ *per Cent.* and Brokerage	10	10993	14	6
23	9	By Thread in Comp. between *James Severn* and self, each half, for Charges	11	17	14	6
31	9	By House-Expenses, paid sundry Charges this Month	7	21	18	—
	R	By Balance rem. in hand, carried to the next mo.	—	9696	17	3¾
				20759	17	3¾

1789		Per Contra Cr.				
Aug. 6	8	By Ship *James*, paid sundry Charg. in refitt. her	6	207	5	—
28	11	By Ship *Hopewell*, paid *Andrew Collins* in full	13	1200		
31	11	By House-Expences, paid sundry Charges this Month	7	21	17	6
	R	By Balance remaining in hand, carried to the next Month	—	11804	6	5¼
				13233	8	11¼

1789		Per Contra Cr.				
Sept. 5	12	By Sir *Humphrey Parsons,* paid him in full	3	172	—	—
11	12	By *Yorkshire Cloth,* paid Charges on bringing 150 Pieces Home	15	27	4	6
11	12	By *Yorkshire Cloth,* for the Accompt of *Nathaniel Keeble,* for Charges	15	11	4	8
15	13	By Sugar in Comp. paid Custom and other Charges in bringing it Home	15	66	16	6¼
20	13	By *Thomas Preston,* Esq; paid him in full	5	2185	16	
30	14	By House-Expenses, paid sundry Charg. this mo	7	22	12	6
	R	By Balance rem. in hand, carried to the next mo.	—	11318	12	3
				13804	6	5¼

1789		Cash	Dr.		l.	s.	d.
Oct. 1	—	To Balance brought from the last Month			11318	12	3
1	14	To Timothy Hart and Comp. received in part	12	300			
3	14	To Yorkshire Cloth, received in full for 50 Pcs.	15	425		—	
6	14	To William Warner, received my Legacy in full	4	1000		—	
10	14	To Old S. S. Annuity, received half a Year's Div. on 12000l. due Michaelmas last	10	180		—	
14	14	To Bank Annuity, received half a Year's Div. on 10000l. due Midsummer last	9	150		—	
18	14	To William Harman, received in full . .	15	400		—	
22	14	To Thomas Jones, received in Part . .	13	300		—	
26	15	To Martin Unwin, received in part . .	5	100		—	
					14573	12	3

1789		Cash	Dr.				
Nov. 1	—	To Balance brought from the last Month			13827	1	1
4	15	To Samel Fairman, received in full . .	4	100		—	
10	16	To Sundry Accompts		38	5		
18	16	Serge	3	16	6	8
27	15	To Martin Unwin, received in part . .	5	100		—	
28	16	To Jaques Van Broek, received in full . .	16	161	2	3½
					14242	18	½

1789		Cash	Dr.				
Dec. 1	—	To Balance brought from the last Month .			12715	4	6½
1	16	To Timothy Hart and Comp. received in part	12	300			
6	16	To John Hammond Esq. received in full . .	5	30		—	
9	17	To Sundry Accompts		507	8	4
13	17	To Thomas Preston, Esq. received for the Repairs of my Dwelling-House	5	17	9	6
20	18	To Martin Unwin, received in part . .	5	100		—	
24	18	To Isaac Reynolds, received in full . .	5	42		—	
27	18	To James Allen, received in full . . .	6	8		—	
28	19	To Thread in Comp. between James Severn and self	11	900		—	
					14620	2	4½

The End of the

1789			Per Contra		l.	s.	d.	Cr.
Oct. 6	14	By William Warner, paid in full	4		300			
28	15	By Voyage to Barbadaes	18		19	17	6	
31	15	By House-Expenses, paid Sundry Charges this Month	7		26 15		8	
	R	By Balance remaining in Hand, carried to the next Month			13827	1	1	
					14173	12	3	

1789			Per Contra					Cr:
Nov. 1	15	By William Lowfield Esq; paid him in full	4		400	—		
7	15	By Thomas Johnson, paid in part	5		100	—		
20	16	By Sir Robert Johnson, paid him in full	3		1600	—		
30	16	By House-Expenses, paid sundry Charges this Month	7		27	13	6	
	R	By Balance remaining in Hand, carried to the next Month			12715	4	6½	
					14242	18	-½	

443

1789			Per Contra					Cr.
Dec. 10	17	By Thomas Johnson, paid my Insurance on a Freight lost	5		276			
17	18	By Timothy Hart and Comp. paid them	12		1120	2	—	
18	18	By Oranges and Limons, paid Freight, Custom, &c.	16		36	6	6	
30	19	By William Baker, Esq; paid him in full	4		463	17	4	
31	19	By House-Expenses, paid sundry Charges this Month	7		22	8	4	
	R	By Balance remaining in Hand, carried to the next Month			12701	8	2½	
					14620	2	4½	

Second Cash-Book.

THE

BOOK of HOUSE-EXPENSES.

1789	House-Expences Dr. to Cash.	l.	s.	d.	l.	s	d.
Mar. 1	For a Scrubbing brush	0	1	0			
2	mending a pair of Bellows . . .	0	0	6			
3	a new Tea-kettle	0	7	6			
4	mending the Crane, and 3 Hooks	0	5	0			
	Fish	0	2	6			
6	3 Washing tubs	0	9	0			
7	tinning a large Pot and 4 Sauce-pans	0	4	8			
					1	10	2
9	a Goose and 2 Ducks	0	6	0			
10	a Turkey	0	6	0			
11	the Baker's Bill	0	19	8			
	the Butcher's Bill	6	1	6			
13	3lb. of Sausages	0	1	6			
14	a peck of Oysters	0	3	0			
	a peck of Onions	0	0	6			
					7	18	2
16	a new Fire-shovel and tongs . .	0	8	6			
17	a large Stew-pan	0	8	6			
	the Apothecaries Bill	3	10	0			
19	a Load of Hay	1	10	0			
20	2 Load of Straw	1	0	0			
21	the Farrier's shoeing Whitefoot	0	2	6			
	curing the Coachman's broken shin	1	1	0			
	mending the Clock	0	10	6			
					8	11	0
23	a new Jack-line	0	2	0			
24	the Cook's Bill	0	17	6			
	a Turbot	0	10	6			
26	a Dozen large Eels	0	7	6			
27	a Dozen Limons	0	1	6			
28	a Firkin of Butter	1	8	0			
29	a Cheshire Cheese, wt. 50lb. at 4d. per lb.	0	16	8			
	the Baker's Bill	1	1	6			
31	a Quarter's Rent	10	0	0			
					1	5	2
					3?	?	6

Note, A Continuation of the House-Expenses is needless; since enough has been said already to inform the Judgment of the Learner concerning the nature of such a Book: the rest may be easily supposed.

The End of the second Book of House-Expenses.

444

A

SYNOPSIS,

OR

COMPENDIUM

OF

MERCHANTS ACCOUNTS:

CONTAINING

Particular RULES

FOR THE

True Stating of DEBTOR and CREDITOR,

In all the CASES that can happen in

the whole Courfe of a

MERCHANT'S DEALING.

The Accompts of Merchants are of three Sorts, **viz.**

I. PROPER; wherein the Merchant trades by and for himfelf; which is either Domeftic, i. e. Inland and at Home;
or Foreign, i. e. Abroad.

II. FACTORAGE; wherein the Merchant acts as a Factor in
Commiffion, for one that employs him; and this alfo is
either Domeftic or Foreign.

III. IN COMPANY; wherein two or more Merchants join
together in Trade; and have each a fhare of the Gain,
or bear a Share of the Lofs, in Proportion to his Share
in the Stock, as is taught in the Rules of Fellowfhip.

I. Of PROPER ACCOUNTS.

1. DOMESTIC.

In receiving and paying Money.

CASE I. When an Inventory is taken of the ready Money, Goods, Voyages, and Debts, belonging or owing to me;

Rule, Dr. those several Parcels and Parties. Cr. Stock or principal.

Cafe 2. When an inventory is taken of the Debts owing to me;

Rule, Dr. Stock or principal, Cr. the several parties to whom the same are due.

Cafe 3. When Money is received of one man for the use of another, or for his own Ufe.

Rule, Dr cafh, Cr. the perfon for whofe Ufe it is received. The fame when Money is received for Goods formerly fold.

Cafe 4. When money is paid to one Man for the Ufe of another, or for his own Ufe.

Rule, Dr the Perfon for whofe Ufe it is paid, Cr. Cafh. The fame where Money is paid for Goods formerly bought.

Cafe 5. When Money is lent.

Rule, Dr. Borrower for the Principal, Cr Cafh.

Cafe 6. When money is borrowed;

Rule, Dr Cafh, Cr. the Lender for the principal.

Cafe 7. When Intereft is received for money lent.

Rule, Dr. Cafh Cr. Profit and Lofs. The fame for prompt payment received.

Cafe 8. When Intereft is become due to me, and booked before received.

Rule, Dr. the Perfon who owes it, Cr. Profit and Lofs.

Cafe 9. When intereft is paid for money taken up;

Rule, Dr. Profit and Lofs, Cr. Cafh. The fame for prompt payment paid.

Cafe 10. When Intereft is become due from me to another; and booked before paid.

Rule, Dr Profit and Lofs, Cr. the Perfon to whom it is due.

Cafe 11. When charges are paid on Goods in my Peffeffion;

Rule, Dr. those Goods Cr Cafh.

Cafe 12. When Charges are paid on petty Difburfements in Trade;

Rule, Dr. Charges of Merchandize, Dr. Cafh.

Cafe 13. When Charges are paid on Houfe-Keeping, and all Expenfes thereunto belonging.

Rule, Dr. Profit and Lofs or Houfe-Expenfes, Cr. Cafh.

Cafe 14 When India Stock, Bank Stock, South Sea Stock or Annuity is bought.

Rule, Dr. fuch Stock or Annuity, Cr. Cafh. The fame if there be a Call of 5l. &c. per Cent. upon my fhare in any Capital Stock.

Cafe 15 When Intereft is become due to me on fuch Stock or Annuity, and booked before received.

Rule, Dr. that Stock or Annuity, Cr. Profit and Lofs.

Cafe 16. When India Stock, Bank Stock, South Sea Stock or Annuity is fold;

Rule, Dr. Cafh Cr. fuch Stock or Annuity.

Cafe 17. When my Debtor compounds with me, and I receive Part of the Debt for the whole.

Rule, Dr. Cafh for what I receive, Dr. Profit and Lofs for what I lofe Cr. the perfon by Sundry Accompts, who compounds for the whole Debt'

Case 18. When I compound with my Creditor, and pay him part of the Debt for the Whole ;

Rule, Dr. the Person who receives, to sundry Accompts for the whole, Cr. Cash for what I pay, Cr. Profit and Loss for what is abated.

Case 19. When a Legacy is bequeathed to me ;

Rule, Dr. the Executor, Cr. Profit and Loss.

Case 20. When a Legacy is received ;

Rule, Dr. Cash, Cr. the Executor. If received before entered, Dr. Cash, Cr. Profit and Loss.

Case 21. When I receive a Legacy for the use of another, myself being the Executor ;

Rule, Dr. Cash, Cr. the Legatee.

Case 22. When I pay a Legacy for the use of another, myself being the Executer ;

Rule, Dr. the Legatee, Cr. Cash.

Case 23. When I receive Money by Assignment ;

Rule, Dr. Cash, Cr. the Assignor.

Case 24. When I gave an Assignment or Order on my Debtor to my Creditor ;

Rule, Dr. the Person to whom the Assignment is given, Cr. the Person upon whom the same Assignment is charged.

Case 25. When I pay Money to another, by the Assignment or Order of my Creditor ;

Rule, Dr. the Person who makes the assignment, Cr. Cash.

Case 26. When I receive a Promissary Note in payment, and book it ;

Rule, Dr. the Drawer or Endorser of that Note, Cr. the Person of whom you receive it in Payment.

Case 27. When I Deliver the said Note in Payment afterward ;

Rule, Dr. the Person who receives it, Cr. the said Drawer or Endorser.

Case 28. When I pay Charges on House-keeping, and all Expenses thereunto belonging.

Rule, Dr. Profit and Loss, Cr. Cash.

In buying and selling Goods.

Case 29. When I buy Goods for present Money :

Rule, Dr. the Goods bought, Cr. Cash. The same with Lottery Tickets, which may be esteemed as Goods.

Case 30. When I buy Goods for Time, *i. e.* on Trust ;

Rule, Dr. the Goods, Cr. the Seller. The same when several Payments are to be made by me, only mentioning in the Journal the several Times of Payment. The same also when Goods are taken in lieu of a Debt, either in Part or in the Whole.

Case 31. When I require an Abatement on Goods bought on time, after they are booked, on the Accompt of defect ;

Rule, Dr. the seller, for the Abatement, Cr. the Goods bought. If the Accompt of Goods be closed, Dr. the seller, Cr. Profit and Loss.

Case 32. When I buy Goods for part ready Mony, and Part Trust ;

Rule, Dr. the Goods, Cr. the Seller for the whole. Then Dr. the Seller for what I pay, Cr. Cash for the same sum. Or Dr. the Goods to sundry Accompts, Cr. Cash for what I pay, and Cr. the Seller for what remains unpaid.

U

Cafe 33. When I buy Goods for part ready Money, Part Truft, and Part by Affignment;

Rule, Dr. the Goods to fundry Accompts. Cr. Cafh for what I pay 'Cr. the Perfon whofe Bill I have affigned and Cr. the felling Man for the reft.

Cafe 34. When I fell Goods for prefent Money;

Rule, Dr. Cafh, Cr. the Goods. They fame with Lottery Tickets, which may be efteemed as Goods.

Cafe 35. When I fell Goods for time, *i. e.* on Truft;

Rule, Dr. the Buyer, Cr. the Goods. The fame when feveral Payments are to be made to me, only mentioniog in the Journal the feveral Times of Payment. The fame alfo when Goods are fold in lieu of a Debt, either in part, or in the Whole.

Cafe 36. When I make an Abatement on Goods fold on Time, after they are booked, on the Accompt of defect;

Rule, Dr. the Goods for the abatement, and Cr. the Buyer. If the Accompt of Goods be clofed, Dr. Profit and Lofs, Cr. the Buyer

Cafe 37. When I fell Goods for Part ready Money, and Part Truft;

Rule, Dr. the Buyer for the Whole, Cr. the Goods; Then Dr. Cafh for what I receive, Cr. the Buyer for the fame fum. Or Dr. Cafh for the Money received, Dr. the Buyer for what remains unpaid, Cr. the Goods by fundry Accompts for the whole.

Cafe 38. When I fell goods for part ready Money, Part Truft, and Part by affignment;

Rule, Dr. Cafh for what is received, Dr. the Perfon on whom I have taken the affignment, Dr. the buyer for the reft, Cr. the Goods by fundry Accompts for the whole.

Cafe 39. When I buy feveral forts of Goods for ready Money;

Rule, Dr. each of them for its refpective value; Cr. Cafh by fundry Accompts for the whole.

Cafe 40. When I buy feveral forts of Goods upon Truft;

Rule, Dr. each of them for its refpective value, Cr. the Seller by fundry accompts for the whole.

Cafe 41. When I fell feveral forts of Goods for ready Money;

Rule, Dr. Cafh to Sundry Accompts for the whole Value, Cr. each Sort for its refpective Sum.

Cafe 42. When I fell feveral forts of Goods on Truft;

Rule, Dr. the Buyer to fundry Accompts for the whole Value, Cr. each Sort for its refpective fum.

Cafe 43. When I want Rebate to be made on the prefent Payment of Money, for Goods bought upon Time;

Rule, Dr. the Seller to Sundry Accompts for the whole Sum, Cr. Cafh for the Sum paid, Cr. Profit and Lofs for the Rebate.

Note, This is fuppofed to happen a Day or two after the Goods are bought and booked.

Cafe 44. When I make Rebate on the prefent receiving of Money for Goods fold upon Time;

Rule, Dr. Cafh for the fum received, Dr. Profit and Lofs for the Sum rebated, Cr. the Buyer by fundry Accompts for the whole Sum.

Note, T is is fuppofed to happen a Day or Two after the Goods are fold and Booked.

Cafe 45. When I buy Goods of a Debtor, for a Debt due to me, their Value amounting to more than the Debt, and the Overplus is paid back in Money prefently;

Rule, Dr. the Goods to Sundry Accompts for the whole Sum, Cr. the Seller for fo much as his Debt was, Cr. Cafh for the Overplus.

Note, If feveral forts of Goods had been bought, and the Overplus returned by me, then firſt, Dr. each Sort for its reſpective value, Cr. the Seller by Sundry Accomp's for their whole Value; Secondly, Dr. the Seller for the Overplus paid back, Cr. Caſh for the ſame Sum.

Caſe 46. When I ſell Goods to a Creditor, for a Debt due to him, their Value amounting to more than the Debt, and the Overplus is returned to me in Money preſently;

Rule, Dr. the Buyer for ſo much as is owing to him, Dr Caſh for the Overplus received, Cr. the Goods ſold by Sundry Accompts for the whole Sum.

Note, If ſeveral Sorts of Goods had been ſold, and the Overplus returned to me, then firſt, Dr. the Buyer to Sundry Accompts for their whole Value, cr. each Sort for its reſpective Value. Secondly, Dr. Caſh for ſo much as is received, and Cr. the Buyer for the ſame ſum.

Barter.

Caſe 47 When I give one Sort of Goods for another of equal Value;
Rule, Dr. the Goods received, Cr. the Goods delivered.

Caſe 48. When I give one ſort of Goods for another Sort of greater or leſs Value;
Rule, Firſt, Dr. the Perſon who receives my Goods, Cr. thoſe Goods: Secondly, Dr. the Goods received by me, Cr. the Perſon who delivers them.

Caſe 49. When I give one Sort of Goods for ſeveral other ſorts of equal Value;
Rule, Dr. each particular Sort of Goods received for its reſpective Value, Cr. the Goods delivered by ſundry Accompts for the whole Value.

Caſe 50. When I give one Sort of Goods for ſeveral other Sorts of greater or leſs Value.
Rule, Firſt. Dr. each particular Sort of Goods received for its reſpective value as above, Cr. the Seller by Sundry Accompts for the whole. Secondly, Dr. the ſame Perſon as Buyer, and Cr. the Goods which he has bought.

Caſe 51. When I give ſeveral Sorts of Goods for one Sort of equal Value;
Rule, Dr. the Goods received to Sundry Accompts for their Value, Cr. each particular Sort of Goods delivered for its reſpective Value.

Caſe 52. When I give ſeveral Sorts of Goods for one Sort of greater or leſs Value;
Rule, Firſt, Dr. the Perſon to Sundry Accompts, to whom the Goods are delivered for their whole Value, Cr. thoſe Goods ſeverally for their reſpective Sums: Secondly, Dr. the Goods received, Cr. the Seller.

Caſe 53. When I give ſeveral Sorts of Goods for ſeveral other Sorts, either of equal, greater or leſs Value;
Rule, Firſt, Dr. each particular Sort of Goods received for its reſpective Value, Cr. the ſeller of them by Sundry Accompts for the whole Value: Secondly Dr. the ſame Perſon, as Buyer of the Goods delivered to him, to Sundry Accompts for the whole Value of them, Cr. each particular Sort for its reſpective Value.

Caſe 54. When I ſell Goods of one ſort for Part Goods of another Sort, and Part ready Money;
Rule, Dr. the Goods bought for their Value, Dr. Caſh for the Sum received, Cr. the Goods ſold by Sundry Accompts for their Value.

Caſe 55 When I ſell Goods of one Sort for Part Goods of another Sort, Part ready Money and Part Time;
Rule, Dr. the Goods bought for their Value, Dr. Caſh for the ſum

449

received, Dr. the felling Man for the reft, Cr. the Goods fold by Sundry Accompts for their Value.

Cafe 56. When I fell Goods of one Sort for Part Goods of another Sort, Part ready Money, Part time, and Part by Affignation;

Rule, Dr. the Goods bought for their Value, Dr. Cafh for the Sum received, Dr. the felling Man for what he owes, and Dr. the Perfon drawn on for his Sum, Cr. the Goods fold by Sundry Accompts for their Value.

Cafe 57. When I buy Goods of one Sort, for Part Goods of another Sort, and Part ready Money

Rule, Dr. the Goods bought to Sundry Accompts, Cr. the Goods fold for their Value, Cr. Cafh for the Money paid.

Cafe 58. When I buy Goods of one Sort, for Part Goods of another Sort, Part ready Money, and Part Time:

Rule, Dr. the Goods bought to Sundry Accompts, Cr. the Goods fold for their Value, Cr. Cafh for the Money paid, and Cr. the felling Man for the reft.

Cafe 59. When I buy Goods of one Sort, for part Goods of another Sort, Part ready Money, Part time, and Part by Affignation.

Rule, Dr. the Goods bought to Sundry Accompts, Cr. the Goods fold for their Value, Cr. Cafh for the Money paid, Cr. the felling Man for what is due to him, and Cr. the perfon drawn on for this Sum.

450

Shipping.

Cafe 60. When I buy a Ship for ready Money;

Rule, Dr. the Ship, Cr. Cafh.

Note, The fame for a Ship fitted out in which I have a fhare.

Cafe 61. When I buy a Ship for Part ready Money, and Part Time;

Rule, Dr. the Ship to Sundry Accompts, Cr. Cafh for the Money paid, Cr. the felling man for the reft.

Note, This is the fame as Cafe 32 foregoing which fee.

Cafe 62. When I fell a Ship for ready Money;

Rule, Dr. Cafh, Cr. the Ship.

Cafe 63. When I fell a Ship for Part ready Money, and Part Time;

Rule, Dr. Cafh for the Money received, Dr. the buying Man for what remains due, Cr. the Ship by Sundry Accompts for the Whole.

Note, This is the fame with cafe 37 foregoing, which fee.

Freight.

Cafe 64. When I receive Freight;

Rule, Dr. Cafh. Cr. the Ship,

Cafe 65. When I pay Freight;

Rule, Note, This comes under the Head of *Charges of Merchandize,* as hereafter, or more properly, that particular Voyage where the Goods are confined.

Legacy.

Cafe 66. When I receive a Legacy in Houfes, Lands, or Goods;

Rule, Dr. thofe Houfes, Lands, or Goods, Cr. Profit and Lofs.

Obligation.

Case 67. When I buy an Obligation of another for ready Money;

Rule, Dr. the Perſon to pay to Sundry Accompts, Cr. Caſh for the Sum paid, Cr. Profit and Loſs for the Sum abated.

Case 68. When I ſell an Obligation for ready Money, but for Loſs;

Rule, Dr. caſh for the Sum received, Dr. profit and Loſs for the Sum loſt, cr. the Perſon to pay, by Sundry Accompts, for the whole Sum.

2. F O R E I G N.

Goods.

CASE 1. When Goods are ſent to Sea for my own Accompt, which were formerly entered in my Books:

Rule, Dr. Voyage to —— conſign'd to —— cr. the Goods.

Case 2. When Goods are ſent to Sea for my own Accompt, which were bought for preſent Money, with all charges paid thereon.

Rule Dr. Voyage to —— conſign'd to —— Cr. Caſh.

Case 3. When Goods are ſent to Sea for my own Accompt, which were bought on Truſt;

Rule, Dr. Voyage to —— conſign'd to —— Cr. the ſelling Man.

Case 4. When Goods are ſent to Sea for my Factor's Accompt, which were formerly entered in my Books;

Rule. Dr. Factor's Accompt Current, Cr. the Goods.

Case 5. When Goods are ſent to Sea for my Factor's Accompt, which were bought for preſent Money, with all Charges paid thereon;

Rule, Dr. the Factor's Accompt Current, Cr. Caſh.

Case 6. When Goods are ſent to Sea for my Factor's Accompt, which were bought on Truſt;

Rule, Dr. Factors' Accompt Current, Cr. the ſelling Man.

Premium of Inſurance.

Case 7. When my Goods are inſured by another Perſon, and I pay the premium preſently;

Rule, Dr. Voyage to —— conſign'd to —— Cr. Caſh.

Case 8. When my Goods are inſured by another Perſon, and I do not pay the Premium preſently;

Rule, Dr. Voyage to —— conſign'd to —— Cr. the Inſurer.

Case 9. When I pay the Premium, upon Advice that my Goods are ſafely arrived,

Rule, Dr. the Inſurer, Cr. Caſh.

Case 10. When the Goods of another Perſon are inſured by me, and I receive the Premium preſently;

Rule, Dr. Caſh, Cr. Inſurance.

Case 11. When the Goods of another Perſon are inſured by me, and I do not receive the Premium preſently;

Rule, Dr. the Perſon whoſe Goods I have inſured, Cr. Inſurance.

Case 12. When I receive the Premium afterwards;

Rule, Dr. Caſh, Cr. the paying Man.

Money.

Case 13. When I receive a Premium with Advance for the Inſurance of Goods formerly ſent to Sea; *i. e.* if I receive the Premium in Dollars, and ſell them for more, and receive the Sterling immediately;

Rule, Dr. Caſh to Sundry Accompts, Cr. the man who paid the Dollars for what he paid them at, Cr. Profit and Loss for the Gain in the Payment.

Case 14. When I fell them for Gain, and receive the Sterling sometime afterwards;

Rule, Dr. Cash for the Gain only, Cr. Profit and Loss for the fame Sum.

Note, The other Part of this Cash was entered in my Books before.

Case 15. when I fell the aforefaid Dollars for more to my creditor;

Rule, Dr. the receiving Man to Sundry Accompts, Cr. Cash for the Value of the Dollars, as they were at first received, Cr. Profit and Loss for my Gain in the Payment.

Note, If my Creditor had received the faid Dollars immediately, the Remitter must be made Cr. inftead of Cash.

Case 16. When I receive a Premium with *Loss,* for the Infurance of Goods formerly fent to Sea; *i. e.* if I receive the Premium in Dollars, and fell them for lefs, and receive the Sterling immediately.

Rule, Dr. Cash for what I fold them at, Dr. Profit and Loss for the Loss, Cr. the paying Man by Sundry Accompts for what I at first received them at.

Note, If Fraud be admitted in this Cafe i. e. I be impofed on by him that paid them to me it will hold good.

Case 17. When I fell them for Loss, and receive the Sterling sometime afterward.

Rule, Dr. Profit and Loss for the Loss only, Cr. Cash for the fame.

Note, the Value of the Dollars which I have received them at was entered in my books before.

Case 18. When I fell the aforefaid Dollars for Loss to my creditor;

Rule, Dr. the receiving Man for what I fold them at, Dr. Profit and Loss for my Loss on the fale. Cr. Cash by Sundry Accompts for their first value.

Note, If my Creditor had received the faid Dollars immediately the Remitter must be made Cr. inftead of Cash.

The whole Cost of Infurance.

Case 19. When Goods of my own, that were infured, are cast away at Sea;

Rule, Dr. the Infurer, Cr. Voyage to——

Case 20. When Goods of my own, that were not infured, are cast away at Sea;

Rule, Dr Profit and Loss, Cr. Voyage to——

Case 21. When the Infurance is paid to me before I enter the Circumftance in my Books;

Rule, Dr. Cash; Cr. Voyage to——

Case 22. When the Infurance is paid to me after I have entered it;

Rule, Dr. Cash, Cr. the Infurer.

Case 23. When I hear of another man's Goods infured by me, being cast away, and pay the Adventurer immediately.

Rule, Dr. Infurance, Cr. Cash.

Case 24. When I hear of another man's Goods, infured by me, being cast away, and I do not pay the Adventurer immediately.

Rule, Dr. Infurance, Cr. the Adventurer.

Goods wherein my Factor is concern'd for me.

Case 25. When my Factor buys Goods for my Accompt, or I fend Goods to him to be difpofed of for me;

Rule, Dr fuch Goods in the Hands of fuch Factor, or elfe Voyage to ——for Prime Coft and Charges, Cr. fuch Factor or Voyage.

Case 26. When thefe Goods are fold;

Rule, Dr. the Factor's Accompt Current, Cr. Voyage to——or elfe Cr. Goods in the Hands of fuch Factor.

Note, An Accompt Current is that by which an *Agent* balances or makes even with his Employer.

Case 27. When Abatements are made on the abovefaid Goods, through Defects afterwards found;

Rule, Dr. Profit and Lofs Cr. Factor's Accompt Current.

Note, The fame for bad Debts, Charges of Remittance, &c.

Case 28. When Goods of mine, in the hands of one Factor, are fent to another Factor;

Rule, Dr. Voyage to —— [the place of the Latter, or receiving Factor] Cr. the former or fending Factor.

Case 29. When I receive Goods in return from my Factor;

Rule, Cr. thofe Goods, Cr. the Factors Accompt Current for prime Coft and Charges, as *per* Invoice, by a double Margin for the foreign Money, and the Sterling.

Case 30 When I pay Charges on the above Goods;

Rule, Dr. thofe Goods, Cr. Cafh.

Money between me and my Factor.

453

Case 31. When I draw Bills of Exchange upon my Factor, and receive the Contents prefently;

Rule, Dr. Cafh, Cr. the Factor's Account Current.

Case 32. When I draw Bills of Exchange upon my Factor, and get them accepted, but not received;

Rule, Dr. the Acceptor, Cr. the Factor's Accompt Current.

Case 33. When the Contents of fuch accepted Bills are received by me fometime afterward;

Rule, Dr. Cafh, Cr. the paying Man or Acceptor.

Case 34. When my Factor draws Bills of Exchange upon me for Goods bought by him abroad, and I pay the Contents prefently;

Rule, Dr. the Drawer, Cr. Cafh.

Case 35. When I accept the Bills as above, but do not pay them prefently;

Rule, Dr. the Drawer, Cr. the Perfon to whom payable,

Case 36. When I pay thofe accepted Bills afterwards;

Rule, Dr. the Perfon to whom payable, Cr. Cafh.

Case 37. When I remit Money to my Factor, for Goods by him fent to me;

Rule, Dr. fuch Factor, Cr. Cafh.

Case 38. When Bills of Exchange are drawn by one of my Factors on another;

Rule, Dr. the Factor drawing, Cr. the Factor drawn on; charging and difcharging in fuch Coin as the Bills were received and paid in.

Case 39. When Bills of Exchange are drawn by one of my Factors on another, and the Money is remitted to me, which I receive immediately.

Rule, Dr. Cafh, Cr. the Factor drawing.

Case 40. When Bills of Exchange are drawn by one of my Factors on another, and I receive the Contents at Ufance;

Rule, Dr. the accepting Man, Cr. the Factor drawing.

Case 41. When I have Money in my Hands to negotiate with, and deliver it for Bills of Exchange;

Rule, Dr Account of Exchanges, Cr. Cash.

Case, 42. When I dispose of those Bills for Money;

Rule, Dr. Cash Cr. Accompt of Exchanges.

Case 43. When I pay Bills of Exchange in honour of the Drawer or Indorser;

Rule, Dr. such Drawer or Indorser to Sundry Accompts, Cr. Cash for the Principal and Charges, Cr. Profit and Loss for the Commission.

II. OF FACTORAGE ACCOMPTS.

1 Domestic.

CASE 1. When I pay Charges on Goods received on Commission;

Rule, Dr. Goods for the Accompt of —— Cr. Cash.

Case 2. When I sell Goods in Commission for ready Money;

Rule, Dr. Cash, Cr. Goods for the Accompt of ——

Case 3. When I sell Goods in Commission for Trust;

Rule, Dr. the Buyer, Cr. Goods for the Accompt of ——

Case 4. When I sell Goods in Commission for Part ready Money, and Part Trust;

Rule, Dr the Buyer for what he owes, Dr. Cash for what is received, Cr. Goods for the Accompt of—by Sundry Accompts.

Case 5. When I barter Goods in Commission for other Goods;

Rule. Dr. the Goods bought, Cr. Goods for the Accompt of——

Case 6. When I send Goods of my own to my Employer, with the Charges paid on shipping them;

Rule, Dr. Goods for the Accompt of——to Sundry Accompts, or Dr. my Employer's Accompt Current to Sundry Accompts, Cr. the Goods sent out, Cr. Cash for the Charges.

Case 7. When I buy Goods for ready Money, and send them directly to my Employer, with the Charges paid on them;

Rule. Dr. Goods for the Accompt of——Dr. my Employers Accompt Current, Cr. Cash for the Principal and Charges.

Case 8. When I buy Goods upon Trust, and send them directly to my Employer, with the Charges paid on them;

Rule, Dr. Goods for the Accompt of——to Sundry Accompts, or Dr. my Employer's Accompt Current to Sundry Accompts, Cr. the Seller for their Value, Cr. Cash for the Charges.

Case 9. When Bills are drawn on me by my Employer, for Goods sold, and are payable at Usance;

Rule, Dr. Employer's Accompt Current, or Goods for the Accompt of——Cr. the Person presenting the Bill.

Case 10. When I pay the said Bill presently;

Rule, Dr. the Employer's Accompt Current, or Goods for the Accompt of——Cr. Cash.

Note 1. The same is to be observed when Money is remitted by me to my Employer before he draws on me.

2. When Bills of Exchange are booked upon acceptance (as sometimes it may be necessary) draw two Accompts, one of Bills payable, and the other of Bills receivable in the Ledger: the former must be made Dr. to my Factor's Accompt Current, and the latter must be made Cr. by it.

Case 11. When Goods in Commission are all sold, how must the Accompt be closed?

Rule, Dr. those Goods to Sundry Accompts, Cr. Cash, or Charges of Merchandize for the further Charges on them, as Porterage, Cartage, &c. Cr. Profit and Loss for the Commission and Ware-house-room.

2. Foreign.

CASE 1. Goods in my possession sent to my Factor, by Order of my Employer;

Rule, Dr. Voyage to ——— consign'd to ——— for the Accompt of ——— (my Employer) to Sundry Accompts, Cr. Goods for the Accompt of ——— (my Employer) Cr Cash for the Charges.

Case 2. When those Goods are insured and I pay the Premium presently;

Rule, Dr. Voyage to ——— consign'd to ——— for the Accompt of ——— (my Employer) Cr. Cash.

Case 3. When I do not pay the Premium till afterwards;

Rule, Dr. Voyage to ——— (as above) Cr. the Insurer.

Case 4. When I receive advice from my Factor, that the Goods sent to him for my Employer are sold;

Rule, Dr. such Factor for my Employer's Accompt, Cr. Voyage to ——— for the Accompt of ——— (my Employer.)

Case 5. When my Factor informs me that he hath made an abatement for Defects, &c. found afterwards;

Rule, Dr. Voyage to ——— for the Accompt of ——— (my Employer) Cr. such Factor for the Accompt of ——— my Employer;

Case 6. When Goods are returned to me from my Factor, for Goods sold by him for my Employer.

Rule, Dr. the Goods received for the Accompt of my Employer, Cr. that Factor for the Accompt of my Employer.

Case 7. When I pay Charges thereon;

Rule, Dr. Goods received for the Accompt of my Employer, Cr. Cash.

Case 8. When Goods return'd from my Factor are consign'd directly from him to my Employer;

Rule, Dr. such Employer's Accompt Current, Cr. Factor for my Employer's Accompt.

Case 9. When Commission is due to me from my Employer; for Goods sold by my Factor;

Rule, Dr. Voyage to ——— for Accompt of ——— (my Employer) Cr. Profit and Loss.

Case 10. When I make Abatements afterwards, and for bad Debts;

Rule, Dr. Factor's Accompt Current, Cr. the Person to whom the Abatement is made, or whose Debt is lost.

Case 11. When I pay Charges on Remittances, and Postage of Letters;

Rule, Dr. Factor's Accompt Current, Cr. Cash, or Charges of Merchandize.

Note. When Goods in Commission are all sold, the Produce clear of all Charges is called the *Neat Proceed*, for which Dr. Goods for the Accompt of ——— Cr. Factors Accompt Current.

III. COMPANY ACCOMPTS.

1. Myself keeping the Accompt, and having the Disposal of the Goods.

CASE 1. When Goods in Company are bought by me for ready Money;

Rule, Dr. those Goods for the Cost, and Charges (if there be any) Cr. Cash. Then Dr. Partner's Accompt Current, Cr. his Accompt in Company for his share due to me.

Case 2. When Goods in Company are bought by me on Trust;

Rule, Dr. Those Goods for the Cost, and Charges (if there be any)

Cr. the felling Man : Then Dr. Partner's Accompt Current, Cr. his Accompt in Company for his Share due to me.

Cafe 3. When Goods in Company are fold by me for ready Money ;

Rule, Dr. Cafh, Cr. Goods in Company : Then Dr. Partner's Accompt in Company, Cr. his Accompt Current for his Share due from me to him.

Cafe 4. When Goods in Company are fold by me on Truft ;

Rule, Dr. The Buyer. Cr. Goods in Company : then Dr. Partner's Accompt in Company, &c. for his Share due to him as above at Cafe 3.

Cafe 5. When Goods in Company are fold to myfelf ;

Rule, Dr. thofe Goods for proper Accompt, Cr. Goods in Company : Then Dr. Partner's Accompt in Company, &c. as above.

Cafe 6. When Goods in Company are fold to my Partner ;

Rule, Dr. his Accompt Current, Cr. Goods in Company : Then Dr. Partner's Accompt in Company, &c. as above.

Cafe 7. When Goods in Company are fold by me for Part ready Money and Part Time ;

Rule, Dr. Cafh for what is received, Dr. the Buyer for what remains due, Cr. Goods in Company by Sundry Accompts for the full Value : Then Dr. Partner's Accompt in Company, Cr. his Accompt Current for his fhare due to him.

Cafe 8. When Goods of my own are brought into Company ;

Rule Dr. Goods in Company, Cr. Goods proper : then Dr. Partner's Accompt Current, Cr. his Accompt in Company for his particular Share due to me.

Case 9. When the Whole is furnifhed by me ;

Rule, Dr. Goods in Company, Cr. the felling Man if bought on Time, Cr. Cafh if bought for prefent Money ; Then Dr. Partners Accompt Current, &c. as above at cafe 8.

Case 10. When Goods of my Partner's are brought into Company ;

Rule, Dr. Goods in Company, Cr. Partner's Accompt in Company : Then Dr. Partners Accompt Current, &c. as at Cafe 8.

Case 11. When the Whole is furnifhed by my Partner ;

Rule, Dr. Goods in Company, Cr. Partner's Accompt Current for the Whole : Then Dr. Partner's Accompt Current, &c as at Cafe 8.

Case 12. When Goods in Company are all fold ; if there be gain ;

Rule Dr. the Goods in Company to Sundry Accompts, Cr. Partner's Accompt in Company for his Share, Cr. Profit and Lofs for my Share.

Case 13. When Goods in Company are all fold ; if there be Lofs,

Rule, Dr. Partner's Accompt in Company for his Share of the Lofs, Dr. Profit and Lofs for my Share, Cr. the Goods in Company by Sundry Accompts.

Note. After the Entries belonging to thefe two laft Cafes are Made, the Accompt of Goods in Comp. and Partner's Accompt in Com's. will ftand balanced.

Case 14. When Goods in Company are fent over-fea to be fold, I paying the Charges ;

Rule, Dr. Voyage to —— in Company to Sundry Accompts for the whole Charge, Cr. Goods in Company for their Value, Cr. Cafh for the Charges : Then Dr. Partner's Accompt Current, Cr. his Accompt in Company for his Share of Coft and Charges due to me.

Case 15. When I buy Goods for Company Accompt with ready Money, and fhip them off, paying the Charges of fhipping ;

Rule, Dr. Voyage in Company for the whole Charge, Cr. Cafh for the fame Sum : Then Dr. Partner's Accompt Current, &c. as at Cafe 14.

Cafe 16. When I buy Goods for Company Accompt, on Truft, and ship them off before they are entered in my Ledger, paying the Charges of shipping;

Rule, Dr. Voyage to —— in Company to Sundry Accompts for the whole Charge, Cr. the Seller for the prime Cost, Cr. Cash for the after-charges: Then Dr. Partner's Accompt Current, &c. as at Case 14.

Case 17. When I receive Goods from our Factor for Company Accompt, in return for Goods sent and sold, with Charges paid by me at the Receipt thereof;

Rule, Dr. Goods received in Company to Sundry Accompts for their prime Cost and Charges, Cr. Factor at —— for company Accompt for the Cost and Charges, as per Invoice, Cr. Cash for the Charges paid at their Receipt: Then Dr. Partners Accompt Current, &c. as at Case 14.

Case 18. When Goods are sent from my Factor in one Place, to our Factor in another Place;

Rule, Dr. Voyage to —— consign'd to our Factor, Cr. my Factor at —— his Accompt Current: Then Dr. Partner's Accompt Current, &c. as at Case 14.

Case 19. When Goods are sent by our Factor in one place, to my Factor in another place, in Return for Goods sold for Company Accompt;

Rule, Dr. Voyage to —— consign'd to —— my Factor at —— Cr. our Factor at —— Then Dr. Partner's Accompt in Company, Cr. his Accompt Current for his share of the said Goods.

Case 20. When goods are sold by our Factor, as per his advice.

Rule, Dr. Factor at — his Accompt Current, Cr. Voyage to — in company.

Case 21. When I receive advice that my Factor hath afterwards made some abatements;

Rule, Dr. Voyage to —— Cr. Factor at —— his Accompt Current.

Case 22. When I receive Money of my Partner for his share of Goods formerly bought;

Rule, Dr. Cash, Cr. Partner's Accompt Current.

Case 23. When Money is remitted to me, by our Factor for Goods sold;

Rule, Dr. Cash, Cr. Factor at—his Accompt Current: then Dr. Partner's Accompt in company, Cr. his Accompt Current for his Share due to him.

Case 24. When Money is remitted to me, by our Factor for Goods sold, but payable at Usance.

Rule, Dr. the accepting person, Cr. Factor at —— his Accompt Current: Then Dr. Partner's Accompt in Company, &c. at as Case 23.

Case 25. When I pay Money on Sight of my Partner's Bill;

Rule, Dr. Partner's Accompt Current, Cr. Cash.

Case 26. When I give to my Creditor an Assignment on my Partner, for his Share of the Goods in Company;

Rule, Dr. the Receiver of the Assignment, i. e my Creditor, Cr. Partner's Accompt Current.

2. My Partner keeping the Accompt, and having the disposal of the Goods.

CASE 1. When I pay my Share in Money;

Rule, Dr. Partner's Accompt in Company. Cr. Cash.

Case 2. When I furnish my Share in Goods;

Rule, Dr. Partner's Accompt in Company, Cr. the Goods.

Case 3. When I furnish both my own and my Partner's share;

Rule, Dr. Partner's Accompt in Company for my share, Dr. Partner's Accompt Current for his Share, Cr. the Goods by Sundry accompts.

Case 4. When my Partner furnishes my share, as well as his own;

Rule, Dr. Partner's Accompt in Company, Cr. Partner's Accompt Current for my Share only.

Case 5. When my Partner sends me an Accompt of the Sale of Goods in Company;

Rule, Dr. Partner's Accompt Current, Cr. his Accompt in Company for my Share of the neat Proceed.

Case 6. If there be gain on the above Sale;

Rule, Dr. Partner's Accompt in Company, Cr. Profit and Loss.

Case 7. If there be Loss;

Rule, Dr. Profit and Loss, Cr. Partner's Accompt in Company.

Case 8. When my Partner draws on me for my Share of Goods in Company, and I pay the same presently;

Rule, Dr. Partner's Accompt Current, Cr. Cash.

Case 9. When my Partner draws on me. as above, at Usance;

Rule, Dr. Partner's Accompt Current, Cr. the demanding Person.

The general Balance of the whole Ledger, in order to transfer the same into new Books.

OBSERVATION 1. All Accompts are balanced either by *Balance*, or by Profit and Loss; except Accompts in Company, which are balanced by the Goods in Partnership for my Partner's Gain, or to those Goods for his Loss thereon.

Observ. 2. When Accompts with Persons are made even by Receipts or Payments, those Accompts stand balanced already.

Observe. 3. When Accompts remain unfinished;

Case 1. If it be of Money remaining in Hand;

Rule, Dr. Accompt of Balance, Cr. Cash.

Case 2. If it be of Persons who are debtors;

Rule, Dr. Accompt of Balance, Cr. their Accompts.

Case 3. If it be of Persons who are Creditors;

Rule, Dr. their Accompts, Cr. Balance.

Case 4. If it be of Goods, which are sold, and their is Gain;

Rule, Dr those Goods, Cr. Profit and Loss.

Case 5. If it be of Goods, which are all sold, and there is Loss;

Rule, Dr. Profit and Loss, Cr. those Goods.

Case 6. If it be of Goods, Part sold, and Part unsold;

Rule, For what is sold Dr. and Cr. as above: For what is unsold Dr. balance. Cr. the Goods at the prime cost.

Note. The same when all the Goods remain unsold.

Observ. 4. The Accompts of Insurance, Charges of Merchandize, Interest, House-Expenses, &c. are all balanced by Profit and Loss.

Observ. 5. The Accompts of Profit and Loss, and Balance are balanced by Stock, they being made Drs. to, or Crs. by Stock, as their particular Balances direct.

Observ. 6. The Accompt of Stock is balanced by the several balances of profit and Loss, and Balance, being brought thereto.

Observ. 7. The Accompt of Balance in the old Books, will be the Inventory in the new ones.

F I N I S.

ADDENDUM

Written text of Dr. side of "Balance" entry, page 346, with accompanying notes.

To Cash remaining in Hand, car-
  ried to the next Ledger
To Canary, unsold, 5 pipes, at
  25*l. per* Pipe
To Hops, unsold, 44 Bags, wt.
  132*G.* 2*qrs.* [,] at 28*s. per G.*
To *French* Wine, unsold, 10 Hhds.
  at 30*l. per* Hhd.
To Drugget, unsold, 20 Pieces,
  qt. [quantity] 280 Yards,
  at 3*s.* 4*d. per* Yard
To Sir *Robert Johnson*, due to me
To Sir *Humphrey Parsons*, due to
  me
To *William Baker* Esq; due to me
  on Bond
To *William Warner*, due to me, to
  be paid *April* 20th next
To *Brandon George*, due to me
To *Samuel Fairman*, due to me
To *Lisbon* Wine, unsold, 25 Hhds.
  at 7*l. per* Hhd.
To *William Lowfield* Esq; due to me
To *Thomas Johnson*, due to me
To *John Hammond*, [comma used] Esq.; due
  to me, to be paid *April* 20th next
To *Martin Unwin*, due to me
To *Norwich* Crape, unsold, 56 Pcs.[,]
  qt. 896 Yds.[,] at 3*s.* 6*d. per* Yard

To *Isaac Reynolds*, due to me
To Duroy, unsold, 20 Pieces, qt.
  300 Yards, at 6*s. per* Yard
To Sagathee, unsold, 90 Pieces, qt.
  1080 Yards, at 2*s.* 6*d. per* Yard
To Serge, unsold, 90 Pieces, qt.
  1260 Yards, at 1*s. per* Yard.

[*Editor's note*. For consistency, periods twice following the word 'Pieces' were replaced by commas.]

Note 1[.] Every *Article* under the head of *Balance*, on
    the *Dr.* side, is derived or brought from the *Cr.*
    Side of that particular Accompt, which is made
    Cr. by Balance.
2. These *Articles* taken together, make up the Whole
    of your present *Estate* in *Money*, *Goods*, and *Debts*
    due to you; and in your next *Books*, that is, in
    your *Journal* and *Ledger*, they must each of them
    be made *Dr.* to *Stock*, because each Particular is
    a Part thereof.

9

THE REV. RICHARD TURNER'S *NEW INTRODUCTION,* 1794

A NEW
INTRODUCTION
TO
BOOK KEEPING,
AFTER THE
ITALIAN METHOD,

William BY *Hart.*

DEBTOR AND CREDITOR:

Junos 12. 1805.

IN WHICH

The THEORY of that Art is not only elucidated, but the PRAC-
TICE made eafy and familiar, by the Addition of a
SET OF BOOKS,
Exhibiting the various Incidents which ufually fall in a Courfe of
Bufinefs.

THE WHOLE

Laid down in a Manner fo eafy and intelligible as to be
underftood in a few Days.

To which is added,
Several FORMS of BILLS, &c.

By the Rev. R. TURNER, LL. D.
Author of a " VIEW of the EARTH"—" A VIEW of the HEAV-
ENS"—" The HEAVENS SURVEYED"—PLAIN TRIGONOME-
TRY," &c. &c.

The FIRST AMERICAN EDITION,
FROM THE THIRD ENGLISH EDITION.

Deliver all Things in NUMBER *and* WEIGHT, *and put all in* WRITING
that thou GIVEST OUT, *or* RECEIVEST IN.—ECCLES. xlii. 5.

PRINTED at *BOSTON,*
BY I. THOMAS AND E. T. ANDREWS.
FAUST'S STATUE, No. 45, NEWBURY STREET.

1794.

To the **MASTERS**

INTRUSTED WITH THE

EDUCATION of **YOUTH,**

AND TO THE

YOUTH THEMSELVES,

THIS ſhort INTRODUCTION to BOOK
KEEPING (after what is uſually called
the ITALIAN METHOD) by which Learn-
ers may ſoon become acquainted with
the firſt Principles of that moſt valuable
ART; and from thence be enabled to
underſtand any other Method, as well as
the Poſting of any Accounts, how com-
plicated or abſtruſe ſoever, is

Moſt reſpectfully dedicated

and

devoted to their Services,

by

The AUTHOR.

465

BOOK KEEPING,

ACCORDING TO THE

ITALIAN METHOD.

THIS method of keeping books by way of *Debtor* and *Creditor*, was firſt invented by the Italians, and is ſo regular and exact, that the merchant can always be ſatisfied what he gains or loſes by every perſon he trades with, or merchandize he deals in, and conſequently knows, at any time, with very little trouble, what he is worth to a farthing.

It is, therefore, no wonder that moſt men, who have any inclination to trade, are very deſirous of being maſters of this uſeful qualification ; for it muſt certainly be a great ſatisfaction to every perſon to ſee how much he gains by each commodity he deals in ;— how he improves by a year's revolution in trade, and what is the true ſtate of his affairs and circumſtances at all times ; becauſe, from hence he always knows how to enlarge or contract his expences, with certainty, ſuitable to his income.

The books made uſe of in this way of keeping accompts are chiefly three, viz. The *Waſte Book*, *Journal*, and *Ledger*.

Of the WASTE BOOK.

In the *Waſte Book*, which is ruled with a margin and three columns for *l. s. d.* is written down every occurrence of trade, by way of memorandum, juſt as it happens, in the common courſe of your buſineſs.

Of

Of the JOURNAL.

The *Journal* being ruled after the fame manner, is a book in which every cafe of the *Wafte Book* is more methodically expreffed, with particular mention of the proper Debtor, Creditor, and Sum of Money, in one line, and the other circumftance of the affair in another; or in as many as are neceffary.

Of the LEDGER.

The *Ledger* is ruled with a double Column in the margin, one for the month, the other for the day, and alfo with a column for the folio, before thofe for *l. s. d.*—This book, as it is the largeft, fo it is the moft material; and contains the particular ftated accompt of every perfon you deal with, and every commodity you trade in.—Every accompt of this book confifts of two parts, a debtor and a creditor. If the accompt be of a perfon, the debtor fide fhews what he owes you, the creditor what you owe him. If it be an accompt of goods, the debtor fide fhews what charge you have been at for them, and the creditor what returns they have made.—*Note.* For the ready finding any accompt in the *Ledger*, there muft be an alphabet prefixed, directing to the folio where the accompt itfelf is pofted.

The firft thing neceffary to a juft method of book keeping is an inventory of your whole eftate; that is, an exact and particular account of all your effects; as cafh, wares, debts, &c. This makes up your whole property, and is what we call ftock.

In entering the INVENTORY, *obferve,*

Firft. What money, goods, and wares you have in poffeffion, or are owing to you, make each particular accompt debtor to ftock, and ftock creditor by each accompt.   *Secondly.*

Secondly. What you owe to any perſon, make ſtock debtor for ſo much to the perſon, and the ſame perſon creditor by ſtock.

Thirdly. What money is owing to you, make the perſon owing debtor, and ſtock creditor.

In entering or poſting the ſeveral articles, obſerve this *general rule* :

Whatſoever comes to you is debtor, and when you aſk upon what accompt it comes to you, the anſwer ſhews the creditor.—Whatſoever you part with, or goes from you is creditor ; when you aſk upon what account it goes from you, the anſwer ſhews the debtor.—Thus, If you buy 1 cwt. of cheeſe for 25s. cheeſe comes to you, therefore, cheeſe is debtor, and caſh goes from you, therefore caſh is creditor.

Note. This one rule will carry you through the whole myſtery of book keeping ; as it is evident from the following application of it to every particular circumſtance, that uſually happens in trade.

Entering Commodities BOUGHT IN.

Firſt. What you buy for ready money, that account is debtor and caſh creditor.

Secondly. What you buy upon truſt, that accompt is debtor and the perſon ſelling is creditor.

Thirdly. What you buy for part money, and part truſt, the commodity is debtor, and caſh creditor for the ſum paid, and the perſon ſelling is creditor for the reſt.

Entering Commodities SOLD OUT.

Firſt. What you ſell for ready money, that accompt is creditor, and caſh debtor.

Secondly. What you ſell upon truſt, that accompt is creditor, and the perſon buying is debtor.

Thirdly.

Thirdly. What you fell for part money and part truft, the commodity is creditor for the whole value ; and for the money, cafh is debtor, and the perfon buying is debtor for the reft.

EXCHANGING *or* BARTERING.

The commodity you part with is creditor, and the commodity received is debtor.

BORROWING *and* LENDING.

Firft. What you lend, cafh is creditor, and the perfon borrowing is debtor.

Secondly. What money you borrow, cafh is debtor, and the perfon lending is creditor.

On B I L L S.

Firft. When you draw a bill payable at any time on a perfon that owes you money, the perfon on whom the bill is drawn is creditor, and accompt of bills receivable is debtor.—When the bill is paid, accompt of bills receivable is creditor, and cafh, or the perfon to whom the bill is paid, is debtor.

Secondly. When a perfon draws a bill on you, payable at a certain time, the perfon that draws the bill is debtor, and accompt of bills payable is creditor. —When you pay the bill, cafh is creditor, and accompt of bills payable is debtor.

Thirdly. When a perfon, indebted to you, draws a bill on a third perfon to pay you fo much, and the bill is accepted, the perfon that draws the bill, or the accompt on which the money is due, is creditor, and accompt of bills receivable is debtor.—When you receive the bill, then accompt of bills receivable is creditor, and cafh debtor.

On accidental LOSSES, PROFITS, *and other* EXPENCES.

Firft. What money you gain, win, or receive gratis, cafh is debtor to profit and lofs, and profit and lofs creditor by its value.   *Secondly,*

Secondly. What money or commodity you give away, lofe, or is fpoiled, &c. is creditor, and profit and lofs is debtor for its value.

On FOREIGN TRADE.

Firft. When goods are fent to your factor abroad, make the voyage debtor and the goods creditor.

Secondly. When you have advice that your factor has received the goods, then he becomes debtor to the voyage, and the voyage creditor.—If he gains by felling the goods, he becomes debtor to profit and lofs on account of the gain.

Thirdly. If he returns the goods, he is creditor and the goods are debtor.

On HOUSEHOLD EXPENCES.

What money or commodity you make ufe of, or is fpent in your family, &c. is creditor, and profit and lofs is debtor for its value.

Note. You may erect an account of houfehold expences, and make it debtor inftead of profit and lofs.

Note alfo, That you never meddle with the accompt of cafh, but when money is either received or paid.

On ERRORS.

If you have entered any thing in your *Ledger* under a wrong title, or any otherwife falfe, you need not blot it out, but make this mark *(X)* in the margin againft it, and write on the contrary fide, Error *per contra*, with the fum againft it ; and the fame mark in the margin ; fo will the accompt be right without blotting, as if you had made no fuch error at all.

To remove an ACCOMPT *from one Folio to another.*

When in your *Ledger* any accompt comes to the foot of the page, and there is not room to finifh it, balance, or clofe up the accompt in that place thus ; —add up the debtor and creditor fides, and fubftract the lefs fum out of the greater, and make the lefs

B debtor

471

debtor to, or creditor by itself for the difference carried to such a page ; so will the accompt be balanced. Then turn to a new pair of pages in the *Ledger*, and put the title of the accompt as before, and make it debtor to, or creditor by itself.

To Balance the LEDGER.

When every transaction is entered into the *Ledger* out of the *Journal*, the next thing is to balance your *Ledger*, (that is) to make it even throughout the whole book.—To this end, you must erect a new accompt at the end, by the title of Balance debtor, *per* contra creditor. To the debtor of this accompt will be brought all the money, goods, and debts belonging, or are remaining due to you ; and on the creditor will appear all the debts you owe. By this, and the accompt of profit and loss, will all the other accompts be evened in the following manner.

To Balance your CASH.

First. Add up the debtor and creditor side of the first accompt which is cash, and substract the one from the other ; make balance debtor to cash for the money remaining in your hands, and cash creditor by balance for the same sum, which will make both sides of the accompt even.

Secondly. For balancing goods, observe 1st, When none are sold the accompt is evened by making balance creditor for the whole remaining, at the first cost.—2dly, When all are sold, then the accompt is balanced by charging it debtor to profit and loss for the gain, or creditor for the loss.—3dly, When only part are sold, first make the accompt creditor by balance for what remains at prime cost, and balance debtor, and charge the goods debtor to, or creditor by profit and loss for the money gained or lost on what are sold.

Thirdly.

472

Thirdly. For balancing the accompts of men, observe firſt, when the debtor ſide is heavieſt, *i. e.* when
they owe you any thing, then make their accompt
creditor by balance, and balance debtor for the ſum
remaining.—2dly, When the creditor is heavieſt, *i. e.*
when you owe them, then charge their accompt debt-
or to balance, and balance creditor by the difference.
—3dly, When both ſides are even, then you are only
to add the debtor and creditor ſides together and ſet
down the ſame ſum, and it is done.

The laſt accompt ſave two to be balanced is profit
and loſs.—Add up the debtor by itſelf, and the creditor by itſelf, and deduct the leſſer ſum out of the
greater, and note the difference; then if the debtor
be more than the creditor, make ſtock debtor for ſo
much loſt, but if the creditor be more than the debt-
or, make ſtock creditor for ſo much gained.

The laſt accompt to be balanced is balance itſelf.
—Add up ſeverally the debtor and creditor ſide, and
make the creditor ſide equal to the debtor by making
balance creditor by ſtock, and ſtock debtor; then add
up the debtor and creditor ſides of the ſtock, and if
the ſums are equal, your accompt is rightly ſtated;
otherwiſe it is wrong, and you muſt ſearch till you
find out the error.

Of Opening a new Set of Books.

The manner in which a new inventory is to be
formed from the ſaid balance, in order for opening
new books, is thus:—Make the particulars on the
debtor ſide of balance, being the ſeveral branches of
your eſtate, ſeverally debtors to ſtock, and ſtock creditor; and make the particulars on the creditor ſide
of balance, being the ſeveral debts you owe, ſeverally
creditors by ſtock, and ſtock debtor.

473

474

☞ 'TIS customary with Merchants to distinguish their
Books by the Letters of the *Alphabet*. The *first* Set they
mark with A ; the *second* with B ; the *third* C ; and so on.

THE
WASTE-BOOK.*

* W H E N you poſt any accompt out of a *Waſte-Book*, into the *Journal*, you muſt make this mark (√) againſt it, or write *Poſted* in the margin, to ſhew that, *That Accompt is Journaliſed.*

London, *June* the 1st, 1794.

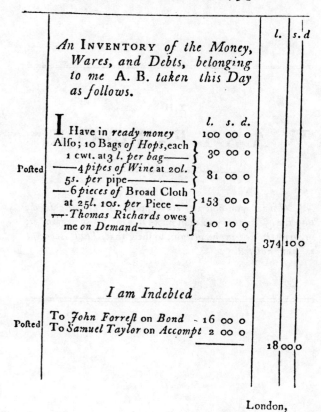

		l.	s.	d
An INVENTORY *of the Money, Wares, and Debts, belonging to me* A. B. *taken this Day as follows.*				
		l.	*s.*	*d.*
I Have in *ready money*	100	00	0	
Alfo; 10 Bags *of Hops,* each 1 cwt. at 3 *l. per bag*	30	00	0	
4 *pipes of Wine* at 20*l.* 5*s. per pipe*	81	00	0	
6 *pieces of* Broad Cloth at 25*l.* 10*s. per Piece*	153	00	0	
Thomas Richards owes me *on Demand*	10	10	0	
		374	10	0

Posted

I am Indebted

Posted

To *John Forreft* on *Bond* — 16 00 0
To *Samuel Taylor* on *Accompt* 2 00 0

18 00 0

London,

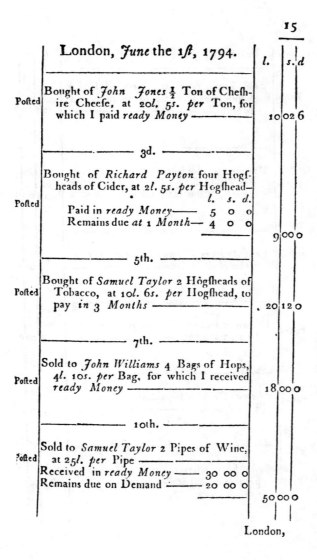

478

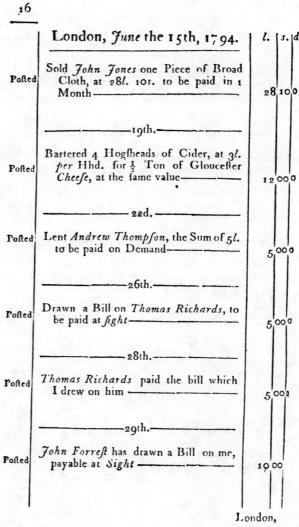

		l.	s.	d
	London, *June* the 15th, 1794.			
Poſted	Sold *John Jones* one Piece of Broad Cloth, at 28*l*. 10*s*. to be paid in 1 Month ———	28	10	0
	——————— 19th. ———			
Poſted	Bartered 4 Hogſheads of Cider, at 3*l*. *per* Hhd. for ½ Ton of Glouceſſer *Cheeſe*, at the ſame value———	12	00	0
	——————— 22d. ———			
Poſted	Lent *Andrew Thompſon*, the Sum of 5*l*. to be paid on Demand———	5	00	0
	——————— 26th. ———			
Poſted	Drawn a Bill on *Thomas Richards*, to be paid at *ſight*———	5	00	0
	——————— 28th. ———			
Poſted	*Thomas Richards* paid the bill which I drew on him ———	5	00	0
	——————— 29th. ———			
Poſted	*John Forreſt* has drawn a Bill on me, payable at *Sight* ———	19	00	

London,

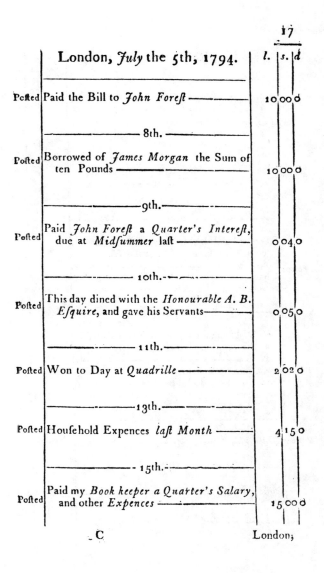

London, *July* **the 5th, 1794.**

		l.	*s.*	*d*
		17		
Posted	Paid the Bill to *John Forest* ———	10	00	0
	——— 8th. ———			
Posted	Borrowed of *James Morgan* the Sum of ten Pounds ———	10	00	0
	———9th.———			
Posted	Paid *John Forest* a *Quarter's Interest,* due at *Midsummer* laft ———	0	04	0
	—— 10th.———			
Posted	This day dined with the *Honourable A. B. Esquire,* and gave his Servants———	0	05	0
	——— 11th.———			
Posted	Won to Day at *Quadrille* ———	2	02	0
	———13th.———			
Posted	Houfehold Expences *laft Month* ———	4	15	0
	- 15th.-			
Posted	Paid my *Book keeper a Quarter's Salary,* and other *Expences* ———	15	00	0

_C

London;

480

			l.	s.	d
	London, *July* the 16*th*, 1794.				

| W C. | Shipped two hundred Weight of Cheſhire Cheeſe, in the *Golden Lion*, *John Lane*, Maſter, conſigned to *William Cowley*, at the *Hague*, marked as in the Margin. | | | | |

Poſted The Cheeſe valued at ———— 2 10 0
Paid Freight and Cuſtom ——— 0 12 0

3 2 0

——————— 20th. ———————

Received Advice that my *Factor* has received the Cheeſe ſafe at the *Hague*—
Poſted Sold for ———————— 6 10 0
Charges————————— 0 18 6
being deducted makes ————

5 11 6

——————— 23d. ———————

Received from my Factor *William Cowley*, at the *Hague*, a Cheſt of Sugar, Weight Neat ———————————
Poſted 3cwt. 2qu. 0lb. valued at ———— 4 8 0
Paid Freight and Cuſtom here — 1 3 6

5 11 6

——————— 25th. ———————

Poſted Received a *Legacy* left me by *my Uncle*—

5 0 0

——————— 27th. ———————

Poſted Paid *Church* and *Poor* ————————

0 2 6

End of the WASTE BOOK.

THE
JOURNAL.*

481

* It is common for *Book Keepers*, in the Margin of their *Journals*, to have References to the *Folios* of their *Ledgers* where the Article is entered both *Debtor* and *Creditor*; but there is no abfolute Neceffity for such References; for, the *Alphabet* in the *Ledger* directs to the *Folio* of the *Debtor*, and the *Column* in the *Debtor* fhews the *Folio* of the *Creditor*; but left fome fhould look upon the Book not complete without them, they are fubftituted here as ufual.

The *upper* Figure fhews at what Folio the Accompt is made Debtor, the *lower* where the fame is entered Creditor.

London, *June* the 1ſt, 1794.

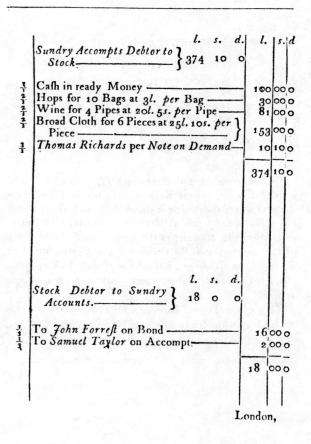

482

		l.	s.	d.	l.	s.	d
	Sundry Accompts Debtor to Stock.⎫	374	10	0			
¼	Caſh in ready Money ———				100	00	0
²⁄₁	Hops for 10 Bags at 3*l.* *per* Bag ———				30	00	0
²⁄₁	Wine for 4 Pipes at 20*l.* 5*s.* *per* Pipe ———				81	00	0
²⁄₁	Broad Cloth for 6 Pieces at 25*l.* 10*s.* *per* Piece ——⎫				153	00	0
³⁄₁	*Thomas Richards* per *Note on Demand*—				10	10	0
					374	10	0

		l.	s.	d.	l.	s.	d
	Stock Debtor to Sundry Accounts.⎫	18	0	0			
¹⁄₃	To *John Forreſt* on Bond ———				16	00	0
³⁄₁	To *Samuel Taylor* on Accompt. —				2	00	0
					18	00	0

London,

London, *June* the 1ft, 1794. | *l.* | *s.* | *d* |

| | | *l.* | *s.* | *d.* | | *l.* | *s.* | *d.* |

$\frac{4}{1}$ | Chefhire Cheefe Debtor to Cafh for half a Ton ——— 10 2 6 | 10 | 2 | 6

——————— 3d. ———————

Cider Debtor to Sundry Accounts 9 0 0

$\frac{4}{1}$ To Cafh paid ——————— 5 0 0
$\frac{4}{4}$ To *Richard Payton* remains due at 1 Month ———— } 4 0 0 | 9 | 0 | 0

——————— 5th. ———————

$\frac{5}{3}$ Tobacco Debtor to *Samuel Taylor* for two Hogfheads to pay in *three Months* at 10*l.* 6*s. per* Hogfhead ——— | 20 | 12 | 0

——————— 7th. ———————

$\frac{1}{2}$ Cafh Debtor to Hops 18*l.* received for 4 Bags at 4*l.* 10*s. per* Bag ——— | 18 | 0 | 0

——————— 10th. ———————

Sundry Accounts Debtor to Wine 50 0 0

$\frac{1}{3}$
$\frac{3}{2}$ Cafh received in Part for two Pipes 30 0 0
Samuel Taylor for the reft *on Demand* ——————— } 20 0 0 | 50 | 0 | 0

——————— 15th. ———————

$\frac{5}{2}$ *John Jones* Debtor to Broad Cloth for one Piece valued —— 28 10 0 to be paid in *one Month* ——— | 28 | 10 | 0

London,

483

London, *June* the 19th, 1794.

		l.	*s.*	*d*

		l.	*s.*	*s.*
$\frac{4}{4}$	Cheese Debtor to Cider —— for four Hogsheads —— Received in Barter half a Ton of *Gloucester* of the same Value ———	12	0	0
		12	0	0

——————— 22d. ———————

		l.	*s.*	*d.*
$\frac{6}{1}$	*Andrew Thompson* Debtor to Cash to be paid *on Demand* ———	5	0	0
		5	0	0

——————— 26th. ———————

| $\frac{6}{3}$ | Bills receivable Debtor to *Thomas Richards* for one drawn on him to be paid at Sight: ——— | | | |
| | | 5 | 0 | 0 |

——————— 28th. ———————

| $\frac{1}{6}$ | Cash Debtor to Bills receivable, received the Bill of *Thomas Richards* | | | |
| | | 5 | 0 | 0 |

——————— 29th. ———————

| $\frac{3}{6}$ | *John Forrest* Debtor to Bills payable, for one to be paid by me at Sight ——— | | | |
| | | 10 | 0 | 0 |

——————— *July* 5th. ———————

| $\frac{6}{1}$ | Bills payable Debtor to Cash, paid *John Forrest* the Bill ——— | | | |
| | | 10 | 0 | 0 |

——————— 8th. ———————

		l.	*s.*	*d.*
$\frac{1}{7}$	Cash Debtor to *James Morgan* for borrowed of him ———	10	0	0
		10	0	0

London,

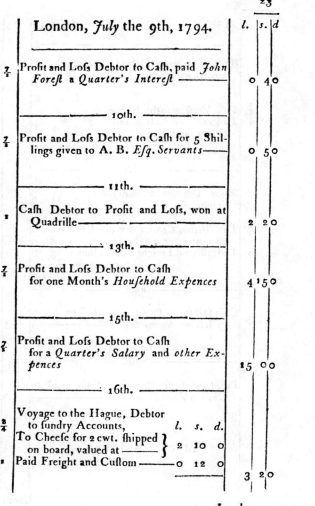

	London, *July* the 9th, 1794.	l.	s.	d
7/1	Profit and Lofs Debtor to Cafh, paid *John Foreft* a *Quarter's Interest* ——	0	4	0
	——————— 10th. ———————			
7/1	Profit and Lofs Debtor to Cafh for 5 Shillings given to A. B. *Efq. Servants*——	0	5	0
	——————— 11th. ———————			
1	Cafh Debtor to Profit and Lofs, won at Quadrille——————————	2	2	0
	——————— 13th. ———————			
7/1	Profit and Lofs Debtor to Cafh for one Month's *Houfehold Expences*	4	15	0
	——————— 15th. ———————			
7/1	Profit and Lofs Debtor to Cafh for a *Quarter's Salary* and *other Expences*	15	0	0
	——————— 16th. ———————			
8/4	Voyage to the Hague, Debtor to fundry Accounts, l. s. d. To Cheefe for 2 cwt. fhipped } on board, valued at ——— } 2 10 0			
1	Paid Freight and Cuftom ——— 0 12 0	3	2	0

486

London, *July* the 20th, 1794.

l. | *s.* | *d*

William Cowley Debtor to Sundry Accounts.

		l.	*s.*	*d.*
$\frac{8}{8}$	To a Voyage to the Hague———	3	2	0
7	To Profit and Loſs gained by } ſelling the Goods	2	9	6

5 | 11 | 6

——— 23d. ———

		l.	*s.*	*d.*
	Sugar Debtor to Sundry Accounts	5	11	6

| $\frac{8}{8}$ | To *William Cowley*, for one Cheſt received neat 3 cwt. 2 qu. valued at | 4 | 8 | 0 |
| 1 | To Caſh paid Freight and Cuſtom | 1 | 3 | 6 |

5 | 11 | 6

——— 25th. ———

| $\frac{1}{7}$ | Caſh Debtor to Profit and Loſs for a *Legacy* left me by *my Uncle* ——— | 5 | 0 | 0 |

——— 27th. ———

| $\frac{7}{1}$ | Profit and Loſs Debtor to Caſh paid to *Church and Poor* ——— | 0 | 2 | 6 |

End of the JOURNAL.

London,

THE
LEDGER.*

* EVERY Entry in the *Ledger* must be wrote *double* ; the *Debtor*, or Accompt *charged*, the *Creditor*, or Accompt *discharged* : So that *every Debtor* must have its *correspondent Creditor*, and every *Creditor* must have its *Debtor*, and each of them answering exactly the other.

The Column placed before those for *l. s. d.* on the *Debtor* side is marked [**Cr.**] and refers to the *Folio* where the same Account has Credit. That on the *Creditor* side marked [**Dr.**] refers in like manner to the *Folio* where the same is made *Debtor*.

It may not be improper to advise the *Book Keeper*, when Posting up his Accompts in the *Ledger*, always in the *first place* to post up his *Debtors*, then give the proper Credit : For, if through haste, or some interruption, a mistake arises on the *Credit*, it is not of such bad consequence as when it happens on the *Debtor* ; for the one may be a *total Loss*, when the other is but *an Error* in the Accompt.

D

A	B	C
	Fol.	*Fol.*
	Broad Cloth —— 2	Cash ———————— 1
	Bills receivable – 6	Cheese ——————— 4
	Bills payable – 6	Cider ————————— 4
	Balance ————— 9	Cowley (*William*) 8

D	E	F
		Fol.
		John Forreſt — 3

G	H	I
	Fol.	*Fol.*
	Hops ————————— 2	Jones (*John*)—5

K	L	M
		Fol.
		Morgan(*James*)7

N	O	P
		Fol.
		Payton (*Richard*) 4
		Profit and Lofs 7

Q	R	S
	Fol.	*Fol.*
	Richards (*Thomas*) 3	Stock ———— 1
		Sugar ———— 8

T	V	W
Fol.	*Fol.*	*Fol.*
Taylor (*Samuel*) 3	Voyage to the ⎫ 8	Wine ———— 2
Tobacco ———— 5	*Hague* ⎭	
Thompfon (*Andrew*) 6		

X	Y	Z

		Stock	Dr.	Cr	l.	s.	d
1794							
June	1	To Sundry Accompts as *per Jour-nal*					
		To *John Forrest* on Bond		3	16	00	0
		To *Samuel Taylor* on Accompt		3	2	00	0
		To Balance *for the Neat of my Estate*		9	367	07	0
					385	07	0

490

		Cash	Dr.		l.	s.	d
June	1	To Stock in ready Money		1	100	00	0
	7	To Hops received for 4 Bags at 4*l.* 10*s.* per Bag		2	18	00	0
	10	To Wine received in part for 2 Pipes		2	30	00	0
	28	To Bills receivable for 1 received of *Thomas Richards*		6	5	00	0
July	8	To *James Morgan* for 10*l.* borrowed of him		7	10	00	0
	11	To Profit and Loss won at *Quadrille*		7	2	02	0
	25	To Profit and Loss for a Legacy left me by *my Uncle*		7	5	00	0

				l.	s.	d
		Per Contra **Cr.**	Dr			
1794						
June	1	By Sundry Accompts as *per Journal*				
		By Cash in ready Money ———	1	100	00	0
		By Hops 10 Bags at 3*l.* per Bag ———	2	30	00	0
		By Wine 4 Pipes at 20*l.* 5*s.* per Pipe	2	81	00	0
		By Broad Cloth 6 Pieces at 25*l.* 10*s.* per Piece———	2	153	00	0
		By *Thomas Richards* per Note on Demand———	3	10	10	
		By Stock *gained by Trade*	9	10	17	0
				385	07	0

491

				l.	s.	d
		Per Contra **Cr.**				
June	1		4	10	02	6
	3	By Cheese paid for half a Ton	4	05	00	0
	22	By Cider paid in part for 4 Hhds.				
		By *Andrew Thompson* 5*l.* to be paid on Demand———	6	5	00	0
July	5	By Bills payable, paid *John Forest* his Bill drawn on me ———	6	10	00	0
	9	By Profit and Loss, paid a *Quarter's Interest* to *John Forrest*, due last *Midsummer* ———	7	00	04	0
	10	By Profit and Loss 5*s.* given to *A. B. Esqr's. Servants* ———	7	00	05	0
	13	By Profit and Loss for 1 Month Household Expences———	7	4	15	0
	15	By Profit and Loss for a *Quarter's Salary* to my Book Keeper, and other Expences ———	7	15	00	0
	16	By Voyage to the Hague paid Freight and Custom———	8	00	12	0
	23	By Freight and Custom paid ———	8	1	03	6
	27	By Profit and Loss paid Church and Poor ———	7	00	2	6
		By *Balance remains in my Hands*	9	117	17	6
				170	2	0

492

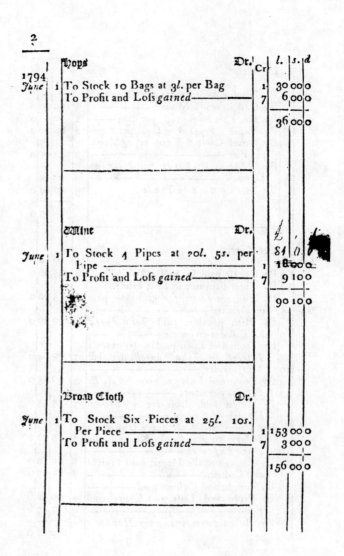

Hops	Dr.	Cr	l.	s.	d
1794					
June 1	To Stock 10 Bags at 3l. per Bag	1	30	00	0
	To Profit and Loss *gained*	7	6	00	0
			36	00	0

Wine	Dr.	Cr	£		
June 1	To Stock 4 Pipes at 20l. 5s. per Pipe	1	81	00	0
	To Profit and Loss *gained*	7	9	10	0
			90	10	0

Broad Cloth	Dr.				
June 1	To Stock Six Pieces at 25l. 10s. Per Piece	1	153	00	0
	To Profit and Loss *gained*	7	3	00	0
			156	00	0

					Dr	l.	s.	d

Per Contra   **Cr.**

1794
June 7. By Cash received for 4 Bags, at 4*l.*
     10*s.* per Bag ——————— 1 | 18 | 00 | 0

By *Balance remains* 6 Bags, at 3*l.*
     per Bag ———— ———— 9 | 18 | 00 | 0

36 | 00 | 0

Per Contra   **Cr.**

June 10 By Sundry Accompts, as per *Jour-*
     nal —   *l. s. d.*

By Cash received in Part } 30 0 0   1
     for 2 Pipes }

By *Sam. Taylor* remains } 20 0 0   3 | 50 | 00 | 0
     due on Demand }

By *Balance remains* 2 Pipes ——— 9 | 40 | 10 | 0

90 | 10 | 0

Per Contra   **Cr.**

June 15 By *John Jones* 1 Piece to be paid in
     one Month——————— 5 | 28 | 10 | 0

By *Balance remains* 5 Pieces ——— 9 | 127 | 10 | 0

156 | 00 | 0

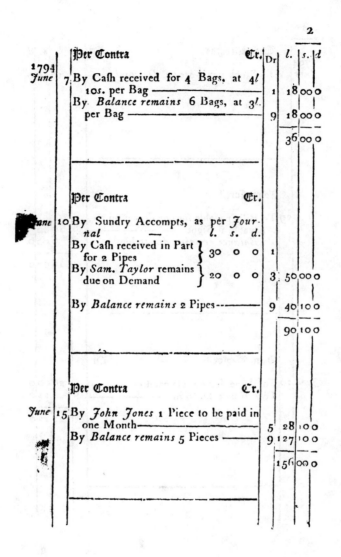

493

494

Tho. Richards	Dr.	Cr	l.	s.	d
1794					
June 1 To Stock *per Note on Demand* ——		1	10	10	0

John Forest	Dr.		l.	s.	d
June 29 To Bills payable for one drawn on me, payable at Sight ———		6	10	00	
To *Balance remains due* to him		9	6	00	0
			16	00	0

Sam. Taylor	Dr		l.	s.	d
June 10 To Wine due on Demand ———		2	20	00	0
To *Balance* due to him ———		9	2	12	0
			22	12	0

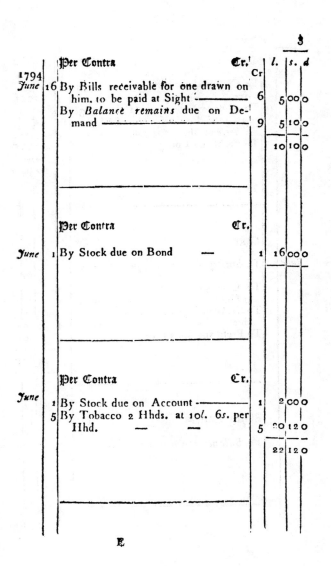

Per Contra   **Cr.**   Cr   *l.*   *s.*   *d*

1794
June 16 By Bills receivable for one drawn on
       him, to be paid at Sight ———   6   5 00 0
     By *Balance remains* due on De-
       mand ———————————   9   5 10 0

                                      10 10 0

Per Contra   **Cr.**

June   1 By Stock due on Bond   ——   1   16 00 0

Per Contra   **Cr.**

June   1 By Stock due on Account ———   1   2 00 0
     5 By Tobacco 2 Hhds. at 10*l.* 6*s.* per
       Hhd.   ——   5   20 12 0

                                        22 12 0

E

Cheese		Dr.	Cr	l.	s.	d

1794
June 1 To Cash paid for half a Ton of *Cheshire* ——— | 1 | 10 | 02 | 6

19 To Cider Bartered, 4 Hhds. at 3*l.* per Hhd. For half a Ton of *Cheshire Cheese* at the same value ——— | 4 | 12 | 00 | 0

To Profit and Loss *gained* | 4 | 00 | 02 | 0

| | | 22 | 04 | 6 |

496

Cider		Dr.

June 3 To Sundry Accounts as *per Journal*

                    l.   *s.*   *d.*

To Cash paid in Part for 4 Hhds. ——— 5 0 0 | 1

To *Richard Payton* remains due ——— 4 0 0 | 4 | 9 | 00 | 0

To Profit and Loss *gained* | | 3 | 00 | 0

| | | 12 | 00 | 0 |

Richard Payton		Dr

To *Balance remains* due to him | 9 | 4 | 00 | 0

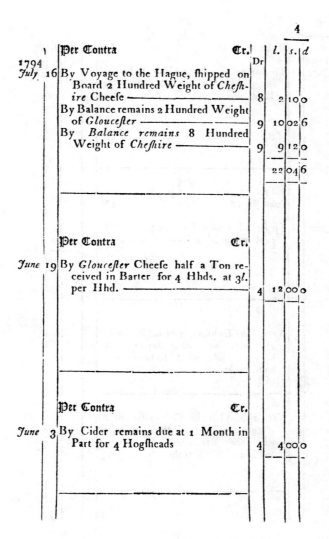

			Dr	*l.*	*s.*	*d*
	Per Contra	**Cr.**				
1794						
July 16	By Voyage to the Hague, shipped on Board 2 Hundred Weight of *Cheshire* Cheese ——————		8	2	10	0
	By Balance remains 2 Hundred Weight of *Gloucester* ——————		9	10	02	6
	By *Balance remains* 8 Hundred Weight of *Cheshire* ——————		9	9	12	0
				22	04	6

	Per Contra	**Cr.**				
June 19	By *Gloucester* Cheese half a Ton received in Barter for 4 Hhds. at 3*l.* per Hhd. ——————		4	12	00	0

	Per Contra	**Cr.**				
June 3	By Cider remains due at 1 Month in Part for 4 Hogsheads		4	4	00	0

497

		Tobacco	Dr.	Cr	l.	s.	d
1794 June	5	To *Samuel Taylor* 2 Hhds. to be paid in 3 Months, at 10*l.* 6*s.* per Hhd.		3	20	12	0

		John Jones	Dr.		l.	s.	d
June	15	To Broad Cloth, for one piece to be paid in one Month——— ——— ——		2	28	10	0

Note, The Debtor side of *all Accompts of Goods,* shews what they *cost* ; the Creditor side what *Returns* they have made.

Note also, That the Debtor side of all *Accounts of Men,* is the *Charge,* or what they stand indebted to you; and the Creditor is the *Discharge.*

	Per Contra	Cr.	Dr	l.	s.	d
1794	By *Balance remains* 2 Hogsheads, at 10*l.* 6*s.* per Hhd. ————		9	20	12	0

	Per Contra	Cr.		l.	s.	d
	By *Balance remains* due to me ———		9	28	12	0

Note. When the Debtor fide of Accompts belonging *to Men exceeds*,
then the Balance is due to *me* : but
if the Creditor fide is *moſt*, the
Balance is due *to him*.

500

			Cr	l.	s.	t
Andrew Thompson		Dr.				
1794 June 22	To Cash 5l. lent him to be paid on Demand ———		1	5	00	0
Bills receivable		Dr.				
June 26	To *Thomas Richards*, for one drawn on him, to be paid at sight ———		3	5	00	0
Bills payable		Dr.				
July 5	To Cash paid *John Forrest*, his Bill drawn on me payable at sight———		1	10	00	0

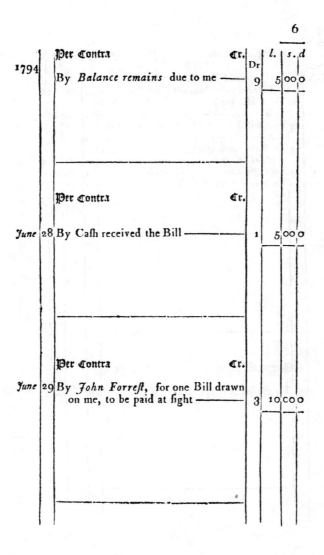

			Dr	l.	s.	d
	Per Contra	**Cr.**				
1794	By *Balance remains* due to me ——		9	5	00	0
	Per Contra	**Cr.**				
June 28	By Cash received the Bill ——————		1	5	00	0
	Per Contra	**Cr.**				
June 29	By *John Forreſt*, for one Bill drawn on me, to be paid at ſight ————		3	10	00	0

501

				l.	s.	d
		Profit and Loss	Dr. Cr.			
1794			Cr			
July	9	To Cash paid *John Forrest* a Quarter's Interest, due last *Midsummer* ———	1	00	04	0
	10	To Cash for 5*s.* given to *A. B. Esq.* Servants ———		00	05	0
	13	To Cash for one Month of *Household Expenses* ———	1	4	15	0
	14	To Cash for a *Quarter's Salary* to my *Book-Keeper* and *other Expenses*—	1	15	00	0
	27	To Cash paid to the Church and Poor	1	00	02	6
		To Stock *gained by Trade* ———	1	10	17	0
				31	03	6

502

		l.	s.	d
James Morgan	Dr. Cr.			
To *Balance remains* due on Demand	9	10	00	0

Per Contra   **Cr.**

1794			Dr	l.	s.	d
July	11	By Cash won at *Quadrille*	1	2	02	0
	20	By *William Cowley* gained by selling my Goods at the *Hague*	8	2	09	6
	25	By Profit and Loss for a Legacy left me by my *Uncle*	1	5	00	0
		By Hops *gained*	2	6	00	0
		By Wine gained	2	9	10	0
		By Broad Cloth gained	2	3	00	0
		By Cheese gained	4	0	02	0
		By Cider gained	4	3	00	0
				31	03	6

503

Per Contra   **Cr.**

July	8					
		By Cash borrowed	1	10	00	0

F

	Balance	Dr.	Cr	l.	s.	d
1794	To Cash remaining in my hands		1	117	17	6
	To Hops, 6 Bags remain, at 3l. per Bag ————		2	018	00	0
	To Wine, remains 2 Pipes, at 20l. 5s. per Pipe ————		2	040	10	0
	To Broad Cloth remains 5 Pieces, at 25l. 10s. per Piece————		2	127	10	0
	To Thomas Richards remains due on Demand ————		3	005	10	0
	To Gloucester Cheese, remains 10 cwt. at 20l. 5s. per Ton————		4	010	2	6
	To Cheshire Cheese, remains 8 cwt. at 24l. per Ton ————		4	009	12	0
	To Tobacco, remains 2 Hhds. at 10l. 6s. per Hhd. ————		5	020	12	0
	To John Jones, remains due to me		5	028	10	0
	To Andrew Thompson, remains due to me ————		6	005	00	0
	To William Cowley remains due to me ————		8	001	03	6
	To Sugar remains in my Hands————		8	005	11	6
				389	19	0

    These Articles on the *Debtor* side are the several Branches of my *present Estate.*

	Per Contra Cr.	Dr	l.	s.	d
1794	By *John Forrest* remains due to him	8	6	00	0
	By *Samuel Taylor*, remains due to him	3	2	12	0
	By *Richard Payton*, remains due to him — —	4	4	00	0
	By *John Morgan*, remains due to him	7	10	00	0
	By *Stock for the Neat of my Estate*	1	367	07	0
			389	19	0

These Articles on the *Creditor* side (except the last, which is the Neat Value of my Estate,) are the several *Debts* I owe.

End of the LEDGER.

FORMS

OF

DIFFERENT BILLS, &c.

An Inland Bill of Exchange.

Boſton, *June* 18, 1794.

£. 10 10 0

Sir,

At Sight *(or ten Days after Date)* pay to Mr. *Thomas Turner*, or Order, Ten Pounds Ten Shillings, for Value received, and place it to Account as adviſed by *(or without further advice from)*

Your humble Servant,

SAMUEL JEWKES.

To Mr. *James Clark*,
Merchant in *Worceſter.*

A Foreign Bill of Exchange.

Rotterdam, *June* 20, 1794.

For £ 1272 13 4 *Flemiſh*, at 33s. 4d. *per* £ *Sterling.*

At Uſance *(or* 60 *or* 30 *days after ſight)* pay this my firſt Bill of Exchange to Mr. *Thomas Shaw*, or his order, Twelve Hundred and Seventy-two Pounds, Thirteen Shillings, and Four Pence *Flemiſh*; Exchange at Thirty-three Shillings and Four Pence per Pound Sterling, for Value received, and place it to the Account of

Your humble Servant,

HERMAN VANDERSTAGEN.

To Meſſrs. *Andrea* and *Jean Varelſt*,
Merchants, in *London.*

₊ USANCE is a customary Time for the Payment of Foreign Bills of Exchange circulating from one Nation to another, and is sometimes one Month, sometimes two or three Months, according to the custom of different Countries.

A Promissory Note of Hand.

For Value received I promise to pay William Weaver or Order, fifty two pounds ten shillings on Demand (or one Month after date) with Interest.

JAMES WARING.

£. 52   10   0

☞ A Promissory Note, having *Order* inserted, is indorseable from one Person to another : and if *Value received* is not mentioned, it is of no Force.

A General Receipt.

Received of Mr. *A. B.* the sum of five pounds ten shillings, in full for, &c. and all demands.

C. D.

N. B. A general receipt will discharge all debts, except such as are on specialty, *i. e.* bonds, bills and other instruments that may properly be called acts or deeds, viz. Those that require to be executed in a solemn manner, where the sealing and delivery are the most essential parts of the act ; and on that account can only be destroyed by something of equal force, viz. some other specialty, such as a general release, &c. Neither will it discharge indorseable promissory notes, or inland bills.

Bill

Bill of Parcels.

Boston, 20th *July*, 1794.

BENJAMIN FAIRDEALER,

Bought of JOHN GAYLESS,

		l.	*s.*	*d.*
22	Yards velvet at 22*s.*	24	4	0
20	Yards satin at 10*s.* 6*d.*	10	10	0
10	Yards muslin 12*s.*	6	0	0
12	Yards broadcloth 15*s.*	9	0	0
6	Pair men's silk stockings 9*s.*	2	14	0
6	Pair do. worsted do. 5*s.*	1	10	0
		£53	18	0

510

Received his Note for the amount payable in three Months.

JOHN GAYLESS.

———————

A Bill for Borrowed Money.

Received and borrowed, of *C. D.* three hundred and fifty dollars, which I hereby promise to pay on demand. Witness my hand this ——— day of July, 1794.

t. B.

———————

350 Dollars.

———————

FINIS.

Accounting Books Published by Garland

■ ■ ■ ■ ■ ■ ■ ■ ■ ■ ■ ■ ■ ■ ■ ■ ■

NEW BOOKS

■ *Altman, Edward I., *The Prediction of Corporate Bankruptcy: A Discriminant Analysis.*
New York, 1988.

■ Ashton, Robert H., ed. *The Evolution of Accounting Behavior Research: An Overview.*
New York, 1984.

■ Ashton, Robert H., ed. *Some Early Contributions to the Study of Audit Judgement.*
New York, 1984.

■ *Bodenhorn, Diran. *Economic Accounting.*
New York, 1988.

---

* Included in the Garland series Foundations of Accounting
† Included in the Academy of Accounting Historians, Classics Series, Gary John Previt, ed.

■ *Bougen, Philip D. *Accounting and Industrial Relations: Some Historical Evidence on Their Interaction.*
New York, 1988.

■ Brief, Richard P., ed. *Corporate Financial Reporting and Analysis in the Early 1900s.*
New York, 1986.

■ Brief, Richard P., ed. *Depreciation and Capital Maintenance.*
New York, 1984.

■ Brief, Richard P., ed. *Estimating the Economic Rate of Return from Accounting Data.*
New York, 1986.

■ Brief, Richard P., ed. *Four Classics on the Theory of Double-Entry Bookkeeping.*
New York, 1982.

■ Chambers, R. J., and G. W. Dean, eds. *Chambers on Accounting.*
New York, 1986.
   Volume I: Accounting, Management and Finance.
   Volume II: Accounting Practice and Education.
   Volume III: Accounting Theory and Research.
   Volume IV: Price Variation Accounting.
   Volume V: Continuously Contemporary Accounting.

■ *Clark, John B. (with a new introduction by Donald Dewey). *Capital and Its Earnings.*
New York, 1988.

■ Clarke, F. L. *The Tangled Web of Price Variation Accounting: The Development of Ideas Underlying Professional Prescriptions in Six Countries.*
    New York, 1982.

■ Coopers & Lybrand. *The Early History of Coopers & Lybrand.*
    New York, 1984.

■ Craswell, Allen. *Audit Qualifications in Australia 1950 to 1979.*
    New York, 1986.

■ Dean, G. W., and M. C. Wells, eds. *The Case for Continuously Contemporary Accounting.*
    New York, 1984.

■ Dean, G. W. , and M. C. Wells, eds. *Forerunners of Realizable Values Accounting in Financial Reporting.*
    New York, 1982.

■ Edey, Harold C. *Accounting Queries.*
    New York, 1982.

■ Edwards, J. R., ed. *Legal Regulation of British Company Accounts 1836-1900.*
    New York, 1986.

■ Edwards, J. R. ed. *Reporting Fixed Assets in Nineteenth-Century Company Accounts.*
    New York, 1986.

■ Edwards, J. R., ed. *Studies of Company Records: 1830-1974.*
    New York, 1984.

- Fabricant, Solomon. *Studies in Social and Private Accounting.*
  New York, 1982.

- Gaffikin, Michael, and Michael Aitkin, eds. *The Development of Accounting Theory: Significant Contributors to Accounting Thought in the 20th Century.*
  New York, 1982.

- Hawawini, Gabriel A., ed. *Bond Duration and Immunization: Early Developments and Recent Contributions.*
  New York, 1982.

- Hawawini, Gabriel A., and Pierre A. Michel, eds. *European Equity Markets: Risk, Return, and Efficiency.*
  New York, 1984.

- Hawawini, Gabriel A., and Pierre Michel. *Mandatory Financial Information and Capital Market Equilibrium in Belgium.*
  New York, 1986.

- Hawkins, David F. *Corporate Financial Disclosure, 1900-1933: A Study of Management Inertia within a Rapidly Changing Environment.*
  New York, 1986.

- *Hopwood, Anthony G. *Accounting from the Outside: The Collected Papers of Anthony G. Hopwood.*
  New York, 1988.

- Johnson, H. Thomas. *A New Approach to Management Accounting History.*
  New York, 1986.

■ Kinney, William R., ed. *Fifty Years of Statistical Auditing.*
New York, 1986.

■ Klemstine, Charles E., and Michael W. Maher. *Management Accounting Research: A Review and Annotated Bibliography.*
New York, 1984.

■ *Langenderfer, Harold Q., and Grover L. Porter, eds. *Rational Accounting Concepts: The Writings of Willard Graham.*
New York, 1988.

■ *Lee, T. A., ed. *The Evolution of Audit Thought and Practice.*
New York, 1988.

■ Lee, T. A., ed. *A Scottish Contribution to Accounting History.*
New York, 1986.

■ Lee, T. A. *Towards a Theory and Practice of Cash Flow Accounting.*
New York, 1986.

■ Lee, T. A., ed. *Transactions of the Chartered Accountants Students' Societies of Edinburgh and Glasgow: A Selection of Writings, 1886-1958.*
New York, 1984.

■ *Loft, Anne. *Understanding Accounting in Its Social and Historical Context: The Case of Cost Accounting in Britain, 1914-1925.*
New York, 1988.

■ McKinnon, Jill L.. *The Historical Development and Operational Form of Corporate Reporting Regulation in Japan.*
New York, 1986.

■ *McMickle, Peter L., and Paul H. Jensen, eds. *The Auditor's Guide of 1869: A Review and Computer Enhancement of Recently Discovered Old Microfilm of America's First Book on Auditing by H. J. Mettenheimer.*
New York, 1988.

■ *McMickle, Peter L., and Paul H. Jensen, eds. *The Birth of American Accountancy: A Bibliographic Analysis of Works on Accounting Published in America through 1820.*
New York, 1988.

■ *Mepham, M.-J. *Accounting in Eighteenth-Century Scotland.*
New York, 1988.

■ *Mills, Patti A., trans. *The Legal Literature of Accounting: On Accounts by Diego del Castillo.*
New York, 1988.

■ *Murphy, George J. *The Evolution of Canadian Corporate Reporting Practices: 1900-1970.*
New York, 1988.

■ *Mumford, Michael J., ed. *Edward Stamp—Later Papers.*
New York, 1988.

■ Nobes, Christopher, ed. *The Development of Double Entry: Selected Essays.*
New York, 1984.

■ Nobes, Christopher. *Issues in International Accounting.*
New York, 1986.

■ Parker, Lee D. *Developing Control Concepts in the 20th Century.*
New York, 1986.

■ *Parker, Lee D., ed. *Financial Reporting to Employees: From Past to Present.*
New York, 1988.

■ *Parker, Lee D., and O. Finley Graves, eds. *Methodology and Method in History: A Bibliography.*
New York, 1988.

■ Parker, R. H. *Papers on Accounting History.*
New York, 1984.

■ Previts, Gary John, and Alfred R. Roberts, eds. *Federal Securities Law and Accounting 1933-1970: Selected Addresses.*
New York, 1986.

■ *Reid, Jean Margo, ed. *Law and Accounting: Nineteenth-Century American Legal Cases.*
New York, 1988.

■ *Sheldahl, Terry K., ed. *Accounting Literature in the United States before Mitchell and Jones (1796): Contributions by Four English Writers, through American Editions, and Two Pioneer Local Authors.*
New York, 1988.

■ Sheldahl, Terry K. *Beta Alpha Psi, from Alpha to Omega: Pursuing a Vision of Professional Education for Accountants, 1919-1945.*
New York, 1982.

■ Sheldahl, Terry K. *Beta Alpha Psi, from Omega to Zeta Omega: The Making of a Comprehensive Accounting Fraternity, 1946-1984.*
New York, 1986.

■ *Sheldahl, Terry K., ed. *Education for the Mercantile Countinghouse: Critical and Constructive Essays by Nine British Writers, 1716-1794.*
New York, 1988.

■ Solomons, David. *Collected Papers on Accounting and Accounting Education (in two volumes).*
New York, 1984.

■ Sprague, Charles F. *The General Principles of the Science of Accounts and the Accountancy of Investment.*
New York, 1984.

■ Stamp, Edward. *Edward Stamp—Later Papers. See* Michael J. Mumford.

■ Stamp, Edward. *Selected Papers on Accounting, Auditing, and Professional Problems.*
New York, 1984.

■ *Staubus, George J. *Activity Costing for Decisions: Cost Accounting in the Decision Usefulness Framework.*
New York, 1988.

■ Storrar, Colin, ed. *The Accountant's Magazine—An Anthology*.
New York, 1986.

■ Tantral, Panadda. *Accounting Literature in Non-Accounting Journals: An Annotated Bibliography*.
New York, 1984.

■ *Vangermeersch, Richard G. *Alexander Hamilton Church: A Man of Ideas for All Seasons*.
New York, 1988.

■ Vangermeersch, Richard, ed. *The Contributions of Alexander Hamilton Church to Accounting and Management*.
New York, 1986.

■ Vangermeersch, Richard, ed. *Financial Accounting Milestones in the Annual Reports of the United States Steel Corporation—The First Seven Decades*.
New York, 1986.

■ *Walker, Stephen P. *The Society of Accountants in Edinburgh, 1854-1914: A Study of Recruitment to a New Profession*.
New York, 1988.

■ Whitmore, John. *Factory Accounts*.
New York, 1984.

■ *Whittred, Greg. *The Evolution of Consolidated Financial Reporting in Australia: An Evaluation of an Alternative Hypothesis*.
New York, 1988.

■ Yamey, Basil S. *Further Essays on the History of Accounting.*
New York, 1982.

■ Zeff, Stephen A., ed. *The Accounting Postulates and Principles Controversy of the 1960s.*
New York, 1982.

■ Zeff, Stephen A., ed. *Accounting Principles Through the Years: The Views of Professional and Academic Leaders 1938-1954.*
New York, 1982.

■ Zeff, Stephen A., and Maurice Moonitz, eds. *Sourcebook on Accounting Principles and Auditing Procedures: 1917-1953 (in two volumes).*
New York, 1984.

■ *Zeff, Stephen a., ed. *The U. S. Accounting Profession in the 1890s and Early 1900s.*
New York, 1988.

REPRINTED TITLES

- *American Institute of Accountants. *Accountants Index, 1920* (in two volumes).
    New York, 1921 (Garland reprint, 1988).

- American Institute of Accountants. *Fiftieth Anniversary Celebration.*
    Chicago, 1937 (Garland reprint, 1982).

- American Institute of Accountants. *Library Catalogue.*
    New York, 1919 (Garland reprint, 1982).

- Arthur Andersen Company. *The First Fifty Years 1913-1963.*
    Chicago, 1963 (Garland reprint, 1984).

- Bevis, Herman W. *Corporate Financial Reporting in a Competitive Economy.*
    New York, 1965 (Garland reprint, 1986).

- Bonini,. Charles P., Robert K. Jaedicke, and Harvey M. Wagner, eds. *Management Controls: New Directions in Basic Research.*
    New York, 1964 (Garland reprint, 1986).

- *The Book-Keeper and the American Counting Room.*
    New York, 1880-1884 (Garland reprint, 1988).

■ Bray, F. Sewell. *Four Essays in Accounting Theory*. London, 1953. *Bound with* Institute of Chartered Accountants in England and Wales and the National Institute of Economic and Social Research. *Some Accounting Terms and Concepts*.
    Cambridge, 1951 (Garland reprint, 1982).

■ Brown, R. Gene, and Kenneth S. Johnston. *Paciolo on Accounting*.
    New York, 1963 (Garland reprint, 1984).

■ Carey, John L., and William O. Doherty, eds. *Ethical Standards of the Accounting Profession*.
    New York, 1966 (Garland reprint, 1986).

■ Chambers, R. J. *Accounting in Disarray*.
    Melbourne, 1973 (Garland reprint, 1982).

■ Cooper, Ernest. *Fifty-seven years in an Accountant's Office. See* Sir Russell Kettle.

■ Couchman, Charles B. *The Balance-Sheet*.
    New York, 1924 (Garland reprint, 1982).

■ Couper, Charles Tennant. *Report of the Trial ... Against the Directors and Manager of the City of Glasgow Bank*.
    Edinburgh, 1879 (Garland reprint, 1984).

■ Cutforth, Arthur E. *Audits*.
    London, 1906 (Garland reprint, 1982).

■ Cutforth, Arthur E. *Methods of Amalgamation*.
    London, 1926 (Garland reprint, 1982).

■ Deinzer, Harvey T. *Development of Accounting Thought.*
New York, 1965 (Garland reprint, 1984).

■ De Paula, F.R.M. *The Principles of Auditing.*
London, 1915 (Garland reprint, 1984).

■ Dickerson, R. W. *Accountants and the Law of Negligence.*
Toronto, 1966 (Garland reprint, 1982).

■ Dodson, James. *The Accountant, or, the Method of Bookkeeping Deduced from Clear Principles, and Illustrated by a Variety of Examples.*
London, 1750 (Garland reprint, 1984).

■ Dyer, S. *A Common Sense Method of Double Entry Bookkeeping, on First Principles, as Suggested by De Morgan. Part I, Theoretical.*
London, 1897 (Garland reprint, 1984).

■ *† Edwards, James Don. *History of Public Accounting in the United States.*
East Lansing, 1960 (Garland reprint, 1988).

■ *† Edwards, James Don, and Robert F. Salmonson. *Contributions of Four Accounting Pioneers: Kohler, Littleton, May, Paton.*
East Lancing, 1961 (Garland reprint, 1988).

■ *The Fifth International Congress on Accounting, 1938 [Kongress-Archiv 1938 des V. Internationalen Prüfungs- und Treuhand-Kongresses].*
Berlin, 1938 (Garland reprint, 1986).

- Finney, A. H. *Consolidated Statements.*
  New York, 1922 (Garland reprint, 1982).

- Fisher, Irving. *The Rate of Interest.*
  New York, 1907 (Garland reprint, 1982).

- Florence, P. Sargant. *Economics of Fatigue and Unrest and the Efficiency of Labour in English and American Industry.*
  London, 1923 (Garland reprint, 1984).

- *Fourth International Congress on Accounting 1933.*
  London, 1933 (Garland reprint, 1982).

- Foye, Arthur B. *Haskins & Sells: Our First Seventy-Five Years.*
  New York, 1970 (Garland reprint, 1984).

- *† Garner, Paul S. *Evolution of Cost Accounting to 1925.*
  University, Alabama, 1925 (Garland reprint, 1988).

- Garnsey, Sir Gilbert. *Holding Companies and Their Published Accounts.* London, 1923. *Bound with* Sir Gilbert Garnsey. *Limitations of a Balance Sheet.*
  London, 1928 (Garland reprint, 1982).

- Garrett, A. A. *The History of the Society of Incorporated Accountants, 1885-1957.*
  Oxford, 1961 (Garland reprint, 1984).

- Gilman, Stephen. *Accounting Concepts of Profit.*
  New York, 1939 (Garland reprint, 1982).

■ Gordon, William. *The Universal Accountant, and Complete Merchant ... [Volume II].*
     Edinburgh, 1765 (Garland reprint, 1986).

■ Green, Wilmer. *History and Survey of Accountancy.*
     Brooklyn, 1930 (Garland reprint, 1986).

■ Hamilton, Robert. *An Introduction to Merchandise, Parts IV and V (Italian Bookkeeping and Practical Bookkeeping).*
     Edinburgh, 1788 (Garland reprint, 1982).

■ Hatton, Edward. *The Merchant's Magazine; or, Tradesman's Treasury.* London, 1695 (Garland reprint, 1982).
Hills, George S. *The Law of Accounting and Financial Statements.*
     Boston, 1957 (Garland reprint, 1982).

■ *A History of Cooper Brothers & Co. 1854 to 1954.*
     London, 1954 (Garland reprint, 1986).

■ Hofstede, Geert. *The Game of Budget Control.*
     Assen, 1967 (Garland reprint, 1984).

■ Howitt, Sir Harold. *The History of the Institute of Chartered Accountants in England and Wales 1880-1965, and of Its Founder Accountancy Bodies 1870-1880.*
     London, 1966 (Garland reprint, 1984).

■ Institute of Chartered Accountants in England and Wales and The National Institute of Social and Economic Research. *Some Accounting Terms and Concepts.* See F. Sewell Bray.

■ Institute of Chartered Accountants of Scotland. *History of the Chartered Accountants of Scotland from the Earliest Times to 1954.*
    Edinburgh, 1954 (Garland reprint, 1984).

■ *International Congress on Accounting 1929.*
    New York, 1930 (Garland reprint, 1982).

■ Jaedicke, Robert K., Yuji Ijiri, and Oswald Nielsen, eds. *Research in Accounting Measurement.*
    American Accounting Association,
    1966 (Garland reprint, 1986).

■ Keats, Charles. *Magnificent Masquerade.*
    New York, 1964 (Garland reprint, 1982).

■ Kettle, Sir Russell. *Deloitte & Co. 1854-1956.* Oxford, 1958. *Bound with* Ernest Cooper. *Fifty-seven Years in an Accountant's Office.*
    London, 1921 (Garland reprint, 1982).

■ Kitchen, J., and R. H. Parker. *Accounting Thought and Education: Six English Pioneers.*
    London, 1980 (Garland reprint, 1984).

■ Lacey, Kenneth. *Profit Measurement and Price Changes.*
    London, 1952 (Garland reprint, 1982).

■ Lee, Chauncey. *The American Accomptant.*
    Lansingburgh, 1797 (Garland reprint, 1982).

■ Lee, T. A., and R. H. Parker. *The Evolution of Corporate Financial Reporting.*
    Middlesex, 1979 (Garland reprint, 1984).

■ *† Littleton, A. C.. *Accounting Evolution to 1900.*
    New York, 1933 (Garland reprint, 1988).

■ Malcolm, Alexander. *The Treatise of Book-Keeping, or, Merchants Accounts; In the Italian Method of Debtor and Creditor; Wherein the Fundamental Principles of That Curious and Approved Method Are Clearly and Fully Explained and Demonstrated ... To Which Are Added, Instructions for Gentlemen of Land Estates, and Their Stewards or Factors: With Directions Also for Retailers, and Other More Private Persons.*
    London, 1731 (Garland reprint, 1986).

■ Meij, J. L., ed. *Depreciation and Replacement Policy.*
    Chicago, 1961 (Garland reprint, 1986).

■ Newlove, George Hills. *Consolidated Balance Sheets.*
    New York, 1926 (Garland reprint, 1982).

■ North, Roger. *The Gentleman Accomptant; or, An Essay to Unfold the Mystery of Accompts; By Way of Debtor and Creditor, Commonly Called Merchants Accompts, and Applying the Same to the Concerns of the Nobility and Gentry of England.*
    London 1714 (Garland reprint, 1986).

■ *Proceedings of the Seventh International Congress of Accountants.* Amsterdam, 1957 (Garland reprint, 1988).

■ Pryce-Jones, Janet E., and R. H. Parker. *Accounting in Scotland: A Historical Bibliography.*
    Edinburgh, 1976 (Garland reprint, 1984).

- *Reynolds, W. B., and F. W. Thornton. *Duties of a Junior Accountant* [three editions].
    New York, 1917, 1933, 1953
    (Garland reprint, 1988).

- Robinson, H. W. *A History of Accountants in Ireland.*
    Dublin, 1964 (Garland edition, 1984).

- Robson, T. B. *Consolidated and Other Group Accounts.*
    London, 1950 (Garland reprint, 1982).

- Rorem, C. Rufus. *Accounting Method.*
    Chicago, 1928 (Garland reprint, 1982).

- Saliers, Earl A., ed. *Accountants' Handbook.*
    New York, 1923 (Garland reprint, 1986).

- Samuel, Horace B. *Shareholder's Money.*
    London, 1933 (Garland reprint, 1982).

- *The Securitites and Exchange Commission in the Matter of McKesson & Robbins, Inc. Report on Investigation.*
    Washington, D. C., 1940 (Garland reprint, 1982).

- *The Securities and Exchange Commission in the Matter of McKesson & Robbins, Inc. Testimony of Expert Witnesses.*
    Washington, D. C., 1939 (Garland reprint, 1982).

- Shaplen, Roger. *Kreuger: Genius and Swindler.*
    New York, 1960 (Garland reprint, 1986).

- Singer, H. W. *Standardized Accountancy in Germany. (With a new appendix.)*
    Cambridge, 1943 (Garland reprint, 1982).

■ *The Sixth International Congress on Accounting.*
London, 1952 (Garland reprint, 1984).

■ Stewart, Jas. C. (with a new introductory note by T. A. Lee). *Pioneers of a Profession: Chartered Accountants to 1879.*
Edinburgh, 1977 (Garland reprint, 1986).

■ Thompson, Wardbaugh. *The Accomptant's Oracle: or, a Key to Science, Being a Compleat Practical System of Book-keeping.*
York, 1777 (Garland reprint, 1984).

■ *Thornton, F. W. *Duties of the Senior Accountant.* New York, 1932. *Bound with.* John C. Martin. *Duties of Junior and Senior Accountants, Supplement of the CPA Handbook.*
New York, 1953 (Garland reprint, 1988).

■ Vatter, William J. *Managerial Accounting.*
New York, 1950 (Garland reprint, 1986).

■ Woolf, Arthur H. *A Short History of Accountants and Accountancy.*
London, 1912 (Garland reprint, 1986).

■ Yamey, B. S., H. C. Edey, and Hugh W. Thomson. *Accounting in England and Scotland: 1543-1800.*
London, 1963 (Garland reprint, 1982).